D1557090

THE RURAL ECONOMY
OF ENGLAND

COLLECTED ESSAYS

JOAN THIRSK

THE HAMBLEDON PRESS

Published by The Hambledon Press
35 Gloucester Avenue, London NW1 7AX
1984

ISBN 0 907628 28 1 (Cased)
ISBN 0 907628 29 X (Paper)

History Series 25

British Library Cataloguing in Publication Data

Thirsk, Joan
    The rural economy of England.—(History series; 25)
    1. Country life, England—History
    2. England, Rural conditions
    3. Great Britain—History—16th century
    4- Great Britain—History—17th century
    5. Great Britain—History—18th century
    I. Title   II. Series
    330.942   HC253

Typeset by Ebony Typesetting
Trion House, 13 Dean Street, Liskeard, Cornwall PL14 4AB

Printed and bound in Great Britain by
Robert Hartnoll Ltd., Bodmin, Cornwall

CONTENTS

110022944

PREFACE

The preparation for publication of these essays, written over a period of thirty years, prompts many reflections on the wayward paths of historical research. The historian commonly sets out on a main highway, but is soon enticed into alluring byways. Yet any one of those byways is likely to lead to another main highway, approached this time from an unusual direction. In short, every new problem opens up unexpected views of others, and one is led in fresh directions. Yet at the end of it all, the final path that is traced frequently turns out to be a circuit, turning around one clearly identifiable central theme.

Such is the case here. The essays chosen for this volume all focus on some aspect of rural economy and rural society. They dovetail with longer studies, that have appeared in book form, exploring the agricultural base and industrial by-employments that sustained English rural society as a whole before 1800.[1] But English society is no monolith, and it is a gross simplification to force it into one mould. That is why some of the essays here anatomise small districts and small communities, like the fenlands of Axholme, the pastoral districts of Staffordshire, and the Vale of Tewkesbury in Gloucestershire. Although one starts at a high level of generality, varied local conditions soon force themselves upon the attention. One does not proceed far before noticing the influence of special local circumstances that differentiate one district from another. The general historian must from time to time become a local historian, and focus on small detail; in that way experience is greatly enlarged, and the tapestry of history elaborated and enriched.

I first learned this lesson when exploring the sale of confiscated lands during the Interregnum (Chapter VII). Most of these forced sales were carried out between 1646 and 1656, when Parliament

---

[1] See, in particular, J. Thirsk, ed., *The Agrarian History of England and Wales, IV, 1500–1640*, Cambridge, 1967, and *idem. V. 1640–1750*, Cambridge, 1984; J. Thirsk, *Economic Policy and Projects. The Development of a Consumer Society in early Modern England*, Oxford, 1978.

desperately needed money, and saw a solution by selling the forfeited lands of the Crown, the Church, and private Royalists. My main search was conducted at a general level; it set out to examine the disposal of all confiscated Royalist land in south-eastern England. Yet it was most rewarding when it moved from generalities to explore local detail. One such investigation involved an estate in the vicinity of Bletchley and Stony Stratford in Buckinghamshire. Winslow, Whaddon, and Bletchley manors were granted as a gift to Major General Philip Skippon in return for his services in the Civil War. Skippon subsequently dismembered the estate, selling twenty different parcels to twenty-seven different buyers, mostly local yeomen and husbandmen. The result of this transaction was so unlike that achieved by sales elsewhere, that the whole affair called for closer scrutiny of the circumstances. It was not unreasonable to suspect that somewhere behind this unusual distribution of land among many small purchasers, a hand was deliberately at work; a principle was felt to be at stake. Was Skippon himself the most influential figure? He was evidently a reticent man in political life, but, nevertheless, held firm convictions in private.[2] Did the tenants of these manors join together in political and social solidarity? Or did both seller and buyers share a common sympathy?

In 1952 when I published this research I did no more than glimpse a network of social and economic circumstances that might illuminate these land transactions. But since much of my subsequent work has been devoted to exploring economic and social structures in other rural areas, I now see, in the light of those comparisons, a much denser tangle of relevant factors in Buckinghamshire. This area of the county was still partly forested; its former owner had been a distant figure, the non-resident Duke of Buckingham. It could have been expected to harbour people who stood up for themselves, and showed determination to defend their livelihoods. The county of Buckinghamshire as a whole nurtured some outspoken Levellers, who inveighed against greedy gentlemen swallowing up all the land and depriving the poor of every common right. They were responsible for two pamphlets, *Light Shining in Buckinghamshire* (1648) and *More Light Shining in Buckinghamshire* (1649). Neither of these explicitly names its authors or gives its place of origin. They have usually been cited alongside another pamphlet, avowedly drawn up by 'the middle sort of men' from another wooded district of Buckinghamshire, the

---

[2] See DNB *sub nomine* and Skippon's will, PRO, PCC Nabbs 1660, 193.

Chilterns, issued in 1649. Yet another broadside, this time by the Diggers, was issued from Iver, near Uxbridge, at the gateway to the Chilterns, in 1650. Not surprisingly, all four pamphlets have tended to be linked together.[3]

But now that we know so much more of the characteristics of woodland communities as a whole, it is not wildly imaginative to suggest that North Buckinghamshire (which is, in fact, a south-easterly continuation of the Northamptonshire forests of Salcey and Whittlewood), also espoused Leveller-Digger ideas. The writers of the two Leveller pamphlets shining a light in Buckinghamshire were plainly much concerned with oppressive distant lords, who appointed lawyers to be stewards of their manors, and left these to tyrannize over tenants at manorial court leets. They evidently had no experience of patriarchal resident gentlemen of the kind depicted in the Vale of Tewkesbury (Chapters XV & XVI). Their lords were great men who received commissions, grants, and patents from the King, were invested with lofty names and titles such as dukes, princes, etc., and through royal support considered themselves entitled to 'rob, spoil, extort and tyrannize over the poor people'. These are all covert allusions, but they could so easily be read as a description of the Dukes of Buckingham.[4] The writers were also evidently much concerned with the consequences of Parliament's sales of confiscated land, and expressed the hope that the bishops' and crown's lands, and the commons, parks, woods, and forests would not be swallowed up by great ones who would enclose them. They were convinced that 'the apostate Parliament men' were sharing the spoils among themselves. This was prophetic indeed, since Major General Philip Skippon was given, that is, did not have to buy, the Duke of Buckingham's estate. Finally our suspicion of a Leveller-Digger connection in north Buckinghamshire is strengthened by a passage in another Digger tract, 'A Letter taken at Wellingborough' (1650) in which sympathizers described their journey through the Home Counties to raise money for the Diggers at work on St. George's Hill in Cobham, Surrey. The towns through which they passed, looking for generous donors of money, included Newport Pagnell, Stony Stratford, and Winslow, the very area we have been describing, in which the Duke of

[3] C. Hill, *The World turned Upside Down*, London, 1972, pp. 94, 99–103, 92; G. H. Sabine, ed., *The Works of Gerrard Winstanley*, Cornell U.P., Ithaca, New York, 1941, pp. 605–06; K. Thomas, 'Another Digger Broadside', *Past and Present*, 42, 1969, pp. 57–68.
[4] For the full texts of these two pamphlets, see Sabine, *op. cit.*, pp. 611 ff.

Buckingham had held sway.[5]

In the years following the conveyance of the Duke of Buckingham's lands to Skippon, some of the new purchasers from Skippon – freeholders and copyholders – were active enclosers of coppices and waste. Leveller pamphlets had inveighed against enclosure, but a more benevolent attitude towards it supervened in the Commonwealth period, when it was taken for granted that sufficient common would be set aside to satisfy the poor. This provision certainly characterised enclosures in north Buckinghamshire. They were carried out in accordance with the many theoretical arguments publicised at the time. These recommended schemes to provide more farms for husbandmen, allowed land to be enclosed for the purpose, but insisted that the poor be treated fairly. This particular grant of a royalist estate had, indeed, allowed humble men 'to share in the lands and estates of gentlemen and rich men'. Thus the episode leaves a trail of clues that carry us far beyond the problems of royalist estates and their purchasers. They give a glimpse of a district of North Buckinghamshire with a distinctive structure and distinctive social aspirations.[6]

The standard image of rural England as a country of villages and common fields, of authoritarian lords and dull peasants, and of one agricultural routine of corn-growing and livestock-keeping has emerged in the last three decades of historical research as no more than a convenient stereotype. The English countryside is highly diverse, and, most significant of all, shows great variety over short distances. In one single county like Kent, one can travel 30 miles only and pass from a marshland landscape, with its appropriate economy and society, into the forested clay lowland of the Weald, possessing communities with another distinctive mode of life, and thence on to chalk downlands, with yet a third quite different social structure and agricultural system. Still one has traversed no more than half the county from south to north. When one has grasped the full diversity of England as a whole, then much of the dynamism in the kingdom's economic and social development in the sixteenth and seventeenth centuries may be seen to have come from localized changes, setting up a chain of reactions and interactions between neighbouring, varied

---

[5] For the text, see Sabine, pp. 439 ff.
[6] For enclosure in Whaddon, etc., see PRO Chancery Proceedings, Hamilton Div., 16/107; 424/6; Collins Div., 85/58; for the literature on agricultural improvement in the 1650s, see Thirsk, *Agrarian History, V, op. cit.*, Chapters 16 and 19.

but closely-interdependent, regions and communities. Each and all of them became increasingly reliant on the others, as first one and then another was more insistently, and then permanently, drawn into the mainstream of commercial marketing.

The interlocking and subtly complementary relationships that were devised between neighbouring agricultural regions, and also between towns and their surrounding countryside, solidified some structures for long periods. Partly for this reason common fields persisted in some cases into the nineteenth century; their produce complemented the agricultural products of enclosed farming regions. But changing relationships forced farmers to be flexible in a multitude of small ways (as were the livestock-breeding regions which changed to dairying, and the sheep-keeping countries which turned from wool to mutton production). As historians of agriculture and rural industry have probed reality more deeply, they have come to accept the notion of a kaleidoscope of regional specialities and of processes of economic change.

Views of social structure, however, still tend to favour stereotypes, and it is probably here that a fresh eye is most needed. In my essay on the family, written in 1964 (Chapter XVIII), I deplored the neglect of that subject at that time. No such complaint would be appropriate now; the literature is voluminous. But it is still much concerned with a few stereotypes. Similarly, our study of different social classes, both rural and urban, has not yet moved far beyond one standard image. Yet the gentry delineated in Chapters XV and XVI, who inhabited the Winchcombe–Tewkesbury area of Gloucestershire in the seventeenth century, clearly did not match the conventional portrait of manorial lords that is drawn so often from the East Midland and southern counties. And we cannot much longer be satisfied with one image of the English peasant – again a Midlander, usually from Leicestershire – who strained to survive on fifty acres, when we know that others could live respectably on five acres – for example, in the fens – because they had at their disposal an infinity of natural resources extending far beyond their corn and livestock. Signs are accumulating, however, that closer attention is being paid to the more refined analysis of social structures and social relations in towns and countryside. Just as we now recognise a variety of different agricultural systems, similarly, we must expect to identify not one style of social relationships between the rural classes but many. Social theorists, like Marx who identified class war, and Kropotkin who emphasised mutual aid, were poles apart, but the explanation lies in the fact that reality spans a very wide spectrum.

I frequently call to mind the words of the venerable, and in the 1920's and 1930's very lonely, investigator of agricultural history, Dr. George Fussell, that one needs to live to be 200 years old before one can do full justice to the historical evidence of our rural past. But since none of us will live to be 200 years old, we know we can never hope to produce our best work. I readily recognise that if I had known more of the social structure of farming regions when I wrote in 1952 on the sale of royalist lands, I would have drawn more significance from the regional characteristics of certain transactions. If in 1970 (Chapter XII) I had known as much as I know now about the horticultural revolution in southern Europe in the sixteenth century, I would have distilled more meaning from the evident enthusiasm for new fruits and vegetables that was shown in England in the seventeenth century. I comfort myself with the evidence of these essays that horizons do steadily widen, while at the same time small details in the foreground of our canvasses are continuously being filled in, until, in the graphic words of R. H. Tawney, we are able to put every button on every uniform.[7] None of the essays presented here depicts all the detail that might be assembled. I rest content with the thought that the work of one generation serves as an outline, awaiting improvement by the next.

[7] J. M. Winter, ed., *History and Society. Essays by R. H. Tawney*, London, 1978, p. 70.

ACKNOWLEDGEMENTS

The author and publisher are grateful to the following for permission to reproduce essays first published by them.

I   British Agricultural History Society (in the *Agricultural History Review*, III, 1955).

II and Phillimore and Company Ltd., Bridge Place, Canterbury (in
III   Phillimore's Hand Books, 5).

IV and Past and Present Society (in *Past and Present*, no. 29, 1964,
V   and no. 33, 1966). IV, V, XVIII and XX World Copyright: The Past and Present Society, Corpus Christi College, Oxford, England.

VI   Historical Association (in the General Series of Pamphlets, no. 41, 1958).

VII   Economic History Society (in the *Economic History Review*, 2nd Ser., V, no. 2, 1952).

VIII   University of Chicago Press (in the *Journal of Modern History*, XXVI, no. 4, 1954).

IX   Lincolnshire Architectural and Archaeological Society (in *Reports and Papers*, 6, i, 1955). By Permission of the Jews Court Trust, Lincoln.

X   British Agricultural History Society (in the *Agricultural History Review*, I, 1953).

XI   University of Keele (in the *North Staffordshire Journal of Field Studies*, 9, 1969).

XII   British Agricultural History Society (in *Land, Church and People. Essays presented to Professor H.P.R. Finberg*, ed. Joan Thirsk, *Agricultural History Review*, 18, 1970, Supplement).

XIII   Cambridge University Press (in *Essays in the Economic and Social History of Tudor and Stuart England, in Honour of R.H. Tawney*, ed. F. J. Fisher, 1961).

XIV   Manchester University Press (in *Textile History and Economic History. Essays in Honour of Miss Julia de Lacy Mann*, ed. N.B. Harte and K.G. Ponting, 1973).

XV   Longman Group Ltd. (in *Rural Change and Urban Growth, 1500–1800. Essays in English Regional History in Honour of W.G. Hoskins*, ed. C.W. Chalklin and M.A. Havinden, 1974).

XVI   Bristol and Gloucestershire Archaeological Society (in *Essays in Bristol and Gloucestershire History. The Centenary Volume of the Bristol and Gloucestershire Archaeological Society*, ed. Patrick McGrath and John Cannon, 1976).

XVII   Leicester University Press (in *The Making of Stamford*, ed. Alan Rogers, 1965).

XVIII   Past and Present Society (in *Past and Present*, 27, 1964).

XIX   The Historical Association (in *History*, LIV, 1969).

XX   Past and Present Society and Cambridge University Press (in *Family and Inheritance. Rural Society in Western Europe, 1200–1800*, ed. Jack Goody, Joan Thirsk, and E.P. Thompson, 1976).

XXI   University of Reading (in the Stenton Lectures Series, 11, 1978).

LIST OF ABBREVIATIONS

AASR   Architectural and Archaeological Societies' Reports and Papers of the Counties of Lincoln and Northampton

AHEW   Joan Thirsk, ed., *The Agrarian History of England and Wales, IV, 1500–1640*, Cambridge, 1967.

AHR   Agricultural History Review

BIHR   Bulletin of the Institute of Historical Research

BM   British Museum, now the British Library

Cal. SP Ven.   Calendar of State Papers Venetian (London, 1864–98)

CSPD   Calendar of State Papers Domestic

DNB   *Dictionary of National Biography*

LAO   Lincolnshire Archives Office, The Gaol, Lincoln

LRO   Lincolnshire Records Office, The Gaol, Lincoln.

L. & P. Hen. VIII   Letters and Papers of Henry VIII (London, 1862–1910)

LRS   Lincoln Record Society

N. Staffs. Jl.F.S.   North Staffordshire Journal of Field Studies

PRO   Public Record Office, Chancery Lane, London

RO   Record Office

Trans. N. Staffs. F.C.   Transactions of the North Staffordshire Field Club

TBGAS   Transactions of the Bristol and Gloucestershire Archaeological Society

VCH   *Victoria County History*

I

THE CONTENT AND SOURCES OF ENGLISH AGRARIAN HISTORY AFTER 1500

PRESENT knowledge concerning the agrarian history of England after 1500 owes most to a group of historians who published books on the subject in the period 1907–15. An earlier generation of scholars, including Seebohm, Vinogradoff, and Maitland, had devoted their attention to the origins of the manor and its development in the Middle Ages. The next generation broadened its interests to cover later periods and other aspects of agrarian life: agricultural techniques, and the economics of farming, as well as tenurial relationships. The history of farming from the earliest times was surveyed by W. H. R. Curtler in *A Short History of English Agriculture* (1909), and by R. E. Prothero (later Lord Ernle) in *English Farming Past and Present* (1912). Enclosure, and particularly the effects of Parliamentary enclosure, were discussed by Gilbert Slater in *The English Peasantry and the Enclosure of the Common Fields* (1907), by A. H. Johnson in *The Disappearance of the Small Landowner* (1909), and by E. C. K. Gonner in *Common Land and Inclosure* (1912). The economics of peasant versus capitalist agriculture were examined by the German scholar Hermann Levy in *Large and Small Holdings*, first published in 1904 and enlarged in an English translation in 1911. A *History of the English Agricultural Labourer* by the German political economist W. Hasbach appeared in an English translation in 1908, with a preface by Sidney Webb. It was followed in 1911 by *The Village Labourer*, a more concentrated study of the effects of Parliamentary enclosure on the same class by J. L. and Barbara Hammond. Professor R. H. Tawney pushed the investigation back in time, and in *The Agrarian Problem in the Sixteenth Century* (1912) analysed the impact of the price revolution on the rural classes. Finally, the American historian H. L. Gray made a study of English field systems in a book of that name, published in 1915.

These were landmarks in the writing of modern agrarian history, and since all appeared within a few years of each other, it looked as though a strong school of agrarian history had been established. In fact, however, the subject languished for the next twenty years. This may have been due in part to the authoritative nature and seeming finality of the works then published—they are still the standard text-books on their subjects, and are likely to remain so for years to come —but the more likely explanation is that they were a by-product of hot political debate, which lost energy and urgency when war brought prosperity to the farmer in 1914. The writings of these historians made their appearance during an agricultural depression, in the midst of earnest, anxious discussion about the future of agriculture, which taxed the historian with questions about the past. What had happened to the stout English peasantry of the golden Tudor age? Had the Parliamentary enclosure of the open fields, so long acclaimed as a wholly progressive measure, benefited society as much as it had benefited the land? Had peasant proprietorship possessed some virtue, unseen till now when disaster befell? Did the past, in short, hold the lost key to agricultural prosperity?

Writing in an atmosphere charged with 'anticipations, whether true or false, of coming change,'[1] none of these scholars could fail to be aware of the topical nature of their researches. Some, having reached their conclusions, threw their opinions into the political debate. Lord Ernle wrote in the conviction that 'a considerable increase in the number of peasant ownerships, in suitable hands, on suitable land, and in suitable localities, was socially, economically, and agriculturally advantageous.' Hasbach held that an increase in peasant proprietorship was not only desirable, but inevitable, a view which was not shared by the writer of the preface to his book, Sidney Webb. Gilbert Slater summed up his opinion in the sentence 'British agriculture must be democratised,' which allowed for the increase of small holdings and allotments, together with some form of agricultural co-operation 'suitable to modern conditions,' which he did not further define.[2]

These views read oddly nowadays, but in the circumstances of the time they were not illogical. The tide of opinion, among historians at least, was running in favour of small holdings, because these had withstood the rigours of economic depression better than the large farms.[3] With the outbreak of war in 1914, however, the discussion was postponed because the problems of agriculture were temporarily

[1] R. E. Prothero, *English Farming Past and Present* (2nd ed., 1919), p. 393.
[2] *Ibid*, p. vii; W. Hasbach, *A History of the English Agricultural Labourer*, p. x; Gilbert Slater, *The English Peasantry and the Enclosure of the Common Fields*, p. vii.
[3] See Hermann Levy's explanation in *Large and Small Holdings*, pp. 1–2, 211.

solved. After the war, the controversy did not again engage the historians.

The significance of the meagre harvest of writing on agrarian history after 1915 is easily misunderstood, however. After a lull of some twenty years, fresh advances in understanding of the subject began to be made in the 'thirties through more modest local studies, many of which were prepared as university theses and never published. Their scope was narrow, geographically speaking—the history of a county or smaller unit, covering no more than a century or two—but they immensely enriched the content of agrarian history by underlining the great diversity of farming practice and social structure between regions. In consequence, scholars turned away from the writing of general works on a national scale and concentrated instead on regional studies, mostly written up into articles for local historical societies. Even so, the harvest of writing between 1918 and 1945 could not be called abundant. The more remarkable growth of interest in the subject has taken place since 1945, and has been coincident with the development of local history. Under its influence, agrarian historians have been drawn from the study of single aspects of the rural economy such as field systems, rents, tenures, or social classes towards the study of the local community in all its aspects.[4] At the same time, monographs on medieval estates have demonstrated the wisdom of this approach by showing the complex circumstances in which regional variations emerge. They have shown that the current facts of landownership, land distribution, tenure, and agricultural prices do not alone account for regional eccentricity, that some of its causes lie deeper, in soil and physical environment, the history of early settlement, size of population, and local customs of inheritance.[5]

The scope of agrarian history has broadened, therefore, but so also have the sources of information. New classes of documents have been discovered, and more assiduous use is being made of evidence on the ground. Fresh paths have been opened up, and more pitfalls dug for the unwary.

[4] A pioneer study was J. D. Chambers, *Nottinghamshire in the Eighteenth Century*, 1932. It was not concerned with agrarian history alone, but was the study of a community from all points of view, inspired by the belief that local history could enlarge our understanding of national history.
[5] See, in particular, R. H. Hilton, *Social Structure of Rural Warwickshire in the Middle Ages*, Dugdale Society Occasional Papers, No. 9, 1950; G. R. J. Jones, 'Some Medieval Rural Settlements in North Wales', *Institute of British Geographers: Transactions and Papers*, No. 19, 1953, pp. 51–72; G. C. Homans, 'The Rural Sociology of Medieval England', *Past and Present*, No. 4, 1953, pp. 32–43.

Study of the ground evidence is as yet in its infancy. Our present meagre apparatus of knowledge does not allow us to interpret the landscape without much preliminary information from documents. Perhaps this will always be so. On the other hand, it is conceivable that new methods will be devised, at least for dating features in the landscape, which will relieve some of the pressure on documents. As things are at present, the history of fen reclamation, or of sheep farming on the Cistercian granges of Yorkshire, can be placed in their exact topographical setting by reference to the fendikes, the sheephouses, and sheepwalk boundary marks which survive on the ground. But without documents—and this is the problem which obstructs the interpretation of ridge and furrow—much evidence of the landscape is unusable.[6]

This is not to say that the general survey of a region as it is today will not help the historian to reconstruct in imagination the condition of the land in the sixteenth century. The disposition of most villages, rivers, and meadows, for example, remains the same. The principal changes that must be allowed for in the appearance of the country-side are those brought about by enclosure, land drainage, and the use of artificial fertilizers. Sixteenth- and seventeenth-century writers on husbandry have made us familiar with contemporary techniques and tools of husbandry.[7] Knowing their limitations, and with a rough mental picture of the countryside before the improvements of the nineteenth century, we shall be prepared for some of the more obvious regional differences. On grounds of common sense, it is likely, for example, that farmers in coastal villages with wide stretches of saltmarsh will favour sheep fattening rather than crop growing; that farmers in the ill-drained fenland will specialize in cattle rather than corn, since seasonal flooding exposes their fields to continuous risk. Farmers on the clays may concentrate on corn or stock, or give equal attention to both according to the state of the market and their personal preferences, but a farmer in the chalk country will have less choice. His arable is restricted by the amount of manure he can get from the cattle and sheep which he feeds on the downland commons. If no stint of animals is in operation, a convention, not always strictly adhered to, required him to limit them to the number he could winter on his arable land.

[6] For an excellent combination of documentary and ground evidence, see H. E. Hallam, *The New Lands of Elloe*, Department of English Local History, Occasional Paper No. 6, University College of Leicester, 1954.

[7] For a bibliographical discussion of these writings, see G. E. Fussell, *The Old English Farming Books from Fitzherbert to Tull*, 1947; *More Old English Farming Books from Tull to the Board of Agriculture*, 1950.

If physical conditions prepare us for certain conclusions about sixteenth-century husbandry in a particular district, we may look for confirmatory evidence in the manorial surveys, which show the proportion of cultivated land on the manor which was devoted to arable, meadow, and pasture. Manorial surveys were intended to inform the manorial lord of the way in which his land was tenanted and rented. The fullest survey, though rare to find, will give the size of each tenant's holding, the acreage of each man's arable, meadow, pasture, and closes, the type and conditions of tenure, the rents and dues, the area of common pasture, and the stint of animals allowed to each tenant according to the size of his arable holding. The most detailed and informative manorial surveys belong to the sixteenth and seventeenth centuries. In the eighteenth century their place was taken by valuations, which contain equivalent information, or by rentals, but these omit descriptions of the uses and disposition of the land.[8]

An examination of some manorial surveys of the Midlands suggests that in districts of mixed husbandry it was usual for somewhere between 60 and 80 per cent of the cultivated land (i.e. excluding the common pastures and waste) to be devoted to crops. In a pastoral region the proportion of ploughland was not likely to exceed 45 per cent, and might fall as low as 10 per cent. To measure the full significance of these variations, however, it is necessary to know what proportion of the arable land was sown each year. Some land was sufficiently fertile to be fallowed every fourth year, other land was fallowed every third or even every second year. Unfortunately, the number of fields is not a reliable guide to the rotation. It is frequently true that a village possessing fields with two or three clear directional names, such as North and South Fields, or East, West, and South Fields, will have two- or three-course rotations respectively. But since villages might modify the rotation when there were more mouths to be fed, or because of an increase or diminution in the supply of manure, or as a result of piecemeal enclosure, guesswork by the sixteenth century is dangerous. A statement about the rotations will sometimes be found in a manorial survey, or in a manorial court roll. It may occur incidentally in the bills of plaintiff and defendant in a lawsuit, or it may not be mentioned anywhere.[9]

---

[8] A number of surveys have been printed by local societies. See, for example, *Surveys of the Manors of Philip, First Earl of Pembroke and Montgomery, 1631–2*, ed. E. Kerridge, Wilts Archaeolog. and Nat. Hist. Soc., Records Branch, ix, 1953.

[9] See also below, page 8.

In both arable and pastoral farming regions it is usual, in the sixteenth century, to find some 8 to 15 per cent of the cultivated land in meadow, while the rest of the land, apart from the open arable, is taken up with temporary ley,[10] or with pasture closes. These may lie at the back of the farmhouse, or they may consist of consolidated strips taken out of the open fields and held in severalty. By the sixteenth century, in the Midlands at least, the area of commons and waste in districts of mixed husbandry was small, while in pastoral areas it was extensive. The chief reason for this was that pastoral areas had their husbandry thrust upon them by the physical conditions, and if the land was not suited to crops, not only was there less incentive to engage in assarting, but there were often positive advantages to the majority in keeping their grazing in common.[11] In districts of mixed farming where the waste was potential arable land, gradual encroachments in the course of the centuries had brought much of it into cultivation, and by the sixteenth century there was only a limited quantity of common pasture left.

Manorial surveys indicate broad differences in land-use, but it is on the probate inventories, which record the crops and stock on individual farms, that the more detailed picture of husbandry depends. Inventories are lists drawn up by neighbours of the possessions of a deceased person who has left a will. They list his furniture and household possessions room by room, the animals and implements in the yard, the animals and crops in the fields, and the quantity of grain, hemp, flax, wool, wood, and hay in store. The animals are usually counted and classified with great care. Less often, the exact acreages of the crops growing in the fields are given.[12]

The inventories available to the historian at present are those of wills proved in local probate courts, and housed either in the local probate registries or in local record offices. Inventories of wills

[10] For the use of leys in open fields, see W. G. Hoskins, *Essays in Leicestershire History*, 1951, pp. 140–4.

[11] See the preamble of the Inclosure Prevention Act, 1684, repealing certain clauses of an act of 15 Chas. II (an Act for settling the draining of the Great Level) which had allowed manorial lords to enclose a part of the commons for themselves. '. . . such taking and cutting of the said commons and wastes into small pieces is since found to be very prejudicial to the owners and country, being a great waste of ground in division, which are hard to be kept as fences between party and party, the roadways and passages through such commons as set forth being very low, and generally in bad ground, not passable or well to be amended, whereby such divisions are of little value.' —Samuel Wells, *The History of the Drainage of the Great Level*, 1830, II, pp. 519–20.

[12] A sample of Essex inventories has been printed in *Farm and Cottage Inventories of Mid-Essex*, ed. F. W. Steer, Essex County Council, 1950.

proved in the Prerogative Court of Canterbury, which include those of the more substantial gentry, are at Somerset House, London, but are not available for inspection. The inventories begin in the 1530's, and are most informative in the sixteenth and seventeenth centuries. They become less detailed in the course of the eighteenth century, and cease about 1830.

Since the inventories have only recently been explored by economic historians, certain problems are as yet unsolved concerning their reliability for use in comparative studies between different periods and different districts. The question is of fundamental importance for agrarian history, since the character of farming regions will not be fully uncovered without the aid of comparative statistical material from different districts. Yet the answer must wait upon further use of the inventories, and the comparison of results with information derived from other sources. It is a case of having to use the tools in order to learn how to use them.

The main question is whether the inventories fairly represent all classes of the community. A recent study of this question showed that in one Nottinghamshire village hardly more than a quarter of the population which died between 1572 and 1600 left wills, while in the period 1660–1725 the proportion was just over a fifth. Yet the most cursory examination of inventories will show a wide variety of social classes represented: not only gentry and yeomen, but husbandmen, craftsmen, labourers, and widows. The first question then can be reduced to this: how poor and how numerous were the very poor who were omitted? The second question is whether the inventories of the seventeenth and eighteenth centuries were equally representative of the same classes. Can a comparison be safely made between standards of wealth at two different periods, or did the habit of leaving wills gradually lose its hold on the poorer classes? Did more and more of the gentry and even the yeomen apply for probate to the Prerogative Court of Canterbury? In this connection, it is prudent to notice conclusions drawn from the inventories of four Nottinghamshire parishes, even though the sample is a small one. They showed that the proportion of craftsmen and labourers represented in them fell considerably as between the period 1575–1639 and 1660–99. This may reflect similar changes in the class structure of the four parishes. But if so, it is the reverse of the class changes which we have been taught to expect.[13] So far as our experience extends at the moment, it

---

[13] Class representation in the inventories is considered in Maurice Barley, 'Farmhouses and Cottages, 1550–1725', *Economic History Review*, 2nd Series, vii, 1955, pp. 291–306. A sample of inventories from four Nottinghamshire parishes, 1575–1639,

would seem to be safer to make comparisons between regions than between centuries.

Of greatest value to the agrarian historian is the information in the inventories concerning the numbers of stock, the acreage of crops, the quantity of grain and other farm produce in store, and the implements and tools of husbandry and of the dairy. Judging from the inventories of Leicestershire and Lincolnshire in the sixteenth century, the two most important crops grown by the Midland peasant were barley and pulses. Wheat ranked third in importance, rye fourth, and oats fifth. But although this order of precedence was widely observed, the average area of sown land, and the portion of land devoted to each crop, varied significantly between regions. In Lincolnshire, for example, barley occupied 58 per cent of a sown area of twenty-six acres on the wolds and heath; 54 per cent of a sown area of eight acres in the fens, 42 per cent of a sown area of sixteen acres in the clay vales, and 30 per cent of a sown area of seventeen acres in the marshland. In the Leicestershire claylands the figures were much the same as for the Lincolnshire clays. The average sown area was about twenty acres, of which some 38 per cent was sown with barley.[14]

Experience so far suggests that single inventories are of little use for indicating the crop rotations of the open fields. More often than not, there is an awkward disproportion in the amount of land which the peasant had under spring and winter crops.[15] This was probably due to the disproportions in the amount of land he held in each field—the result of much buying and selling of land over the centuries. It meant that the peasant whose land lay wholly in the open fields did not reap the same harvest every year. Alternative explanations of the disproportion are that parts of his arable land were enclosed, and not subject to the same rotations as the land in the open fields, or that not all the arable lay in one village and subject to the same field course.

The study of single inventories is necessary to explain individual

Continued

showed the classes represented in the following proportions: gentry 5 per cent; yeomen 11.4 per cent; husbandmen 15.7 per cent; craftsmen 11 per cent; labourers 21.5 per cent; widows 11.6 per cent; not stated 23.7 per cent. If the last two groups are omitted from the figures, the proportions are as follows: gentry 7.7 per cent; yeomen 17.6 per cent; husbandmen 24.3 per cent; craftsmen 16.9 per cent; labourers 33.2 per cent. These figures seem to give generous weight to the lower classes. The proportion of labourers agrees with the evidence of the 1524 subsidy that one-third of the population of most villages depended at least in part on wages for a living.

[14] W. G. Hoskins, *op. cit.*, pp. 137, 160, 168, 171.

[15] See the attempt to deduce rotations from inventories in Julian Cornwall, 'Farming in Sussex, 1540–1640', *Sussex Archaeological Collections*, XCII, 1954, pp. 71–2.

idiosyncracies in stock keeping, but average figures for a whole region are the vital clue to regional specialization. Nearly all Midland peasants who left wills at death kept a cow or two, fewer people kept sheep and pigs, and fewer still horses, while goats were almost, if not entirely, unknown. These generalizations mask striking regional differences. For example, in sixteenth-century Lincolnshire the average flock of sheep in the claylands was twenty-six, whereas in the marshland, the centre of sheep fattening, it was forty. The average farmer in the more wooded claylands kept six pigs, where the fenland peasant with meagre resources of wood and scrub kept only four. Cattle of all kinds were more numerous on the farms of the fen and marsh than on the wolds and heath. It is from these and other comparative observations that regional variations in Lincolnshire finally emerge, and lay bare the contrast between the dairying and sheep husbandry of the fenland, the sheep and cattle fattening of the marshland, the sheep and barley farming of the wolds and heath, and the mixed husbandry of the clay vales.[16]

Having obtained some idea of land use and the specialized husbandry of a region, the historian must consider the size and social structure of its villages, for changes in population and land distribution in the next two centuries exerted a profound influence on the organization and techniques of farming. The size of village communities can be gauged from ecclesiastical returns giving the number of families or communicants in the parish. In 1563 the archdeacons of the dioceses throughout the kingdom were asked to submit a return of the number of families in each parish, and although the order was not everywhere complied with, the returns for many dioceses have survived.[17] In some, the enquiry was followed by others, which, so long as the figures are directly comparable, allow changes in population to be observed at different dates in the course of the next two hundred years. In the diocese of Lincoln,[18] for example, the number of communicants was returned in 1603, the number of communicants and nonconformists in 1676, the number of families in 1705–23, and the number of families in 1788–92. In districts where no such returns exist, the hearth tax returns, which are tax assessments covering various years between 1662 and 1674, and

---

[16] The regions of Lincolnshire are analysed in greater detail in Joan Thirsk, *English Peasant Farming*, London, 1957, reprinted 1981.

[17] These returns are in British Museum, Harleian MSS 594, 595, and 618.

[18] The diocese of Lincoln included the counties of Lincolnshire, Leicestershire, Bedfordshire, Buckinghamshire, Hertfordshire, and Huntingdonshire.

which give the names of all householders paying the tax, together
with those who were exempt on grounds of poverty, can be used to
give a rough idea of the number of houses per village in the mid-
seventeenth century.[19]

For a picture of the social structure of a village or district,
information has to be drawn from two imperfect sources. The
manorial survey gives the size of farm holdings rented directly from
the lord, but it tells us nothing about the sub-letting and exchange-
letting which went on among tenants, and which is known to have
been considerable. This is a serious shortcoming, but it does not
empty the survey of all useful content. It may not tell the exact truth
concerning the distribution of land among the tillers of the soil, but at
the same time it is unlikely to distort the picture out of all recognition.
In the fenland of Holland, for example, where there were frequently
three, four, or five manors per village, the manorial survey shows a
large proportion of very small allotment-like holdings. Since it is
probable that many peasants held land of more than one manor, a
single manorial survey undoubtedly exaggerates the smallness of the
holdings. Yet at the same time, it serves to illustrate reliably enough
the contrast between the small holdings of the fen and the large farms
of the neighbouring wolds.[20]

The second source of information on the class composition of the
village is the subsidy assessment of 1524, which was a completely new
assessment in that year, village by village, of all persons possessing
goods or lands, or earning wages, worth at least twenty shillings a
year. In the country districts, though not in the town, this assessment
seems to have included the great majority of householders, and
although the meaning of the valuations placed on goods and land is
not yet fully understood, they seem to offer a rough and ready guide to
the relative distribution of wealth in the village. They emphasize the
contrast, for example, between the social structure of the small wold
villages of Lincolnshire, which possessed a rich squire, one or two
yeomen and husbandmen, and a group of wage labourers, and the
large fen villages with every grade of wealth represented in a

---

[19] The Hearth Tax Returns are discussed in C. A. F. Meekings, *Surrey Hearth Tax,
1664*, Surrey Record Society, XVII, parts 41–2, 1940.

[20] In fact, however, the fenland yields another type of record, peculiar to the district,
the acre book, which is an assessment for sewer tax compiled on a *parish* basis, and
listing every acre of land in the parish and the tenants' names. For evidence of land
distribution based on surveys, see, for example, Joan Thirsk, *Fenland Farming in the
Sixteenth Century*, Occasional Paper No. 3, University College of Leicester, 1953,
pp. 39–40.

gradually descending scale.[21]

The broad picture of a region, showing the size of the average village community, its class structure, and predominant system of husbandry in the sixteenth century, lays the foundation for the third and most important task of all, to trace the process of change in the course of the next three and a half centuries, and if possible analyse its causes. To do this, account must be taken of the many aspects of social and economic development which, by their interaction, brought about alterations in farming practice: changes in market demand, for example; changes in food habits and standards of living; changes in the distribution of land between classes, and changes in the size of classes; and finally, more important than any of these as the agent of agricultural revolution, the changing relationship between the supply of land and the size of the population. Any community which earns its living almost exclusively from agriculture will be most profoundly affected in its husbandry by alterations in its resources of land or people.

Many of these changes can be traced for the seventeenth century in the same classes of documents as were used to compile the account of the Tudor period, particularly manorial surveys, probate inventories, and ecclesiastical returns of population. The progress of enclosure may be judged from the returns of the enclosure commissioners of 1517, 1548, 1565, and 1607,[22] from lawsuits concerning land, from surveys, and terriers (including glebe terriers),[23] and for the second half of the seventeenth century onwards from formal enclosure agreements, found among family papers or among Chancery Decrees in the Public Record Office.[24]

A great wealth of material on agrarian matters will be found in lawsuits: in the bills and answers of plaintiff and defendant, and sometimes in enquiries carried out locally by specially appointed commissioners in an effort to reach a settlement. They may describe and account for changes in crop rotations and fallowing, enclosure

---

[21] For examples of the use of the subsidy assessment, see W. G. Hoskins, *op. cit.*, pp. 127–30; Joan Thirsk, *op. cit.*, pp. 43–4.

[22] These records were used extensively in Maurice Beresford, *The Lost Villages of England*, 1954, *passim*, but see in particular pp. 106, 142, and footnotes 1, 2, and 3, p. 423.

[23] For a description of glebe terriers, see M. W. Beresford, 'Glebe Terriers and Open-Field Leicestershire', *Studies in Leicestershire Agrarian History*, Trans. Leics. Archaeolog. Soc. for 1948, 1949, pp. 77–125.

[24] For examples of enclosure agreements enrolled in Chancery, and their resemblance to later Parliamentary enclosure awards, see *Victoria County History of Leicestershire*, II, 1954, pp. 218, 225.

disputes and agreements, the engrossing of farms, gains of land by reclamation along the coast, losses through erosion, and the improvement of waste, commons, and fen inland. Disputes about broken sales contracts may disclose the most important markets for agricultural produce, and the principal channels of trade with neighbouring counties and London. Areas where the pasture shortage was becoming acute will be disclosed in lawsuits concerning the unauthorized use of commons by outsiders, or the overcharging of the commons by the inhabitants. Since many changes in farming techniques in the course of the sixteenth and seventeenth centuries were due fundamentally to the shortage of land, brought about by the increase of population and the growing commercial incentive to use the land more productively, it is essential to ascertain the urgency of this problem in a region. In some pastoral areas, a grazing shortage was unknown in the Tudor period and the commoners' animals were still unstinted. In others, stints were in operation, but they were generous. In the clay Midlands, however, there were many signs of increasing economy in the use of both arable and pasture. The insufficiency of arable in some townships led to a reduction in the number of fallows in the open fields. Pasture scarcity led sometimes to the introduction of a stint, limiting the numbers of cattle, horses, and sheep which each commoner might keep on the common, or a reduction in the number previously permitted. Sometimes the crisis precipitated the partial or complete enclosure of a village, since enclosure enabled each farmer to use his land as he pleased. Short of this, it might persuade individuals to lay more and more of their arable strips under temporary grass or ley. They were then obliged to tether their animals for grazing immediately their neighbours sowed corn in the remaining strips in the furlong, but neither lost any common rights by the change in land-use, for after harvest both the leys and the grain stubble were thrown open to the stock of the whole town.

For the eighteenth and nineteenth centuries, the evidence of agrarian change is to be found in Parliamentary enclosure awards, land tax assessments, rentals, tithe awards, and crop returns, and in officially printed population censuses, Parliamentary papers on the state of agriculture, agricultural statistics from 1866 onwards, and newspapers.[25]

Parliamentary enclosure awards, which may be found in parish

---

[25] The list of sources described below is of manuscript, not printed sources, which are too numerous to be dealt with adequately here.

chests, among private muniments, or among the records of the Clerk of the Peace, set out all the new allotments of land and the new roads to be made. They have been much studied of late, mainly as a check upon the opinion held by earlier historians such as J. L. and Barbara Hammond that enclosure 'broke the back of the peasant community.'[26] The execution of enclosures, their cost, and social consequences have all come under scrutiny. The approach to the last problem has been made by comparing the distribution of land at the time of the enclosure award with that which can be inferred from the apportionment of land tax between 1780 and 1832. The tendency nowadays is to praise the fairness of the enclosure commissioners (Dr J. D. Chambers has gone so far as to call Parliamentary enclosure 'a milestone in the recognition of the *legal* rights of humble men'), to treat sceptically the complaints of contemporaries about the high cost of enclosure, and to play down the contribution of enclosure towards the decline of the peasantry. Apart from the fact that enclosure often tended at first to increase, rather than reduce, the number of land-owning peasants, it is now recognized that their decline was already under way in the late seventeenth century. At the same time, it is important to remember that all recent studies of this subject have been of a statistical nature, and have traced the fortunes of classes, not of individuals. They have ignored the personal tragedies of enclosure, with which contemporaries were much concerned, because the administrative documents, while illustrating the transfer of land from one class to another, do not readily disclose, and certainly do not explain, transfers of land within a single class. The peasant, ruined by enclosure, who gave up his holding to another of his class, does not proclaim his tragedy loudly enough to be heard in the pages of the land tax. His story is more likely to be found in the pamphlet literature of the time.[27]

Tithe awards, which were nineteenth-century agreements for the commutation of tithes in kind, give the amount of tithable land in the parish, its current use as arable, meadow, or pasture, and the money charge to be borne by each landowner after commutation. When the whole of the parish is tithable, the award gives a complete picture of land use and the size of farms.

---

[26] J. L. & Barbara Hammond, *The Village Labourer*, Guild Book edition, 1948, I, p. 101.
[27] J. D. Chambers, 'Enclosure and Labour Supply in the Industrial Revolution', *Econ. Hist. Rev.*, 2nd Series, V, 1953, pp. 319–43, and the works cited in the footnotes. The phrase quoted is on p. 327; W. E. Tate, 'The Cost of Parliamentary Enclosure in England', *ibid.*, 1952, pp. 258–65.

During the French wars when the grain shortage and consequent high prices threatened to cause serious social disturbance, crop returns were collected by the Home Office covering the years 1793, 1794, 1795, 1800, and 1801. A full account has been given recently of the origin of the returns, and of contemporary opinions on their reliability,[28] but although some of the returns have been printed and commented upon, no attempt has been made so far by modern historians to investigate their accuracy. It is known that the total acreage returned for each parish was rarely a complete record of the total land under crops. It is likely, however, that the returns indicate reliably the proportionate importance of each crop.

It is impossible in a short article to give due consideration to all the diverse aspects of change which fall within the province of agrarian history. Some of the problems enumerated here will be found amplified in accounts of regional economies already published. But the study of a fresh district will always prompt new questions or suggest fresh answers to old problems of explaining the seeming eccentricity of local farming practice and social organization. At the same time, the student will encounter problems of interpretation which defy solution until more regional surveys are available for comparison. He will notice more acutely than before the lamentable gaps in our knowledge of even general agricultural trends. Writing on the sixteenth century has so far been almost exclusively concerned with enclosure and rent. The seventeenth century has received hardly any attention: the first forty years have been treated as a tailpiece to the boom of the sixteenth century, the next twenty years as a bleak and barren interlude, and the last forty years as a period of preparation for the so-called eighteenth-century agricultural revolution. This revolution has been seen only through the eyes of four exceptional farmers, Lord Townshend, Coke of Holkham, Jethro Tull, and Robert Bakewell, and is therefore hopelessly out of focus. Later eighteenth- and nineteenth-century writing has dwelt mainly on the changes in land-ownership effected by Parliamentary enclosure, and on nineteenth-century depressions affecting the corn-growing districts. In a sense, however, local studies have postponed immediate consideration of problems of general development by

[28] W. E. Minchinton, 'Agricultural Returns and the Government during the Napoleonic Wars', *Agricultural History Review*, I, 1953, pp. 29–43. This article lists all the returns in print at that time, to which the following should be added: R. A. Pelham, 'The 1801 Crop Returns for Staffordshire in their Geographical Setting', *Coll. for History of Staffs.*, 1950–51, pp. 231–42.

showing that England has not one agrarian history but many, that the old corn-growing areas of the Midlands are not the whole of England. No new survey of English agrarian society and agriculture will be entitled to the name which does not take full account of the diversified character and fortunes of its many regions.

II
SOURCES OF INFORMATION ON
POPULATION, 1500–1760

THERE are many as yet unanswered questions relating to population trends in the period 1500–1760. It is generally accepted that the total population of England rose throughout the period 1500–1640, though the rate of increase was not constant and slowed down in the last forty years. It is also well established that population began to grow again after 1700 and more rapidly after 1750. But what happened between 1640 and 1700? And to what extent was the rise of the sixteenth century and the trend upward or downward in the seventeenth and early eighteenth centuries at the same rate in all parts of the country? It is certain that the pace of increase and decrease differed between town and country. It is probable that the pace differed in different districts of the countryside, in part because of local differences in the death rate if not of the birth rate—though this subject has never been properly investigated—more certainly because of immigration into and emigration out of the village. There are, for example, contemporary statements to the effect that people were attracted into areas where the commons were still extensive and squatters could acquire common rights without much difficulty. A description of the manor of Epworth in Axholme, written in 1675, tells us that there were five hundred cottages in the manor, many of them erected within recent years, and that 'the liberty the common people have of graving (i.e. digging) in the common is that which draws multitudes of the poor sort from all the countries adjacent to come and inhabit in the Isle'.[1] One further factor gave rise to local differences in the rate of population change. It is known that villages varied in their attitude towards newcomers wishing to settle among them. In some villages immigration was carefully controlled or entirely prohibited by a resident manorial lord who was anxious not to harbour too many landless people lest they should later become a charge on the parish. In others, where manorial control was weak or

[1] John Rylands Library, Manchester, Ry. Ch. 2550.

non-existent, newcomers were accommodated willingly. Such villages sometimes grew rapidly in size, and in the nineteenth century were called 'open villages.' They were so well furnished with agricultural labourers above their local needs that they supplied gangs for work on more distant farms, where, for the first time, old commons on chalk and limestone upland and in the fens were being brought under the plough.

In short, there are three factors which must have given rise to local differences in the rate of population change even though the general trend was everywhere the same. These were differences in the death rate if not also of the birth rate; local differences in the attractiveness of certain villages and towns to those seeking a home and employment; local differences in manorial policy towards newcomers.

If local population changes can be determined more exactly for this period, they will help towards posing and answering some of the more general questions bearing on economic and social development in the same period, for population changes are one of the mainsprings of economic change. One example will serve to illustrate the connection. Villages which grew rapidly—sometimes by as much as half—in the sixteenth century had somehow to find a living for their extra households. To do so, many were driven to colonize hitherto neglected waste, to devise more economical ways of using their older cultivated lands (by taking a crop in the fallow year, for example), sometimes to enclose their commons and fields, sometimes to develop other forms of industrial employment such as the knitting of stockings or the weaving of cloth. It is probably no accident that framework hosiery knitting spread into many Leicestershire villages in the second half of the seventeenth century when those villages had reached the limit, within the framework of current technical knowledge, in the economical use of their land resources. In short, if one is to explain fully why farming organization and methods changed more rapidly at some periods than at others, it is essential to estimate the influence of rising population and the rising demand for food in both town and country.

It follows, therefore, that any study of village population can contribute something towards establishing the connection between economic change and changes in the size of population. The two immediate questions to be answered are: (1) At what rate did population increase or decrease in the period 1500–1760? (2) To what extent were there regional variations of increase and decrease?

A number of sources exist for this purpose. The birth and death registers of any parish may be used to estimate the natural increase or decrease of population. But to estimate total populations at different periods between 1500 and 1603 there are some ecclesiastical censuses, and some tax lists which are considered to be almost as complete as a census of households.

The subsidy assessment of 1524 was a new village by village assessment of all persons having land, movable goods, or wages worth £1 a year or more. The definition given to movable goods was comprehensive. It included such things as household goods, coin and plate, stock of merchandise, farm stock, including crops already harvested. It excluded only standing corn and personal attire. Men with property in more than one place were assessed in the village in which they normally lived. Everyone was taxed on the source of wealth—land, goods or wages—which would yield the most.[2]

The subsidy was collected in all counties in England except Northumberland, Cumberland, Westmorland, Chester and the bishopric of Durham. Further exceptions were the Cinque Ports, Brightelmstone and Westbourne in Sussex, the wardens of Rochester Bridge and the town of Ludlow. The Act did not apply in Wales, Ireland, Calais, Guernsey or Jersey.[3] Payment was spread over a period of four years. In the first two years all taxpayers contributed something; in the third and fourth years the tax fell only on those having land or goods worth £50 or more. Hence the assessments for 1524 and 1525 list all taxpayers. Those for 1526 and 1527 list only the wealthiest.

It is generally believed that the subsidy assessments of 1524 and 1525 affected all but the paupers in the population. Since the average daily wage at this period was 6d., and a man working for three hundred days a year earned £7 10s., most wage labourers must have come within the scope of the subsidy. Nevertheless, it is also true that some puzzling problems concerning the incidence of the assessment remain. The Yorkshire lists are so brief that it is obvious that the assessment was not comprehensive in this particular county. There may be other counties which will prove similarly unrewarding, but only by local investigation, only by comparing the subsidy lists with other population censuses can this be more certainly determined. The subsidies that have been examined for certain Midland and southern

[2] For a general discussion of the significance and completeness of this subsidy assessment, see *Lay Subsidy Rolls for the County of Sussex*, 1524–5, ed. Julian Cornwall, *Sussex Record Society*, LVI, Introduction.

[3] *Statutes of the Realm*, III, 230–239.

counties suggest that here at least the assessment was efficiently made.[4] The subsidy for Wigston Magna, in Leicestershire, for example, lists 67 names compared with 80 families in the census of 1563, after some rise in population can reasonably be expected to have taken place.

The second class of documents giving information on total population are the Chantry Certificates of 1547. A chantry was 'a small chapel or enclosure within a church and sometimes a distinct and separate building at a distance from the church in which an altar was erected and consecrated and a priest appointed to chant certain prescribed services for the welfare of individuals, specified by name, whilst they were living, and also for the repose of their souls after death'.[5] The first chantries act of 1545 authorized the King, during his life, to appoint a commission to survey and seize for the King's use all the endowments and property of the chantries. The dissolution of the monasteries had evidently caused the founders and patrons of chantries to anticipate the King and to reclaim property which they or their ancestors had given for pious uses. Being in urgent need of funds to prosecute his wars against France and Scotland, the King was equally determined to acquire this wealth for his own use. The chantries were surveyed, but the King's death rendered the act of 1545 void. A second act was passed in 1547 and a further survey taken. This time the parson and the churchwardens of the parishes were required to state, among other things, the number of housling people in the parish. This is assumed to mean the number of communicants, i.e. the number of people over about fourteen years of age.

It remains for local historians to determine by comparison with other population returns for this period how accurate these chantry certificates were. The editors of the volumes which have already been printed have disagreed about their accuracy,[6] but it is unlikely that a general verdict can be passed which will apply everywhere. The

[4] For an assessment that has been printed, see note 2, above; also *Subsidy Roll for the County of Buckingham, anno* 1524, eds. A. C. Chibnall and A. V. Woodman, *Bucks. Record Society*, VIII, 1950; James Tait, *The Taxation of Salford Hundred, Chetham Society*, N.S., XXXIII, 1924; S. H. A. H(ervey), *Suffolk in 1524, Suffolk Green Books*, X, 1910. The original assessments are in the Public Record Office in Class E179. There is an index to this class of records on the open shelves of the Round Room.

[5] *A History of the Chantries within the County Palatine of Lancaster*, ed. Rev. F. R. Raines, Chetham Soc., LIX, 1862, Vol. I, p. iii.

[6] Certificates which have been printed include *The Chantry Certificates*, ed. Rose Graham, *Oxfordshire Record Society*, I, 1919; *The Survey and Rental of the Chantries . . . in the co. of Somerset*, ed. Emanuel Green, *Somerset Rec. Soc.*, II, 1888; *The*

counting of heads may have been done with great care in one parish and by guesswork in the neighbouring parish. Admittedly, the large round numbers for town populations are suspicious. But the figure of 83 housling people for Standlake and 63 for Minster Lovell in Oxfordshire look like attempts to make an exact enumeration.

A second census of people was taken in 1563 in every diocese of England at the request of the Privy Council. This time the return was of the number of families, not communicants. The census formed part of a general report on the state of the church in every parish, and in some of their replies the archdeacons stated that they had insufficient time to prepare a list of numbers of households and would submit this separately. Some late returns were amalgamated with the other documents, others, if they were ever sent, were never put in their correct place and are therefore missing from the group. Of this census, the returns for Leicestershire and Buckinghamshire have appeared in print.[7] A further parish by parish report was called for in 1603, this time incorporating the number of communicants and recusants. The volumes in which the 1563 returns are bound also contain some of the 1603 returns. They are in the British Museum Manuscripts Room in Harleian 594, 595 and 618. All the 1563 returns that have ever been found are here, but some for 1603 exist in other repositories. Those for the diocese of Lincoln, for example, are at Lincoln and were printed in a volume of the Lincoln Record Society.[8] It is worth making local enquiries in whatever place the diocesan records are kept for other returns for 1603 besides those in the British Museum, and, indeed, for further population returns of a later date, for in some dioceses a census continued to be taken at intervals throughout the seventeenth, eighteenth, and into the nineteenth centuries.

The volumes in the British Museum contain the following returns: Households in 1563 in the dioceses of Bangor, Bath and Wells, Canterbury, Carlisle, Chester, Coventry and Lichfield, Durham and Ely in Harl. 594; 1563 returns for the dioceses of St. David's and Worcester in Harl. 595; 1563 returns for the diocese of Lincoln in Harl. 618; 1603 returns of communicants for the dioceses of Bangor

Certificates of the Commissioners appointed to survey the chantries . . . in the co. of York, part II, ed. W. Page, *Surtees Soc.*, XCII, 1895. The originals of these certificates are in the Public Record Office among the records of the Court of Augmentations.

[7] *Victoria County History of Leicestershire*, III, 1955, pp. 166–7; Julian Cornwall, 'An Elizabethan Census', *Records of Bucks.*, XVI, 4, 1959.

[8] *The State of the Church*, ed. C. W. Foster, *Lincoln Record Soc.*, XXIII, 1926. *See also* V.C.H. *Leics.*, pp. 168–9.

and Gloucester in Harl. 594; 1603 returns for the dioceses of Norwich and Winchester in Harl. 595.

Since the ecclesiastical censuses of 1563 and 1603 dealt with families and communicants, they cannot be exactly compared. But it is possible to turn the number of communicants in 1603 into households. In Leicestershire a figure of 2.8 communicants per household has been arrived at by comparing two later censuses, which are very close to each other in date, the Hearth Tax Return of 1670, enumerating households (to be discussed later) and the ecclesiastical census of 1676 enumerating communicants. When this figure of 2.8 was used to turn the number of communicants in 1603 into households, it was possible to demonstrate that in Leicestershire between 1563 and 1603 the number of families had increased by about 58 per cent.[9]

For anyone attempting a population study of a single parish or a larger district, the two most instructive articles which may serve as models relate to the county of Leicestershire. The first is the chapter on Population by C. T. Smith in the Victoria County History of *Leicestershire*, Volume III. This chapter prints the whole of the 1563 and 1603 returns for that County. The second is an article by Dr. W. G. Hoskins on 'The Population of an English Village, 1086–1801. A Study of Wigston Magna'. *Trans. Leics. Archaeolog. and Hist. Soc.*, XXXIII, 1957, 15–35. These two studies demonstrate better than anything else the methods and the results of an analysis of population.

Those who do not trust this juggling with figures which are not directly comparable must be content with a direct comparison of population in 1524 and 1563. But the two censuses of 1563 and 1603 can be related separately to later censuses of communicants and families, though these comparisons of course bridge much longer periods of time.

Sources of information on population between 1603 and the first national census of 1801 consist almost entirely of tax assessments and ecclesiastical censuses. But it is worth mentioning, first of all, another type of record, unique of its kind—the Protestation Return of 1641–2 —which was in effect a census of all the male inhabitants of the

[9] Dr. Hoskins in the article cited more fully below used a more complicated method of converting the 1603 figures, though the final result is the same as that used by C. T. Smith. He reckoned that the communicants constituted one third of the members of a household and that there were $4\frac{1}{4}$ persons per household.

villages of England and Wales over eighteen years of age. It is not a record that can safely be compared with other censuses, but to the village historian with an intimate knowledge of all the families living in one place it may be of great value as a check upon, or an aid to the understanding of, other records on population.

The Protestation was an oath required of all adult males in 1641, pledging them to defend the true reformed Protestant religion, His Majesty's royal person, and the power and privileges of Parliaments. The document that was returned from each village to Westminster was a list of names of all male inhabitants over the age of eighteen, indicating those who had subscribed to the oath and those who had refused. Some of the returns, for good measure, list the occupations of the oathtakers, not because these details were asked for, but because, thank goodness, there are always over-zealous officials who like to give more information than is required. Among the returns for Lincolnshire, for example, occupations are given for twenty-one villages. In some the inhabitants are divided into two categories only —householders and servants. But in others more precise descriptions are given. North Witham, for example, had forty-four oathtakers, of whom three were described as gentry, two as clergy, eight as husbandmen, five as cottagers, and sixteen as sons and servants. Faldingworth had seventy-four oathtakers, including two gentry, fourteen husbandmen, twenty-eight cottagers, nineteen servants, one labourer and three sojourners.

The original copy of the Protestation Return is deposited at the House of Lords Record Office, where it is available to all students by appointment. Some returns, however, have already appeared in print. The most recent is that for Oxfordshire, which is accompanied by an introduction explaining in further detail the procedure used for the taking of the Protestation.[10] Other returns in print relate to Northumberland, Surrey, Durham, Sussex (the western rapes only), Huntingdonshire and Halifax township.[11]

Anyone wishing to use these figures of adult males in order to gauge the total population of a place in 1642 will find that so much doubtful arithmetic is necessary that the task is hardly worth doing. It might, of course, be possible to do something with the figures of a whole county, since small errors will cancel themselves out, but it is

---

[10] *Oxfordshire Protestation Returns*, 1641–2, ed. Christopher S. Dobson, *Oxfordshire Record Soc.*, XXXVI, 1955.

[11] See *Surtees Soc.*, CXXXV; *Surrey Archaeolog. Coll.*, LIX, 1962; *Sussex Record Soc.*, v; *Trans. Cambs. and Hunts. Archaeolog. Soc.*, v; *Halifax Antiquarian Soc.*, 1919.

impossible to escape large errors when dealing with single villages. In short, the village historian will find it well worth while to look at the Protestation Return if he has other information for the same period requiring clarification, but this is not a census that can be compared with others.

A much more useful record of population is the Hearth Tax Return, which covers the period 1662–74. This tax was first levied in 1662 and abolished in 1689. For part of the time the task of collection was farmed out to contractors and no returns survive. But for certain years in the sixties and seventies there are assessments, county by county, village by village, deposited in the Public Record Office in Chancery Lane, London, in Class E179. There is an index to these records on the shelves of the Round Room.

The hearth tax assessment gives the names of all occupiers (not landlords) of houses and the number of hearths in each house. It is considered to be a reliable record of the number of households in a village, though one must, of course, count both those who paid tax and those who were exempt on the grounds of poverty. Some of the early lists are incomplete, inasmuch as they do not include a list of exemptions. In addition this record may be used as a guide to the size of houses (judged by the number of hearths per house), while the proportion of exemptions (usually about a third of all households in rural areas) has been used as a guide to the scale of the pauper problem. When using the hearth tax assessment for towns, however, some caution must be exercised in estimating total population, for many houses were divided among more than one family, and the assumption that one hearth taxpayer represented one family may not always be valid.

An explanation of the significance of the hearth tax returns is contained in the introduction by C. A. F. Meekings to *The Surrey Hearth Tax*, 1664.[12] The most recent volume to be published on the hearth tax is a transcript of the returns for two divisions in the Hemlingford Hundred of Warwickshire—the first of a series designed to cover the whole county.[13] Others are in print for Newcastle-on-Tyne, Somerset, Staffordshire, Bedfordshire, Suffolk, Dorset, Oxfordshire and Leicestershire.[14]

---

[12] *Surrey Hearth Tax*, 1664, ed. C. A. F. Meekings, *Surrey Record Society*, XVII, 1940.

[13] *Warwick County Records: Hearth Tax Returns*, Vol. 1. *Hemlingford Hundred: Tamworth and Atherstone Divisions*, ed. Margaret Walker, 1957.

[14] For Newcastle-on-Tyne, see *Archaeologia Aeliana*, 3rd Ser., VII, pp. 49–76; for Somerset, see *National Records, I*, ed. R. Holworthy and E. Dwelly, 1916: for Staffs., see

The first *ecclesiastical* census of population after the Restoration was that taken in 1676 throughout the see of Canterbury. So far as is at present known the same enquiry was not carried out in the see of York. This census—usually known as the Compton Return—was a return of the number of communicants, nonconformists and recusants in every village in the southern province. The original manuscript is deposited in the William Salt Library at Stafford, but some of the returns have appeared in print.[15] Since this census was compiled on the same basis as that for 1603, direct comparison between the two is possible. It is also possible to devise a multiplier for converting communicants, etc., into households by comparing the Compton Return with the Hearth Tax assessment. It was by this method that the writer of the article on Population in the *Victoria County History of Leicestershire* arrived at the conclusion that in Leicestershire, at any rate, there were 2.8 communicants per household.

Later ecclesiastical censuses exist for many counties and parts of counties, but no complete list of them has ever been compiled and local enquiry in the diocesan archive offices is necessary. For the County of Lincoln there is a return on families for 1705–23, and another for 1788–92.[16] Oxfordshire has a return of 1738 in print, which includes the number of houses per parish, and in some cases the number of families and the number of communicants.[17] This arch-deaconry also has a return of 1854, although the national census of 1851 renders its population evidence superfluous.[18] The diocese of York, which covers most of Yorkshire, all Nottinghamshire and part of Northumberland, has a visitation return of 1743, also in print, giving the number of families (or in a few cases the number of

---

Trans. William Salt Archaeolog. Soc., 1921, 1923 and 1927; for Beds., see *Beds. Hist. Rec. Soc.*, XVI, 1934; for Suffolk, see *Suffolk Green Books*, No. XI, Vol. XIII, 1905; for Dorset, see *Dorset Nat. Hist. and Arch. Soc.*, 1951; for Oxfordshire, see *Oxon Record Soc.*, XXI, 1940; for Leicestershire, see *Victoria County History*, III, pp. 170–2.

[15] *Victoria County History of Leicestershire*, III, pp. 173–4. *See also* 'Religious Census of Leicestershire in 1676', *Trans. Leics. Archaeolog. Soc.*, VI, 1884–8, pp. 296–306; 'Compton Return, 1676', *Lincolnshire Notes and Queries*, XVI, 1921, pp. 33–511; 'The Compton Census of 1676,' ed. C. W. Chalkin, *Kent. Arch. Soc. Rec. Publications*, XVII, 1960; *Berks, Bucks. & Oxon. Archarolog. Jnl*, IV, 1899.

[16] Both deposited in the Lincolnshire Archives Office, The Gaol, Lincoln. The return for 1705–23 is printed in *Speculum Diocesos Lincolniensis*, Lincs. Record Soc., IV, 1913.

[17] *Bishop Secker's Visitation Returns*, 1738, ed. Rev. H. A. Lloyd Jukes, *Oxon Record Soc.*, XXXVIII, 1957.

[18] *Bishop Wilberforce's Visitation Returns for the Archdeaconry of Oxford*, ed. E. P. Baker, *Oxon Record Soc.*, XXXV, 1954.

inhabitants) per parish.[19] The diocese of Exeter, covering Devon and Cornwall had a visitation in 1821, which records the number of families in each parish.[20] These examples are enough to show that ecclesiastical censuses—at least after 1660—were not uncommon, and to suggest that it is worth while searching for other unprinted records of this kind in diocesan record offices.

One last word of warning is necessary: it is easy when working in detail on population figures to lose sight of the fact that they are rough estimates only. But so long as this is borne constantly in mind, the *more significant, broad* population changes can be demonstrated to good effect. And for anyone working on a county, or a region larger than a parish, population figures can be used for compiling a most instructive population density map which will serve as a pointer to areas of congested population and land shortage. For such a map one can obtain the parish acreages by using one of the nineteenth century directories of the county concerned. One of about 1850 is recommended, for by that time the parishes had been accurately surveyed and yet no great parish boundary changes had taken place. With acreage and population figures, a density map showing families or communicants per thousand acres can be constructed which will help towards the understanding of some of the stresses and strains borne by rural communities between the sixteenth and eighteenth centuries.[21]

POSTSCRIPT

A thorough investigation of the ecclesiastical census of population in 1676 has now been completed by Dr. Anne Whiteman. It has revealed good surviving returns for the diocese of York and a reasonable number for the diocese of Carlisle. One listing of a Lancashire chapelry in Chester diocese shows that an enquiry was initiated there too, but no evidence has been found to show whether one was conducted in Durham diocese.

All the known parish returns, assembled by Dr. Whiteman under the title *The Compton Census of 1676: a critical Edition*, are to be published by the British Academy in its *Records of Social and Economic History, New Series*.

[19] *Archbishop Herring's Visitation Returns*, 1743, ed. S. L. Ollard and P. C. Walker, *Yorks Archaeolog. Soc. Record Ser.*, LXXI, LXXII, LXXXV, LXXXVII.

[20] *The Diocese of Exeter in 1821*, Vol. I, *Cornwall*, Vol. II, *Devon*, ed. M. Cook, *Devon and Cornwall Rec. Soc.*, N.S. III, IV, 1958, 1960.

[21] See the maps of Lincolnshire population densities in 1563 and 1801 in Joan Thirsk, *English Peasant Farming*, 1957, pp. 11, 199.

III
UNEXPLORED SOURCES IN LOCAL RECORDS

IF I had a long list of neglected sources in local record offices, my paper would be so serious a reflection on the work of local archivists and historians that I would not expect to escape lynching. In fact, I do not think there is any large class of records in local record offices that one could say was utterly unexplored. Our archivists have so well publicized their large, and growing, collections of documents in the last fifteen years in guides and annual reports that there is little chance nowadays of anyone alighting on a major source of information that is not known and has not been used before. So well-known are our sources, indeed, that Mr. Michael Robbins began an article in the *Bulletin of the Middlesex Local History Council* (no. 14, December 1962) saying: 'Of the written sources of information available to the local historian, most flow in what one may call the usual channels; the kinds of archive material that any good handbook will call attention to as potential for every district, from the contents of the parish chest onwards. These may be supplemented, with luck, by the papers of a big house, or a local solicitor's accumulation, or sale records, and plans'. And, of course, these chance survivals too are well represented in the collections of the local record office. The truth is that for the local historian the most neglected sources lie not in local record offices, but in the Public Record Office, where large classes of documents are relatively unused because their quantity is daunting, and their indexes are inadequate. Cases in Chancery Proceedings and the Court of Requests, for example, are invaluable to the local historian for their topographical and personal informa-tion, as well as for the factual narratives they contain about the causes in dispute. Much of our best material on the internal marketing of food and agricultural produce, for example, lies in these records—in complaints by merchants about farmers' broken contracts for the sale of grain or stock, in the complaints of ordinary people about cattle drovers who allowed their beasts to graze in unauthorized places on their journeys across the kingdom—we have hardly begun to scratch the surface of this material. And no wonder, for it takes months merely to go through the list of the Chancery cases of the Six Clerks in the seventeenth century looking for a particular district or subject, and this is but a tithe of all the records of the Courts of Westminster.[1]

If it be agreed then that most of the various classes of records of local archives are relatively well known, there are, nevertheless, some which are not as fully used as they should be because the questions they answer have not received proper attention. My remarks are mainly concerned with this type of neglect—the fault of the historian rather than the archivist.

The local historian, though he does not usually recognise it, has much in common with the social anthropologist. Both make studies of small communities, and in both cases, very often, they study an economy that is fairly primitive. One of the first tasks which the anthropologist sets himself when he first makes the acquaintance of a new community is to study the family, the strength of the ties that bind its members together, the duties and obligations that are commonly accepted by members of a family, and the way in which family property is owned, and handed on from generation to generation. English historians are concerned with most aspects of the life of a community, but not, strangely enough, with the family. In ignoring it, I think we are closing our eyes to an institution that had great influence on the social and economic development of local communities. I suspect that different parts of England, not to mention Wales and Scotland, would show notable differences in the strength of family ties, possibly in the composition of the household living under one roof, and certainly in customs of inheritance. And this collection of problems, large though it is, still does not touch the question of changes in the structure of the family at different periods, a matter on which French historians have already advanced some positive views.[2]

We are not without sources of information on the family. One of the finest is wills. We have recently had a study of the charitable bequests in wills of the sixteenth and seventeenth centuries, but no one has yet looked for any consistent pattern in the way that testators

---

[1]　See, for example, *Staffordshire suits in the Court of Star Chamber temp. Henry VII and Henry VIII*, ed. W. K. Boyd (William Salt Archaeolog. Soc. NS. x, 1907), p. 104); and *Chancery proceedings temp. Elizabeth, A.D. 1560 to A.D. 1570*, ed. W. K. Boyd (William Salt Archaeolog. Soc. NS. x, 1907), p. 92.

[2]　*Cf.* Philippe Ariès, *Centuries of childhood* (1962) and the references cited therein, particularly R. Prigent, 'Le renouveau des idées sur la famille', *Institut National d'Etudes Démographiques*, Cahier no. 18 (1954).

provided for their kin, a matter which doubtless disturbed their sleep rather more than their charitable bequests. Attitudes towards the family, and the quality of the relationship between parents and children, are often revealed in the phraseology of wills, and I believe that a comparative study of two contrasted districts in, for example, Westmorland and Hertfordshire, would yield rewarding, and perhaps surprising results. The recent study made by Mr. W. M. Williams of the families living in Gosforth, Cumberland, showed such different patterns of behaviour among children from those generally familiar to us who live in modern industrialized communities that it is not unreasonable to ask whether a similar gulf did not separate the highland peasant family two or three centuries ago from the small merchant living in a commercial centre like London or Bristol.[3]

The structure of the family is also revealed in the way in which people bequeathed their property. Did they usually try to provide in some way for all their children, both male and female, and, if so, how? Was it customary to provide girls with money, and boys with land? Or did all the land go to the eldest son? Is the conventional story about the tyranny of primogeniture and the unhappy fate of younger sons, driven to seek their fortunes in other occupations or in other places, a true picture of all classes of English society, or is it not rather a generalization that applies only to the gentry? I suspect so. And I suspect that the conventions about providing for sons and daughters differed from district to district, possibly also from period to period. Here again, a comparative study is needed.

Another source of information on the descent of land among peasant families is the manorial court roll. This class of record has been used to tell us something about agricultural practice, and the way in which the community disciplined its members, but I know only one study of recent years concerned with the way in which customary holdings passed back and forth over the generations, and the effect of these movements on the size of farms. There are striking contrasts at the present time in the size of farmholdings in different parts of the country: the small landowner may have disappeared from some places, but he shows remarkable tenacity in others. This has to be explained, and some comparative studies of how customary holdings passed from hand to hand in different manors—in pastoral

---

[3] W. K. Jordan, *Philanthropy in England, 1480–1660* (1959); W. M. Williams, *The sociology of an English village: Gosforth.*

compared with arable regions; in districts where land was plentiful
and in those where it was scarce; in manors where partible inheritance
was the custom, and in manors where primogeniture was observed—
would help us to understand a little better the more significant
historic factors affecting the distribution of farm ownership.[4]

I have recently begun a study of the court rolls of the manor of
Tottenham in Middlesex, where the manorial custom was Borough
English. The library committee at Tottenham is enlightened enough
to have embarked on a programme of publishing its very fine
collection of rolls. My purpose is to discover the significance of
Borough English. No one seems to know. The lawyers know what it
was, but have taken no interest in its *effects* on land holding. Did this
custom of descent to the youngest son mean that a man's holding
remained intact from generation to generation, or was it frequently
divided up before death so that the older children could also be
provided for? It is already clear to me that Middlesex in the sixteenth
century is not the best choice of place and time for studying the
influence of such a custom on the distribution of land. Other
influences were more powerful. There were too many merchants of
London hovering in the background waiting for tasty morsels to fall
from the tables of peasants long before they uttered their last breath.
Nevertheless, I do not despair of reaching some conclusion about the
effects of Borough English, though I realize that other districts would
probably produce clearer and more decisive conclusions. There is, in
fact, no lack of examples. It is noticeable how often Borough English
crops up as a custom of inheritance in forest districts, for example, in
Rockingham Forest, Northamptonshire, in Ashdown Forest, Sussex,
and in the Forest of Dean, Gloucestershire. I doubt whether the
landhungry outsider interfered as much with the working of this
custom in these districts as did the Londoner in Tottenham.[5]

Study of the family should also take account of the size of the
elementary family of parents and children, and its age structure.
There may well be regional differences in the size of the family, even
though we find it convenient at present to use an average figure, and
apply it everywhere. Wills can tell us something about the numbers of
children who survived into adolescence and beyond, but the age

[4] J. Z. Titow, 'Some differences between manors and their effects on the condition
of the peasant in the thirteenth century', *Agric. Hist. Rev.* X(I) (1962).
[5] *Court rolls of the Manors of Tottenham*, ed. F. H. Fenton, ii. 1377–99; vi. 1510–31;
viii. 1547–58; P. A. J. Pettit. 'The economy of the Northamptonshire Royal Forests,
1558–1714', Oxford D. Phil. thesis, 1959, p. 360; G. R. Corner, 'On the custom of
Borough English', *Proc. Suffolk Inst. Archaeology*, ii; Glos. City Library, RF 30, 4.

structure of the family is a rather more difficult problem. Yet no one should assume that it would be much the same for all communities at any given period. Mr. Titow has recently compared, with the aid of medieval custumals, the marriage alliances that took place in the manors of Taunton in Somerset, of Witney in Oxfordshire, and Wargrave in Berkshire in the thirteenth century. Taunton was a manor in which virtually all the land had been taken into cultivation; it has no reserves. Witney and Wargrave, on the other hand, had land awaiting colonization. The young men of Taunton were constantly marrying widows, presumably for the sake of their land, outliving them, then taking a young second wife, who frequently outlived her husband, but then robbed the eldest son of the chance of succeeding to his father's holding at a reasonable age. He in turn was driven to marry a widow. On the manors of Witney and Wargrave, where there was land for the taking, men married wives of their own age, and remarriages were far less common. Apart from the different age structure of the family in these two contrasted examples, and its effect on the inheritance prospects of the children, it seems possible that these differences also affected the rate at which population increased in land-hungry communities on the one hand, and in land-sated communities on the other.[6]

And this brings me to another source of information not adequately used at present, the various censuses of population taken at the behest of the church. I tried to compile a complete list some years ago of all the ecclesiastical censuses that existed in print and in the archive offices, but it proved impossible. Some are well known, like the Compton Census of 1676 in the William Salt Library; some are now being publicized in print, like the visitation of 1821 for Cornwall and Devon; some are less familiar, like the census for Lincolnshire of 1788 92, but are listed in record office publications; and some, I suspect, exist in the records of clerical visitations, but are not listed anywhere. An excellent example of the work that can be done with these censuses, when critically used, is Dr. Hoskins's article on the population of Wigston Magna. At present Wigston Magna stands as a typical example of an East Midland village, yet at some periods in its history, in the seventeenth century, for example, I do not think its fortunes were typical. But we cannot be sure without more such studies of village population.[7]

[6] J. Z. Titow, *op. cit.*
[7] *The Diocese of Exeter in 1821*, ed. Michael Cook (Devon and Cornwall Rec. Soc., NS iii, iv, 1958, 1960); W. G. Hoskins. 'The population of an English village, 1086–1801: a study of Wigston Magna', *Leics. Archaeolog. and Hist. Soc.*, xxxiii (1957).

Censuses of population are not the only ecclesiastical records that are somewhat neglected by the historian. There are others that suffer similarly, due to lack of knowledge of their scope. Returns to visitation articles, for example, contain information about schools and their curricula. Ecclesiastical suits, particularly in tithe, are often a mine of information on land use and the relative importance of different crops in a parish. Probate inventories have, of course, received a great amount of attention in recent years, but not enough as yet from the town historian who could write a social history based on this source alone. Inventories of inns, for example, show, indirectly, the astonishing amount of business by inn-keepers in boarding chapmen and merchants in the towns of the seventeenth century. And their lists of goods and chattels tell us directly much about the furnishings of the period. Compare, for example, the two inventories, separated from each other by rather less than a hundred years, of the innkeepers of the White Hart Inn at Petworth in 1670 and 1758. The inn had 24 rooms and outbuildings at both dates; but in 1670 the lodging chambers had much more colourful names than in 1758. There were the Griffin, the Cock, and the Falcon, the Bell, the Dolphin, the Hart, the Luce, the Angel, the Star, and the Marigold Chamber. In 1758 only the names of the Hart, the Angel, and the Marigold chambers survived, while the other rooms had presumably lost the paintings justifying their names: prints, pictures, and maps were taking the place of murals. The hall of 1670 was called the dining room in 1758, the parlour had become the best parlour, and a beaufet (a buffet) had been introduced. The pewter of 1670 was being replaced by pottery drinking mugs in 1758, and there were more copper and glass vessels by that time also. There were leather chairs and stools in 1670, but none in 1758. On the other hand, there was tea, coffee, and a punchbowl in 1758, the brewhouse was better equipped, and there was more liquor. Perhaps the bar in 1758 did more business than in 1670, and the hotel less, for there were only 24 sheets in 1758 compared with 63 in 1670.[8] It is not often that one is fortunate enough to find two inventories of the same place at different dates, but any random sample of town inventories at different dates will point similar contrasts. As for the industries of the town, probate inventories are among the best sources of information on the variety of crafts practised and their relative importance.

Lastly, I would like to turn to a quite different source, which is

[8] G. H. Kenyon, 'Petworth town and trades', *Sussex Archaeolog. Coll.*, xcix (1961), pp. 126–35.

neglected because many examples still repose unknown and
unsuspected in private hands. I mean nineteenth-century diaries. I
have learned casually of the existence of some of these, and colleagues
of mine have advertised for them in local papers, and gathered in a
considerable harvest. They can be invaluable, as I learned from the
diary of a Lincolnshire farmer of the later-nineteenth century, which I
found in the hands of his descendants in London. The diary was a
copious record of the private thoughts of the writer, of his day-to-day
activities on the farm, and of his journeys on Sunday when, as a
Methodist lay preacher, he went to give the sermon in the chapels of
neighbouring villages. One could not help but get a vivid impression
of this conscientious but rather over-earnest Victorian Liberal Non-
conformist—an enthusiast for modern methods of farming with
machinery, who nevertheless maintained a paternal attitude towards
his workers. He was deeply religious and thoughtful about the
problems of life, but also sententious beyond belief. When his son
overturned a bottle of ink, as he was writing up his diary, he wrote: 'I
pray God that he may be preserved from making a worse spill in
future life. I trust he may never besmirch his character'. He was also
painfully preoccupied with his own minor physical ailments, and his
wife's indispositions. There are many melancholy pages about their
aches and pains, punctuated at one point by a few pages written in
elated mood when the diarist thought he had discovered the cause of
them all. His clothing was too tight-fitting, and inhibited the flow of
oxygen around the body. But a few pages on, he was again as
depressed as ever. After all this, it was a great relief to learn from his
son that he lived to be ninety years old, and his wife to be eighty-
seven.

I have not given you much idea of the great value of this diary for
the study of agricultural history—it was full of comments on the
economic difficulties of the 1870s, on the anxieties of people who
feared that machinery would replace men on the farm, and on the
growth of agricultural unionism. And when the diarist moved from a
farm on the Lincolnshire wolds down into the marsh, there were some
shrewd sociological comments on the differences in the class
structure of the two types of country. Diaries, indeed, are neglected
(though I am aware that there is a bibliography of them),[9] and are
worth searching for. But they do not belong in the category of

[9] W. Matthews, *British diaries: an annotated bibliography of British diaries written between 1442 and 1942* (1950).

documents awaiting the attention of the dillgent historian, but rather of records awaiting discovery by the archivist. And at this point it is surely time for the historian to desist.

POSTSCRIPT

The diary of a Lincolnshire farmer referred to above, p. 33, is now published. See Jean Stovin (ed.), *Journals of a Methodist Farmer, 1871–1875*, Croom Helm, London, 1982.

P.A.J. Pettit's thesis is now more readily available as a book. See *The Royal Forests of Northamptonshire. A Study in their Economy*, Northants Rec. Soc., XXIII, 1968.

IV

THE COMMON FIELDS[1]

IT is now nearly seventy years since H. L. Gray published his detailed
study of *English Field Systems*, and nearly forty-five years since the
first appearance of *The Open Fields* by C. S. and C. S. Orwin.[2] Both
books made an attempt to explain the origin of the common-field
system, Gray regarding it as a ready-made scheme of cultivation
imported by the Anglo-Saxons from the Continent, the Orwins
considering it as a common-sense method of farming in pioneer
conditions when cooperation was the best insurance against hunger
and famine. Both theories still command a certain measure of
support for the simple reason that no alternatives have yet been
offered in their place. But in the last two decades and more, a number
of studies on agrarian subjects have contained evidence that does not
fit comfortably in the old framework, and a fresh appraisal of the
subject is overdue. Moreover, since all countries in western Europe
have the same problem to solve—they have all had experience of
common-field systems existing side by side with enclosed farms—it
behoves us to take account of the large amount of foreign literature
that has accumulated in recent years, since it may not be irrelevant to
the English situation.

But first a definition of the common-field system is necessary. It is
composed of four essential elements. First, the arable and meadow is
divided into strips among the cultivators, each of whom may occupy
a number of strips scattered about the fields. Secondly, both arable
and meadow are thrown open for common pasturing by the stock of
all the commoners after harvest and in fallow seasons. In the arable
fields, this means necessarily that some rules about cropping are
observed so that spring and winter-sown crops may be grown in

---

[1] For many helpful comments and criticisms, I wish to thank Mr. Trevor Aston, Dr.
A. R. H. Baker, Mr. T. M. Charles-Edwards, Dr. Cunliffe Shaw, Professor Rodney
Hilton, Dr. W. G. Hoskins, and Professor M. M. Postan, and most of all Professor H.
P. R. Finberg, who has read every one of the innumerable drafts of this paper.

[2] H. L. Gray, *English Field Systems* (Cambridge, Mass., 1915); C. S. and C. S.
Orwin, *The Open Fields* (Oxford, 1938).

separate fields or furlongs. Thirdly, there is common pasturage and waste, where the cultivators of strips enjoy the right to graze stock and gather timber, peat, and other commodities, when available, such as stone and coal. Fourthly, the ordering of these activities is regulated by an assembly of cultivators—the manorial court, in most places in the Middle Ages, or, when more than one manor was present in a township, a village meeting.

Since all four elements—strips, common rights over the arable and meadow, common rights over the pasture and waste, and disciplinary assemblies—are necessary to make a fully-fledged common-field system, it is unthinkingly assumed that they have always existed together. This, however, is almost certainly not the case. The oldest element in the system is in all probability the right of common grazing over pasture and waste. It is the residue of more extensive rights which were enjoyed from time immemorial, which the Anglo-Saxon and later Norman kings and manorial lords curtailed, but could not altogether deny. By the sixteenth century we are familiar with commons that were enjoyed by one township alone. But even at this date there are examples of commons which were still enjoyed by two or three townships, such as Henfield common, grazed by the commoners of Clayton-le-Moors, Altham, and Accrington, Lancashire. Earlier still we have examples of commons that were used by the townships of a whole Hundred, such as the common called Kentis Moor in Kentisbeare, which belonged to the Hundred of Hayridge, Devon, in the early fourteenth century, and the common of the Hundred of Colneis, Suffolk, so described in 1086. A century earlier than this we hear of commons which were reserved to the inhabitants of a whole county: thus, the men of Kent had common rights over Andredsweald, and the men of Devon over Dartmoor. There is some reason to think, then, that common rights over pasture and waste were ancient, were once extensive, but underwent a process of steady erosion, which even in the sixteenth century was not everywhere complete.[3]

The existence of strips in the arable fields and meadows is first attested in one of the laws of King Ine of Wessex, issued between A.D. 688 and 694. Since the interpretation of the passage is of some importance, it must be quoted in full:

---

[3] L. Dudley Stamp and W. G. Hoskins, *The Common Lands of England and Wales* (London, 1963), pp. 5–13; *Trans. Devon Assoc.*, xxxii (1900), p. 546. I wish to thank Prof. H. P. R. Finberg for this reference.

If ceorls have a common meadow or other shareland to enclose, and some have enclosed their share while others have not, and cattle eat their common crops or grass, let those to whom the gap is due go to the others who have enclosed their share and make amends to them.

The meaning of the passage is not crystal clear, and with our knowledge of later common-field systems in mind, it is, of course, tempting to assume that one such is depicted here. In fact, there is nothing in this law to prove the existence of a mature common-field system. It states explicitly that peasants could have shares in arable and meadow, bearing 'common crops or grass', but it does not say that all the fields of the community were organized together for the purposes of cropping and of grazing when the land lay fallow. It is perfectly possible that one set of parceners or neighbours shared one field, while another group shared another field. Indeed, this is the meaning taken for granted by Vinogradoff, who described the law as one imposing on parceners the duty of maintaining the hedges of a meadow. If this interpretation is correct, then such arrangements as parceners may or may not have made about cultivating and grazing their lands in common were likely to be their own private concern.[4]

There is nothing in Ine's law, then, to support the idea that in the late seventh century common grazing after harvest was practised in common fields or meadows on a village basis. And where no evidence exists, there is no place for assumptions. There are examples from the later Middle Ages onwards, in the fens of south Lincolnshire and in Kent, of strip fields in which there were no common rights of pasture and none were felt to be necessary. If and when cultivators grazed their arable, they tethered their beasts on their own parcels. In another county, where common rights over the arable were customary in the later Middle Ages, there are hints that they had been established only recently. It is the opinion of Dr. Cunliffe Shaw that when, in the period 1250–1320, manorial lords began to make grants of common rights over ploughland in the Royal Forest of Lancaster, such rights were an innovation. Before this, common grazing had been confined to the *Moors*—the relatively small pastures attached to every Lancashire vill. In short, there is a case for thinking that in the earliest strip fields cultivators may not have enjoyed common rights over all the arable fields of the township. If so, an essential ingredient

---

[4] Ine's laws, c. 42 (ed. Liebermann, i, pp. 106–9). This law is translated and discussed in F. M. Stenton, *Anglo-Saxon England*, 2nd edn. (Oxford, 1947), p. 277; P. Vinogradoff, *The Growth of the Manor* (London, 1905), p. 174. See also H. R. Loyn, *Anglo-Saxon England and the Norman Conquest* (London, 1962), pp. 156–7.

of the mature common-field system was missing.[5]

Early evidence of communally-agreed crop rotations is also elusive. The authors of some detailed studies of medieval estates as late as the fourteenth and fifteenth centuries have confessed themselves completely unable to disentangle any system of cropping, despite the presence of fields divided into strips. In some cases, it is clear that the lands of the demesne were subject to a rotation while tenants' lands lack any signs of having been similarly organized. In other cases, even the demesne lands seem to have been cropped haphazardly. Miss Levett's study of the manors of St. Albans Abbey, for example, showed that in 1332 the demesne fields were divided into three main groups (*prima, secunda, et tertia seisona*), presumably for the purpose of a three-course rotation, but there was no indication that the tenants' lands were similarly grouped. She concluded her study of all the manors of St. Albans with the judgement that the three-field system was imperfectly developed or else decaying. Professor Hilton, writing of the distribution of demesne arable on the manor of Kirby Bellars, Leicestershire, and observing the variety of crops, both spring and winter sown, which were grown in the same field, was driven to conclude that 'the lord of the manor had a flexible agricultural system within the framework of the supposedly rigid three-field system.' On the estates of Stoneleigh abbey at Stoneleigh. Warwickshire, he concluded that there was no regular division of the common fields into two, three, or four large fields, that widely separated furlongs were cropped together, and that tenants' holdings were unevenly distributed throughout the fields. Miss Davenport in her study of Forncett manor, Norfolk, thought that 'probably Forncett was a three-course manor', but at the same time admitted that there were no clear indications of three great fields, cultivated in rotation. On the contrary, there were abundant references to fields which were numerous and small. A more recent study of the fields of Church Bickenhill, Warwickshire, has shown 'not the classic arrangement of two or three large open fields; instead . . . we are confronted by a bewildering complexity of many small open fields or furlongs . . . there is no way of discovering whether the six or seven apparently independent open fields were separate cropping units in the

[5] Joan Thirsk, *English Peasant Farming*, p. 14; A. R. H. Baker, 'The Field Systems of Kent' (London Ph.D. thesis, 1963), pp. 23–6. See also A. R. H. Baker, 'The Field System of an East Kent Parish (Deal)'. *Archaeologia Cantiana*, lxxviii (1963). pp. 96–117; 'Open Fields and Partible Inheritance on a Kent Manor', *Econ. Hist. Rev.*, 2nd ser., xvii (1964), pp. 1–23; 'Field Systems in the Vale of Holmesdale', *Agric. Hist. Rev.*, xiv (1966); Dr. Cunliffe Shaw in correspondence with the author.

fourteenth century, and if so how they were related to each other.'
Moreover, in all but one of the few deeds in which the holdings of
tenants were specified in detail, there was no equality in the acreage
which each tenant held in each field. From all these examples, then,
we have to conclude that another ingredient of the common-field
system—regulated crop rotations—was missing from at least some
villages in the later Middle Ages.[6]

The account of Church Bickenhill carries us a stage further,
however, because its authors pursue the problem beyond 1500, and
demonstrate how the field pattern was later immensely simplified. A
deed of 1612 and a survey of 1677 showed that Church Bickenhill's
ploughland then consisted of three common arable fields, whose
many furlong names had been discarded. In short, a simplification of
field lay-out and/or nomenclature had occurred somewhere between
the fourteenth and seventeenth centuries.[7]

Our knowledge of the origins of the common-field system is
woefully incomplete, but what there is does not support the view that
the four elements composing the system were present in all villages
from the very beginning of settlement. In many places, some of the
essential elements seem still to be missing in the later Middle Ages,
Yet from the sixteenth century onwards manorial documents contain
more and more explicit rules and regulations about the workings of
the system until in the seventeenth and eighteenth centuries they are
at their most emphatic and lucid. On the eve of Parliamentary
enclosure some maps of common-field villages present a more
orderly pattern of strips, furlongs, and fields than anything available
earlier. Here then are grounds for the hypothesis that the system
evolved slowly. Common rights of pasture on the waste were ancient;
arable fields seem to have been divided into strips before any village
agreements were reached to regulate rotations and graze the stubble
and fallow in common. The careful supervision exercised by manorial
officers over all aspects of common-field farming is not everywhere
apparent in early manorial documents, and in some manors not until
the sixteenth century: court roll material survives from the thirteenth
century onwards, and although there is much evidence of penalties

---

[6] A. E. Levett, *Studies in Manorial History* (Oxford, 1938), pp. 338–9, 184; R. H.
Hilton, *The Economic Development of some Leicestershire Estates* (Oxford, 1947), p.
152; R. H. Hilton, *The Stoneleigh Leger Book* (Dugdale Soc. Publications, xxiv, 1960),
p. lv; F. G. Davenport, *The Economic Development of a Norfolk Manor, 1086–1565*
(Cambridge, 1906), p. 27; V. H. T. Skipp and R. P. Hastings, *Discovering Bickenhill*
(Dept. of Extra-Mural Studies, Birmingham Univ., 1963), pp. 15–18.
[7] Skipp and Hastings, *op. cit.*, pp. 20, 22.

imposed on those who damaged the property of others, particularly at harvest time, there are few hints of crop rotation or common pasture rights. Since this view of the common-field system as a gradual development is already the considered opinion of German scholars, has won the assent of Scandinavian and Yugoslavian colleagues, and is now being more seriously considered by the French, it is worth paying some attention to their argument and the evidence for it. While some of the steps in the argument have to rest upon the balance of probability, most lie upon a sound foundation of archaeologial and documentary evidence.[8]

In Germany the first farms for which there is archaeological proof from the later Iron Age were farms in severalty. Some were isolated, some were grouped in hamlets. By the sixth century of our era German settlements were still small, consisting not of twenty or thirty households, as Meitzen once supposed, but of two or three families with perhaps twenty inhabitants all told. As population increased, new households were at first accommodated in the old settlements. It was this increase which led to the emergence of nucleated villages. Other changes accompanied the growth of population. Farms were split up to provide for children, and fields were divided again and again. Ancient field names, such as *Spalten*, meaning *slits*, point to this development, while later documents and plans amply prove it. A multitude of German examples can be cited of townships consisting at one stage of large, undivided, rectangular fields, which became subdivided into hundreds of strips in two centuries or less. There are Yugoslavian examples, authenticated by detailed maps, which show this transformation taking place in the nineteenth and twentieth centuries in an even shorter period.[9]

If it be asked why the division of holdings resulted in the creation of

[8] I wish to thank Professor W. O. Ault for allowing me to see his manuscript before publication. See *Open-Field Husbandry and the Village Community, Trans. Amer. Philos. Soc.*, NS, 55, part 7, 1965. For Continental literature on commonfield systems, see Gunner Bodvall, 'Periodic Settlement, Land-Clearing, and Cultivation with Special Reference to the Boothlands of North Hälsingland', *Geografiska Annaler*, xxxix (1957), pp. 232, 235; Svetozar Ilešič, *Die Flurformen Sloweniens im Lichte der Europäischen Forschung* (Müncher Geogr. Hefte, xvi, 1959), *passim*; E. Juillard, A. Meynier and others, *Structures Agraires et Paysages Ruraux* (Annales de l'Est, Mémoire xvii, 1957), p. 54.

[9] W. Abel, *Geschichte der deutschen Landwirtschaft* (Stuttgart, 1962), pp. 15–16, 27, 70–74; Annaliese Krenzlin, *Die Entstehung der Gewannflur nach Untersuchungen im nördlichen Unterfranken* (Frankfurter Geogr. Hefte, xxxv, 1961), part I, p. 110; A. Krenzlin, 'Zur Genese der Gewannflur in Deutschland', *Geogr. Annaler*, xliii (1961), pp. 193–4; S. Ilešič, 'Die jüngeren Gewannfluren in Nordwestjugoslavien', *ibid.*, pp. 130–7.

long strips rather than small rectangular fields, then the answer of German scholars is that the strip was a more convenient shape for cultivation by the plough. It did not, as English historians have sometimes argued, influence the lay-out of fields at the time of colonization, but it did influence the method of partitioning holdings at a later date.[10]

As farms were divided into smaller units and population rose, the production of food had to be increased. The arable land was enlarged by assarts and the fields became more numerous. The waste diminished, and the arable had to be worked more intensively. The former field-grass economy, under which land had been used alternately for arable crops and then left for years under grass, gave way gradually to a more intensive rotation of arable crops and fewer years of grass until finally a two- and later a three-course rotation, allowing only one year of fallow, was arrived at. It is unlikely, however, that in the first instance this system of cropping was communally organized. More probably it was adopted by individuals or by parceners cooperating for mutual convenience in one field.[11]

Eventually, as fields multiplied whenever new land was taken into cultivation from the waste, and as the parcels of each cultivator became more and more scattered, regulations had to be introduced to ensure that all had access to their own land and to water, and that meadows and ploughland were protected from damage by stock. The community was drawn together by sheer necessity to cooperate in the control of farming practices. All the fields were brought together into two or three large units. A regular crop rotation was agreed by all and it became possible to organize more efficiently the grazing of stubble and aftermath. Thereafter, the scattering of strips, which had at one time been a handicap, became a highly desirable arrangement, since it gave each individual a proportion of land under each crop in the rotation. Some exchanges of land took place to promote this scattering. The partition of holdings was in future contrived to preserve the same effect. And when new land was colonized in the Middle Ages by the inhabitants of old-established settlements, it was not uncommon for this too to be divided into strips. Indeed, such was the force of example that the inhabitants of some East German villages, colonized for the first time in the high Middle Ages under lordly direction, allotted their arable from the start in intermingled

---

[10] Krenzlin, *Die Entstehung der Gewannflur*, p. 96; Abel, *op. cit.*, p. 72.
[11] Krenzlin, *op. cit.*, pp. 104–7, 111–7.

strips.[12]

German scholars also recognize the possibility that, when cropping regulations were introduced and peasants did not have adequate representation in all the fields, a complete re-allotment of strips may have taken place, a new pattern of occupation being introduced to replace the old. One case of re-allotment occurred in unusual circumstances in 1247 when the abbot of the monastery owning the village of Isarhofen ordered a fresh apportionment of holdings on the grounds that war and the desertion of farms had caused such confusion that no one knew the boundaries of his land. Similar re-arrangements in more peaceful circumstances may perhaps be inferred from fourteenth-century documents showing tenants' holdings that were more or less equally distributed throughout the fields.[13]

The evolution of common fields in Germany was a long-drawn-out process. Many came into existence gradually after sites, deserted in the Middle Ages, had been re-occupied. It is possible to observe the gradual parcelling of rectangular fields into strips as late as the seventeenth and even the eighteenth centuries. But for our purpose, of comparing German with English experience, it is more important to be able to date the earliest examples of a complete common-field system. Unfortunately, the German evidence is, if anything, more scanty than the English in the Middle Ages. There is enough to suggest the existence of fields, divided into strips, in the high Middle Ages. Examples of crop rotations are found on monastic demesne as early as the eighth century and may be assumed to have spread to tenants' holdings by 1300 when rising population compelled people to use their land with the utmost economy. A rotation on tenants' land may be inferred from documents from the Wetterau *circa* 1300 showing tenants' holdings that were divided more or less equally between three fields. Finally, since the multiplication of strips seems to be associated in Germany with periods of increasing population, in the sixteenth, and again in the eighteenth and nineteenth centuries, it

---

[12] Abel, *op. cit.*, p. 75; F. Steinbach, 'Gewanndorf und Einzelhof', *Historiche Aufsätze Aloys Schulte zum 70 Geburstag gewidmet* (Düsseldorf, 1927), p. 54; Krenzlin, *op. cit.*, p. 114; *Kolloquium über Fragen der Flurgenese am 24–6 Oktober, 1961, in Göttingen*, ed. H. Mortensen and H. Jäger (*Berichte zur deutschen Landeskunde*, xxix, 1962), p. 313. I wish to thank Dr. Karl Sinnhuber for drawing my attention to this report of the latest German conference on the origin of common fields.

[13] Abel, *op. cit.*, p. 75. It has been suggested that the Swedish re-organization of strips, known as *solskifte*, was also associated with the introduction of a communal crop rotation: Staffan Helmfrid, *Östergotland 'Västanstång', Geogr. Annaler*, xliv (1962), p. 260.

is argued by Dr. Annaliese Krenzlin that the first complete common-field system probably developed in the previous period of rising population, somewhere between the tenth and thirteenth centuries. It will be noticed that, in answering this final and most important question of all, the documents fail and German scholars are driven to an assessment of probability.[14]

With the steps of this argument in mind, it is now time to review the English evidence, looking for clues to the gradual evolution of the common-field system. The task is difficult because so many of the earliest references impart only scraps of ambiguous information, and it is tempting when the presence of one element of the common-field system is proved, to take the others for granted. This temptation must be resisted.

Nucleated villages and common fields are generally believed to have been an innovation of the Anglo-Saxons, who introduced to England a system of farming with which they were already familiar in their homeland. This theory could only prevail so long as German scholars adhered to the argument, put forward in its clearest form by August Meitzen in 1895 in *Siedelung und Agrarwesen der Westgermanen und Ostgermanen, der Kelten, Römer, Finnen, und Slawen*, that the field systems portrayed in German maps of the eighteenth and nineteenth centuries, so strongly reminiscent of English common-field villages of the same period, were a more or less faithful representation of the lay-out of fields from the time of original settlement. Modern German scholars who have consulted earlier maps and plans than those available to Meitzen, however, no longer hold this view. As we have seen, they now regard the common-field system as the outcome of a long and slow process of development. In these circumstances, it is no longer possible for English scholars to argue that the Anglo-Saxons brought from Germany in the sixth century a fully-fledged common-field system.

Anglo-Saxon laws refer to parceners, to 'common meadow', and 'shareland', the charters to land lying 'acre under acre', to land lying

---

[14] Abel, *op. cit.*, p. 75; Krenzlin, *op. cit.*, pp. 102–7, 111; *Kolloquium, op. cit.*, pp. 232, 246. Controversy still rages among German scholars, but the main differences of opinion concern explanations for the different shapes of common fields, a subject which is almost totally ignored by English scholars. One exception, however, is *Valley on the March* (London, 1958) by Lord Rennell of Rodd, chapter iv. See also Harald Uhlig, 'Langstreifenfluren in Nordengland, Wales, und Schottland', *Tagungsbericht und Wissenschaftliche Abhandlungen, Deutscher Geographentag, Würzburg, 29 Juli bis 5 August 1957*, pp. 399–410.

in 'common fields', 'in common land', in 'two fields of shareland', to headlands and gores. The significance behind these terms and phrases is uncertain, but it is just as legitimate to interpret them as a description of lands in which parceners were associated as to conclude that a mature common-field system embracing the whole village was in existence. With even more reason, this interpretation can be put upon the chapter in the 'Venedotian' lawbooks, which has frequently been used to illustrate the cooperative method of farming from which emerged the common-field system in Wales. This chapter on co-tillage (*cyfar*) described how land, when ploughed with a team assembled by a group of cultivators, was then divided between them, one strip being allotted to the ploughman, one to the irons, one to the exterior sod ox, one to the exterior sward ox, and one to the driver. Since we are also told about 'whoever shall engage in co-tillage with another', and about 'tillage between two co-tillers', it is reasonable to assume that these laws refer to partnerships between a few cultivators, such as parceners, and not to a system of cultivation involving the whole township. But in any case, these Welsh regulations can no longer be safely used as evidence for tenth-century conditions, since most if not all of them are of much later date.[15]

If laws and charters fail to establish the existence of a mature common-field system, they nevertheless give ample evidence of the division of land into strips. Was this due to division of land at death, or, as Continental scholars assume, to the effects of partible inheritance? Almost nothing is known from any period as yet about the customs of the English peasantry when devising land by will. But there were few manors in the Middle Ages, whatever the official manorial custom of inheritance, which did not allow customary tenants to create trusts on their death beds and so dispose of their land in any way they pleased, and at all times freeholders were entitled to dispose of their land freely. Primogeniture was never popular with the peasantry: it was the subject of adverse comment by pamphleteers during the Interregnum, when it was called 'the most unreasonable descent.' Even in the nineteenth century, a writer on promigeniture in England was constrained to remark that 'primogeniture is not rooted in popular sentiment or in the sentiment

[15] Vinogradoff, *op. cit.*, p. 262, note 29; H. P. R. Finberg, *Gloucestershire* (London, 1955), pp. 39–40; F. Seebohm, *The English Village Community* (Cambridge, 1926 edn.), pp. 118–21; *The Welsh History Review*, 1963, 'The Welsh Laws', *passim*, esp. p. 55; J. G. Edwards, 'The Historical Study of the Welsh Lawbooks', *Trans. Roy. Hist. Soc.*, 5th ser., xii (1962).

of any large class except the landed aristocracy and those struggling
to enter their ranks'. We are left with a shrewd suspicion that the
English peasant preferred, if he could, to provide for more than one
of his children.[16]

As for the influence of partible inheritance, this is a subject almost
totally neglected by English historians, who have been too readily
persuaded of the supremacy of primogeniture by the lawyers and by
medieval evidence from the later twelfth century onwards from a few
highly manorialized and carefully administered ecclesiastical estates
where partible inheritance did not find favour with the landlord. It is
generally thought that partible inheritance was once the dominant
custom in England. Domesday Book shows that it was still a common
custom among members of the upper classes in the eleventh century.
It is usual to argue that the custom began to be displaced after the
Conquest when land held by knight service was made subject to the
rule of primogeniture. By the end of the thirteenth century lawyers
applied the rule of promogeniture to all free land unless special proof
was given of a custom of partibility. Primogeniture thus became the
law of England in cases of intestacy. So far the argument is
unexceptionable. But it would be a mistake to pay too much attention
to the lawyers' assertions concerning the subsequent supremacy of
primogeniture, particularly among the peasantry. Partible
inheritance was still the custom of the manor in the sixteenth century
in many of the less densely-settled pastoral areas of the north—
Furness, Rossendale, highland Northumberland and the West and
North Yorkshire dales—as well as in parts of Kent and the East
Anglian fenland. Indeed, I have argued elsewhere that it was liable to
persist in all weakly-manorialized areas where the lord's authority
was frail, and land was plentiful—usually only pastoral regions by the
Tudor period.[17]

But even if we concede only a small place in our calculations for the
effects of inheritance in partitioning land, we have to be prepared for
large consequences. H. L. Gray has demonstrated its effects in a

---

[16] Margaret James, *Social Problems and Policy during the Puritan Revolution,
1640–60* (London, 1930), pp. 26, 98, 310 (I wish to thank Mr. Christopher Hill for
drawing my attention to these references); J. W. Probyn, ed., *Systems of Land Tenure in
Various Countries* (London, 1876), p. 375.

[17] Professor G. C. Homans and Dr. H. E. Hallam are honourable exceptions to this
generalization at the beginning of this paragraph; T. H. Aston, 'The Origins of the
Manor in England', *Trans. Roy. Hist. Soc.*, 5th Ser., viii (1958), pp. 78–9; W.
Holdsworth, *History of English Law*, iii (London. 1903), p. 173; Joan Thirsk, 'The
Farming Regions of England', in *The Agrarian History of England and Wales, vol. iv,
1500–1640* (1967).

township of 205 acres in Donegal, Ireland, which was at one time divided between only two farms. In 1845, after two generations of partitioning, these two farms had dissolved into twenty-nine holdings consisting of 422 separate parcels. The plan of the township without accompanying explanation would suggest a common-field township on the way to being enclosed. In fact, it was an enclosed township on the way to becoming a common-field one. Similar effects were described by the inhabitants of the Welsh lordship of Elvell, Radnorshire, before the statute of 27 Hen. VIII put an end, in law if not in practice, to the custom of gavelkind in Wales. It was not unusual, declared the natives, for a small tenement to be divided into thirty, forty, and sometimes more parcels in three or four generations. They had seen the lordship, numbering 120 messuages, increase to 400.[18]

If the partition of inherited land could have the effect of dividing fields into a multitude of strips, what evidence is there to show that it had this effect in England? There are some illustrations to show single fields which became subdivided into strips: an example, cited by Professor Hilton, concerns Swannington, Leicestershire, where an assart, *Godbertes Ryding*, held in severalty by Roger Godeberd in the thirteenth century, was found later subdivided among several tenants and incorporated in the common fields. In this case the reason for the partition is unknown. More conclusive is the example of a number of villages in the East Riding of Yorkshire in which the creation of strips led on to the emergence of a complete common-field system. These villages lay in a district that was devastated in 1069 and lay waste for almost a century. When the land underwent reclamation in the mid-twelfth century, charters show that the tenants occupied farms in severalty. They provided for their sons by dividing their lands and, when necessary, reclaiming more. Their assarts bore the names of those who first cleared the land, and by the end of the thirteenth century they too were divided among several occupiers, all heirs of the original tenant. Indeed, the townships were full of selions and bovates. And although this is not adequate evidence by itself of a fully-fledged common-field system, it was well established by the sixteenth century. Here then is convincing proof that when farms in

---

[18] H. L. Gray, *op. cit.*, pp. 190–1; E. G. Jones, *Exchequer Proceedings (Equity) concerning Wales, Henry VIII-Elizabeth* (Univ. of Wales, History and Law Series, iv, 1939), p. 313; I owe this reference to the kindness of Mr. Glanville Jones. For a discussion showing that this custom of inheritance had exactly the same effect upon land in China, see Hsiao-Tung Fei, *Peasant Life in China* (London, 1943), pp. 194–5.

severalty are divided among heirs, fields of arable strips can emerge in a comparatively short time out of farms in severalty, and eventually become absorbed into a full common-field system.[19]

These examples from the East Riding carry us silently over several vital stages in the evolution of the common-field system. They explain the appearance of intermingled arable strips, but they do not tell us how and when the cultivators resolved upon rationalizing this complex arrangement by adopting a common crop rotation and agreeing to share common rights after harvest throughout the village fields. To illuminate this phase of development we have to examine evidence from other places and periods.

When once the number of tenants and the number of arable fields in a village increased substantially, the problem of ensuring access to land and water and of preventing encroachments must have become acute. Our knowledge of assarting which took place in the thirteenth century tells us much, if we have imagination enough, for many assarts were divided into strips at the outset, others in the course of several generations. But we can also illustrate the problem more exactly. Professor Finberg has drawn attention to an unusual charter, probably belonging to the early eleventh century, which describes the boundaries of an estate at Hawling, Gloucestershire. It defines the area of *field*, or pasture, in the south of the parish, and the area of woodland in the north. These boundaries exclude a piece of land in the centre occupied by the village and its arable. Thus, we are able to compare the arable land of Hawling in the early eleventh century with the lay-out of the parish some seven hundred years later, when in 1748 a new plan of the common fields of Hawling was drawn. There were then three arable fields. The original nucleus of arable was now Middle Field, the smallest of the three; the West Field was part of the former *feld*, and stretched to the parish boundary; the East Field was also an assart from the *feld* in the south-east of the parish. The arable was some five or six times its size in the eleventh century, and we may guess that the parcels or strips of individual tenants were perhaps ten or even twenty times as numerous.[20]

Ine's law hints at cooperation between parceners or neighbours who possessed strips in the same fields. And it may be that (as the

[19] *Vict. County Hist. of Leicester*, vol. ii, p. 158; T. A. M. Bishop, 'Assarting and the Growth of the Open Fields', *Econ. Hist. Rev.*, vi (1935–6), pp. 13 ff. For the effects of partible inheritance on Kentish fields, see articles by A. R. H. Baker cited in note 5.
[20] H. P. R. Finberg, *The Early Charters of the West Midlands* (Leicester, 1961), pp. 188–96.

later Welsh evidence suggests), such cooperation extended to choice of the crops to be grown in a particular field and assistance in cultivation. If men cooperated to this extent, did they also pasture their fields in common after harvest, and if so, how? We cannot attempt to answer these questions until we have considered whether the stubble was grazed at all. It afforded useful feed for animals but was not indispensable if pasture and waste were plentiful. The fields needed the manure to keep them in good heart and it was obviously more convenient to graze stock on the fields than to cart the manure from elsewhere. But the need for manure might not be urgent until the fields were fairly intensively cropped. Under a rotation of crops and long years of grass, men could have managed without. Thus, until population grew and land had to be used economically, we can envisage the possibility that the stubble in the arable fields was not grazed. But by the thirteenth century, certainly, and how much earlier we do not know, the value of dung was fully recognized and received due attention in Walter of Henley's treatise on husbandry.[21]

We must now consider the second question: when and how was the stubble grazed? When once parceners and neighbours cooperated in cultivating their fields, *and* also recognized the need to graze the stubble, we may assume that in some places, at least, common grazing would suggest itself naturally. It may not always have happened this way: the example of Kentish fields, in which stubble was always grazed in severalty, springs to mind. But grazing in common was obviously convenient, for it eliminated the tedious and always unsatisfactory business of hurdling strips to contain the sheep and of tethering great cattle.

We are still dependent on Ine's law (apart from the dubious later Welsh evidence) for our assumption that cultivation of the arable and the grazing of the fields in common concerned only parceners and neighbours who were sharing fields, and did not necessarily involve the whole community of tenants. This belief is strengthened by Bracton's treatise on the *Laws and Customs of England*, written in the mid-thirteenth century, which also discusses rights of common pasture on the same basis, that is, as a grant of a right from one person to another or between members of a small group who are parceners or neighbours. Indeed, his examples make it abundantly clear that the word *common* had a more restricted meaning than that which historians normally accord it.[22] Medieval charters and court rolls

[21] *Walter of Henley's Husbandry* . . . , ed. E. Lamond (London, 1890), pp. 18–23.
[22] Henry de Bracton, *De Legibus et Consuetudinibus Angliae*, G. C. Woodbine (New

lend further support to this view by yielding examples of such agreements between neighbours possessing intermingled or adjoining
land. The charters of Missenden Abbey, Buckinghamshire, record a
grant of land in Missenden in 1161 from Turstin Mantel. With it
Mantel granted rights of common over all his own land, presumably
because it lay intermingled with, or adjoining, that newly granted to
the abbey. In 1284 each side agreed to forgo rights over the other's
arable, and the monks received permission to build a dyke and hedge
to divide their land from Mantel's. In another charter from the same
cartulary, dated 1170–79, Alexander de Hampden confirmed a grant
to the monks of Missenden Abbey of a virgate of land in Honor,
minus four acres which Alexander kept for himself. He substituted in
their place four acres from his demesne elsewhere. He allowed the
monks to pasture a certain number of animals on his land 'in wood
and field (*in bosco et plano*)', and in return Alexander received rights
of common over the third field of the abbey grange, which lay next to
Alexander's land, when it was not in crop. Another agreement
(1240–68) recorded in the same cartulary was between Thomas
Mantel and Robert Byl. Thomas held land within the bounds of
Robert Byl's estate and agreed to enclose his portion with a ditch and
not to claim rights of pasture beyond it. Here, then, are three agreements, each of which refer to the grant of rights of common over
arable between two parties. Bearing in mind the possibility that such
agreements between neighbours might continue in some places long
after they had given way in others to a common-field system on a
village basis, we may treat as equally relevant other examples of later
periods.[23]

In the Wakefield manor court rolls of 1297 a dispute between
Matthew de Bosco and Thomas de Coppeley concerning grazing
rights in open time (i.e. after harvest) was settled by an agreement that
in open time 'they ought to intercommon'. Another quarrel at
Alverthorpe in the same manor in December 1307 concerning
common rights in a certain *cultura* of the arable fields was set down in
the court rolls not as a quarrel between the complainant, Quenylda de
Alverthorpe, and the whole township but between her and four other

Continued

Haven, 1915–22), vol. iii, pp. 129–30, 166–70, 182, 184. The Welsh evidence seems to
come from rather the same period (above, n. 15).
[23] E. C. Vollans, 'The Evolution of Farm Lands in the Central Chilterns in the
Twelfth and Thirteenth Centuries', *Trans. Institute of British Geographers*, xxvi (1959),
pp. 204–5, 208, 222, citing charters from *The Cartulary of Missenden Abbey*, part i, ed.
J. G. Jenkins (Bucks. Arch. Soc., Records Branch, ii, 1938), pp. 66–8, 184–5, 128.

named persons. In 1299 in the manor court of Hales, Worcestershire, Richard de Rugaker made amends to Geoffrey Osborn because he drove off Geoffrey's animals from a field which was common between themselves *and others* (not, it should be noted, between them and the whole township). Similarly, when German Philcock of Stanley, in Wakefield manor, was accused in November 1306 of making a fosse in the fields of Stanley, he said it was not to the injury of *his neighbours*, because it was always open in open time. Yet again, Prior Walter and the canons of Selborne Priory, Hampshire, granted in 1326 to Henry Wyard and his wife Alice common pasture for all their beasts except pigs and goats in the field (described in detail) belonging to the Prior, in exchange for a release from Henry and Alice of all their right in sixteen acres of land in Theddene and in the common pasture above *La Bideldone*. Finally, another citation from a later period, from the court orders of Lowick, Furness, in 1650, wherein it was laid down that Christopher Harries, Bryan Christopherson, and James Penny 'shall stint their after grass when their corn is gotten equally according to their share'.[24]

Alongside the early grants of common pasture rights between individuals and small groups, we must set examples of grants of wider scope, some embracing all tenants, though not, so far as our evidence extends, embracing all fields, others proving conclusively that all tenants commoned all fields. In a grant dated between 1235 and 1264 Roger de Quincy forbade his tenants in Shepshed to pasture their animals on the fields of the monks of Garendon 'except in the open season when neighbours common with neighbours'. This saving clause—*'set in seysona quando campi aperti sunt et vicini cum vicinis communicare debent'*—stresses once again the rights of neighbours to common with one another. Nevertheless, it is significant that the right of common pasture mentioned here is a grant to *all* tenants to pasture the fields of the monks. A custumal of the late thirteenth century (temp. Edward I) tells us that tenants of land in Crowmarsh, Oxfordshire, had common of pasture on the stubble of the lord's land as soon as the grain had been gathered. A custumal of Laughton, Sussex, dated 1272, declared that rights of common pasture over the demesne were the privilege of the free tenants in return for services to

[24] *Court Rolls of the Manor of Wakefield*, vol. ii, *1297–1309* (Yorks. Arch. Soc. Rec. Ser., xxxvi, 1906), pp. 20, 131, 58; *Court Roll of the Manor of Hales, 1270–1307*, part ii (Worcs. Hist. Soc., 1912), p. 391; *Calendar of Charters and Documents relating to the Possessions of Selborne and its Priory* (Hants. Rec. Soc., 1894), p. 41—see also p. 38, and Hants. Rec. Soc., 1891, pp. 38–9, 49, 64; G. Youd, 'The Common Fields of Lancashire', *Trans. Hist. Soc. Lancs. and Cheshire*, cxiii (1962), p. 10.

the lord. Finally two convincing examples of tenants' common rights over all fields. According to the customs of Stanbridge and Tilsworth, Bedfordshire, in 1240 'when a field of Tilsworth lies out of tillage and to fallow, then likewise a field of Stanbridge ought to lie out of tillage and fallow, so that they ought to common horn under horn'; the court roll of Broughton, Huntingdonshire in 1290 lists the names 'of those who sowed in the fallow where the freemen and bondmen ought to have their common pasture'. If we assimilate these examples into one generalization, we may say that rights of grazing over arable land were still being shared by neighbours in the twelfth century, but before the middle of the thirteenth century there were villages in which all tenants shared common rights in all fields. Further search, of course, may well produce evidence of the latter in the twelfth century. Alternatively, we may reach the same goal by approaching the problem from another direction.[25]

The grazing of all the fields of a village in common could not take place until they were all incorporated into a scheme of cropping which ensured that all the strips in one sector lay fallow at the same time, that all the strips in another were sown in autumn, or in spring, and that the fields were harvested and cleared at the same time. Thus, in places where common rights over the arable were still a matter of agreement between neighbours, we should not expect to find crop rotations organized on a village basis. We need not be surprised, then, that many villages in the Middle Ages appear to have contained numerous fields, not apparently arranged in any orderly groups, and that no distinction was preserved between furlongs and fields. In such cases, it is likely that the distinction was of no practical significance.

Not all manors, however, exhibit the same puzzling appearance of disordered cultivation even in the thirteenth century. Some early references to cropping imply that an intensive rotation of one or two crops and a fallow was observed on ecclesiastical demesne in the twelfth century. A lease of Navestock Manor, Essex, in 1152, for example, mentions winter and spring corn and a season of fallow. An extent of 1265–6 shows that some lands of the monastery of St. Peter at Gloucester, situated in Littleton and Linkenholt, Hampshire, were cropped for two years out of three. In 1299 a two-course rotation,

[25] L. C. Lloyd and D. M. Stenton, *Sir Christopher Hatton's Book of Seals* (Northants. Rec. Soc., xv, 1950), p. 14; *Custumals of Battle Abbey in the Reign of Edward I and Edward II*, ed. S. R. Scargill-Bird (Camden Ser., N.S., xli, 1887), pp. 89, xxxv; *Custumals of the Manors of Laughton . . .* , ed. A. E. Wilson (Sussex Rec. Soc., lx, 1961), pp. 3–4; G. C. Homans, *English Villagers of the Thirteenth Century* (Cambridge, Mass., 1942), pp. 422, 57–8.

including one year of fallow, prevailed on various Worcester
episcopal estates. And, indeed, since three thirteenth-century
treatises of husbandry imply that a regular two or three-course
rotation was an essential of good farming, we may guess that it was
fairly commonplace practice among responsible farmers by that
time.[26]

None of these examples, however, can be taken as proof that
tenants' lands were subject to the same rotation, or, indeed, any
rotation. But on Lincolnshire manors in the twelfth and thirteenth
centuries we find clues to the division of all the village land into two
halves for cropping purposes, and here we are on firmer ground:
tenants' lands must have been drawn into the same field courses as
that of their lords. Sir Frank Stenton assures us that the practice of
dividing the land of the village into two halves was not unusual in
Lincolnshire: it was common in every part of Lindsey, and less
frequently found in Kesteven; it has not been found in Holland, but
we should not expect this, for there is no evidence of a common-field
system ever having developed in the fens. To illustrate this arrangement, two of Sir Frank Stenton's earliest examples must suffice. Early
in Henry II's reign (between 1154 and 1170) Thorald, son of Warin,
gave to the nuns of Bullington in East Barkwith '15 acres of arable
land on the one side of the village and as much on the other side and
half the meadow which belongs to all my land of the same village, and
pasture for a hundred sheep with all things pertaining to the same
land'. In 1156–7 Peter Cotes granted to Catley priory 20 acres of land
on one side of the village of Cotes and 20 acres on the other. The
purpose of equally dividing the land between two halves of the village
is made clear in at least two leases which said that the land was to be
cropped in alternate years.[27]

If we now discount the possibility that these holdings had been
equally divided between the two halves of the village from the time of
original settlement, we have to explain how this equal division had
been brought about. German scholars, as we have mentioned

[26] *The Domesday of St. Paul's . . .* , ed. W. H. Hale (Camden Ser., 1858), p. 133;
Historia et Cartularium Monasterii Sancti Petri Gloucestriae, ed. W. H. Hart (Rolls
Series, 1863–7), vol. iii, pp. 35–6, 41; *The Red Book of Worcester*, ed. Marjory Hollings
(Worcs. Hist. Soc., lxxii, lxxiv, 1934), pp. 125, 126, 151; *Walter of Henley's Husbandry*,
pp. 6–9, 66–7, 84–5.
[27] *Transcripts of Charters relating to the Gilbertine Houses . . .* , ed. F. M. Stenton
(Lincs. Rec. Soc., xviii, 1920), pp. 94, 83; *Registrum Antiquissimum . . . of Lincoln*, vol.
iv, ed. C. W. Foster (Lincs. Rec. Soc., xxxii, 1937), pp. 69–70, 233. Other possible
twelfth-century examples are listed in H. L. Gray, *op. cit.*, pp. 450–509, but the
evidence given there is not sufficient to prove anything either way.

already, envisage the possibility that at some stage in the evolution of a common-field system a radical re-distribution of land was necessary in order to facilitate the introduction of new common-field regulations on a village basis. Such a re-organization is not inconceivable in English villages; it would not have been repugnant to tenants. We are already familiar with the annual re-apportionment of meadow by lots, which was customary in many English villages. The re-allotment of arable land was a common, though not, of course, annual, practice in Northumberland—a normal common-field county—in the sixteenth century and later: in a number of villages the fields were divided into two halves and the strips re-allocated in order to give tenants land in one half or the other and reduce the distances they had to walk to their parcels. It was also customary in parts of the northern counties, possessing an infertile soil, to change the arable fields at intervals by putting the old ploughland back to common pasture and taking in a new field from the common. It is clear that people did not always cling tenaciously to their own plots of land.[28]

Clues to the re-allotment of land in the Middle Ages are not explicit, but indirect. They are of two kinds. Some documents show holdings comprising strips that lay in a regular order between the strips of other tenants. Professor Homans has cited several examples from the thirteenth and fourteenth centuries. Seebohm drew attention to an outstanding example from Winslow, Buckingham-shire, where in 1361 John Moldeson held seventy-two half-acre strips, of which sixty-six had on one side the strips of John Watekyns, while on the other side forty-three lay next to the strips of Henry Warde and twenty-three next to those of John Mayn. However, knowing as we do from the experience of German, Welsh, and Irish villages that, in a matter of two generations, a pattern of land occupation could be changed out of recognition through conveyances of pieces and the division of fields among parceners, we cannot believe that this orderliness dates from the time of original settlement. Indeed, we could say with some confidence that the allotment of land, depicted in a document in 1361, had taken place not more than one hundred years before. Do these examples, then, denote deliberate re-allotments of village land in the not very distant past for the sake of facilitating common-field regulations? It is possible. But there are

---

[28] M. W. Beresford, 'Lot Acres', *Econ. Hist. Rev.*, xiii (1943), pp. 74–9; Lord Ernle, *English Farming Past and Present* (London, 1961 edn.), pp. 26, 230; R. A. Butlin, 'Northumberland Field Systems', *Agric. Hist. Rev., xii (1964), pp.* 99–120; H. L. Gray, *op. cit.*, pp. 208–9.

equally plausible, alternative explanations. They may be the result of a redistribution of land following the Black Death, for many new tenancies had to be created after this calamity. Alternatively they may represent isolated examples in their villages of the partition among heirs of one holding comprising scattered fields. Such an effect can be demonstrated from English documents occasionally, from German records frequently. In short, none of these cases is any use for clinching an argument.[29]

Other clues to the re-distribution of village land lie in the evidence of holdings that were equally divided between two or more sectors of the village lands. But when we look for such examples, they turn out to be far from numerous. The vast majority of tenants' holdings did not consist of strips evenly divided between two or more cropping units. The distribution was more often highly irregular, and this fact has been a constant source of bewilderment to historians. Even the examples from Lincolnshire of estates comprising equal amounts of land in two halves of the village prove to be less tidy than we imagined. Peter Cotes's grant of land in Cotes, already quoted, consisted of forty acres divided into two equal halves. But the details of the parcels composing it are as follows: $13\frac{1}{2}$ acres lay on the north side of the village upon Lechebek, 3 acres less one rood upon Northills; on the south side 9 acres lay upon Lekbek, 8 acres upon Rodewale, 3 acres next Gilbert's court, and a further selion on the other side of the trench opposite the toft. Far from indicating an orderly allocation of tenants' lands throughout the village, the composition of this estate strongly suggests a collection of pieces, deliberately selected at this date or earlier to make an estate that conformed to some prior division of all the village lands. It prompts the suggestion that the division of village fields into halves, and later into thirds or quarters was intended to facilitate cultivation and grazing, but was implemented without much regard to the distribution of individual tenants' strips. After all, it would not have been difficult, within a generation, for the individual to rectify any irksome imbalance of crops by buying, leasing, or exchanging land. Moreover, additional land was being asserted at the same time: some of it was held in severalty; some of it was asserted by cooperative effort and immediately divided into strips and added to the existing

[29] G. C. Homans, 'Terroirs ordonnés et Champs orientés: une Hypothèse sur le Village anglais', *Annales d'histoire économique et sociale*, viii (1936), pp. 438–9; Seebohm, *op. cit.*, p. 27, P. F. Brandon, 'Arable Farming in a Sussex Scarpfoot Parish during the late Middle Ages', *Sussex Arch. Coll.*, c (1962), p. 62.

field courses. There were plenty of occasions for re-shaping a lop-sided holding, even though many peasants did not apparently deem it necessary to do so. If this is a reasonable hypothesis, it removes some of the problems of explaining how field courses could be re-organized from time to time without any elaborate preliminaries or consequences. When we encounter a decision in the court roll of the manor of Crowle, Isle of Axholme, in 1381 to divide the fields into four parts in order to fallow a quarter each year, and when the villagers of Marton, north Yorkshire, in the fourteenth century appointed men 'to do and ordain as best they can to cast the field into three parts so that one part every year be fallow', we do not have to look for a wholesale re-allocation of tenants' land.[30]

This survey of some of the early evidence of common-field practices does not allow us to say with any certainty when the first village took a decision to organize the cultivation *and* grazing of its arable fields on a village basis. A much more thorough examination of all the evidence will be necessary before this stage is reached. All we have been able to do so far is to recognize in documents of the twelfth and thirteenth centuries some of the steps in the development of a common-field system. The earliest case cited here of regulated cropping by the whole village is dated 1156–7. It may have involved common grazing as well, but we cannot be certain. The first unmistakable statement about commoning by a whole village dates from 1240. With some assurance, then, we can point to the twelfth and first half of the thirteenth centuries as possibly the crucial ones in the development of the first common-field systems.

To reach this stage of our argument, we have been obliged to use scraps of information from many different manors and villages, and it may not have escaped the notice of the observant reader that some of the illustrations used here are drawn from districts of England in which the final system did not usually contain two or three arable fields on the classic model, but one or many fields. Some explanation is called for. The distinction between the two- and three-field system, on the one hand, and systems with other numbers of fields on the other, is not, I submit, a fundamental one that indicates a different origin, as H. L. Gray maintained. The two systems coincide with, and arise out of, the distinction between arable and pasture farming types. The two- and three-field system characterized arable, that is mixed farming, districts. Villages with more or fewer common fields were

---

[30] Lincs. Archives Office, Crowle manor I, 34; Homans, *English Villagers*, p. 56.

mainly pasture-farming communities. I have argued elsewhere that the principal difference between the communal farming practices of the forest and pastoral areas, on the one hand, and the arable areas on the other was that in the latter the common-field system reached a more mature stage of development. In the pastoral areas, common arable fields were not unknown, but they were small in comparison with the acreage of pastures. Grassland was the mainstay of the economy and arable crops were grown for subsistence only. Hence the arable fields did not have to be cropped with the utmost economy; their small area lessened the problem of ensuring access to all tenants' parcels; and the stubble did not have to be economically grazed owing to the abundance of other pasture. For these reasons, there was no urgent necessity to control rigorously the cultivation of the plough-land. In the pastoral villages of the Lincolnshire fenland, for example, no attempt was ever made to order the strip fields on a village basis.[31]

If pastoral areas were slow to regulate their ploughland as a village concern, we begin to understand why enclosure was for them a painless and peaceful process. For agreements between two persons or a small group to extinguish common rights over the arable were far more easily reached, as the charters of Missenden abbey readily demonstrate, than agreements between all the inhabitants of the village. Far-reaching conclusions follow from this argument if it is pursued to its logical end. The areas of England which we are accustomed to label as 'early enclosed'—central Suffolk, most of Essex, Hertfordshire, parts of Shropshire, Herefordshire, Somerset, Devon, and Cornwall—were pastoral districts in the sixteenth century, and were 'early enclosed' only because they had never known a fully developed common-field system.

Finally, it is necessary to revert again to the unanswered question, posed in this paper, namely the date of the earliest complete common-field system to be found in England. It is clear that the mature system was liable to come into operation at different times in different parts of the kingdom. Professor Hilton's introduction to the Stoneleigh Leger Book shows that common fields in this forest area were in process of creation in the period 1250–1350. Mr. Elliott's study of Cumberland common fields hints at an even later process of evolution, as well as supplying some excellent examples of one phase in gestation when closes were shared between several tenants. Mr.

---

[31] Thirsk, 'The Farming Regions of England,' cited in note 17. The importance of arable husbandry in forcing the growth of the common-field system is also stressed in Ilešič, *op. cit.*, (cited in note 8 above), pp. 73, 75, 114.

Glanville Jones has recently argued that Welsh bond hamlets with their open field share-lands are well documented in the Middle Ages and go back to the Early Iron Age; if the argument presented here is at all acceptable, then we may recognize in this case too the first signs of a field pattern that might evolve later into a common-field system. For there is no reason to regard Wales, or England, for that matter, as a special case. One point is established beyond reasonable doubt by the comparisons drawn here between English and Continental experience, namely, that in those West and East European countries in which field systems have been analysed with some care, the evolution of the common fields appears to have followed much the same course. In all cases the presence of a sufficiently large and growing population, compelled to cultivate its land more intensively, was a pre-condition of growth: this condition seems to have been first fulfilled in the twelfth and thirteenth centuries. It should also be said that there is no reason to think that the social framework in which common-field systems emerged necessarily influenced their form. They could evolve in a thoroughly authoritarian society, in which the lord allotted land to his men—there are German examples to show this occurring in a pioneering community under the close surveillance of the lord. They could just as well take shape in a society of free colonists, such as that depicted in the East Riding of Yorkshire in the twelfth and thirteenth centuries.[32]

---

[32] Hilton, *The Stoneleigh Leger Book*, p. liv; G. Elliott, 'The System of Cultivation and Evidence of Enclosure in the Cumberland Open Fields in the Sixteenth Century', *Trans. Cumb. and Westm. Antiq. and Arch. Soc.*, N.S., lix (1959), pp. 85, 87, 95, 99; Glanville Jones, 'Early Territorial Organization in England and Wales', *Geogr. Annaler*, xliii (1961), pp. 175–6.

V

THE ORIGIN OF THE COMMON FIELDS

I HAVE to thank Dr. Titow for giving me a claim to more space in *Past and Present* and so enabling me to elaborate upon some of the problems raised by my article in No. 29 (December, 1964).* It was intended to open a fresh discussion on the origins of the common-field system. Why, how, and when did it take this form? Dr. Titow offers two different answers to these questions, which are designed to meet all cases. Farmers, founding a settlement for the first time, laid out standard holdings in intermingled strips equally divided between the rotational fields and then expanded the area of land in cultivation in succeeding generations (p. 94). In short, the system was fully worked out in men's minds before they imposed it on the land. The second explanation meets the case of villages in the East Riding where the documents suggest that a group of farmers with ring-fence farms in the mid-twelfth century had turned themselves into a common-field village by the sixteenth century, if not a great deal earlier. Dr. Titow explains the situation thus:

> straggling ['straggling' is surely a gratuitous adjective] settlers cultivated a few acres of assart. . . . As soon as a settlement increased in size to become a village community, it tended to adopt the open-field system of cultivation, presumably because this seemed to the settlers the most appropriate system for community farming—and it must have been a system known to them from their general knowledge of their experience in whatever place they came from (p. 93).

Thus, in the first explanation the common-field system is taken as an idea already fully formulated before it was put into operation. In the second case three vital questions are ignored: first, why did the growth of a village community make people want community farming in place of their existing arrangements; second, how did the change take place, quietly by a process of evolution, or by a decisive break with the past and a fresh start; third, when was the system adopted? Dr. Titow has decided that it was devised long before any documents begin and that all communities who subsequently

---

* Chapter IV above and J. Z. Titow, 'Medieval England and the Open-Field System', *Past and Present*, no. 32 (December, 1965).

adopted it were copying the examples of others. This he rightly calls a simple explanation. But it is simple only because it dismisses as insoluble all the problems which I was trying to explore. Perhaps they *are* insoluble, but I am not yet satisfied that we have to accept this as the final verdict. Most of our documentary evidence has been examined by historians with the same strong preconceptions as Dr. Titow, namely, that the common-field system was in full operation before our documents begin. My article was intended to encourage the re-examination of the evidence without preconceptions. I know this is a difficult exercise, but it may in the end advance our knowledge and for that reason I consider it worth doing. It has led me to incur the charge from Dr. Titow that I have forced my own unorthodox and novel interpretations upon words which have perfectly straightforward meanings (pp. 92, 102). I admit that my scepticism has grown so great that I question all accepted meanings. But I hoped to show that interpretations other than the orthodox ones are possible. I do not wish my interpretations to become a new orthodoxy unless and until they have been better tested.

I do not propose here to enter into a debate with Dr. Titow about the precise meanings of particular phrases in single documents. These will only be made clear by the re-examination of far more evidence than that which I cited. Instead I wish to take up some of Dr. Titow's more general statements which I consider disputable, and which, if not contested now, may confuse subsequent discussion by others.

1.   I deplore Dr. Titow's statement that evidence from the Continent of Europe is irrelevant to my discussion of the origins of the common-field system. I am tempted to provoke Dr. Titow further by declaring that we may also learn something from the study of peasant cultivation in present-day Asia, Africa, and South America, where examples abound of intermingled strips, though not, I believe, usually accompanied by common rules about rotations and grazing. But if we narrow the scope of our enquiry a little, and agree that the common-field system is not a world phenomenon, it is at least a European one.

2.   Dr. Titow makes several references (pp. 87, 93) to the areas (which he does not himself define) which are commonly held to have practised a common-field system. Northumberland, Wales, East Anglia, and Kent, he says, are not areas of common fields. In fact, of course, there are excellent examples of common-field systems in all these areas except Kent. Moreover, the old generalizations about the geographical distribution of common fields need thorough revision,

for much that was once accepted as evidence of common fields merely illustrates the presence of intermingled strips; it does not necessarily follow that such strips were part of a common-field system. This has been demonstrated in recent studies of the Lincolnshire fenland and of Kent, where intermingled strips were independently cultivated by their occupiers and were not subject to common rules.[1] Since it is essential to make these differences clear by the use of a precise terminology, I have followed the usage recommended in the Glossary of Terms published in the *Agricultural History Review*,[2] and have employed the term *common field* for land worked under a common-field system, reserving *open field* for land lying in strips but not subject to common grazing rights. Dr. Titow's persistence in regarding the terms *open field* and *common field* as freely interchangeable (p. 86, note †) will confuse rather than clarify the interpretation of the evidence.

3. The word *common* which appears so often in medieval documents has for Dr. Titow a perfectly straightforward meaning (p. 96). It described land worked under the common-field system. But Dr. A. R. H. Baker has demonstrated that in Kent a *common field* simply meant a field of intermingled strips.[3] How can we be certain, without examining the matter again, that in the earliest medieval documents it did not have the same meaning? Professor Hilton has recently traced changes in the meaning of the word 'freedom' in the Middle Ages.[4] I suggest that we must be equally watchful for changing meanings of agrarian terms.

4. I agree with Dr. Titow that the rule of impartible inheritance came to dominate customary land in champion areas while partible inheritance persisted in the pastoral regions (p. 96). But this dominance was far from complete in the thirteenth century, and in any case some manors had less customary land and more free land than others. Moreover, within the framework of this broad generalization, changes of emphasis can be observed at different periods. Dr. Faith has suggested that in periods when land was

---

[1] Chapter IV above.

[2] R. A. Butlin, 'Some Terms used in Agrarian History. A Glossary', *Agric. Hist. Rev.*, xi (1961), pp. 98–104.

[3] A. R. H. Baker, 'Field Systems in the Vale of Holmesdale', *Agric. Hist. Rev.*, xiv (1966), pp. 7, 9.

[4] R. H. Hilton, 'Freedom and Villeinage in England', *Past and Present*, no. 31 (July, 1965).

plentiful peasants were less concerned to keep their land in the family than in periods of land shortage when heirs insisted on their inheritance rights.[5] In the thirteenth century when population was increasing, in some places very rapidly as Dr. Titow has shown in his excellent description of customary tenancies on the manor of Taunton,[6] a modest revival of partible inheritance could easily have aggravated the organizational problems of cultivation in champion areas by increasing the number of parcels. There are signs in the Tudor period that partible inheritance, coupled with the rise of population, brought to a head a number of problems which were merely latent in periods when numbers were stable or falling: the size of holdings was falling alarmingly, and complaints to this effect were explicit; but implicit in these complaints was also an increase in the number of parcels. This, indeed, may be the reason why descriptions of the workings of the common-field system accumulate at this period—because the organizational difficulties created by increasing numbers of people made stricter rules necessary. Our experience of life in England at the present day does not help much towards the understanding of the common-field system, but it does at least reinforce this point that a rise of population calls forth a host of regulations and restrictions affecting the use of land.

Borough English, the third custom of inheritance, is treated by Dr. Titlow as having the same effect as primogeniture, resulting in a holding passing undivided to one son (p. 93). Here again there is some room for doubt about the universal truth of this statement. Dr. Faith has argued persuasively that the descent of land to the youngest son is a 'fossilized' form of partible inheritance for part of the rule of gavelkind was special provision for the youngest son.[7] I would like to be reassured that holdings subject to Borough English always passed intact to the youngest son and were not used before death to provide a nucleus of a holding for other sons. On the manor of Taunton Dr. Titow showed how in a period of acute land shortage sons without an inheritance in prospect married widows with land. This was an admirable solution, but it was only made possible by the custom of the manor relating to widows' rights. Not all widows on all manors

[5] Rosamund Faith, 'Peasant Families and Inheritance Customs in Medieval England', *Agric. Hist. Rev.*, xiv (1966), pp. 86–92.
[6] J. Z. Titow, 'Some Differences between Manors and their Effects on the Condition of the Peasant in the Thirteenth Century', *Agric. Hist. Rev.*, x (1962), pp. 1–13. See also J. Z. Titow, 'Some Evidence of the Thirteenth-Century Population Increase', *Econ. Hist. Rev.*, 2nd ser., xiv (1961–2), pp. 218–24.
[7] Rosamund Faith, *op. cit.*

could offer the same inviting prospect to land-hungry young men. My suspicions about Borough English are deepened by the fact that it was still a strong custom in forest areas in the sixteenth century, and these were notorious for their many small holdings. Did Borough English have anything to do with it? This paragraph is full of possibilities and suspicions rather than certainties, but there is some justification here for looking again at the alleged dominance of single-son inheritance in champion areas in the thirteenth century. I would like this door left open despite Dr. Titow's desire to close it.

5. My definition of the common-field system is based on the way things worked in the sixteenth and seventeenth centuries when our documents make the arrangements reasonably clear (p. 89). This is the way our textbooks present it, and the way we are led to believe it worked from the beginning. Dr. Titow thinks it quite unhistorical to believe that changes did not take place over a period of several centuries (p. 89). So do I. But he allows only for a certain untidiness, overlying an original tidy arrangement. I envisage the casual development of a field system which arrived at its most systematic form at varying dates in different villages between about the thirteenth and eighteenth centuries. I do not believe that the emergence of the common-field system necessarily involved a major reallocation of holdings; I endeavoured to make this clear in my article. On the other hand I do not exclude the possibility that this happened in some cases. Nor did I argue that all land was held in severalty before the thirteenth century.[8] On the contrary, I see evidence of intermingled strips over which neighbours, sharing one or more fields, may have organized their own rotations and common grazing. This is a kind of half-way house between land in severalty and land under a common-field system. It may not involve the intervention of the village community or manorial court. Does this perhaps explain why the first entries (referring to agricultural disputes) in the manor court rolls of the later twelfth and thirteenth centuries are concerned with asserting only the lord's rights against individuals who have damaged *his* crops and injured *his* stock? Claims by other tenants against their neighbours were the exception. This, however, raises the question why, how, and when the manor court took up issues which

---

[8] I entirely agree with Dr. Titow that the bulk of ancient peasant land was already in the form of a standard customary holding as early as 1086 (p. 98). But I know no evidence to prove that at this date the virgates and bovates consisted of intermingled strips, as he implies. This is not made clear until the twelfth and thirteenth centuries when we first see them at closer quarters.

were really a village concern. If the common-field system, as Dr. Titow envisages it, existed from time immemorial, perhaps a village commune upheld rules of cultivation until its authority was taken over by the manorial court. Or were the rules first taking shape, as I have argued, when the manorial court was developing its authority for enforcing them? Questions phrased in this way are perhaps impossible to answer. But an assembly of information about the antiquity of the village commune would contribute helpful circumstantial evidence.

From a desire to make my original article as concise as possible I did not make explicit all the problems that surround this subject. Nor have I done so here. There are questions about the development of the common-field system after the Black Death, for example. Did it collapse in some places, only to revive again in the sixteenth century? Clearly, my questions do not make the path of the agrarian historian easy. But the answers which Dr. Titow puts forward, and which rest, as he admits, on a balance of probabilities, do not seem to me lifelike. I shall continue to search for material by which to test my hypothesis, and hope that medieval historians who are far more conversant with the sources than I, will lend a hand.

POSTSCRIPT

A reappraisal of the origins and development of common field systems is now taking place, and a considerable literature has accumulated since 1964. This work is best represented by the ten essays contained in Trevor Rowley (ed.), *The Origins of Open-Field Agriculture*, London, 1981, which also contains an up-to-date bibliography.

VI

TUDOR ENCLOSURES

In the first two decades of this century, Tudor enclosures received more than their share of attention from economic historians. Since then there has been no attempt to reconsider the old judgments in the light of new knowledge, and by constantly rehearsing old views we are now in danger of oversimplifying a complex problem.[1] In the crudest accounts the movement is described thus: all over England men were enclosing their land and turning it into sheep pasture, because the wool of the sheep was more profitable to grow than any other produce of the farm. Enclosures were carried out with ruthless disregard for the rights and interests of the smaller farmers and cottagers, and were the cause of much misery and social unrest.

A moment's reflection must raise doubts concerning the accuracy of this account, for, apart from the fact that not all land is suitable for sheep, we learned some twenty years ago from the study of the London food market in the sixteenth century that there was much specialization in food production in the different regions of England.[2] The Londoner's mutton came from Gloucestershire and Northamptonshire, his fruit and hops from Kent, his vegetables from Essex, his dairy produce from East Anglia, his bread corn from Sussex, Kent and Norfolk, the barley for his beer from Lincolnshire. This picture of agricultural diversity and regional specialization, which is equally familiar in present-day Britain, does not accord well with the England described in the enclosure story. The truth is that enclosures took many different forms. They were carried out for many different reasons. They frequently resulted in a change of land use but not always in a change from corn-growing to sheep-keeping. In short, they varied greatly in character and importance from one part of England to another.

Briefly, one may define enclosure as a method of increasing the

---

[1] See the bibliography at the end of this chapter.
[2] F. J. Fisher, 'The Development of the London Food Market, 1540–1640', *Econ. Hist. Rev.*, V, 1934–5, pp. 46–64.

productivity or profitability[3] of land. This definition would apply accurately to all forms of enclosure. To appreciate both its social and economic significance in the sixteenth century, however, it is necessary to bear in mind that not all parts of England at that time were at the same stage in agrarian development. The process by which the open field system gave way to consolidated farms in separate ownership was long and slow in some areas, and relatively rapid and painless in others. In the southern and eastern counties of Essex, Surrey, Sussex and Suffolk and in the south-western counties of Devon and Cornwall examples of common field farming were hard to find in 1500. The densely settled parts of the Midlands were then at a far more advanced stage of enclosure than the thinly populated counties of the north. Finally, there were yet other districts where it is believed that common fields had never existed, though it is probable that such areas lay always in thinly-populated pasture-farming regions where the arable fields were small in size.[4]

Over a large part of central and northern England, there was still much commonable waste and common field in the sixteenth century. Indeed, much survived into the eighteenth and nineteenth centuries. And because enclosure was a long drawn-out affair in many places, some regular stages in the process of evolution through the centuries can be discerned. In the first days of settlement it can be assumed that most villages had small arable fields and meadows, while the remainder of the village lands—the pasture and the waste—was extensive. Indeed, the waste of one village was not clearly marked off from the next, so abundant was it on all sides that a strict definition of boundaries between townships was for a long time unnecessary. Intercommoning by the stock of neighbouring villages or parishes

---

[3] By 'increase in the productivity of land' I do not mean to suggest that the yield of crops per acre necessarily increased. It may have done but this is difficult to prove. I mean simply that the land was more efficiently cultivated. Pasture closes were grazed more carefully than commons. Arable closes were better manured and might carry a crop in the fallow year. In the words of John Hales in the *Discourse of the Commonweal of this Realm of England*—'Experience sheweth that tenauntes in common be not so good husbandes as when every man hath his part in several.' Also experience showed that land was not always being put to its best use. Old arable fields were not as productive as ploughed-up grassland. See the reasons for the proposed enclosure of the lands of Mudford in Somerset in 1554 in *Tudor Economic Documents*, ed. Tawney & Power, I, pp. 61–2.

[4] H. L. Gray's map of open field England in *English Field Systems* (1915) has been proved incorrect. The map printed by C. S. and C. S. Orwin in *The Open Fields* (1938), p. 65, is much more detailed and accurate, though it too requires some minor revision. There are no counties in England in which some traces of common field cultivation have not been found. See Chapters 4 and 5 above.

continued for centuries in many places, since it saved the expense of constructing a boundary bank between them. As population increased, the arable fields had to be enlarged at the expense of the pasture and waste until a point was reached where the common grazings failed to feed all the stock of the inhabitants. Intercommoning between parishes often caused disputes and litigation at this point, and commons were formally carved up between townships. The next step was to control the number of stock which individuals might graze on the commons. Part of, and later all, the common waste was turned into regulated common pasture where animals were stinted, and feeding was restricted by agreement to certain periods of the year when other grazings, the stubble of the open fields, for example, and the aftermath of the meadows, were not available. Further increases in the human and animal population of the township might later compel fresh reductions in the stints previously agreed upon. Finally, when land shortage again became critical and all these measures of economy had been tried, the final expedient was the enclosure and division of both common pastures and common fields among individuals. It might be carried out on individual initiative with the lord's consent or without, and it might raise an outcry or pass unnoticed. Alternatively, it might be carried through by communal agreement, a method which became more common in the later years of the sixteenth century, and was fairly usual in the seventeenth. In either case enclosure meant that all common rights over the fields or commons were extinguished. When enclosure of the fields took place by agreement, it was often accompanied by a re-arrangement of strips so that some consolidation of holdings could be effected. When common pastures were enclosed, parcels were allotted to all who claimed common rights, including both cottagers and peasants holding strips in the open fields. In all cases, each man was master of his own piece of land, to hedge or fence it, and cultivate it as he pleased.

It may be that no single English village passed through all the stages described here in converting its arable fields and commons into consolidated farms. But in the sixteenth century every one of these stages in development could be illustrated by examples from different regions of England. The partitioning of commons between several parishes was a frequent occurrence in the Pennine areas in the Tudor period. Henfield Common in the Lancashire parish of Whalley, for example, was divided between the townships of Clayton-le-Moors, Altham and Accrington between 1576 and 1594. Thealmoor, near

Oldham, was divided between the lords of Chadderton, Alkrington, and Nuthurst prior to 1526.[5] The enclosure of part of the waste in order to create some regulated common pasture, where the quality of the grazing could be improved and better shelter provided for stock, was undertaken in James I's reign on Bowes Moor in Yorkshire and in Charles I's reign at Wath-upon-Dearne, near Rotherham.[6] In Elizabeth's reign, energetic colonization of the waste in order to increase the ploughland was carried out at Burton Leonard in the West Riding, where the number of holdings was increased from 60 to 84 oxgangs. The inevitable sequel was a pasture shortage which compelled the inhabitants to reduce the stint of cattle allowed to every oxgang from seven beasts to four.[7] The introduction of cattle stints on formerly unstinted common pastures was discussed in parts of the Lincolnshire fenland at the end of the sixteenth century, though nothing came of the proposal.[8] A reduction in the old cattle stints owing to the increase in the number of stock was forced on the villagers of Burton Leonard, Bishop Wilton on the Yorkshire wolds, and Foston in the western clay vale of Lincolnshire.[9] Finally, the division of the common fields and pastures among individuals was under way in countless villages all over the country. In some cases, it was carried out by agreement, as at the enclosure of Bradford Moor in Yorkshire in 1589, when all the tenants assembled on the moor and reached an almost unanimous decision to enclose. In others it was a matter of individual initiative. On many Lancashire manors in Rossendale piecemeal enclosure of an acre or two of waste, or the enclosure of a few strips in the arable fields, was extremely common. These closes were made by tenants with the lord's consent and most of them aroused little or no opposition. In other cases, eager land-lords were prepared to buy consent, as did William Brocas of Theddingworth in Leicestershire, who in 1582 granted 'diverse gratuities and leases of good value' to secure his tenants' co-operation. The enclosures which caused indignation and the breaking down of hedges were those in which a lord or his tenant rode roughshod over the rights of others. These were the cases which en-

---

[5] Lancs. County Records Office, DD Pt., Bdle 18; H. T. Crofton, 'Moston and White Moss', *Trans. Lancs. & Cheshire Antiq. Soc.*, XXV, p. 51.

[6] P.R.O., *Exchequer Depositions*, 17 Jas. I, Hil. I; Sheffield Central Library, WWM, C2, 257 (3).

[7] P.R.O., *Exchequer Depositions*, 38 Eliz., Easter I.

[8] Joan Thirsk, *English Peasant Farming*, p. 112.

[9] P.R.O., *Exchequer Depositions*, 38 Eliz., Easter I; 14 Jas. I, Mich. 8; Thirsk, *op. cit.*, p. 97.

raged public opinion and lingered long in popular memory. They also supplied the fuel that inflamed the writings of contemporary pamphleteers. Nevertheless a determined tenantry, jealous of its rights and willing to raise a 'common purse' to pay the costs of litigation, got many such wrongs righted. A victory of this kind seems to lie behind the decree of 1569–70 ordering Thomas Saville of Woodkirk to lay open an enclosure of a hundred acres which he had made on the commons of Allerton township in the parish of Bradford. The decree was awarded 'after complaint by the tenants and freeholders thereof.'[10] The many other enclosure cases heard in the courts at Westminster combine to portray a far from docile peasantry, invoking 'ancient custom' to good effect. They did not all submit and depart from their villages with tears and lamentation.

Since enclosure of one kind or another was in progress over the greater part of England in the Tudor period, all attempts at generalization about the movement are hazardous. Nevertheless it is certain that some kinds of enclosure were more typical of some regions than of others. The partition of waste between intercommoning parishes, the construction of regulated common pastures on formerly unregulated waste, the taking in of waste on a large scale in order to increase the arable land—these forms of enclosure were most frequent in the more thinly settled parts of highland England—in the Pennine districts of the north, for example, from which most of the cases quoted above are taken. Land there was extensively rather than intensively cultivated. There were still abundant wastes awaiting improvement to accommodate any increase of population. If, for the greater convenience of working, enclosure of the arable fields took place in such areas, it was frequently done by amicable agreement or by piecemeal enclosure initiated by individuals and it raised no great opposition. The inhabitants were not yet oppressed by a threatening land shortage, and did not consider their interests seriously injured. This fact, indeed, affords a clue to the way in which enclosure probably took place in the Middle Ages before population pressure and the existence of a growing class of poor landless villagers underlined the distressing social consequences of enclosure more

[10] P.R.O., *Duchy of Lancaster*, 44, 440; *Victoria County History of Leicestershire*, II, p. 203; G. H. Tupling, *The Economic History of Rossendale*, Chetham Soc., LXXXVI, *passim*; Leeds Public Library, *Stansfield Collection*, C, 4, I, 797. For an example of a common purse collected by tenants to pay the costs of an enclosure suit, see the case brought by the tenants of Holme-on-Spalding Moor against enclosers of their common—P.R.O., *Exchequer Depositions*, 19 Jas. I, Trin. 5. For other examples see R. H. Tawney, *Agrarian Problem in the Sixteenth Century*, p. 330, note 2.

heavily than the economic advantages.

In parishes of moderate population density where the problem of grazing shortage was new in the sixteenth century, or in pastoral regions like the fen where the population was large but where, owing to the nature of the economy, the common pastures were still extensive, the introduction of stints on the commons, or the reduction of old ones, was a frequent expedient for sharing the land more equitably. It served as a warning signal of land shortage ahead, but did not betoken any immediate crisis. There are many examples of new stints being introduced in the townships of the Midlands and in the vale lands of northern England in the sixteenth century, for these were areas which had attracted early settlement, and were populous and relatively intensively cultivated. Finally, there were many townships in the same region which experienced an even more serious land shortage, where the waste was already taken up, the common pastures were inadequate, and where enclosure, in consequence, invariably injured someone. In such villages enclosure of any kind was liable to lead to violent protest.

This attempt to differentiate the character of enclosure in the various regions of England assumes that at each stage the ultimate stimulus was a rising population, compelling individuals or whole communities to devise more economical ways of using their land. It was a powerful underlying motive, particularly in the Midlands, but it was not the only one. In the sheep-rearing uplands, where settlement was often thin, and the sheepwalks and hill-grazings extensive, rising prices seem to have exerted more influence than pressure of population. Indeed, to many contemporary writers, the inflation of food-prices, which made farming more profitable and gave the incentive to increase production, seemed a more powerful factor than land shortage, though the two were, of course, closely connected. Then, too, every landlord and every farmer had his own private reasons. Some landlords wanted to increase the value of their land in order to raise rents.[11] The lord of Honington in Lincolnshire, Sir Charles Hussey, confessed himself obliged to enclose land in order to increase his income and meet the cost of expensive lawsuits. Some large

---

[11] See, for example, the enclosure history of Cotesbach in Leicestershire. This is also an excellent example of a village wholly enclosed in the Tudor period, partly by force, partly by the buying out of freeholders, where much of the land was converted to pasture, but not apparently for sheep. Depopulation occurred, but it was the result rather of engrossing and rationalization of an estate. L. A. Parker, 'The Agrarian Revolution at Cotesbach, 1501–1612,' *Trans. Leics. Archaeolog. Soc.*, XXIV, 1948, p. 41 *et seq.*

farmers decided to enclose and convert their land to pasture in order
to reduce their labour costs, for, in the words of a contemporary,
'nothing is more unprofitable than a farm in tillage in the hands of
servants where the master's eye is not daily upon them.'[12]

All the subsidiary motives for enclosure have to be considered
when evaluating regional differences of pace and purpose. But only
the overwhelming compulsion of population increase, together with
accompanying price rises, can explain why enclosure made such swift
progress and was such a burning issue in two separate periods of
history, the sixteenth and the late eighteenth and early nineteenth
centuries. Contemporaries were more acutely aware of the
relationship between population and land use than later historians.
As the inhabitants of Bradford in Yorkshire explained when
defending their decision to enclose the common, the population of
the town had increased and the ancient land in cultivation was no
longer sufficient to maintain them. When the inhabitants of four
Lancashire townships fell out over the sharing of their commons, one
of the causes of acrimony was the fact that forty new tenements had
been built on the demesnes of Sawley Abbey since the Dissolution,
thus aggravating the pasture shortage. People who had once taken a
lenient view of intruders claiming common rights became more
watchful as their waste land diminished while the scale of farming and
stock-keeping increased. A native of Holme-on-Spalding Moor put
the point succinctly when giving evidence in an enclosure dispute
heard in the Court of Exchequer in 1620. He knew not whether a
tenement built on the common some sixty years before had common
by right or 'by sufferance or negligence of the freeholders.' But at the
time the cottage was built 'the freeholders made little reckoning of
common for so small goods as was then put upon the said common by
the said tenants.'[13]

Since enclosures in the sixteenth century were diverse in type and
purpose, it follows that not all enclosing farmers were bent upon
converting their ploughland to pasture. That the Crown was
interested only in enclosure accompanied by conversion was due to
the fact that such a change of land-use led to unemployment and
depopulation, reduced the corn harvest and aggravated local
problems of grain scarcity. At the same time, contemporaries were

[12] P.R.O., *Star Chamber*, 8, 17, 24; Sheffield Central Library, *Strafford Letters* WWM, 20a, no. 17.
[13] *Duchy of Lancaster*, 44, 440; *Exchequer Special Commission*, 2747; *Exchequer Depositions*, 18 Jas. I, Hil. 15.

well aware that enclosure was not the only cause of these troubles. Engrossing was equally important, for, when two or more farms were thrown together, the superfluous farmhouses were either reduced to the status of cottages or left to decay. Thus the number of holdings in a township was reduced, the smaller farmers were deprived of a livelihood, land hunger and unemployment ensued. The result was a further increase in social tension.

When the first enclosure commission was appointed in 1517, its enquiries concerned enclosure and imparking and embraced the whole of England except the four northern counties. The Crown was not sufficiently well-informed at that time to recognize nice regional differences in the geographical pattern of enclosure, nor to appreciate subtle differences between enclosing and engrossing.[14] The commission appointed in 1548 was directed to enquire into engrossing as well as enclosing and imparking, but it did not complete its work, and the only returns which have survived relate to Warwickshire and Cambridgeshire. Even more short-lived was the commission of 1565, the only known returns of which relate to Buckinghamshire and Leicestershire. Nevertheless, it may not be without significance that these fragmentary reports relate to counties in central and eastern England. For in 1607, following upon the Midland Revolt, the enclosure commissioners finally centred their attention upon this area. Their articles of enquiry included both engrossing and enclosing, and their work was limited to seven counties, Warwickshire, Leicestershire, Lincolnshire, Northampton-shire, Buckinghamshire, Bedfordshire and Huntingdonshire, counties which had lain at the centre of the disturbances and where, it was now recognized, the problems of enclosure and engrossing were most acute.[15]

The agrarian statutes and proclamations of the period likewise reflect a growing understanding of local differences and changing economic conditions governing the motives for enclosure. The first general statute of Henry VII's reign against the pulling down of towns

---

[14] For the discussion by modern historians whether engrossing also meant enclosing, see below, p. 74.

[15] The commissioners appointed in 1517 were ordered to report on the villages and houses pulled down since 1488, the land then in tillage and now in pasture, and the parkland which had been enclosed for wild animals. For the exact terms, see *The Domesday of Inclosures, 1517–1518*, ed. I. S. Leadam, I, pp. 81–3. For those of 1548, see *Tudor Economic Documents, op. cit.*, I, pp. 39–41. For those of 1607, see L. A. Parker, 'The Depopulation Returns for Leicestershire in 1607', *Trans. Leics. Archaeolog. Soc.*, XXIII, 1947, pp. 14–15.

(1489) aimed at arresting all depopulation and all conversion of arable to pasture irrespective of region and motive.[16] Later statutes, however, attempted to differentiate. In 1536 the Act of 1489 against depopulation and the conversion of ploughland to pasture was re-enacted, but now it applied only to the Isle of Wight and a group of counties in central England, extending from Lincolnshire and Nottinghamshire south to Berkshire, Buckinghamshire, and Hertfordshire, east to Cambridge and west to Worcestershire, and including Leicestershire, Rutland, Warwickshire, Northampton-shire, Bedfordshire and Oxfordshire. A second statute of 1533 attacked engrossing by prohibiting farmers from occupying more than two farms unless they lived in the parishes in which they were situated, and forbidding them to keep more than two thousand four hundred sheep. The preamble of the Act expressly described engrossing as a consequence of 'the great profit that cometh of sheep.' But in 1555, the conversion of arable to pasture was not ascribed to this one cause, but to the profits of cattle and sheep fattening which tempted men to specialize in this branch of farming at the expense of rearing. An Act of that year obliged farmers who kept more than 120 shear sheep to keep at least two milch cows and rear one calf. In 1593 the abundance and cheapness of corn caused Elizabethan legislators at last to shed their fear of enclosure and pasture farming and to repeal their acts to maintain tillage, but this opened the flood-gates to fresh enclosures, and, following the bad harvest of 1595, panic caused them to be revived. Again it was the graziers as well as the sheep-masters who bore the brunt of government opprobrium. It was enacted that land that had been under the plough for twelve years continuously before conversion to pasture should be restored to tillage. Nevertheless, an exception was made of land which had been grassed down in order to regain heart. Moreover, the Act applied in certain counties only—in twenty-three English counties, and in the Isle of Wight and Pembrokeshire. It excluded from its scope much of East Anglia, the south-east and the south-west, as well as Stafford-shire, Shropshire, Cheshire and Lancashire.[17]

In summary, therefore, it may be said that enclosure and the conversion of arable to pasture featured prominently in legislation throughout the Tudor period, but many of the statutes and proclama-tions were selective in their application and they give no grounds for

[16] There was one earlier local act concerning the Isle of Wight (1488) against enclosure and engrossing.
[17] The act was later amended to exclude Northumberland also.

asserting that enclosures were considered to be the responsibility of the sheepmaster alone, nor that sheep were deemed the sole cause of depopulation. Engrossing as a cause of depopulation was deplored in the proclamations of 1514 and 1528, the Act of 1533, the proclamation of 1548, the enclosure commission of the same year, the proclamation of 1551, and the enclosure commission of 1607. Indeed, it is difficult to explain why historians in recent years have so often seemed to forget that engrossing *and* enclosure were regarded by contemporaries as twin evils in the countryside and *equally* injurious to the commonweal. It may be that Professor Gay won a silent victory when, at the turn of this century, he engaged in long argument with I. S. Leadam whether the engrossing of farms necessarily meant that such farms were also enclosed.[18] Gay held that it did, and evidently persuaded others besides himself. More recent work on regional diversity, however, suggests that Gay was wrong in making this dogmatic, universal assumption. To take but one contrary example, the Lincolnshire marshland was a region little troubled by enclosure and conversion in the Tudor period. Nevertheless, it was much concerned with engrossing in 1607. The demand for fattening land was keen, not only from local farmers but from others living on the neighbouring wolds who reared on the hills and fed in the lowlands. In consequence, when farms were thrown together, or marsh pasture near the coast was leased to 'foreigners' living at a distance, houses of husbandry were deprived of their land and left to fall into decay. Here was a region plagued by engrossers and depopulation, but not by enclosers. Indeed, much of the land in the marsh was not enclosed until after 1800.[19]

Like the legislation, the pamphlet literature of the time dealt with a variety of agrarian grievances and did not confine itself to enclosures for sheep pasture. Sir Thomas More's devastating attack on the sheep which devoured men, and on the covetous gentry who enclosed and depopulated without remorse for the sufferings of the poor, lives longest in the memory. But more than one pamphleteer and preacher reserved his strongest language for engrossers of farms.[20] Others wrote not of sheepmasters alone, but of graziers, using the more

[18] E. F. Gay, 'Inquisitions of Depopulation in 1517 and the Domesday of Inclosures', *Trans. R.H.S.*, N.S., XIV, 1900, p. 240 *et seq.*

[19] Joan Thirsk, *op. cit.*, pp. 238, 148–51, 154–6. On the question of engrossing and enclosing, see also the similar conclusions from different evidence of Maurice Beresford in *The Lost Villages of England*, pp. 113–5.

[20] See the sermons of Hugh Latimer, Thomas Lever, and Archbishop Cranmer, and William Harrison's *Description of England*, ed. F. J. Furnivall, 1876, p. 19 *et seq.*

general term to embrace men who specialized in cattle rearing, fattening and dairying. Yet others deplored the sheep, not because sheep inevitably followed enclosure (as they doubtless knew, there were many farmers who overgrazed the commons with larger and larger flocks without enclosing any land), but because sheep drove out cattle and corn.[21]

When agrarian discontent flared into open revolt in 1549, the riots likewise disclosed a tangle of motives and more than one cause of complaint. Ket's followers in Norfolk in 1549 did not feel themselves so much injured by enclosure as by the overgrazing of the commons by greedy lords, the damage done to crops by the keeping of dovecotes and by rabbits kept in unprotected cony warrens, as well as by rising rents. The only reference in Ket's programme to enclosure is ambiguous and appears to relate to closes for the growing of saffron.[22] The Midland Revolt of 1607, however, was directly concerned with enclosure and the conversion of ploughland to pasture. And since the rebellion was concentrated in this one part of England, in Warwickshire, Leicestershire, Northamptonshire and Bedfordshire, we shall illuminate the problem of enclosure by considering why this was so.

In the first place, the Midland counties, generally speaking, were the most densely populated in common-field England by 1500.[23] In Leicestershire there was no waste left except in Charnwood Forest. All the land not under the plough nor reserved for hay consisted of regulated common pasture.[24] The situation was probably little less serious in neighbouring Midland counties. But while an increasing population in already congested townships was liable to precipitate some enclosure, since a change of this kind permitted the more economical use of land, not all densely-settled villages underwent an

[21] See, for example, the writings of Alexander Nowell and also *Certain Causes gathered together wherein is shewed the decay of England only by the great multitude of sheep*, reprinted in *Tudor Economic Documents*, III, p. 51 *et seq.*
[22] Agrarian grievances may have helped to foment trouble in 1536 but enclosure complaints were not openly expressed in the Pilgrimage of Grace, Professor Bindoff in his re-examination of Ket's rebellion has pointed out other special local circumstances to explain why the outbreak in 1549 was centred in Norwich and its neighbourhood. Ket drew his support not from the thinly settled and poor soils of the breckland in south-west Norfolk but from the populous north and east where farms were already small, freeholders numerous and pressure on the land was becoming acute; *cf.* S. T. Bindoff, *Ket's Rebellion, 1549* (Historical Association Pamphlet, General Series: G.12), pp. 9–10, 17–18.
[23] *Cf.* H. C. Darby, *The Historical Geography of England before A.D. 1800*, p. 232.
[24] *Cf.* W. G. Hoskins, 'The Leicestershire Farmer in the Seventeenth Century,' *Agricultural History*, xxv, p. 10.

enclosure crisis in the sixteenth century. Much depended on the type of economy prevailing in the region, the nature of the soil, and the number of freeholders involved. In 1607, for example, the enclosure commissioners reported over 13,000 acres enclosed and converted to pasture in Lincolnshire. Yet almost nothing came to light in the fenland.[25] The reason lay in the pastoral nature of the economy. The fenlands, which lay under water in winter, afforded rich and abundant common grazing in summer. The native peasant got his livelihood from fattening stock on these pastures and required only a little land under crops to supply his household needs and to fodder his beasts in the hardest months of winter. In addition, he had other sources of income in the fish, fowl, and reeds of the fen. He had no need to convert old cornland to grass for he enjoyed unstinted common grazing. If he enclosed at all he was more likely to enclose grassland to increase his corn acreage.[26] In the marshland areas along the Lincolnshire coast, a system of mixed husbandry obtained. The arable usually occupied a larger proportion of the land of a township than in the fen and the grazings were less extensive (in most marshland villages stock were stinted on the common), but this was a recognized sheep and cattle fattening region, and probably had been for centuries. A satisfactory balance between arable and pasture had been struck long ago and charges of enclosing and converting arable to pasture puzzled the inhabitants. Their lands were 'such as time out of mind have been used for feeding and breeding or grazing of cattle and be not fit for tillage.' The local people were much more concerned in 1607 with the engrossing of farms by ambitious yeomen and gentry.[27]

Generalizing from these examples, we may infer that the market conditions of the sixteenth century were not of a kind to alter significantly the pattern of land use in old-established cattle fattening regions. It is probable that meat and wool yielded a satisfactory profit throughout the century. A fair balance between corn and grassland had been struck long before, which it was convenient to maintain. And the fact that most pastures, in the fen at least, were open

[25] J. D. Gould, 'The Inquisition of Depopulation of 1607 in Lincolnshire', *Eng. Hist. Rev.*, July, 1952, p. 395. Land enclosed and converted to pasture amounted to 5,500 acres in Lindsey, 3,360 acres in Kesteven, and 560 acres in Holland, the fenny division of the county.

[26] These points are elaborated in Joan Thirsk, *op. cit.*, p. 6 *et seq.*

[27] *Op. cit.*, p. 154 *et seq.* The quotation may be found in the answer of Francis Megson of Orby when charged with enclosure in Star Chamber in 1608—P.R.O., *Star Chamber*, 8, 17, 23.

commons was not yet regarded as a grave drawback to the majority. This, as we have seen, was due partly to the type of husbandry, but it must be attributed also in part to the class structure of fen society. The villages were composed of many small freeholders who drew more benefit from the use of open commons than they would have done from a small allotment of enclosed grassland. The situation might have been different had the fenland been populated by a smaller community of large farmers who could each have claimed large allotments after enclosure.

If the traditional cattle fattening regions of England were not troubled by enclosure and conversion, in what farming regions did they present a grave social problem? Until a comprehensive study of husbandry and enclosure in the sixteenth century is completed, the answer to this question can only be put forward tentatively. But it would seem that the problem was concentrated firstly in the densely-settled claylands where a mixed farming was generally practised, and where crop rotations that included some years of leys suited the land best and enabled farmers to keep more stock, when market conditions favoured them. The problem was concentrated secondly in the more thinly-populated chalk and limestone uplands where rearing was already the rule and where sheep were now being kept on a larger scale than ever before. In these two farming regions there were substantial differences in the circumstances surrounding enclosure.

The claylands were mostly populous areas of ancient settlement and relatively intense cultivation, where the need to use the land more economically was a powerful stimulus to the would-be encloser. Farmers were coming to recognize that flexibility of land use on the clays was a wise measure for increasing productivity. Some of the clays were so ill-drained as to make bad cornland and promised a greater yield if put down to permanent pasture, others yielded better under a convertible husbandry of alternate crops and leys. Under the common field system farmers had already been able to put this knowledge and experience to good effect by laying down land in the arable fields under temporary grass. Sometimes whole furlongs were left in ley by communal agreement, sometimes individual strips. In the latter case the farmer had to hurdle or tether his animals while they were grazing during the corn-growing season. When the harvest was carried, his strips were thrown open together with the stubble of his neighbours' lands to be depastured by the stock of the whole village. The only drawback to this practice, in some places at least, was that so many beasts had to be tethered that there was constant danger that they would break loose and trample down the corn. The peasants of Fulbeck in Lincolnshire explained that they had to tether three hundred head of draught cattle and milch cows and in 1620 decided it would be easier to enclose their fields.[28] This was the conclusion of many another farmer, though not everyone was able to procure the assent of his fellows.

It is evident from the answers given by farmers in Star Chamber to the charge of enclosing and converting arable to pasture that many changes of land use in the Midlands which were reported to the Enclosure Commissioners in 1607 sprang from the decision to adopt some form of ley farming in enclosures—to rest the overworked ploughland and increase fertility by introducing a few years of leys. The advantages were expounded by Fitzherbert in these words: 'If any of his three closes that he had for his corn be worn or wear bare, then he may break and plough up his close that he had for his leys, or the close that he had for his common pasture, or both, and sow them with corn, and let the other lie for a time, and so shall he have always rest ground, the which will bear much corn with little dung'[29] His opinion was not that of an unpractical crank. It was current among many thoughtful, observant farmers, and, indeed, its wisdom was finally recognized in Tudor statutes against enclosure. The Act of 1597 explicitly allowed the temporary conversion of arable to pasture in order to regain heart,[30] thus following the advice of the Speaker of the House of Commons, who had ventured to put a more moderate view of enclosure now that popular antagonism had somewhat abated, and had condemned the old laws against enclosure for 'tyeing the land once tilled to a perpetual bondage and servitude of being ever tilled.'[31]

There is no need to press the evidence further and to take the more extreme view, once put forward by Miss Harriet Bradley, that the purpose of alternate husbandry was to rest the old arable because it was utterly exhausted by centuries of cultivation. The modern proponents of ley farming have never suggested that it is a desperate remedy for exhausted cornland. It has been recommended rather as a

[28] P.R.O., *Chancery Proceedings*, C. 2, Jas. I, F.13, 5. In Wigston Magna (Leics.) in the seventeenth century one-fifth of the open fields were in leys; *cf.* W. G. Hoskins, *The Midland Peasant*, p. 233.

[29] *Tudor Economic Documents, op. cit.*, III, p. 23.

[30] See above, p. 73.

[31] Cited in Harriet Bradley, *The Enclosures in England–an Economic Reconstruction*, 1918, p. 99.

means of increasing the yield of both arable and pasture, since, by taking the plough all round the farm, the pasture benefits from being cropped (it is much easier to produce a good pasture that will last three or four years than to keep permanent grass in peak condition) while the arable is greatly improved by a period of rest under grass.

By adopting a more intensive system of husbandry on the claylands, farmers were able to keep more cattle and horses, and, if the land was suitable, more sheep—in other words, to produce more of the things that commanded a high price in the sixteenth century. But to place the emphasis on sheep at the expense of cattle is to falsify the picture of the economy of the claylands. Beef and leather were as much a product of the vales of England as mutton and wool. Whether prices favoured the production of cattle rather than sheep, or sheep rather than cattle, is another question which historians have not yet seriously tackled. Indeed, it is doubtful whether any generalizations could ever be made on this subject—so much depended on the type of farm and the place of stock in the management of the land. In the same way, it is impossible to make any accurate statements concerning the relative profit from corn-growing and stock-raising at this time. It is probable, however, judging by contemporary opinion, that throughout the sixteenth century animal products gave a larger margin of profit to clayland farmers than crops.[32] Hence the popular hostility towards encloser and grazier. Not every enterprising farmer was both, but the two were naturally identified in popular complaint.

The second farming region which suffered most from enclosure in the Tudor period was the sheep rearing lands, the less fertile uplands where from time immemorial sheep had ruled the earth. They grazed the hillsides during the day and were folded on the low fields at night. Indeed, without the golden hoof, the land could not have been kept in cultivation. In considering why enclosers gained such a strong foothold here, it is necessary to remember that the uplands were areas of large farms and small and sparsely distributed settlement. The

---

[32] According to Fitzherbert, writing in 1539, 'of all stock the rearing of sheep is most profitable.' While this may well have been true in the 1530's, subsequent legislation (see above p. 73f.) suggests that it did not remain true in the later decades of the century. Dr. Bowden has suggested that the price relationship between wool and wheat changed in the course of the century, causing sheep pastures to expand at the expense of cornland in the first half of the period and to shrink in the second. This conclusion concerning price movements may well be correct but the suggested consequence, namely an increase in arable at the expense of pasture in the later years of the century, is still disputed. It is equally likely that falling wool prices were offset by good prices for mutton. *Cf.* P. J. Bowden, 'Movements in Wool Prices, 1490–1610,' *Yorks. Bulletin of Economic and Social Research*, IV, 1952.

large farmer wanting to enlarge his sheep flock found it easier to enclose great tracks of common or to force the enclosure of the open fields, because his tenants were few and the opposition weak. It is no accident that so many deserted villages are found in the uplands, on the chalk wolds, and on the limestone and Cotswold hills of the Midlands. It would have been difficult, indeed impossible, for a landlord, however ruthless, to depopulate a large village.[33]

The economic incentive to enclose land in the uplands was the same as that which goaded the lowland farmer—the high price of animal products, particularly wool and mutton. In the first three decades of the century the booming textile industry created an almost insatiable demand for wool. It is probable that the market slackened off in the middle of the century as wool production increased and the broadcloth industry became depressed. But it is unlikely that the upland farmer's income was much affected by this. He now had to meet a growing demand for mutton for the townsman's table.[34] In addition, his sheepwalks produced a fine short wool which became more scarce and sought after as the century wore on. Larger sheep flocks in the vales, marshes and fens had increased the proportion of long coarse wool to such an extent that the fine wool of the hill sheep was at a premium.[35] The sheep flock had always been indispensable to the hill farmer, but in the Tudor period it did more than fertilize his fields, it paid his rent, furnished his house and fed and clothed his family as well.

If we seek an example of a county where much enclosure took place but where several different motives were present, it is ready to hand in Leicestershire. It was not one of the main corn-exporting counties since it lacked good transport facilities to London and the coast.[36] Its speciality was cattle and sheep. In west Leicestershire, in the neighbourhood of Charnwood Forest, enclosure strengthened the hand of farmers specializing in dairying and rearing, some of whose land was converted after enclosure to permanent pasture, some

[33] Maurice Beresford, *The Lost Villages of England*, p. 247 *et seq.*

[34] One pamphleteer, writing in mid-century, implied that the popular taste for mutton was growing at the expense of beef. 'The most substance of our feeding was wont to be on beef, and now it is on mutton. And so many mouths goeth to mutton which causeth mutton to be dear.' *Tudor Economic Documents*, III, p. 52.

[35] P. J. Bowden, 'Wool Supply and the Woollen Industry', *Econ. Hist. Rev.*, Second Series, IX, no. I, p. 44 *et seq.* Dr. Bowden's argument must be modified in the light of genetic considerations. See *Agric. Hist. Rev., XIII, 2, 1965, pp. 125-6.*

[36] John Gould, 'Mr. Beresford and the Lost Villages', *Agric. Hist. Review*, III, 1955, p. 112.

adapted to a convertible husbandry.[37] In south Leicestershire, fattening was the main pursuit. Indeed, the permanent pastures of the Market Harborough district have continued to hold their fine reputation to this day. In the eastern uplands, the sheep flock was the farmers' best friend and the price of wool and mutton the chief spur to his enterprise. In this way the whole of Leicestershire was exposed to the currents of agrarian improvement. No doubt a similarly varied pattern would emerge from a more detailed examination of the movement in other Midland counties.

When Edwin Gay examined the enclosure evidence collected by the commissions of enquiry in the Tudor and early Stuart period, he suggested that the complaints against depopulating enclosure were somewhat exaggerated. If one measures the importance of the problem from a national standpoint, this may be a fair judgment. Also it was doubtless true, as John Hales declared in Edward VI's reign, that the worst and most ruthless enclosures had already occurred before the beginning of the reign of Henry VII. But this was cold comfort to the husbandman of the sixteenth century watching the progress of enclosure in and around his own village. Enclosure has first to be recognized as a social problem concentrated in the Midlands. Seen in that narrower context, it cannot be lightly dismissed. In Leicestershire alone, more than one in three of its 370 villages and hamlets underwent some enclosure between 1485 and 1607.[38] The motives and incentives to enclose, as we have seen, were many and complex. But they worked their worst effects in one consolidated belt of country, stretching from the western half of Lincolnshire through Northamptonshire and Leicestershire to Warwickshire and reaching south to include Bedfordshire and Buckinghamshire. The historian who tries to account for trends and changes in a broad context recognizes different types of enclosure and different motives and thereby deepens his understanding of the causes of change. He sees the problem of the sixteenth century as a temporary crisis only. But the Midland peasant lived in the midst of events and saw only one widespread movement to enclose and convert the land to pasture. He saw more cattle and more sheep in the closes. He saw rich farmers taking up more and more land but giving less employment than ever before to the labourer. He could have viewed the matter calmly had he lived in the Lincolnshire fens or the

---

[37] *Calendar of State Papers Domestic, 1629–31*, p. 490.

[38] L. A. Parker, 'The Agrarian Revolution at Cotesbach, 1501–1612', *op cit.*, p. 41, note 2.

Yorkshire dales. He could have viewed the matter in better perspective had he lived to see the amiable enclosure agreements of the seventeenth century. But it was difficult to keep a balanced outlook when one's own livelihood was at stake, and when, moreover, the idea of enclosure had not yet 'hardened and become more durable.'[39]

BIBLIOGRAPHY

The first attempt to examine the contemporary literature and explain the causes of sixteenth-century enclosure was made by Erwin Nasse in a paper *On the Agricultural Community of the Middle Ages and Inclosures of the Sixteenth Century in England* (original edition, 1869; English translation, 1870). Since this essay argued that the purpose of sixteenth-century enclosure was to facilitate ley farming, it deserves more attention than it has received in the last forty years. Nasse's conclusions were accepted by W. Cunningham in *The Growth of English Industry and Commerce* (1st edn. 1882), and with some modifications by W. Ashley in *An Introduction to English Economic History and Theory* (1st edn. 1893). They were afterwards neglected, however, perhaps because a more extreme interpretation of the evidence of ley farming was put forward by Harriet Bradley in *The Enclosures in England—an Economic Reconstruction* (1918). Her argument that enclosure was due to soil exhaustion was challenged and discredited by Reginald Lennard in 'The Alleged Exhaustion of the Soil in Medieval England,' *Economic Journal*, no. 135, 1922.

The discussion took on a more statistical character when the reports of the enclosure commissions of 1517 and 1607 were analysed. See I. S. Leadam, 'The Inquisition of 1517,' *Trans. R.H.S.*, 2nd Ser., VI (1892); VII (1893); VIII (1894); XIV (1900); *The Domesday of Inclosures, 1517–18* (1897); E. F. Gay, 'The Inquisitions of Depopulation in 1517 and the "Domesday of Inclosures",' *Trans. R.H.S.*, 2nd Ser., XIV, 1900; 'Inclosures of England in the Sixteenth Century,' *Quarterly Journal of Economics*, XVII, 1903; 'The Midland Revolt and the Inquisitions of Depopulation of 1607,' *Trans. R.H.S.*, 2nd

[39] Polydore Vergil in 1534, quoted by M. W. Beresford, *op. cit.*, p. 104. These words are adapted from Vergil's remark on the abuses of fifteenth-century enclosure. I do not think that the idea of enclosure became generally acceptable until the mid-seventeenth century, when the last anti-enclosure bill was presented in the House of Commons and rejected.

Ser., XVIII, 1904.

Many of the contemporary pamphlets and sermons referring to enclosure may be found in volumes published by the *Early English Text Society* and the *Parker Society* respectively. A full list is included in Conyers Read, *Bibliography of British History, Tudor Period, 1485–1603* (1933), p. 169 *et seq.*

The most recent research bearing on general problems of enclosure is contained in M. W. Beresford, *The Lost Villages of England* (1954), and P. J. Bowden, 'Movements in Wool Prices, 1490–1610,' *Yorks. Bulletin of Economic and Social Research*, IV, 1952. This article was criticized in two subseqent issues of the *Bulletin*, and a reply published in vol. IX, no. 2, 1957. A fuller description of the diversity of farming types in England and a more detailed account of enclosure history are contained in *The Agrarian History of England and Wales, vol. IV, 1500–1640*, ed. Joan Thirsk, 1967, Chs. I, IV.

POSTSCRIPT

An up-to-date bibliography on enclosure in the sixteenth and seventeenth centuries is available in

J. G. Brewer, *Enclosures and the Open Fields: a Bibliography*, British Agricultural History Society, Reading University, 1972.

M. Turner, *English Parliamentary Enclosure. Its Historical Geography and Economic History*, Folkestone, 1980.

J. A. Yelling, *Common Field and Enclosure in England, 1450–1850*, London, 1977, pp. 234–41.

VII

THE SALES OF ROYALIST LAND DURING THE INTERREGNUM

THE sale by Parliament of crown, church, and delinquents' lands during the Interregnum brought about a redistribution in the owner-ship of land comparable in scale with that achieved by the sales of dissolved monastic land a century earlier. Of the social changes produced by the latter, some seventeenth-century observers were already dimly aware.[1] But with the exception of polemical writers with an axe to grind, and Royalists in exile with but meagre first-hand knowledge, there were few who ventured to generalize about the results of the sales of their own generation. Not that the outward resemblance between the old confiscation and the new passed unnoticed. Henry Neville, who explained to the Lower House in February 1659 his theories on the changed balance of property between Lords and Commons, and attributed it to the sales of monastic land, immediately provoked speculation on this score. 'Query', wrote the Parliamentary diarist, Guibon Goddard, in the margin of his diary, 'whether this equality or almost parity hath not more enforced that argument of late by distributing King, Queen, Bishops' and delinquents' lands?'[2]

A full answer to Goddard's question would require a threefold study of the sales of crown, church and private lands. In this article the scope of the problem has been narrowed to delinquents' lands alone, and the material selected confined to those estates which lay in the twelve south-eastern counties, namely, Hampshire, Berkshire, Oxfordshire, Buckinghamshire, Bedfordshire, Hertfordshire, Essex, Kent, Sussex, Surrey, Middlesex and London. A preliminary survey of the sales in Lancashire suggests that in more pronouncedly Royalist areas the findings would not differ substantially from those appearing here.

[1] See R. H. Tawney, *Harrington's Interpretation of his Age* (1942) (The Raleigh lecture on history . . . British Academy, 1941).
[2] *Diary of Thomas Burton*, ed. J. T. Rutt (1828), III, 133.

Contemporary interest in the Parliamentary sales was not confined to those who, like Guibon Goddard, sought a nice balance of power between Lords and Commons. The decision to sell Royalist property overlay the problem of Parliament's long-term policy towards the Royalist party—a subject which, no doubt, figured prominently in the debates on the sales themselves, and which agitated the Commons on at least one occasion in the later fifties.[3] The disposal of the land raised the hopes of Levellers and Diggers alike, the former perceiving in the sales the chance of turning copyholds by purchase into freeholds, the latter envisaging the possibility of freeing the land entirely from the toils of private ownership.[4] The critics and avowed enemies of Parliament, for their part, found in the sales ammunition for their attacks on the social upstarts who thronged Westminster, and who, in their view, had contrived the sales for their own advancement and devoured all.[5]

The pamphleteers and polemical writers, who levelled these charges, had collected much accurate information on the identity of purchasers and grantees of forfeited land, but their investigations were restricted to the private affairs of a small circle of leading Parliamentary and army figures. In directing their attack against the alleged self-interest and greed of the 'Grandees' and their henchmen, they succeeded in conveying the impression that the bulk of the land had fallen into their hands. Just how widely this view was accepted may be judged by the fact that Chancellor Hyde, writing on the eve of the Restoration of the problems of the land settlement, dismissed the idea that a second restoration of lands would provoke war. The chief beneficiaries of the sales, he argued, were but a few irreconcilable Parliamentarians, who were daily losing influence and popular sympathy.[6]

From a closer inspection of the pamphlet writing of the time, it is evident that the sales of delinquents' lands were less often the specific target of criticism than those of the crown and church. But, since the

[3] Clement Walker, *The Compleat History of Independency* (1661), pp. 9, 45; *Diary of Thomas Burton*, op. cit. I, 230–43.

[4] Pauline Gregg, *John Lilburne and his relation to the first phase of the Leveller movement, 1638–49* (Ph.D. thesis, University of London, 1939), pp. 454–9; *Gerrard Winstanley, Selections from his Works*, ed. Leonard Hamilton (1944), pp. 88, 117.

[5] M.El., *A list of members of the House of Commons, observing which are officers of the army . . . together with such sums of money, offices and lands as they have given to themselves . . .* (1648); W. W. Wilkins, *Political Ballads of the Seventeenth and Eighteenth Centuries* (1860), I, 107, 'The Parliament routed' (1653); Clement Walker, op. cit. IV, 45.

[6] *Clarendon State Papers* (Oxford, 1767–86), III, 687.

Royalist land sales did not take place until 1651, when the volume of ephemeral writing had much diminished, the dearth of direct references probably did not signify any revision of opinion on the part of the critics. Clement Walker, who had inveighed against the self-seeking of the Parliament men, died as the sales of Royalist land were about to begin. The anonymous writer, M.El., who in 1648 compiled a list of public men with the offices and lands they had acquired, and who promised his readers, 'thou shalt see how both Delinquents estates and Bishops Lands are by Members of Parliament shared amongst themselves', never published the sequel.[7] The Levellers who had denounced the sales of bishops' lands because 'Parliament men, Committee men, and their kinsfolkes were the only buyers', had lost strength and voice after 1649, and so had nothing to say of the sales of Royalist land when they began two years later.[8]

The opinions of contemporaries on the outcome of the sales of crown and church lands were generally accepted, both then and later, as applying to all the sales. Modern research on the land market has done little to challenge the old views. It is true that the monopoly held by Parliamentary leaders and army commanders has proved to be less complete than contemporaries supposed, but their share of the spoil, we are told, was only exceeded by that of the London merchants and speculators. Both Dr Chesney and Prof. Arkhangel'sky reached the same conclusion after examining the purchasers noted in the records of the Committee for Compounding. A sample taken by Prof. Arkhangel'sky showed that London merchants represented nearly 51 per cent of all purchasers, while army officers and government officials together accounted for a further 21 per cent. Dr Chesney, without attempting to give precise figures, drew attention to the conspicuous activities of these three classes of purchasers, as well as those of their stable companions, the lawyers, scriveners, and goldsmiths.[9]

Neither of these historians was apparently puzzled by the fact that the Committee for Compounding, which had nothing whatever to do with the sales, possessed a list of purchasers among its records. Had they considered the problem, their suspicions might have been aroused as to the reliability of its information. The Committee's

[7] M.El. loc. cit.
[8] *The Leveller Tracts, 1647–53*, ed. W. Haller and G. Davies (1944), p. 79.
[9] S. I. Arkhangel'sky, 'Rasprodazha zemel'nuikh vladeny storonnikov korolya' (The sale of Royalist lands), *Izvestiya Akademy Nauk (U.S.S.R.) 7 seriya: Otdelenie obshchestvennuikh nauk*, no. 5 (1933), p. 376; H. E. Chesney, 'The Transference of Lands in England, 1640–60', *Trans. Roy. Hist. Soc.* 4th ser. xv, 189.

functions were limited, and were in no way concerned with negotiating the sales of Royalist land. Its task was simply to carry out the sequestration of the property, administer it, and assess the fine to be paid by owners who chose to compound for it. The officers responsible for the sales of land of those Royalists who refused to pay composition, or who, because of their exalted position in the Royalist party, were not allowed to do so, were the Drury House Trustees—a separate committee, which was not brought into existence until the first act for the sale of delinquents' lands was passed in July 1651.[10]

From an administrative point of view, it was necessary for the Drury House Trustees to inform the Committee for Compounding as each sale took place. Instructions were then issued to local officers, informing them of the name of the purchaser, and ordering the lifting of the sequestration order.[11] The fact that the Committee for Compounding often received from Drury House the name, not of the purchaser, but of an agent acting on his behalf, or even the name of someone who had made the first contract, withdrawn at the last moment, and who had then been replaced by another, mattered little to the Committee. Its responsibility was simply to see that the sequestration order was revoked. As a source of information on the identity of purchasers, therefore, these cancellation orders are thoroughly misleading.

It is the indentures of bargain and sale, enrolled in Chancery, which, in the absence of the Drury House papers, afford reliable evidence on the identity of purchasers. Even these do not at first tell the whole story, for it was not uncommon for buyers to remain concealed behind the names of their agents, emerging only in a later indenture to complete the transaction. The obstacles that usually impede a full study of the land market—the difficulties of finding written records of the sales and re-sales, and then of distinguishing between genuine purchasers and trustees—prove less formidable in the case of Parliamentary land sales than in private land dealings. In the first place, the Treason Trustees faithfully observed the Statute of Enrolments of 1536, and registered all bargains and sales in the Court of Chancery. Secondly, because the times were out of joint, and considerable suspicion attached to the legality and permanence of the sales, it was usual for the purchasers of forfeited land to see that all later transactions were enrolled in like manner. The Close Rolls, in

---

[10] *Acts and Ordinances of the Interregnum, 1642–60*, ed. C. H. Firth and R. S. Rait (London, 1911), II, 520–45.
[11] For an example of these orders, see P.R.O. SP 23/18, f. 854.

consequence, hold the key to most of the business done in forfeited land during the Interregnum.

The care taken by purchasers to see that dealings at second and third hand were recorded in Chancery sheds some light on the state of public opinion on the sales. It is doubtful whether purchasers pinned any great faith in their permanence. Political crises in the later fifties were the signal for several requests to Parliament to pass legislation confirming the sales—themselves a pointer to the prevailing uncertainty.[12] If one may judge from the wistful remark of Sir Anthony Ashley Cooper in the Commons in March 1659, hopes of permanence ran higher in the early years of the Commonwealth. 'I have sat sixteen years here,' he declared, 'ventured my life, and bought lands, and my friends and interest have done so. I always hoped whenever you came to a settlement, you would confirm all those sales.'[13] But although it was common enough for purchasers in later years to mourn in public the languishing of their hopes, there is no evidence to suggest that the majority bought without giving due consideration to the hazards of their venture. They weighed the long-term risk against the short-term advantage, and deemed the chance worth taking. There was no trace of self-pity in Sir Arthur Hazlerigg's reply to those who taunted him in the Commons for his large purchases of church lands, for which he was nicknamed 'the bishop of Durham'. 'I know not how long after I shall keep the Bishops' lands. For no King, no Bishop, no Bishop no King; we know the rule.' Like many another purchaser, foreseeing eventual confiscation, he consoled himself that he would not be left destitute. 'I had an estate left me, besides my own acquisition, that will maintain me like a gentleman. I desire no more.'[14]

Uncertainty attached to the sales from the beginning. But it is clear that, if the optimism of purchasers had not prevailed over their hesitations, they would never have bought forfeited land, or, having done so, would quickly have re-sold it. As it was, they were neither slow to buy, nor anxious, having bought, to sell.[15] The full explana-

---

[12] *Diary of Thos. Burton*, I, 410; *A letter from Lord General Monck and the officers to the several and respective regiments and other forces in England, Scotland, and Ireland*, 21 Feb. 1659. In 1659 there was a motion before Parliament that the gifts it had made during the Protectorate should be taken back again. Some members of the Commons wanted the measure back-dated to 1642. *Diary of Sir Archibald Johnston of Wariston*, ed. J. D. Ogilvie (Scottish Hist. Soc. 3rd ser. xxxiv), III, 119.

[13] *Diary of Thos. Burton*, IV, 51–2.

[14] *Diary of Thomas Burton*, II, 423–4.

[15] This statement is based on the evidence of the Close Rolls indentures, which give the date of each transaction. The first sales in south-eastern England began in

tion of the sober activity of the land market, however, lies not in individual assessments of the political situation—for these should have produced a host of re-sales from 1659 onwards—but in a closer examination of the identity of purchasers. There were far more purchasers who bought to keep, than speculators with an eye for quick profit.

In the first place, the most important, though not the most numerous, group of purchasers of Royalist land, was the Royalists themselves. The larger their estates, the greater was their ability to buy their land back, for so long as they were not heavily indebted before the civil war broke out, they had the capital reserves, or more often simply the prestige, to command the necessary credit. Through their agents they borrowed the money and managed the negotiations with Drury House. When the land was safely vested in the possession of trustees, it was mortgaged to the extent of the debt.

Although at times the employment of agents appeared as a half-hearted attempt to conceal the facts of the situation from the authorities, it is unlikely that this was in fact the intention. Since all sales were negotiated in London, it was simply a matter of convenience for purchasers living outside to use the services of an agent. In any case, it was no secret from Cromwell and his colleagues that Royalists were recovering their estates by purchase. Secretary Thurloe received reports of at least two of these transactions, one describing the Marquess of Winchester's re-purchase of his lands, and mentioning the 'very great sumes of money borrowed to pay the purchase', the other recording the efforts of Samuel Foxley as agent to the delinquent, Charles Gerrard, and commenting on the good reward he was to receive for his pains. Indeed, Cromwell himself was alleged to have intervened personally to discharge Lord Arundel of some thousands of pounds which he owed to Drury House for the purchase of his lands.[16]

Continued

February 1652, seven months after the first act for sale. In the country as a whole they reached their peak in 1653. S. I. Arkhangel'sky, op. cit. p. 375. There is no evidence to support the statement of Mr Reynolds in the House of Commons in February 1659, that purchasers came forward unwillingly. 'I bought some lands myself, but was sent for. The contractors said, that if some of us did not break the ice, none would contract.' *Diary of Thos. Burton*, III, 205. This may have referred only to the first sales of bishops' lands, and reluctance to buy may have been overcome by 1651 when the sales had lost their novelty. Cf. G. B. Tatham, 'The Sale of Episcopal Lands during the Civil Wars and Commonwealth', *Eng. Hist. Rev.* XXIII, 1908, 95, where evidence is given of reluctance to buy bishops' lands.

[16] *Thurloe State Papers*, ed. Thos. Birch (1742), IV, 444; I, 307; Edmund Ludlow. *The Memoirs of Edmund Ludlow . . . 1625–72*, ed. C. H. Firth (Oxford, 1894), II. 155. It is

Among the fifty Royalists who forfeited land in south-eastern England, the nobility were by far the most successful in re-purchasing their property. The Marquess of Winchester bought all but two of his fifteen estates in Hampshire and Berkshire, and all his houses in the City of London. The only two properties which eluded him were Halshott farm in Hampshire, in which he had only a life interest, and Englefield Manor in Berkshire, which had been granted by Parliament to his kinsman, Sir Thomas Jervois, and which returned to his hands by a devious route in 1655.[17] Lord Arundel recovered his two manors in Oxfordshire, and Lord Morley and Mounteagle his six manors in Sussex, Essex, and Hertfordshire.[18] The Duke of Newcastle purchased his only estate in southern England in Clerkenwell.[19]

The only member of the nobility who had the opportunity of buying his estates, but who allowed them all to pass into strange hands was the Earl of Craven. He was banking on the strength of the case he had to put before Parliament of wrongful confiscation, for the order for the sale of his property had been passed by a very small majority in the Commons in 1652 after it had been several times rejected. It was reconsidered in December 1653, when the sales were already under way, and again in May 1657. In the event, the lands were not restored to Lord Craven until 1660.[20]

Most of the nobility employed their family solicitors to conduct the business of purchase for them. The Marquess of Winchester enlisted the services of six personal agents, at least one of whom, Daniel Wycherley, father of the Restoration dramatist, William Wycherley, was engaged in his full-time service. Sir John Somerset's agents were John Calvert and Francis Gregg, the business agents of the Arundel family into which Sir John Somerset had married. Lord Arundel, however, relied on his son-in-law, Humphrey Weld, a prominent City

---

evident from the way in which the sales were carried out that they were devised first and foremost as a means of raising money, not of exterminating Parliament's enemies. Any official attempt to prevent Royalists from recovering their land would have run counter to the spirit of the policy. Major-General Desborough's summary of the underlying purposes of Parliament's policy towards the Royalists, 'It is their reformation, not their ruin is desired', was as relevant to the measures of 1651 and 1652 as to those of 1656. *Diary of Thos. Burton*, I, 237.

[17] *Cal. Committee for Compounding*, ed. M. A. E. Green (1889–92), p. 2533; P.R.O. C 54/3810, 23; Chanc. Proc. Bridges Div. 431/48, 1664; C 54/3737, 19; 3853, 27.

[18] P.R.O. C 54/3733, 5; 3734, 12; 3797, 23, 24.

[19] P.R.O. C 54/3814, 13; 3724, 17.

[20] *Cal. Com. Comp.* p. 1617; Bulstrode Whitelocke, *Memorials of English Affairs* (Oxford, 1853), IV, 162; *Diary of Thos. Burton*, II, 128–30.

business man.[21] Lord Morley and Mounteagle was exceptional in employing as his agent John Wildman, known in London circles as a 'common solicitor' because he was ready to undertake a commission for any and every client.

The 'common solicitors' catered mainly for the needs of the gentry. Thomas Knatchbull, who consented to help his delinquent friend, Edward Masters, by buying his estate in Kent in trust for him, described how he 'did imploy one Major Wildman as a solicitor to contract with the Trustees'. Wildman, in fact, was among the best known of solicitors for those wanting to buy land in south-eastern England. The more lucrative business from the north he shared with agents like Samuel Foxley, George Hurd, Gilbert Crouch, and John Rushworth, who were specialists in the purchase of forfeited north country estates.[22]

In the course of time, agents came to be regarded as the indispensable link between purchasers and the Sales Trustees. They had connexions; they knew the ways of Drury House; they could be relied upon to make the best bargain possible. Only a few Royalists managed without them by engaging the services of their friends or relatives. Sir John Gifford of Eastbury managed to buy his Berkshire estate through his nephew and heir, Samuel Dabbs, a London grocer. Sir Lewis Dyve persuaded his son-in-law, Sir John Strangeways, to act for him. Sir Percy Herbert chose his half-cousin, Charles Whitmore, who wisely bought only the most valuable part of Hendon Manor, namely the portion on which the leases were due to fall in in three years' time.[23] All these agents appeared in the records of the Committee for Compounding as buyers in their own right; in fact they were the closest allies of their relatives.

The social upheaval, which contemporaries might have predicted from seeing the first announcement of the sales was much diminished by Royalist tactics. In Hampshire, for example, where twenty-six parcels of land were put up for sale, only nine transfers promised changes of any permanence. Fourteen estates were bought back by

[21] Weld bought numerous Royalist estates; not all were those of Lord Arundel, but all appear to have been bought on behalf of their Royalist owners. *Cal. Com. Comp.* passim.

[22] Chanc. Proc. Collins Div. 143/1A, 1658. Col. Hutchinson's wife described Wildman as 'a great manager of Papists' interests'. I. C. Cole, 'Some notes on Henry Marten, regicide, and his family', *Berks Archaeol. J.* XLIX, 38.

[23] P.R.O. C 54/3743, 28; Chanc. Proc. Hamilton Div. 505/27, 1673; C 54/3684, 19; 3673, 16; H. G. Tibbutt, *The Life and Letters of Sir Lewis Dyve, 1599–1669* (Beds. Hist. Rec. Soc. Publications, XXVII), p. 110.

their owners; two estates were sold for life only. In the four counties
of Berkshire, Hampshire, Oxfordshire and Sussex, twenty-five out of
sixty-four (39 per cent) were bought by their owners direct from the
Trustees. In the four counties of Essex, Hertfordshire, Kent and
Surrey, where small estates belonging to the gentry predominated,
and where the available resources for re-purchase were in consequence less abundant, 25 per cent of the forfeited estates (nine
parcels out of thirty-six) were recovered by direct purchase.

The number of properties bought back by delinquents would
doubtless have been still higher, had not some of the estates been
burdened with debts, and their owners therefore debarred from
purchase. The Treason Trustees were under an obligation to see that
the claims of Royalists' creditors were satisfied before the lands were
put up for public sale.[24] This, however, did not necessarily mean that
the property was thrust into the lap of a London money-lender. Many
a country gentleman had borrowed from a neighbour, sometimes
even continued on terms of close friendship with him. The most
accommodating of these accepted land as payment from the Drury
House Trustees, but at the same time agreed with the Royalist to hold
it only in trust. In this way, a transaction which ostensibly satisfied a
creditor differed little from one in which the land was bought by the
owner. The land was charged with an old-standing mortgage instead
of a new one. Thus, Sir Edward Herbert owed his success in
recovering his houses in London, Middlesex, Yorkshire and Denbigh
to the friendly assistance of his creditor, Thomas Fisher.[25] The
delinquent, Sir John Denham, managed to snatch Horsley Parva
manor, Essex, from Major George Wither by getting his friend, John
Fielder (the guardian of his children) to establish a prior claim to the
land as mortgagee. The fact that the estate ultimately came into the
full possession of Fielder was due less to Denham's financial losses as
a delinquent than to his personal extravagance.[26] It was rarely that
the financial burden borne by Royalist purchasers obliged them to

[24] Firth and Rait, op. cit. II, 523–4.
[25] P.R.O. C 54/3653, 22; Chanc. Proc. Whittington Div. 79/50, 1665.
[26] George Wither, who had been granted the estate at Parliament's request, had
already entered into possession of this property, when Fielder laid claim to it as a
creditor. Wither was dispossessed, and waged a long battle with the Drury House
Trustees in the courts of law, and in the press, for compensation for his losses. Firth
and Rait, op. cit. II, 545; P.R.O. C 54/3738; 3641, 5; Chanc. Proc. Bridges Div. 29/82,
1656; *Cal. Com. Comp.* p. 1790; Thomason Tracts 669 f. 19 (60); J. Aubrey, *Brief Lives*
(Oxford, 1898), I, 218.

sell out before 1660.[27]

When no close alliance existed between Royalist and creditor, the latter took possession of the land on the same footing as a purchaser. But those possessing strong local affiliations were usually content to retain the property as an investment rather than break it up for re-sale. In fact, the policy of local creditors was remarkably consistent throughout south-eastern England, and was directly opposed to that of the London moneylender, who, having been compelled to take land from the Sales Trustees for want of any alternative, had no desire to keep his money tied up in this way, and set about re-selling as quickly as possible. No better example of conformity to this rule could be found than that presented by the creditors of the Earl of Cleveland. His property, which comprised the three adjacent manors of Harlington, Toddington and Dixwells in Bedfordshire, and the two valuable manors of Stepney and Hackney in Middlesex, was sold out almost in its entirety to creditors. Some of them had been temporarily satisfied with leases granted to them by the county sequestration committee as the old ones fell in. Since, however, by 1653 the burden of interest on the debts exceeded the total annual income, the interests of both creditors and delinquent were best served when Parliament decided to sell the property.[28] Creditors were, in this case, so numerous that no more than a fragment of the estate was left over for public sale, and only two out of the total number of beneficiaries were not creditors. One was Mary Deane, the widow of General Richard Deane, who, having been voted an annuity of £600 by Parliament, received as its equivalent Bishop's Hall in Stepney, and twenty-one acres of Toddington land.[29] The other was John Chadwick, a genuine purchaser, but one who brought little profit to the state since he paid the first half of the purchase price with the profits earned from selling forged public faith bills, and immediately set about felling the timber on the land to raise the other half.[30]

The remaining beneficiaries of the Earl of Cleveland's land were his thirty-three creditors, made up of two fairly distinct groups—those on the one hand whose business interests lay predominantly in

[27] For evidence supporting this statement, see Joan Thirsk, *The Sale of Delinquents' Estates during the Interregnum, and the Land Settlement at the Restoration* (Ph.D. thesis, London Univ. 1950), pp. 320–50.

[28] *Cal. Com. Comp.* p. 2157.

[29] P.R.O. C 54/3877, 3; 3716, 1.

[30] P.R.O. C 54/3703, 1; Chanc. Proc. Bridges Div. 593/60, 1659; *Cal. S.P. Dom.* 1654, p. 415.

London, and local gentry and yeomen of the neighbourhood on the other. To the first group belonged Philip Peascod and William Pufford, a London grocer and joiner, who sold out their share of Toddington land within two years; Samuel Baldwin, a lawyer, and later sergeant-at-law, who sold his share within a year; and George Almery, a City man who served as a member of the committee for distributing adventurers' lands in Ireland, who sold his within two years.[31] The biggest claimant was a certain William Smith, who, besides his own claim against the estate, assiduously bought up the debts of others until the total amounted to £32,568. He received in return the two lordships and the lion's share of the lands of Stepney and Hackney. Smith's family were Buckinghamshire gentry with Royalist sympathies, who had been seated at Akely since the early seventeenth century, but William himself was a lawyer and one of the most active land-jobbers then engaged in the land market. He had no hesitation in selling off the entire estate in small parcels.[32]

These re-sales redounded to the benefit of local landowners and farmers—a fact that was unlikely to surprise anyone who knew the course that the market in dissolved monastic land had taken a century before. The first local gains, however, were made by creditors who were the Earl of Cleveland's tenants and neighbours—men such as Francis Astrey, member of a farming family in Harlington, which held land there in the sixteenth century and was still there in the twentieth[33];—George Shaw and William Matthewes, yeomen farmers on the estate;[34] William Denton, a barber-surgeon and member of the Denton family of Hillesdon in Buckinghamshire;[35] and Thomas Farrer, a Buckinghamshire gentleman with lands in Bedfordshire.[36] In Stepney and Hackney, Cleveland's only creditors apart from William Smith were Thomas Mempris, a gentleman actively engaged in local affairs in Mile End, where he held land,[37] and Thomas Fossan, a London skinner, and property owner in Stepney.[38] The fact that none of these creditors relinquished his land until compelled to do so by the march of political events in 1660 was a convincing sign of the strong local attachments of each one of them.

[31] P.R.O. C 54/3731, 22; 3877, 38; 3828, 36; 3827, 8; *Students admitted to the Inner Temple, 1547-1660*, p. 284; C 54/3826, I; C.P. 25(2)/533, Mich. 1656; C 54/3797, 2.
[32] *Cal. Com. Comp.* p. 2167; *V.C.H. Bucks*, IV, 145, 221; P.R.O. C 54/3805, 29.
[33] P.R.O. C 54/3934, 41; *V.C.H. Beds*, III, 442.
[34] P.R.O. C 54/3822, 38, 39.
[35] P.R.O. C 54/3818, 2.
[36] P.R.O. C 54/3819, 43.
[37] P.R.O. C 54/3806, 52.
[38] P.R.O. C 54/3719, 3; *Cal. Com. Comp.* p. 2165.

As soon as the Earl of Cleveland's London creditors prepared to sell out, the local squires and tenant farmers took the initiative. Francis Astrey, who had already accepted from the Drury House Trustees a fifth share in Toddington Manor house, further augmented his estate by buying up the land awarded to Philip Peascod and William Pufford. The estate awarded to the rich London apothecary, Gideon Delaune, was partly, if not entirely, sold out to two tenants of Toddington manor, Thomas Pennington, who had been one of the Earl of Cleveland's bailiffs, and Jeffery Wildman, a tenant farmer.[39] The land allocated to another creditor, William Willoughby (later Lord Willoughby of Parham) was divided and sold in three parcels. One third passed to William Pryor, the tenant; the second to Thomas Pennington, who had already bought some of Gideon Delaune's land; the third part was conveyed to William Saunders, a London draper. But Saunders, true to type, alienated his interest within a year to two Buckinghamshire gentlemen, William and John Theed of Ledburn, members of a modest but well-established landowning family.[40] John Chadwick, now dogged by investigations into his dealings in forged bills, took the wise step of selling out to William Dell, a one-time chaplain to Fairfax and Cromwell, and later Master of Gonville and Caius College, Cambridge, who held a living at Yelden in Bedfordshire.[41]

Meanwhile, in Middlesex, the new owner of Stepney and Hackney manors, William Smith, was managing to dismember the estate on an even more spectacular scale. Between 1653 and 1660 he put his name to forty different bargains and sales. Early in the story he conveyed the lordship of both manors to another landjobber, Captain Richard Blackwell. But although the range of Blackwell's business activities surpassed that of Smith, he could not equal Smith's skill in their management. Soon after the purchase was arranged, it was discovered that Blackwell, in his capacity of commissioner of the customs (he was also a commissioner for prize goods), owed nearly £13,000 to the Exchequer, and was indebted to private persons in another £18,000. He was therefore ordered to transfer the lands once more to William Smith in trusteeship. The sales were resumed, this time in order to pay off Blackwell's debts.[42]

[39] P.R.O. C 54/3877, 38; *Cal. Com. Comp.* p. 2167; P.R.O. C 54/3931, 48; C.P. 25(2)/533, Hil. 1657; C.P. 25(2)/532, Mich. 1653.
[40] P.R.O. C 54/3925, 24, 20; 3828, 16; 3821, 5; 3934, 7.
[41] P.R.O. C 54/3828, 30; *D.N.B.*, article on Dell.
[42] P.R.O. C 54/3989, 9; E 112/445, 222, Hilary 14 and 15 Chas II; H.M.C. Rep. ix, app. 2, 32b.

No restrictions were imposed by the vendors on the size of the parcels sold; more than one item comprised only one house or one acre of ground, though more usual was a group of three or five houses with waste ground attached. In the course of forty separate transactions, parcels of Stepney and Hackney land were sold to forty-seven new owners, of whom twelve were lessees or occupiers of at least part of the premises, and another twelve were residents in the district. Altogether 25 per cent of the purchasers of this property were tenants and 25 per cent local inhabitants.

In accordance with the occupational characteristics of Stepney's inhabitants at this period, most of the purchasers came from the class of wealthy merchants, or were prosperous craftsmen and artisans. The docks and warehouses of the East India Company were situated there, and it is not, therefore, surprising to find many of the company's members and employees taking part in the sales. The most distinguished tenant-purchaser was Henry Johnson, the shipwright and shipowner, who was closely associated with the company, and bought its lease of Blackwall Yard during these years. At the time of the purchase he had not yet reached the pinnacle of his career, when wealth was to bring him the conventional rewards of a knighthood, and the marriage of his granddaughter into the peerage.[43] Other purchasers associated with the East India Company included William Cutler, the garbler of pepper; Sir Thomas Foote, alderman of London and tenant of part of the property which he bought; Thomas Jennings, a London skinner who had once been nominated for election as governor of the company; and Joseph Collins, a ship's captain.[44] The tradespeople and others who earned their livelihood in Stepney included a miller, a glazier, a gardener, a fishmonger, a tailor and several mariners—members of a class which was benefiting rapidly from the expansion of trade and shipping activity in this growing suburb of London.[45] There is no doubt that the parcelling of

[43] P.R.O. C 54/3910, 27; H. Green and R. Wigram, *Chronicles of Blackwall Yard* (1881), I, 9–18. Anne, granddaughter of Sir Henry Johnson, married Thomas Wentworth, third Earl of Strafford, and a distant relative of the Earl of Cleveland. Ultimately Toddington manor came into the possession of her husband by inheritance. Anne Johnson was said to have brought her husband a fortune of £60,000 on her marriage. *D.N.B.*, article on Thomas Wentworth, third Earl of Strafford.

[44] For the association of all these purchasers with the East India Company, see *A Calendar of the Court Minutes of the East India Company, 1635–63*, ed. E. B. Sainsbury (Oxford, 1907–22), passim. For their purchases, see P.R.O. C 54/4032, 14; 4038, 13; 4053; 3809, 34.

[45] P.R.O. C 54/3811, 31; 3868, 27; 3806, 25; 3815, 36; 3813, 5; 4038, 12; 3908, I; 4038, 21.

the estate would have continued steadily if the restoration of the king in 1660 had not brought it to a halt. The lordships of both manors were sold to William Hobson, a former City haberdasher, in February 1660, and in the few months left before the Restoration he showed every sign of continuing the process.[46]

The statement made earlier that there was only moderate traffic in forfeited land may appear to be directly contradicted by the evidence taken from the Earl of Cleveland's estate. But the market in his property was exceptional, for the simple reason that his indebtedness was exceptional. No other single Royalist with land in south-eastern England was so financially embarrassed. At the time of the sales his borrowings with interest were estimated at £112,082. 1s 6½d. The total debts of the remaining forty-nine Royalists were but a quarter of this amount. Moreover, their eighteen creditors included at least two, and probably a further three, who came to friendly agreements with their debtors when once the official transfer of land had taken place. Another three creditors were local people lacking any disposition to sell. Although it was inevitable that creditors should have the strongest temptations to re-sell, the group was not composed exclusively of keen speculators. Economic interest, which had united them, when petitions for the repayment of debts were submitted to Parliament, divided them when once the land was in their hands. Although they were responsible for a vigorous market in the Earl of Cleveland's land, no more than half the Earl's creditors took any part in it. And in south-eastern England as a whole the role of creditors in stimulating sales at second and third hand was small in relation to the total number of transactions.[47]

The eagerness of local people to gain possession of land in their own neighbourhood was a noticeable feature of the sales all over south-eastern England. If land hunger was a lingering malaise of rural society in the seventeenth century, this feature may perhaps be counted, in part, as one of its many manifestations. The Commons had taken steps to assist tenants to buy their land by guaranteeing them pre-emptive rights for thirty days after the announcement of each sale. This provision was by no means a dead letter, and scrupulous regard was paid to it whenever tenants put in their claims.[48] Nevertheless, it is also true that the advantage thus given

[46] P.R.O. C 54/4038, 14, 18, 32.
[47] For a petition of creditors, see *Cal. S.P. Dom.* 1641–3, p. 455. I am indebted to Dr Paul Hardacre for this reference.
[48] It is recorded that when Sir William Monson claimed pre-emptive rights in regard

was insufficient to compensate for the physical and financial handicaps of tenants who had to go to London to make their claims or pay an agent to do it for them, and who also had to raise at least half the purchase money at short notice. Added to this was the fact that the Treason Trustees, judging by the results of the sales, favoured selling large properties *en bloc*.

These handicaps did not affect tenants of properties in London. There the buildings were in any case a dispersed collection. They consisted of the town houses of the nobility, the tenements that had been built around them to house their domestic retinue, and City premises, which were often the abandoned mansions of the court circle, now converted into tenements or business headquarters. The Drury House Trustees were not averse to selling off these houses in penny numbers; and tenants were not troubled with the problem of making their claims for pre-emption in time.

As a result the number of tenants who availed themselves of their pre-emptive rights was far higher in London and Middlesex than elsewhere. Out of fifteen contracts for the sale of houses in the Strand, for example, three were made with tenants, while a fourth tenant secured his tenement by purchase at second hand. In one instance, the purchaser was able to consolidate lands which he already possessed in the Strand by buying three houses, and a coalhouse, yard and stables previously leased to him.[49] In the City, merchants who had leased warehouses and workshops were now able to buy the freehold. A valuable group of storehouses and shops in Barking were sold to a London skinner, who lived in the parish, and to a haberdasher who occupied adjacent buildings.[50] Alderman Thomas Foote, the grocer, bought a house near Gracechurch Street, which he already leased jointly with another grocer.[51] Abraham Babington, a draper, bought the two shops which he rented in Gracechurch Street.[52] Altogether, one-fifth of all the purchasers in London and Middlesex, excluding those who bought the Earl of Cleveland's land, were lessees and

to Chelsea manor, and his claim was passed over in favour of the undertenants, an appeal by Monson brought speedy correction of the error, even though the undertenants had paid in the purchase money. P.R.O. Chanc. Proc. Hamilton Div. 420/45, 1655.

[49] P.R.O. C 54/3809, 23; Chanc. Proc. Collins Div. 196/15, 1671; Mitford Div. 196/115, 1670.

[50] P.R.O. C 54/3688, 14.

[51] P.R.O. C 54/3680, 25.

[52] P.R.O. C 54/3676, II, 29. Babington is not quite a typical case, as he bought with reluctance, and at the earnest wish of the delinquent, or so he alleged at the Restoration, H.M.C. Rep. VII, app. I, 87b.

tenants, and one-third of all the merchants who were buyers were lessees. In a district, in short, where it would have been natural to find speculative buying at its height, purchases by the merchant class made an unusually meagre contribution. Re-sales of a speculative kind were more in evidence among a few land dealers, who were engaged chiefly in the business of the free land market, and who intervened in these sales to buy only the more lucrative properties of the Strand district.[53]

Much capital was made by Parliament's enemies out of the acquisitions of land by prominent Parliamentarians. But the evidence of sales in this one region of the country does little to substantiate their charges. Among the 153 individuals who obtained land at the first sales, only fifteen were leading public figures or government officials. Chief among the latter were officers of the Committee for Compounding and of Drury House, and it is probable that at least some, if not all of these, were simply accepting land in lieu of arrears of pay.[54] On this assumption it is not difficult to explain why their purchases, together with the grants made by Parliament to army commanders and their widows, turned out to be among the least permanent transactions carried out by the Drury House Trustees. Ralph Darnell, the registrar of delinquents' lands, bought a row of five tenements in the Strand, sold one to the tenant and the rest to an outside purchaser five months later.[55] Edward Walford, a travelling messenger of the Sequestrations Committee, bought another house in the Strand only to sell it again. John Baker, the surveyor-general of delinquents' estates, who shared with his brother in the purchase of Hampstead Marshall manor in Berkshire, sold out five months afterwards.[56]

Of those to whom Parliament had given land, Mary Deane

[53] Even the sale of seven houses in the City to Thomas Andrewes, a former Lord Mayor and City financier, proved to be a repayment to the City Chamber of a debt owed by the Royalist owner. P.R.O. C 54/3859, 4. The land dealers mentioned here were not well-known merchants. They attract notice only because of the frequency with which their names occur in indentures of bargain and sales in the Close Rolls. It is possible to trace through their partnerships in single transactions the thread of business interest that linked them all together, but the market in forfeited land was not the chief scene of their operations.

[54] Indentures of bargain and sale do not specify whether the purchase money was paid partly in public faith bills and debentures, or entirely in cash. Financial details were given only when land was conveyed to the creditors of Royalists and to the recipients of Parliamentary gifts.

[55] P.R.O. C 54/3715, 31; 3813, 13.

[56] P.R.O. C 54/3687, 40; *Cal. Com. Comp.* pp. 39, 199; *Cal. S.P. Dom.* 1656–7, p. 63; S.P. 23/18, f. 805; C 54/3849, 4; Chanc. Proc. Collins Div. 160/15, 1662.

disposed of her share of Bedfordshire and Middlesex lands a year later. Cromwell, whose gifts included Newhall manor in Essex, several times contemplated selling it because it brought him so little profit, though in the end, apparently, he did not do so.[57] The boldest plan of estate exploitation was that devised by Major-General Philip Skippon, and carried out on his three manors of Water Eaton, Whaddon, and Winslow in Buckinghamshire. His dealings may stand for the rest, for although they were carried out on a far larger scale than those of other Parliamentary grantees, they differed little in result. The land was again parcelled among local interests.

Viewed from one aspect, there was much in Skippon's behaviour, both in the timing of the sale and in the method of carrying it out, to confirm the charges of greed and opportunism made by Clement Walker, and based on the known facts of Skippon's earlier career. Skippon, declared Walker, 'hath got above £30,000 in his purse, besides £1000 a year land of inheritance given him by Parliament. He hath secured his personal estate beyond the Sea, and his wife and children . . . and is here amongst us but in the nature of a soldier of fortune'.[58] Walker did not live to see Skippon's handling of the estate granted him by Parliament, but he would have considered it fully in character. It was well-timed and shrewdly calculated. He reaped the first crop of fines from the issue of new leases, and when this source of revenue was played out, began early in 1655 to sell off the estate in small parcels, steadily dismembering it in the course of the next two years. By Christmas, 1657, Skippon had sold twenty parcels to twenty-seven buyers, twenty of whom were yeomen and husbandmen already farming in the vicinity, and a further three of whom were craftsmen and tradesmen in the villages. Nine purchasers at least were already tenants. The only London purchaser among them all was John Hatch, a haberdasher, who was nevertheless native to the district, and already held property in it. The three local gentry who made up the remaining buyers included Francis Dodsworth, letting agent of the Duke of Buckingham, who was the former owner. It was Dodsworth and Hatch who alone re-sold parcels of their newly acquired land, carving out new holdings and increasing the number of new owners—all of them local people—by another nine.

It is a simple analysis of motives to see in Skippon's piecemeal sales nothing but calculations of profit. Doubtless these played their part,

---

[57] P.R.O. C 54/3877, 3; 3920, I; 3856, 28; *Oliver Cromwell's Letters and Speeches*, ed. Thos. Carlyle (Everyman's library), III, 137–8.
[58] Clement Walker, op. cit. I, 116–18.

and doubtless too the outcome was far from disappointing. The land had been given to him as a gift worth £1000 p.a. The capital value was not stated, but it would be reasonable to assess it at ten years' purchase, that is to say £10,000.[59] His sales brought in £12,075. 2s. 6d., a sum confirmed by a statement of the tenants themselves.[60] This figure, large as it is, still does not take account of the rents, fines, and timber profits which he had collected in the meantime, nor does it account for the land remaining in his possession. Yet to dismiss these sales as patent evidence of Skippon's acquisitiveness is to ignore one half of the problem. Why did the sales of Skippon's land remain an exclusively local concern? Whereas in other places, purchasers were distributed among a number of different social groups, and the wealthy investor was never completely eliminated, here purchasers formed a solid body of local interests in which the small farmer predominated. Was Skippon perhaps prevailed upon by the organized appeals of his tenants? Was there even some trace of the Leveller principle in their determination to see the land vested in the hands of those who lived upon it? The evidence does no more than hint at it.[61] Although petitions to Parliament revealed the existence of an eloquent group of Leveller supporters in Buckinghamshire, Leveller literature gave no clue to their identity. At the Restoration, Skippon's purchasers appealed against a new confiscation on the grounds that they had bought the land merely to exclude strangers. But this was the politic excuse that was worn threadbare in the course of the year 1660.

The dominant characteristics of land sales in south-eastern England, which are summarized in the tables,[62] were not peculiar to this district alone.[63] Everywhere the Royalists exercised a strong influence in shaping the outcome of the sales. Common sense bade

---

[59] Ten years' purchase was the minimum price laid down by Parliament. Firth and Rait, op. cit. II, 528.

[60] B.M. Add. MS. 5821, f. 190.

[61] Samuel Chidley, the Leveller, carried out a similar re-sale to tenants of parcels of the Crown estate of Greensnorton manor, Northamptonshire. His sympathy for the small man was evident in the fact that he organized an appeal to Parliament on behalf of the small public faith creditors, who wanted repayment of their loans to the government. In these sales, there is no doubt that Chidley considered a principle was at stake.

[62] See tables I, II and III on pp. 106–8.

[63] It is probable that the sales of crown and church lands took a rather different course. They occurred at a time when soldiers possessing debentures and civilians holding public faith bills were being encouraged to use them in part purchase of forfeited land. A flourishing market developed in these bills, which brought many dealers on to the scene. No doubt a considerable amount of land also came their way. If so, then these sales explain the contemporary jibes at the careerists and money makers.

them make strenuous efforts to buy their land. But Parliament played into their hands by compensating their creditors, for in some cases it virtually restored the land to the owner on more favourable terms than he could have secured by direct purchase. Royalists could not foresee that the financial condition of their estates before confiscation would dictate the last word on how much land was to be sold. In fact their debts considerably reduced the profit from the sales; the Earl of Cleveland's lands probably did not even pay the costs of administration. Yet it is doubtful if Parliament or its servants ever perceived how far they had allowed their Royalist victims, on this issue, to become their masters.

The extent to which the nobility, and, to a lesser degree, the gentry, were able to buy their land in spite of the drain on their fortunes through sequestration and financial aid to the king was an example of tenacity, which appears to have been more than equalled in stauncher Royalist areas. In some families the burden of debt rested heavily on succeeding generations, but to outward appearances the sales produced no change at all. The old landowners entered into possession of their property once more; only the finances of the transaction disclosed how much heavier was the price of purchase than the price of paying composition.

That tenants' pre-emptive rights were more than an empty phrase is evident not only from the examples quoted here but also from the sales in Lancashire. Nevertheless, the opportunities of tenants to buy their holdings were seriously limited by the size of the unit sold. The Sales Trustees appear to have been reluctant to break up an estate except for the benefit of creditors. Tenants in south-eastern England, therefore, were most successful in London and Middlesex, where the Trustees had no objection to selling off a row of houses piecemeal. Here, indeed, tenants had a better chance of buying direct from the Trustees than of buying at second hand.

In counties where the most usual unit of Royalist property was a manor, large estates rendered tenants' rights meaningless, but sales at second and third hand went some way to compensate them for their handicaps at the first sale. The three manors sold by Philip Skippon provided tenants with abundant opportunities for purchase.

Continued
But there remains the problem of deciding who bought the lands from the dealers. Mr Tatham's classification of purchasers of episcopal lands is based on the evidence of the Close Rolls, but he does not investigate beyond the first transaction between the Sales Trustees and the purchaser or his agent. G. B. Tatham, 'The Sale of Episcopal Lands during the Civil Wars and Commonwealth', *Eng. Hist. Rev.* (1908), XXIII, 95.

Examples in other counties suggest that although in scale this was unusual, the re-sale of one or two parcels to tenants was not.

Viewed as a whole, the market in forfeited land did not assume great proportions, even though there were some notable cases of estates that were transformed out of recognition by re-sales. This is not surprising, since a large proportion of forfeited land fell into the hands of local people at the outset, who had every reason to retain it intact. It is noticeable that the outstanding examples of re-sales were provided in almost all cases by people who appear to have been strangers to the district in which they bought land.

Solicitors who acted for clients in outlying districts played a notable part in the sales, because they prevented the land from being cornered by a small group of buyers with easy access to Drury House. But the frequent appearance of their names in the records of the Committee for Compounding has won for them an importance wholly disproportionate to their actual interest in the land. In the whole of south-eastern England, there is not one purchase attributed to John Wildman, which can be proved to have been made by him for his own use. Another agent, Samuel Foxley, bought only a quarter interest in Rockland manor, Sussex, whereas the Committee for Compounding ascribed to him the purchase of this entire estate and four others in London and Middlesex. Evidence collected from this one corner of England suggests that agents were hardly at all interested in owning forfeited land when the job of conveyancing was itself so lucrative.

In attempting to assess in precise terms the role of the speculator it has been necessary to differentiate between the speculator and the merchant, because their interests were not always identical. If we take at their face value the purchases of Sir Thomas Foote, Alderman Thomas Andrewes, and Martin Noel, all of them rich and influential merchants, then we have evidence to support the judgement of Mr W. G. Harper on the sales, that 'many of the estates passed out of the hands of the traditional gentry, both lay and clerical, into the possession of rising merchants who had made their money in overseas trade'.[64] From this, it is but a short step to the view that speculation was as common a motive for the purchase or forfeited land as it was for investments in trading ventures. But when account is taken of the purchasers belonging to the merchant class, who bought property because they occupied or leased it already, they cannot be deemed

[64] W. G. Harper, *Public borrowing, 1640–60* (M.Sc. thesis, University of London, 1927), p. 182.

landjobbers.[65] The market in forfeited Royalist land, was no more the special preserve of the speculator than is the market in private land in less disturbed periods. In any case, the merchant buyers were not more numerous than the gentry—the class which is entirely omitted from Dr Chesney's classification of new owners, and which is accorded less than ten per cent of all forfeited land in Prof. Arkhangel'sky's analysis. When the success of the yeomen and small tradesmen is linked with that of the gentry, their gains considerably outweigh those of the merchant class.

Of the substantial purchasing power of the gentry under the difficult economic conditions of the Interregnum, the sales afford copious evidence. Of their stability as a class, and of the hazards of their economic position as individuals, Prof. Tawney has already given account for the century before 1640.[66] In the following two decades, the re-grouping of this class was accelerated by political factors. Its members might be raised by the accidents of political fortune, or might find themselves on the losing side and forfeit everything. Some of the lesser Royalist gentry disappeared into social oblivion as a result of the sales, but a larger number, including most of the nobility, managed to re-assemble all or part of their estates before the Restoration. The wealth which they lost did not rattle in the pockets of those contemporary villains, the Parliamentary fortune seekers; it bulged the coats of some merchants and lawyers, but it also went to swell the purses of many gentry, and some of the more ambitious of their land-hungry tenants.

The suspicions of purchasers that the land would one day be wrested from them crystallized into certainty in the course of the year 1660, by which time, however, many of them had made a satisfactory profit on their purchases. Most delinquents managed to regain possession of their land at the Restoration, and within a year or two all trace of recent events seemed to have been obliterated.[67] The lasting effects of Parliament's policy appeared some twenty to thirty years later, when more than one delinquent was obliged to sell a part of his estate to pay off long-standing debts.

[65] At the Restoration when commissioners were appointed to investigate the sales of crown and church lands, and to consider the claims for compensation from purchasers who were about to be dispossessed, they drew a distinction between purchasers who had bought as tenants, and those who had bought for gain. *Somers Tracts*, 2nd ed. Walter Scott (1809–15), VII, 465–9.

[66] R. H. Tawney, 'The Rise of the Gentry, 1558–1640', *Econ. Hist. Rev.* (1941), XI, 1–38.

[67] Abstracts of title relating to former forfeited land never mention the change of ownership which took place during the Interregnum.

Table I. *A classification of all purchasers holding forfeited land in south-eastern England in* 1660

The number of purchasers who bought land direct from the Trustees in this district was 168. Of these, twenty-one were agents buying on behalf of nineteen Royalists; twenty-seven were purchasers who sold out entirely before 1660; the remaining 141 retained all or part of their acquisitions. By re-sales, a further 116 persons secured parcels of forfeited land, making a grand total of 257 persons holding interests in this property — five times the number of former delinquent owners. The classification of purchasers is based upon what appeared to be their predominant economic interests at the time of purchase.

Classification of purchasers	Number	Percentage of whole
Royalists' agents	20	8
Parliamentary officials, and grantees of land	18	7
London merchants	79	31
Local gentry*	66	25 } 31
Gentry*	13	6
London gentry*	7	3
Local yeomen and artisans	41	16
Lawyers	4	1
Unidentified	9	3
Total	257	100

* 'Local gentry' signifies those who bought land near their homes. 'Gentry' signifies those gentlemen who were not apparently connected with the district in which they bought land. Several of them were creditors of Royalists. London gentry are classed separately.

Table II. *The number of purchasers who bought forfeited land direct from the Treason Trustees, grouped according to the prices paid.**

Figures that take into account not only the status of the purchasers but the price paid for the property cannot be as complete as those given above, because in several sales at first hand, when land was simply granted away to Parliament's nominees, the value was not stated, while the same omission occurred still more often when land was re-sold. Though incomplete, Tables II and III show the expected pattern of land purchase, yeomen buying a few properties direct from the Sales Trustees, and then stopping short at the £1000 mark; gentry falling off at £2000; and merchants buying in strength at prices between £500 and £5000. The merchants scored at the first sales when lands were sold in larger units, whereas yeomen outnumbered them in purchases at second hand. Gentry were equally strong in both sets of transactions, but tended to buy lower-priced properties at second hand.

Purchasers	£1–100	£101–200	£201–300	£301–500	£501–1000	£1001–2000	£2001–3000	£3001–5000	£5000+	Total
Royalists' agents	1	1	3	–	4	4	3	3	1	20
Parliamentary officials and grantees	–	1	2	2	4	–	1	4	1	15
London merchants	1	6	2	2	19	20	–	1	5	56
Local gentry	3	4	–	8	2	12	2	2	2	35
Gentry	–	–	2	–	9	1	–	–	1	13
London gentry	–	–	–	1	–	1	–	–	–	2
Local yeomen and artisans	2	1	3	1	1	–	–	–	–	8
Lawyers	–	–	1	1	1	–	–	1	–	4
Total	7	13	13	15	40	38	6	11	10	153

* In cases where two or more purchasers bought a property, the sum paid has been divided equally between them.

Table III. *The number of purchasers who bought at second and third hand, and who were in possession in 1660, grouped according to the prices paid*

Purchasers	£1–100	£101–200	£201–300	£301–500	£501–1000	£1001–2000	£2001–3000	£3001–5000	£50001+	Total
London merchants	5	1	1	–	1	2	–	1	3	14
Local gentry	12	3	4	5	–	3	1	2	1	31
Gentry	–	–	–	2	2	–	–	–	–	4
London gentry	–	–	–	–	2	–	–	–	–	2
Local yeomen and artisans	11	10	1	5	2	–	–	–	–	29
Lawyers	–	1	–	–	–	–	–	–	–	1
Total	28	15	6	12	7	5	1	3	4	81

VIII

THE RESTORATION LAND SETTLEMENT

IN January 1660, General Monk, the principal negotiant of the Restoration, endeavoured to persuade the gentlemen of Devon that a return of the monarchy was out of the question. Arguing that two new and influential groups had come into being since 1642 — the Puritan sects and the purchasers of crown, church, and delinquents' lands — he declared that no government would survive which did not deal tenderly with their interests.[1] It was not perhaps unreasonable to regard the Puritans as a serious obstacle in the way of a restoration. But were the purchasers of confiscated lands so influential? Their numbers could not be estimated, but it was many times the number of those who had surrendered the land.[2] Moreover, it was likely that 'every acre of land sold was a bond attaching the purchaser to the Commonwealth.'[3] The king's friends and advisers accepted this view and were not disposed to dismiss the land question as a minor matter. Charles was led to believe that much potential support for him attended a satisfactory solution of the problem, and long discussions between himself and his friends at home preceded the Declaration of Breda. But if the new landowners formed a hard core of support for the existing regime, how is it possible to explain their acquiescence in the king's return? The answer to this question lies in the terms of the land settlement, the details of which were never made clear in parliamentary legislation. It is the purpose of this article to piece together, from the fragmentary evidence of debates in parliament and from the litigation and later dealings concerning forfeited land, the terms of that settlement.

[1] W. Kennett, *A register and chronicle ecclesiastical and civil* (London, 1728), p. 32.
[2] The lands forfeited by the two largest landowners in the kingdom, the crown and the church, were broken up for sale into many hundred parcels. By 1660, land in southeastern England, forfeited by fifty royalists, was distributed among 257 people. See chapter 7 above.
[3] S. R. Gardiner, *History of the Commonwealth and Protectorate* (1903), I, 251. Clement Walker reported a remark of Colonel Harvey on the attitude of the City that 'the men most backwards in the Parliaments service, were such of the Presbyterians as had no engagements upon Bishops Lands; whereas others of the same party that have interest in the same lands, are as forward as any the best affected' (Clement Walker, *The compleat history of independency* [London, 1660], II, 13).

At the first whisper of a restoration, Charles appears to have assumed that a full restoration of land would follow his return. In order to encourage his potential friends, he wrote to Mr. Mordaunt in July 1659, promising compensation to all who made a timely show of loyalty to him for what they might lose by such a restoration.[4] Of the complexities of the land problem Charles and his advisers abroad at that time had no conception, since their information was gathered mainly from the propaganda of the anti-Commonwealth men. Dr. John Barwick, writing from England that many landowners would exert themselves on Charles's behalf if they were certain of retaining their land purchases, was informed by Edward Hyde that the chief purchasers were irreconcilable parliamentarians, whom it would be useless to tempt with promises or favours.[5] The view was naïve and was soon dispelled. When, in later correspondence with General Monk, Charles described the land problem as one of the most perplexing with which he had to deal, facts had displaced legend. Charles then recognized that the recommendation that all sales should be confirmed was 'impossible and impracticable.'[6] Yet might not a new confiscation imperil his throne? Had not Colonel Axtell, the regicide, threatened another civil war if the new owners were dispossessed?[7]

Three different statements of policy made by Charles before his return to England mirrored his indecision. The first, of doubtful authenticity, contained a suggestion that purchasers of crown and church lands should surrender their estates but should first be given compensation for money paid out in excess of profits received.[8] The second proposal, contained in a letter of uncertain date in the first half of 1660 from Charles to General Monk, suggested that all purchasers of confiscated land, including royalist land, should rest content with the profit they had already received.[9] The third and final statement was included in the Declaration of Breda, when the whole problem of land sales was referred to parliament, and Charles undertook to accept its decisions.[10] This announcement antagonized no

---

[4] *Clarendon state papers* (Oxford, 1767–86), III, 512–13.

[5] *Ibid.*, III, 687.

[6] Kennett, pp. 97–98.

[7] Great Britain, Public record office, *Calendar of state papers, domestic series, Charles II* (London, 1860), I (1660–61), 116 (hereafter cited as '*CSPD*').

[8] The document was neither countersigned by Charles's ministers nor dated (*Somers tracts* [2nd ed.; London, 1809–15], VI, 539–40).

[9] *Ibid.*, pp. 557–61.

[10] *Parliamentary or constitutional history of England from the earliest times to the restoration of Charles II* [London, 1751–62], XXII, 240 (hereafter cited as '*Old parliamentary history*'); Kennett, p. 132.

one because it settled nothing. It contained none of the definite proposals put forward in Charles's private and semi-official correspondence. But it had the great merit of absolving the king of the responsibility for one of the most vexatious of Restoration problems. Moreover, the earlier statements attributed to Charles on the subject had done good service. Charles had promised compensation for their losses to those who came over to his side quickly. He had also suggested compensation to the owners of crown and church lands. When the exact conditions of the settlement were discussed in parliament, it was customary to refer to the matter as the 'confirmation of sales,' a term which encouraged the optimism of purchasers in the final verdict. An impression was thus successfully conveyed that both purchasers and former owners of confiscated land would be equally satisfied by the outcome.[11]

One of the first bills presented to the Convention Parliament in May 1660 was a 'Bill touching land purchased from the trustees of the late parliament.' It preceded by several days the first reading of the bill of indemnity. The eagerness of the house to settle the matter was not surprising, for, contrary to the advice given to Charles by General Monk, the Convention included more than one purchaser of confiscated lands.[12] The early debates took place in a conciliatory atmosphere. The king's messages to parliament on the subject and the statements issued by the house assured purchasers that their satisfaction was the first consideration. A committee which included John Rushworth, one of the most diligent agents for purchasers of royalist land, was appointed to consider it, and good progress was reported. Yet it was shelved as soon as the bill of indemnity and oblivion was ready, and not until July 11, over two months later, did it come up for discussion again.[13] Speeches from the debate on this occasion afford valuable clues to the contents of the bill and the tenor of the discussion. The bill was evidently sympathetic toward purchasers, but it seemed to advocate compensation to purchasers rather than a

---

[11] This optimism is seen in a letter from Dr. Edward Worth to Henry Cromwell. He was confident of a favourable settlement for Cromwell's Irish lands, and he did not despair of Cromwell's being able to keep the lands formerly belonging to the Earl of Worcester (R. W. Ramsey, *Henry Cromwell* [London, 1933], p. 357).

[12] *Somers tracts*, VI, 559. See Ludlow's accusation that the commons hastened to pass the bill of indemnity 'out of a tender care for their own persons and estates' (*The Memoirs of Edmund Ludlow . . . 1625–72*, ed. C. H. Firth [Oxford, 1894], II, 275).

[13] Great Britain, *The journals of the house of commons*, VIII, 11 (hereafter cited as '*CJ*'); *Somers tracts*, VII, 431; Kennett, p. 147. Before the debate on July 11, a 'bill for the satisfaction of purchasers of crown and other public lands' was read for the first time. It seems indistinguishable from the bill for sales and did not appear again (*CJ*, VIII, 73).

confirmation of sales.[14] Speakers were evenly divided for and against; for, although only one member, Sir Thomas Widdrington, spoke directly for it, others did so indirectly by taking up the case of tenants with ancient leases who had bought estates simply to preserve their titles and who would be unfairly penalized by a summary resumption of lands. Mr. Prynne suggested that only ancient tenants of crown lands should receive compensation, while Mr. Stephens thought that parliament ought to discourage evildoers and instead of confirming estates should punish the purchasers. Colonel West favoured the bill but wanted purchasers to receive indifferent terms of compensation, and this view was endorsed by Sir Thomas Meeres, who was convinced that purchasers had already recouped their initial outlay. Throughout the discussion, in so far as it was recorded, the financial interests of purchasers held pride of place, and no serious consideration was given to the proposal that they should be deprived of their land without recompense.[15] At a later stage in the debate, for reasons not explained, royalist and crown lands were excluded from the scope of the bill.[16] The amended version, applying to church lands only, was referred to a grand committee of the house, which was advised to pay some attention to the petitions of purchasers before it gave final shape to the bill. It was also instructed to consider the terms of compensation to be paid to the purchasers of crown lands. The terms offered to both groups of owners were evidently intended to follow similar lines.[17]

At this time both houses of parliament were giving consideration to two kindred matters — the bill of indemnity and oblivion and the bill for the confirmation of judicial proceedings. The first had but slight bearing on the land settlement. It excluded the regicides from the general pardon, and, since their property was forfeited, such lands as they had bought from the Commonwealth Trustees were quickly restored to their former owners. The Act for the Confirmation of Judicial Proceedings had a more direct bearing on the subject. Former owners of confiscated land needed some safeguard that they

[14] A clause which the Earl of Derby tried to have inserted into this bill in order to exempt his land from the provisions of the act was endorsed 'Act for the confirmation of sales.' The Duke of Buckingham and Lord Craven also tried to procure exemptions (Great Britain, Lancashire County record office, Derby 12, Nos. 16 and 15).

[15] *The parliamentary history of England,* ed. W. Cobbett [London, 1806–20], IV, 80–82.

[16] The only evidence to show that the original bill referred to royalist lands is given in n. 14 above. For evidence of the later exclusion of crowns lands see *CJ*, VIII, 86.

[17] *CJ*, VIII, 86.

would not be debarred by the terms of the act from recovering their property, when once parliament indicated the means. They were pacified with three clauses: nothing in the act was to be construed to confirm or invalidate sales carried out by the treason trustees; any person who was liable to suffer serious wrong by the confirmation of fines, recoveries, and other sentences at law dating from the Interregnum might appeal for a remedy by writ of error or some other accepted procedure, exactly as he would have done in normal circumstances; the failure of persons whose estates had been compulsorily sold to make such an appeal was not to prejudice their right to the land, so long as they prosecuted their claims by way of an action at law, or by lawful entry, within five years after May 29, 1660.[18]

These three clauses suggested to all dispossessed owners a way of redress in the common-law courts. But they were not regarded as the final and complete solution of the land problem. The task of restoring crown and church lands and of satisfying the claims of former tenants and purchasers became a matter for a royal commission, while royalists with sufficient influence had recourse to private acts. Moreover, parliament continued its discussions on the bill for sales. In short, the clauses in the Act for the Confirmation of Judicial Proceedings were treated rather as a warning to purchasers than as a final judgment on the claims of the dispossessed. They suggested a method of recovering land by legal action, but they did not close the door to other methods.

The energy with which parliament first tackled the bill for sales was quickly spent. Finding a way to satisfy purchasers proved more difficult than was anticipated, and on August 6, 1660 the committee appointed to settle the matter turned once more to the commons for advice. The house was bankrupt of ideas and proposed that

---

[18] *Statutes of the realm*, V, 234. Royalists and church landlords had tried, immediately on the king's return, to force entry onto their estates. A proclamation was therefore issued on May 29, 1660, prohibiting such action until parliament had reached a decision on the matter or until an order for eviction was obtained by due course of law. 'This severity,' commented the Venetian ambassador, 'greatly distresses many depressed families which have been in want during his Majesty's exile solely because they remained loyal to him, and who with his return hoped to enjoy their own. They now have the mortification of seeing themselves still shut out and unable to claim anything until it pleases parliament to decide, and God knows what decision it will take upon this.' The issue was then much in doubt (Great Britain, *The journals of the house of lords*, XI, 46 [hereafter cited as '*LJ*']; Great Britain, Public record office, *Calendar of state papers and manuscripts, relating to English affairs, existing in the archives and collections of Venice, and in other libraries of northern Italy* [London, 1931], XXXII [1659–61], 159).

representatives of the church and purchasers should themselves suggest a satisfactory settlement. In the meantime, legislation was passed to prevent church landlords from issuing new leases until the bill for sales was passed.[19]

Before further time could be given to the bill, the king proposed a parliamentary recess, and on September 13 the house ended its sittings until November 6. On the day before they dispersed, the commons and lords suggested that during their absence the king should set up a commission under the great seal to treat with purchasers of church lands. If fair terms could not be decided between the two parties, the principles of an agreement were to be presented to parliament on its return. This decision, coupled with the one made earlier that owners and purchasers of church lands should suggest their own terms of settlement, proved to be the first step toward a new solution — one which obviated the need for a legislative settlement.[20]

The proposal to appoint a commission probably had its origin in the privy council. Many private and joint petitions had been submitted by purchasers to the king, pointing out the hardships which would be caused by a resumption of lands. The king and his counsellors were not disposed to ignore the interests of so large a group. One appeal, signed by several hundred people, persuaded the privy council at its meeting on August 1 to hold conversations between two or three representatives of the purchasers, the barons of the exchequer and the surveyor-general. By the end of August, these discussions were complete, and the king's advisers submitted their report. It was no doubt as a result of this that parliament put forward the idea of a commission.[21]

In his closing speech to parliament on September 13, the lord chancellor promised speedy action to give effect to the proposal. The king, he declared, had given much thought to the problem of sales, and, realizing the difficulties that had prevented members from reaching a conclusion, he promised that as soon as they departed, he would 'put that Business, concerning Sales, into such a Way of Dispatch, that he doubts not you will find a good Progress made in it before your coming together again; and I believe that Persons concerned will be very much to blame, if they receive not good

---

[19] *Old parliamentary history*, XXII, 415–16; *CJ*, VIII, 112.

[20] *CJ*, VIII, 167; *LJ*, VI, 170; *Old parliamentary history*, XXII, 476.

[21] Great Britain, Public record office, PC 2/54, fols. 101, 150 (hereafter cited as 'PRO').

Satisfaction.'[22]

The commission was announced in a proclamation of October 7, 1660. The preamble enlarged upon the king's generosity in considering the compensation of purchasers and gave as explanation his desire to fulfil the promises made in the Declaration of Breda. The commissioners were named and their tasks enumerated. They were to collect the names of all purchasers of land; information on the prices they had paid, how much money had been paid in cash and how much in bills, how many bills had been proved to be forgeries; what profits had been made from rents and resales, timber cutting, and improvements; which purchasers had bought because they were tenants and which had bought for gain. The commissioners were authorized to summon anyone to give evidence who held documents and information relating to the sales. The inquiry was to embrace both crown and church lands, but not delinquents' lands. Since the information would take some time to collect, the proclamation informed purchasers of crown lands that they might collect all arrears of rent, including those due at Michaelmas. A week later, a letter was dispatched from the king to the Archbishop of Canterbury, expressing his wish that those who had been tenants and purchasers of church lands should receive considerate treatment in the grant of leases. The clergy was asked to give priority in the issue of leases to former tenants but, in the case of land sold under the Commonwealth to members of the army, to refrain from issuing any leases for the time being, except to former purchasers or their assigns.[23]

When once parliament resumed its sittings, all petitions from purchasers were handed to the commissioners. The bill for sales, however, remained under discussion by the grand committee of the house. Andrew Marvell, reporting progress to the Hull city council, described the concern of the commons to get the bill through as quickly as possible. Yet no agreement followed. The many amendments added to the original draft were incorporated in the main text, and the new version was placed before the commons on December 11. By that time, the king's intention to dissolve parliament at the end of the month was known, and great haste was necessary if the act was to be passed in time. Yet on December 4, Andrew Marvell wrote no longer of eagerness but of lack of inclination to pass the bill. The explanation came from other sources. The commissioners appointed by Charles II were functioning very

---

[22] *Old parliamentary history*, XXII, 493.
[23] *Somers tracts*, VII, 465–69; Kennett, pp. 273, 279; PRO, PC 2/55, fol. 7.

satisfactorily: *Mercurius Publicus* commented on the satisfaction of both purchasers and former owners; the lord chancellor at the dissolution on December 29 expressed the same view, adding that the commission would continue its work pending the election of the new chamber. In view of its success, both houses of parliament were more than ready to leave the matter in its hands.[24]

When the Cavalier Parliament assembled in May 1661, the lord chancellor made no reference to the land problem. The omission was significant because it had earned comment in all earlier speeches. It was a sign that the issue was regarded as settled. One year after the restoration of the king the matter had abruptly ceased to command attention. The bill for sales was not revived, and no more time was spent on legislation relating to the land settlement.

The protracted discussions that had taken place in parliament had been almost entirely confined to the subject of public lands. Apart from establishing the principle that forfeited land should be restored to its former owners, they brought little comfort to private royalists. Parliament had made it clear that it was not prepared to consider general legislation on their behalf. They were recommended instead to prosecute a claim for recovery within five years in a court of law, though without any guarantee of a favorable outcome. Royalists who had been deprived of the revenues of their estates for eight years and more did not embark on a lawsuit with equanimity. Instead, they looked for other methods, which avoided such uncertainty of outcome, delay, and expense.

Members of the nobility found an answer in private acts. In the words of Lord Craven's petition, this was a means to 'avoid multiplicity of suits.' The house of lords gave the bills a ready hearing, but they were not so well received in the commons. In the first place, the house was fully occupied in discussing bills of a general nature. In the second, we know, on the authority of Clarendon, that private bills caused much acrimonious debate. They threatened to defeat the aim of the king that recriminations in public concerning the events of the

---

[24] *CJ*, VIII, 178, 179, 204; *Old parliamentary history*, XXIII, 7, 91; Andrew Marvell, *The complete works in verse and prose*, ed. A. B. Grosart (London, 1872–75), II, 19, 30; Kennett, p. 326. Ludlow gave a different version of the matter, describing the method used 'to lay those asleep who had purchased the Church-lands, and who promised themselves full satisfaction, according to the message from Breda; commissioners being appointed to that end. But after they had sate once or twice, and heard bitter invectives against the late sales, as sacrilegious, the purchasers finding them for the most part to be of the same opinion, were quite discouraged from any further prosecution of that matter' (E. Ludlow, *Memoirs*, II, 301).

Interregnum should cease. Charles watched closely the passage of these private bills and, in at least one instance, took action to prevent the passing of a bill which had caused much wrangling.[25] In the third place, the marked increase in the number of private bills denoted a tendency, which displeased Charles as much as it, no doubt, displeased the lawyers, to expand the role of parliament as a court of equity. The king's objections were explicitly stated at the prorogation of the Cavalier Parliament in May 1662.[26] But they were in evidence long before this and may have contributed to the early death of many private bills. Of fifty royalists owning land in the southeastern counties, only the Duke of Newcastle, Lord Colepeper, and Lord Arundel obtained private acts.[27]

The sympathy of the house of lords found an outlet instead in a series of orders, which, in straightforward cases, were as effective in restoring the land of the nobility as private acts. The orders were dispatched to the sheriffs in the counties, instructing them to put delinquents in possession of their land. Little resistance was encountered from purchasers, partly, no doubt, as Clarendon explained, because they recognized the measure as one of the king's obligations to his followers, partly also because resistance was fruitless. Those who were obstructive were taken into custody until they submitted.[28]

Private acts and orders of the house of lords solved the problems of a minority—of eight out of a sample of fifty royalists with land in southeastern England. The remainder, however, did not present so large a problem as their numbers might suggest, for some had recovered their property before 1660. Nineteen out of fifty royalists (38 per cent) had managed before 1660 to buy back forty-five out of their one hundred and seventy-nine properties (25 per cent). The situation was quite different from that obtaining on crown and church lands, where no undercover restitution of land had been

---

[25] Great Britain, Historical manuscripts commission, Rept. VII, appendix i, p. 93 (hereafter cited as 'HMC'); *The life of Edward, earl of Clarendon* (Oxford, 1827), II, 152–55.

[26] 'Let not men have too much cause to fear, that the settlements they make of their estates shall be too easily unsettled, when they are dead, by the power of parliaments' (*Somers tracts*, VII, 547).

[27] *Statutes of the realm*, Vol. V, list of personal acts in the index. Altogether, eleven acts for the restoration of estates were passed, of which six concerned lands in Ireland, or England and Ireland.

[28] Lancashire county record office, Derby 12, Nos. 13 and 14; *The life of Edward, earl of Clarendon*, II, 24. For examples of obstruction by purchasers, see *LJ*, XI, 73; HMC, Rept. VII, appendix i, pp. 109, 112.

possible before 1660. These facts partly justify parliament's lack of policy on the subject of private lands. The problem was small compared with that presented by public lands.

Cast upon their own resources, royalists sometimes succeeded in reaching private agreements with purchasers outside the courts of law. Few of these find any place in official documents, but three which were enrolled on the Close Rolls indicate the circumstances in which voluntary agreements were possible. In each case the royalist and the purchaser had mutually beneficial business connections with each other. In the first, Sir Lewis Dyve, the royalist, received a loan from the Commonwealth purchaser, who thus continued in possession of the land as the mortgagee. In the second and third examples, the purchasers had bought the land from the Commonwealth Trustees at the express wish of the delinquent.[29] The absence of many examples of this kind underlines what would in any case be obvious— that unless the purchaser had served, or promised in the future to serve, the interests of the returning royalist, there was no common ground for an agreement between them. Moreover, if private agreements were at all possible, they were usually completed before 1660. This conclusion is strengthened by the statements of royalists who in later years disclosed their efforts to retrieve their land. Their attempts were often abortive, but if they were made, they were made long before 1660.

Royalists who failed to secure a private act or private agreement applied to the courts for a writ of trespass and ejectment. From correspondence passing, before the Restoration, between Sir Thomas Mompesson in England and Sir Edward Nicholas, one of the king's counsellors abroad, it is clear that this procedure fell far short of royalist hopes. 'I am advised,' wrote Mompesson to Nicholas on March 30, 1660, 'to let noe time slippe but to seale leases of ejectment and beginne a shute against those that are in possestion of Tho. Mortimers lands. Some of the tennants have been talked with about it and, I beleeve, will give possession, soe that by that meanes wee shall become the defendants and they that now receive the rent must sue us, if they intend to hold the lands. I desire a word or two of advice from you concerning this businesse as soon as with conveniencie you can, for I shall not proceed in it without your consent, though I am much

---

[29] For Sir Lewis Dyve's transactions, see PRO, C54/4048, No. 32; 4079, No. 12. The other two examples concern (1) the royalist, Henry Winde, and the purchaser, Nicholas Hammond, for which see C54/4067, No. 12; C7, 317, 2; and (2) the royalist, James Bunce, and the purchaser, Abraham Babington, for which see HMC, Rept. VII, appendix i, p. 87; PRO, C54/4056, No. 13.

encouradged that, if I did it, I should goe neere to carrie the shute.'
The reply was dated a few days later. 'Doe well to forbeare to beginne
a sute against those that have possession of your land for that an
ejectment is a sute that will not quickly be decided and, if the tymes
change, you must upon every alteracion of government begin a new
sute; besides I am not without hope you may come to your owne
without a suyte at law, and I am not single in this advise, but Lo.
Chancellor and others here are alsoe of opinion that you should now
forbeare any such course till you see what the next parliament will
resolve in order to his Majesty's establishment.'[30] As we know from
subsequent events, the royal party were disappointed. They had to
take their chance in the courts on the same footing as other claimants
to land, with no certainty that the outcome would be successful.

All the disadvantages of this method of recovery were brought out
in the subsequent experiences of royalists. Though they had a strong
case to plead, the machinery of the law gave equal advantages to their
opponents. Purchasers were entitled to appeal against unfavourable
verdicts and to impose endless delays. The complaint of royalists that
their opponents obstructed a settlement out of a vindictive desire to
involve them in long and expensive lawsuits was a matter of common
form. And while the cases dragged on, the purchaser continued to
enjoy the revenues from the estates.[31]

Although it has proved impossible to find many of these lawsuits in
the records of the courts, there is no doubt that the majority of
royalists successfully regained their land. Two historians writing of
the Restoration settlement in recent years have cast doubt on this
view, and with some justification, for contemporaries, such as
Edward Waterhouse, alleged that more than one parliamentarian
kept his spoil and prospered under both regimes.[32] Such substance as
these allegations possessed can emerge only from a detailed study of
land owned by the more prominent members of Cromwell's party
before and after 1660. The later history of royalist land suggests that

---

[30] *The Nicholas papers. Correspondence of Sir Edward Nicholas, Secretary of State*,
ed. Sir G. F. Warner (Camden Soc.; 3d ser.; London, 1920) XXXI, 206–8. For an
example of a royalist who anticipated a still less favourable settlement, assuming that
he would have to repurchase his land, see Lord Colepeper's will (Somerset House,
London, PCC 1660. No. 235).

[31] See, for example, HMC, Rept. VII, appendix i, p. 147*a*.

[32] David Ogg, *England in the reign of Charles II* (Oxford, 1934), pp. 162–63;
Christopher Hill, 'Land in the English revolution,' *Science and Society*, XIII (winter,
1948–49), 45–46; Edward Waterhouse, *The gentleman's monitor; or, a sober inspection
into the vertues, vices, and ordinary means of the rise and decay of men and families*
(London, 1665), p. 170.

the charge contained no more than a small grain of truth. Seventy per cent of the properties which were sold under the Commonwealth in southeastern England have been traced back to their owners in 1660, and further inquiry would probably yield more.[33] Evidence on land-ownership in wills, proceedings in chancery, judgments in the fire court (for property in the City of London), fines and recoveries, deeds and abstracts of title, and private memoirs all point to the one conclusion. Royalists regained their land in all but exceptional circumstances. The Earl of Cleveland did not recover Hackney manor, nor did he recover Bishop's Hall, Stepney. Even Stepney manor remained for many years entrusted in some way to the agents of William Hobson, the last purchaser.[34] But Cleveland's lands were bestowed by the treason trustees almost exclusively on his creditors. He still had to settle their claims when the land was restored to him in 1660. For this reason, a bill granting permission to sell the land and pay off Cleveland's debts was considered by the convention in the early months of its existence. The fact that so much of Cleveland's estate remained, temporarily or permanently, in the hands of purchasers represented the decisions of the barons of the exchequer, who undertook the task of determining how much money was still due to Cleveland's creditors.[35]

A suit at law was likely to fail only when royalists had prejudiced their titles by confirming sales to purchasers during the Interregnum. Such confirmatory releases, which had been obtained by purchasers at a price, were treated by parliament as 'voluntary sales,' which could not be undone. They came into the same category as the private sales by which royalists had raised money in order to compound for their delinquency.

The decision by parliament that voluntary sales should stand was

[33] Forty-five out of one hundred and seventy-nine estates were recovered before 1660, and at least eighty-one afterward.

[34] William Robinson, *The history and antiquities of the parish of Hackney in the county of Middlesex* (London, 1842–43), I, 304; Somerset House, PCC 1667, No. 137; London County Council, Muniments, BRA 666/26 (hereafter cited as 'LCC, Muniments'). A vague claim was made by Cleveland's heirs to Hackney manor in 1699, but it appears to have descended to the heirs of the Commonwealth purchaser, William Hobson (PRO, C5, 213/56 [1699]). For William Hobson's continuing interest in Stepney manor, see LCC, Muniments, not yet catalogued, Enfeoffment to John Cage, 1665.

[35] The barons of the exchequer drew up a detailed account of all the sums received by creditors in rents and profits and all expenditure on repairs, improvements, and taxation. Small wonder that the empowering act expired before they had completed their task. It was renewed in 1666 for another four years (House of Lords MSS, 13 Car. II, No. 20; 18 Car. II, No. 6).

incorporated in the Act for the Confirmation of Judicial Proceedings. It did not pass without protest from the royalist party, as the parliamentary discussions on a private bill for restoring the property of the Earl of Derby bear witness. Derby's bill had the apparently innocent intention of restoring him to his estates. When it was discussed by a committee of the house of lords, the fact emerged that Derby had asked many of his tenants to buy their farms from the treason trustees and had granted them a release of the property in return for a sum of money equivalent to three years' purchase. The text of Derby's bill contained two controversial clauses: one provided for an investigation into the rents due for the years before 1660; the other invalidated all conveyances of land made by Derby during the Interregnum. These two clauses, since they constituted breaches of the Act of Indemnity and the Act for the Confirmation of Judicial Proceedings, met strong opposition in committee. The judges were called in to give a decision, but although they pronounced that the bills did not contravene the existing acts, no one was apparently persuaded by this verdict. When the bill was debated in the commons in December 1660, it found little favour, even though the Earl of Derby made it known that he intended to refund with interest the purchase money paid by his tenants, while taking into account the profits they had received. The deadlock was ended by the king, who decided to assist the Earl of Derby privately. Purchasers who had been confirmed in possession of their holdings by Derby retained them, while the earl was led to expect a private gift of land or money from the king.[36]

It is useful to bear in mind the reasons for Lord Derby's failure when we come to consider the account given by the Duchess of Newcastle of her husband's experiences at the Restoration. Newcastle was fortunate in procuring a private act for the recovery of his property. His wife, omitting mention of this fact, records that the duke had to go to law to recover his land, that his suits were 'more chargeable than advantageous' to him, and that the courts 'showed no favour to him.' In drawing up an account of all the lands which her

---

[36] *Old parliamentary history*, XXIII, 49–50; House of lords MSS, Minutes of committees, May 16, 1661–May 13, 1664, pp. 23–24. The minutes of the committee on Derby's bill are dated June 1661, but this seems to be a mistake for June 1660, since the king announced that the bill would be dropped on December 29, 1660. Thos. Aspden in *Historical sketches of the House of Stanley and biography of Edward Geoffrey, 14th earl of Derby* (2d ed.; Preston, 1877) does not mention a grant of land by the king but says that, by making economies, Derby was able to buy some of his estates back (pp. 34–35).

husband had held at various times, she showed that lands which he failed to regain in 1660 were worth £2,015 annually. Their capital value of £40,000 represented one-eleventh of Newcastle's total assets. The only acceptable explanation of this loss is that Newcastle had voluntarily alienated the land before 1660 and thus met the same obstacles in the courts as the Earl of Derby encountered in parliament.[37]

Owners who had bought forfeited land at second hand assembled an array of arguments for special treatment, which deserved sympathetic hearing in the courts of equity, although their cause was lost in the courts of common law. With some justice, they argued that they had incurred greater financial hardship than purchasers at first hand. The latter had bought in a great number of cases in the early 1650's and had had some years in which to enjoy the profits. Moreover, they had paid part of the money in public faith bills, bought up at considerably less than face value. Purchasers at second hand had paid as much as the land was worth on the best title and had had little time to reap any profit.[38] Their petitions were no doubt encouraged by the fact that the lords and commons showed considerable sympathy for ancient tenants who had bought crown and church lands. Purchasers of royalist land at second hand were of much the same class, being small farmers who had bought land because they already rented it or because it lay near their existing holdings. There is no evidence, however, that their appeals were heard with any sympathy or elicited practical help. Occasionally purchasers procured from the royalist owner favourable leases. Purchasers at second hand of Stepney manor retained some of their holdings after 1660 in return for a money payment. They were asked to pay the Earl of Cleveland twenty-one year's purchase for lands and thirteen years' purchase for houses and wharfs, if—so the agreement ran—they had not already paid as much to any other person. This last condition suggests that the price paid during the Interregnum was taken into consideration. Although a final settlement between the Earl and his tenants was long delayed—it still had not passed beyond the preliminary stage in 1671—one purchaser at least was satisfied. Sir Henry Johnson, who had bought the Gatehouse in Stepney with

[37] Margaret, duchess of Newcastle, *The lives of William Cavendishe, duke of Newcastle, and of his wife Margaret, duchess of Newcastle*, ed. M. A. Lower (London, 1872), pp. 69–81.
[38] British Museum, London, *Thomason tracts*, E 1030 (II), 'Some considerations offered to publique view' (hereafter cited as 'BM').

other property during the fifties, was rebuilding it with obvious assurance of possession in the seventies.[39]

Purchasers at second hand with more than a small tenement at stake were prepared to fight a long battle in the court of chancery. The heirs of Samuel Wightwick, who had had to surrender Hampstead Marshall manor, charged John Baker, who had sold it to them in 1655, with a breach of covenant. The case which began its course in 1662 was transferred to the common-law courts after four hearings. When a verdict was given in favour of Baker and the Wightwicks were ordered to pay costs, they succeeded in getting a retrial of the case. Judgment two years later was given in favour of Baker, the first purchaser.[40]

A dispute of a more elaborate nature, but arising from similar circumstances, was heard between William Booth and William Sankey, purchasers at different times of the same property in Drury Lane. Their case, too, was passed from chancery to common law court and back again, and judgment at length was given for the second purchaser.[41] These two suits, similar in nature but ending with contrary verdicts, summed up the predicament of all purchasers at second hand. The outcome of suits could not be predicted, since everything depended on the circumstances of the case. A lawsuit might compensate a purchaser for his losses, but it might equally well ruin him.

The key to the terms of the settlement relating to crown and church lands lay in the decision appointing commissioners to investigate in detail the accounts of Commonwealth purchasers. A report was demanded of every penny received and paid out in connection with forfeited land, and from this report commissioners were expected to have little difficulty in deciding whether purchasers deserved compensation or not. As we have already seen, the duties of the commissioners did not extend to the examination of transactions relating to delinquents' estates. Nevertheless, when financial disputes between delinquents and purchasers came into the court of chancery, they were dealt with in exactly the same way. When the Duke of Buckingham claimed his estate from the Commonwealth purchaser, Francis Dodsworth, in 1659, the judgment provided for a full inquiry

---

[39] PRO, E112/455, No. 975; H. Green and R. Wigram, *Chronicles of Blackwall Yard* (London, 1881), p. 17.

[40] PRO, C10, 72/169 (1664); C6, 160/15 (1662); C33/219, fol. 578; C33/221, fols. 12, 211, 537, 665.

[41] PRO, C8, 162/3 (1667); C33/229, fol. 625; C33/231, fols. 44, 203, 467, 505.

into the profits and expenditure of the latter. Similarly, when John, earl of Rochester, heir of the delinquent Henry, Lord Wilmot, claimed equity of redemption in 1666 against three creditor purchasers of his estate in Hertfordshire, an account embracing profits and expenditure over a long period of years was submitted by the latter.[42]

It is fair to assume that a large number of purchasers of crown and church lands received no compensation whatever because their profits during the Interregnum had been more than adequate and that purchasers of delinquents' lands who resigned their interests without protest did so because they knew that no appeals of hardship would stand up to a scrutiny as severe as that carried out by the king's commissioners and the chancery judges.

Nevertheless, the conflict of claims between former tenants and Commonwealth purchasers was not resolved without a quarrel. Clarendon spoke of the bitterness caused by the behaviour of church landlords when both tenants and purchasers expected to be granted leases for the old rent and a moderate fine. The owners, anxious to get quick returns from land of which they had been too long deprived, ignored the claims of both parties and let the land to the highest bidder. The interference by king and parliament in the letting policy of church landlords was, no doubt, prompted by the outcry which these incidents aroused.[43]

Purchasers of crown and church lands who presented a good case of hardship to the commissioners appear, from rather meagre evidence, to have received fair compensation. Ralph Darnell, an assistant clerk to the commons under the Commonwealth, was offered two alternatives—repayment of the original purchase money plus interest at 6 per cent, minus the profits received, or a lease of the manor for three lives. Sarah Grant, whose husband bought a house in the Strand, previously rented from the dean and chapter of Westminster, claimed a new lease at the Restoration and received it for a fine of 'only £80.' John Pym, who bought the former crown manor of Hogsthorpe in Lincolnshire, subsequently held it by lease. The task of the commissioners in weighing the competitive claims of purchaser against former tenant must often have been extremely difficult, however, and may not always have given the purchaser complete satisfaction. How did the dean and chapter of Peterborough decide

---

[42] PRO, C7, 453/71 (1660); C9, 44/99 (1666).
[43] *Life of Clarendon*, II, 7–10.

between the claims of a purchaser, and of a tenant whose case was commended to them by the king because he had assisted the restoration of the monarchy?[44]

It is impossible to tell how often the purchasers of royalist land received compensatory leases. Tenant purchasers of Lord Craven's houses in Spur Alley off the Strand were still his tenants in 1668, but on what terms has not been discovered. Purchasers at second hand of the Earl of Cleveland's estate in Toddington, Bedfordshire, secured leases of ninety-nine years in the place of their freeholds. But, as the following letter shows, the agreement rested entirely on the discretion of the Earl of Cleveland and his steward. The steward wrote to a former purchaser in January 1666:

> Mr. Prior, you may remember I told you both at Toddington and London that you should be justly dealt withall, if you would have patience untill the Earle of Cleavelands Bill was passed. I thought you had beleived mee, and depended upon mee but I find that you have by subtilty procured a conveyance from my Lord of Cleaveland against his will or knowledge that you put into itt, as by writeing under his hand and seale he hath declared, upon which I have been at Councell and am well assured your deeds will be ineffectuall to you and have met my Lord of Cleaveland and my Lord Lovelace before Sir Henneage Finch, who hath told them as much; you will find that this indirect dealing of yours will be recompenced with the destruction of your Estate not only of this you have lately got, but of that you had before, and it shall not be in the power of any body to protect you. And if you doe not immediately come up & deliver up the deeds, that things may be as they were, what I have sayd will infallibly come to pass.[45]

Extreme care was taken by parliament and the crown to announce terms of compensation which would placate the purchasers of crown and church lands. This was regarded as an obligation implicit in the - Declaration of Breda. The explanation for parliament's casual treatment of royalists whose lands had been compulsorily sold and of the purchasers of their land lay in the size and complexity of the problem. The sale of royalists' lands had produced far less social dislocation

---

[44] *CJ*, VIII, 224–25; PRO, C8, 144/52 (1661); LCC, Muniments, BRA 329/19; PRO, E134, 20–21 Chas. II, Hilary 6; CSPD (1661–62), p. 384. Problems connected with the settlement of crown and church lands would be solved if the records of the commission of inquiry could be found. They were listed by Giuseppi among the special commissions of inquiry, Records of the exchequer—king's remembrancer. He had evidently seen them at the public record office, yet they are not now to be found among this class of documents (M. S. Giuseppi, *A guide to the MSS preserved in the public record office* [London, 1923], I, 111).

[45] PRO, E112/357, 48; BM. Add. MS 22186, fol. 12.

than that caused by the sale of public lands, since many royalists bought back their estates before 1660. Moreover, the title to land of royalists who did not retrieve their property required far more detailed investigation than that of crown and church landlords. The Commonwealth sales had been so little concerned with destroying the economic power and prestige of royalists that the latter had had little difficulty, if they were so disposed, in preserving their interest in the land. The sales trustees had themselves recognized this interest by giving mortgaged lands to creditors. The new purchasers recognized this continuing interest by negotiating with royalists for private releases after the official sale had taken place. By 1660 the situation was not the simple one that might have existed if every royalist had resigned all interest in his land and if no purchaser had had any title to the land apart from the one conferred by the trustees. The situation was confused by all kinds of contracts and covenants between royalists and purchasers, some admitted in the sales themselves when creditors were given the land, others negotiated afterward. The problem of restoring royalist lands—in so far as it had not already been solved before 1660—was rendered so complex by the acts of royalists themselves that no simple formula for restitution could have been devised. Process at law was essential to disentangle, in each separate case, the acts of the treason trustees from these voluntary acts of royalists which could not be reversed.

In 1662 a plot to overthrow the monarchy and proclaim a republic was uncovered. The threat of disturbance had passed before the conspiracy came to light, for the plotters, having failed to prepare their manifesto in time, had decided to abandon the project.[46] The interest of this abortive episode lies in the fact that one of the points of the scheduled manifesto was to be a confirmation of sales. If the conspirators expected to win adherents by this proposal, no evidence giving foundation to their hopes at that late date has been found. The acquiescence of purchasers of crown and church land in the restoration of the king was ensured by the setting-up of a commission to inquire into their financial losses. Purchasers of delinquents' land, although not guaranteed compensation, were often dealt with benevolently by reinstated owners. If purchasers had never entertained the possibility that the sales would endure, a good lease was handsome satisfaction.

POSTSCRIPT

For further details on the negotiations for a land settlement, with more emphasis on the fate of Crown and Church lands than on those of private Royalists, see H. J. Habakkuk, 'The Land Settlement and the Restoration of Charles II', *Trans. Royal Historical Soc.*, Fifth Ser., 28, 1978, pp. 201–22.

IX

FARMING IN KESTEVEN, 1540–1640[1]

KESTEVEN is a convenient administrative unit of Lincolnshire with
good natural boundaries. It is divided from Lindsey by the river
Witham, and from Holland by the fen. It is a less satisfactory unit for
the study of farming history. By the sixteenth century, if not
earlier, soil differences had given rise to three types of farming
economy, the first typical of the clay lowlands, the second typical of
the limestone heath, and the third typical of farms which included
fenland as well as clay and limestone. No amount of generalisation
can assimilate these regions into one. The open-field system was still
the broad framework of husbandry in each, but it was a framework
only, within which the detailed routine of farming life was extremely
varied.

This diversity of farming practice does not make for a simple
picture, but it has the great merit of underlining one of the facts of
agrarian history which ought to be a platitude, that by the sixteenth
century regional specialisation had reached an advanced stage. This
specialisation did not consist simply in the production of certain
crops and stock to meet current market demands. These demands
might modify the farmer's programme from year to year, but they
could never eradicate regional differences which had a far older
history. The more deeply engrained characteristics of regions
reflected the facts of physical environment, the size and social
structure of the community inhabiting the district, and the interaction of the one upon the other. Regional differences, in short, were
the outcome of more than eight centuries of human effort in reaching
a compromise with nature.

The study of farming regions inevitably prompts reflection on the
causes that underlie the uneven pace of agrarian change in different
parts of the country. The fact that the arable land was used more
economically in one place than another, that enclosure of the open
fields proceeded more rapidly here than there, that the colonisation

[1] This paper was read to a weekend school on the Kesteven Village, organised by the
Lincolnshire Local History Society at Stoke Rochford Training College in April 1954.

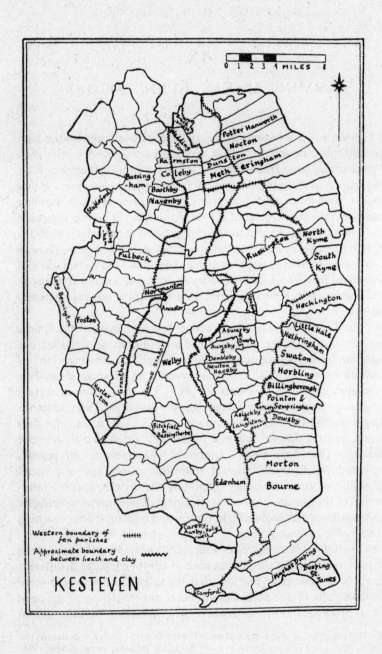

0 1 2 3 4 MILES 8

Potter Hanworth
Nocton
Dunston
Meth eringham
Harmston
Coleby
Boothby
Navenby
Bassing
-ham
Skellesford
Stapleford
Welbourn
Fulbeck
North Kyme
South Kyme
Rushington
Normanton
Heckington
Ancaster
Foston
Aswarby
& Swarby
Aunsby &
Dembleby
Newton &
Haceby
Little Hale
Helpringham
Swaton
Horbling
Billingborough
Pointon &
Sempringham
Dowsby
Welby
Long Bennington
Grantham
ERMINE STREET
Harlax
ton
Aslackby &
Laughton
Bitchfield
& Bassingthorpe
Morton
Bourne
Edenham
Careby
Aunby, Holy
-well
Market Deeping
Deeping
St.
James
Stamford

Western boundary of ┼┼┼┼┼┼
   fen parishes

Approximate boundary ∿∿∿∿
   between heath and clay

KESTEVEN

of the waste was almost complete in Leicestershire in the sixteenth century, when it had hardly begun on the neighbouring Lincolnshire cliff and heath—these are fundamental questions which the historian is called upon to answer. It is probable that more light will be shed on them by the detailed study of farming regions than by the study of changing market demands alone. This essay, which surveys a century of Kesteven's farming history, is intended as a contribution towards that fuller account of English agrarian development which will consider the twofold problem of regional differentiation and uneven growth.

Before examining contemporary documents, it is essential to study the map of Kesteven, for this immediately reveals some of the special topographical features of the division which had an important bearing on husbandry. A ridge of limestone, representing the tapering end of the Cotswold oolite, runs from south to north through the centre of Kesteven. It is broad and much complicated by other geological formations south of Ancaster, but becomes narrow and steep as it nears Lincoln. To the west of the ridge lies a vale of liassic clay, lightened in many places by sand and gravel patches, and intersected by the rivers Witham and Brant, Foston Beck and other small streams which flow into the Trent. On the other side of the limestone ridge lies another long, narrow belt of Oxford and boulder clay, fringed by a further strip of low-lying fen-ground.[2]

As these four main soil belts run from north to south, the villages tend to form parallel lines near the junction of the geological formations. Two lines of villages lie on either side of the limestone heath, the more conspicuous one situated along the western scarp, on the frontier between the Upper lias clays and the limestone, and extending from Bracebridge, through Waddington, Coleby and Boothby to Grantham and beyond. The other lies on the eastern side of the heath, on river gravel somewhat below the junction of the limestone and clay, and stretches from Potter Hanworth, through Nocton and Dunston southward. Yet a third line of villages is set on gravel beds between the clay and the fen, and is most clearly visible between Heckington and Market Deeping.

Since the geological formations are narrow in width, many parishes are so shaped as to include more than one kind of soil. Parishes like Harmston, Coleby, and Boothby extend from the

<hr>

[2] This is a much simplified picture, analysed in greater detail in L. W. H. Payling, 'Geology and place names in Kesteven,' *Leeds Studies in English and kindred Languages*, no. 4, 1935, p. 1 *et seq.*

western clays on to the limestone heath, where Ermine Street, running along the top of the ridge, gives them their eastern boudary. Nocton, Dunston and Metheringham have a similar shape, but are even longer, and stretch from the limestone heath, where Ermine Street is their western boundary, across the central clay vale of Lincolnshire into the fenland. Two of the principal roads through Kesteven—Ermine Street, which joins Stamford and Lincoln, and Mareham Lane, which joins Peterborough with Bourne, Sleaford and Lincoln—run in a north-south direction, and so impose on the villages through which they pass a certain uniformity of field plan. The village street divides the parishes into two halves, and before enclosure divided the open arable between a west and an east field, leaving the meadow and the common at the two extremities.[3] Later the two fields were sub-divided or new ones were added to them. In the sixteenth century, Horbling, for example, had an East and a West Field, and a Mickledale Field. Billingborough had an East and a West Field and a Mill Field. Dowsby had a West Field, East Field, and Millfield, and in addition a Hawefield, which was probably an assart from the heath.[4]

The two most conspicuous series of large rectangular parishes in Kesteven lie to the north of Ancaster on the limestone ridge, and along the fen boundary between Lincoln and Market Deeping. The remaining parishes, in the western lowlands, and south of Ancaster are of irregular shape and usually much smaller. These were the areas which offered a more workable soil, a drier situation, or a better supply of water in the early days of settlement, and which, by the time of Domesday, had the largest populations. These differences in population density have left a permanent mark on the modern map in the small size of parishes, particularly in the wapentakes of Aveland, Aswardhurne, and Beltisloe. Yet some of the parishes which look small today represent modern amalgamations of still smaller parishes: Aswarby, for example, which has been united with Swarby; Aunsby with Dembleby; Newton with Haceby; and Lenton with Keisby and Osgodby.

By the mid-sixteenth century, the distribution of population in Kesteven had changed little from that of Domesday times. The clay

---

[3] Potter Hanworth did not have an East and a West Field, but in the disposition of its arable round the village, its heath common at the western end of the parish and meadow and fen common at the eastern end, it was typical. See the map given in K. Norgate and M. H. Footman, 'Notes for a History of Potter Hanworth,' *A.A.S.R.* XXVI, p. 384.
[4] Lincoln Record Office (LRO), Glebe Terriers, II, 1577–80. ff. 378, 511; I. f.267.

and gravel lowlands of both western and eastern Kesteven were more densely settled than the limestone. Indeed, one would hardly expect otherwise. The only significant development was that some of the clayland parishes extending into the fen had grown more populous. Helpringham, Horbling, Billingborough, Morton, Langtoft, Market Deeping and Deeping St. James were as thickly inhabited as the small parishes of the clay vales. This was undoubtedly due to the presence of extensive fen grazing which exercised the same attraction on the landless peasant as it did in the fenland of Holland and Axholme.[5]

The two clayland zones of Kesteven on either side of the heath were regions of mixed husbandry in the sixteenth and seventeenth centuries, and differed little in their farming practice from the claylands of Leicestershire. On a small group of seven farms in Leicestershire in 1607, all but one had between 62 and 73 per cent of their land under crops. Taking them together, 68 per cent of the land was given over to arable, 13 per cent to ley, 15 per cent to meadow, and rather less than 4 per cent to closes. This pattern of land use resembles that obtaining on the manor of Long Bennington and Foston in 1612, where $67\frac{1}{2}$ per cent of the cultivated land was under crops, $9\frac{1}{2}$ per cent was meadow, 19 per cent pasture and 4 per cent in closes. This is the only example of land use found so far for the Kesteven clay vales.[6]

The size of farm holdings in the claylands reflected a society in which the economic resources of the land were very unevenly distributed. This fact has already been made familiar through taxation documents. The subsidy assessment of 1524 shows that at least a third of the population of most villages had no land or had insufficient to support them, and laboured for wages for part if not the whole of the working week. This conclusion is strengthened by two manorial surveys for this district from the first half of the seventeenth century. At Long Bennington in 1612 nearly thirty-three per cent of the holdings were of five acres of less, that is to say, too small to keep a family independent of other sources of income. At Edenham in 1647, 38 per cent were of this small size. The poorer husbandmen with between five and twenty acres accounted for between 15 and 20 per cent of the tenants of both manors, while the

[5] Compare the statement of a contemporary observer in 1675 on the numbers of poor in the Isle of Axholme. 'The liberty the common people have of graving in the common is that which draws multitudes of the poor sort from all the countries adjacent to come and inhabit in the Isle.'—John Rylands Library, Rylands Charter 2550.

[6] W. G. Hoskins, *Essays in Leicestership History*, pp. 140–41; Public Record Office (PRO), DL 43, 6, 18.

better-off husbandmen and yeomen, farming anything between
twenty and a hundred acres apiece, represented 51 per cent of the
tenants at Long Bennington and 38 per cent at Edenham. One farmer
at Long Bennington and four at Edenham farmed more than a
hundred acres each. Edenham was a large manor, however, and could
accommodate this unusual number of big farmers.[7]

Every farmer's holding of arable, meadow, and pasture closes
carried with it certain rights of grazing on the common, but they were
not as generous as those enjoyed by the parishes which possessed
fenland. There was less land to play with because the parishes were
smaller. Cattle stints had long been customary, and by the sixteenth
century were having to be whittled down to ensure that the demands
of an increasing population did not outrun the supply of grass. At
Foston, for example, where the common had once been large enough
to feed two beasts belonging to every tenant of an oxgang of land,
these beast gates had had to be 'taken out of every man's inheritance'
before 1612 because the grazing would 'not maintain them well for six
weeks together.'[8] At Harlaxton, the villagers had no waste left in
Elizabeth's reign, and were only able to keep a village bull because
two freeholders had surrendered two acres of land for the purpose.
Moreover, one of the common pastures, used as a neat pasture, bore
the signs of ridge and furrow. It too may have had to be taken out of
the arable fields owing to the grazing shortage. Alternatively, it may
have been subject to alternate husbandry. Either way, the change of
land use must have been preceded by some change of tenancy in order
to allow arable held by the demesne lord or his tenant to be turned
into common. Changes like this must have been fairly common over
the centuries. It is an error to assume that the use of the fields and
pastures remained the same from the time of the first printed record
until the beginning of enclosure. There is more than one casual statement in sixteenth century documents to the effect that the common
pastures and waste land had ridge and furrow in them, thus proving
to the satisfaction of the inhabitants that they had once been cropped,
though not within the memory of any living man.[9]

[7] PRO DL 43, 6, 18; LRO 2 Ancaster 4/4. The figures for Edenham exclude the
demesne.

[8] PRO DL 43, 6, 18.

[9] PRO E 178/1334; E 134, 32 Eliz., Hil. 12; E134, 35 Eliz., Easter 12. A survey of
Waddington in 1609 described a cowpasture with signs of ridge and furrow in it.
Pademore, alias Peatmoor in Luddington, Isle of Axholme, was waste land of Crowle
manor, lying in ridge and furrow. PRO DL 42, 119, ff. 20, 22; E 134, 14 Chas. I, Mich.
II.

One of the modifications of open-field husbandry, which was not hindered by ownership rights, and had, indeed, become general practice throughout the Midlands by the sixteenth century, was the laying down of arable strips to temporary grass. Usually this was carried out furlong by furlong, and some general village agreement must have preceded it. But there was nothing to prevent the individual peasant doing the same with his own strips independently of his neighbours. The advantage of the practice was that it increased the pasture area, and at the same time rested the arable for a few years. It was a course recommended by William Fitzherbert, though he wrote in terms suggesting that it was a liberty which only the farmer of enclosed land could enjoy. 'And if any of his thre closes that he hath for his corne be worne or ware bare, than he may breke and plowe up his close that he hade for his layse, or the close that he hadde for his commen pasture, or bothe, and sowe them with corne, and let the other lye for a tyme, and so shall he have alway reist grounde, the which wil beare moche corne with lytel donge.'[10]

It may be that the name 'ley farming' with its modern connotation is too precise a term to apply to the somewhat unsystematic form of alternate husbandry current at this period. No contemporary statement has been found to show how long the ley was kept under grass before being ploughed again. At Waddington, on the limestone ridge, where ley farming was as common as in the claylands, a survey of 1609 described 'lands that have been ploughed, now leys,' but it did not give any hint of the time when the change took place. A dispute occurred at South Witham in Elizabeth's reign, because some of the tenants had sown their leys with corn four or five years previously, and had had it trodden down by their neighbours. But here again there was no information on the age of the ley, only a hint that in some villages, farmers were not allowed to fall out of step with village plans in selecting strips for conversion.[11]

Nevertheless, if the length of the ley was uncertain, its purpose—to extend the pasture area and rest the arable—was not fundamentally different from that of modern ley farming. Moreover, it gave the open-field farmer scope for a more flexible scheme of land management than that conventionally accredited to open-field husbandry, and in that way prolonged the life of the old system. It still had drawbacks, of course. When the fields were thrown open after

---

[10] *Tudor Economic Documents*, ed. R. H. Tawney and Eileen Power, I. p. 23.
[11] PRO DL 42, 119, ff. 20, 22; E 134, 18 and 19 Eliz., Mich. 13; 13 Eliz., Easter 8. For one of the first discussions of ley farming, see W. G. Hoskins, *op. cit.*, p. 123 *et seq.*

harvest, the rich continued to overcharge the fields with their stock at the expense of the poor. The tethering of animals was never entirely satisfactory, for they were always breaking loose and trampling down the corn. The tenants of Fulbeck, who had to tether three hundred draft cattle and milch kine in this way, thought that as much as a third of the harvest was often lost through farmers' carelessness or wilful negligence.[12] It was these shortcomings of the open-field system, together with the fact that it wasted time and land, which precipitated enclosure. The drawback once suggested by historians, that so long as a man's strips lay intermixed with his neighbours he could not convert his arable to grass, has proved to be bad history.

There is no way of discovering how all the arable land of manors situated in the clay vales of Kesteven was divided among different crops. But by using the probate inventories, which are lists compiled after death of the property of peasants who disposed of their goods by will, some account can be given of the stock and crops of individual farmers. Unfortunately, the poorest peasants with few or no possessions are not represented in the inventories. The average peasant of the inventories, therefore, was somewhat better-off than the average farmer of the manorial survey. The manorial survey suggests that the middling-sized farm was 25 acres. The probate inventories suggest that the average farmer had about twenty acres under crops each year, which implies a farm of some fifty acres. The discrepancy in these two results arises from the different scales of social measurement implicit in the two classes of document. But the value of averages in farming studies at this period lies not so much in the absolute figures they give of farms or crop acreages as in the opportunity they afford for comparing results between regions. It is of less importance, therefore, to correlate the evidence of the manorial survey and the inventories than to compare like documents with like for different parts of the country. In short, the fact that the average Kesteven clayland farmer had twenty acres of crops each year need not be taken too literally. What is significant is that the crop acreage of the average Leicestershire clayland farmer was the same, while that of the fenland peasant of Holland was less than half the size. It is by comparisons such as these that we can begin to explain the differing class structure and the different farm economies of neighbouring peasant communities.

If the available inventories do not fully represent all classes of rural

[12] PRO C 2. Jas I, F. 13, 5.

society, they at least yield a good sample of yeomen, husbandmen, and better-off labourers. They suggest that the principal crops grown by these three classes of peasants in the claylands throughout the sixteenth and early seventeenth centuries were barley, peas and wheat. Barley was the grain grown in largest quantity, and occupied 38 per cent, on an average, of the sown land. It was also the principal crop throughout the county, for Lincolnshire was the main source of barley supplies to the Yorkshire brewers and maltsters.[13] Peas took up 31 per cent of the ground, and wheat 21 per cent. Rye was grown on some of the gravel patches amid the clays, and was a more important crop than in other parts of Lincolnshire, but it still did not occupy on an average more than seven per cent of the sown area. Oats occupied another three per cent. Hemp was grown in very small amounts, usually in the garth beside the house. But it was not every man's crop as it was in the fenland.[14]

There was little difference between the crop selection of the Kesteven clayland farmer and the Leicestershire farmer in the Tudor period, except in the proportion of land which each gave to wheat and pulses. The Leicestershire peasant was unaccountably backward in growing wheat, and instead of devoting 21 per cent of his land to this crop, allowed it only eleven per cent, giving the rest to additional pulses.[15]

Stock kept in the Kesteven claylands by the average farmer in the sixteenth century numbered about ten head of cattle, four horses, about twenty-eight sheep, and six pigs. Owing to the presence of woodland, the number of pigs was larger than that found on the limestone, but the number of sheep was smaller, because the better and more extensive sheepwalks lay on the hills not in the vales.

The portrait of the average peasant sketches a type, but obliterates all the individuality in wealth and scale of enterprise of different classes of peasants. The middle rank of farmers in the village were the husbandmen, but at the two extremes there was the richest gentleman or yeoman, and the poorest labourer. We learn something of the wealth of the former in an inventory of the goods of Richard Taylor of Beckingham, the richest farmer in Kesteven in a sample taken from the 1590's. His personal property was valued at £399 7s. 0d., which was more than twelve times the average. His house was large with generous outbuildings, and he had kept abreast of the building

---

[13] *Letters and Papers, Henry VIII*, XV (1540), p. 160.

[14] LRO Miscellaneous probate inventories; Joan Thirsk, *Fenland Farming in the Sixteenth Century*, Occasional Paper, No. 3, University College of Leicester, p. 38.

[15] W. G. Hoskins, *op. cit.*, p. 160 *et seq.*

fashion by having a new parlour built with a chamber above it. He had a pane of glass in a window, separately mentioned because it was worth four shillings. His herd of cattle numbered 148 animals, his horses sixteen, his sheep 128, and his pigs 23. Some of his oxen were let out on hire, and some of his cows as well. Sixty acres were under crops at the time of his death, but his barley land was not yet sown, and would probably have brought the total to something in the neighbourhood of a hundred acres. He was styled a yeoman but he was, in fact, farming on the scale of the squires. Richard Taylor was exceptionally well-to-do, but it was not unusual for the better-off yeomen to have as many horses and sheep as he, though forty cattle were more usual than 140 and eleven pigs more usual than 23. To measure the gulf between the rich farmer, and the poor labourer who nevertheless had some possessions worth valuing, we may take by way of example the inventory of Robert Sturte of Stapleford, who died in 1591. His household goods consisted of two coffers, one cupboard, a shelf, a bed, bedding, and kitchen utensils. His only animals were two kine, his ownly crops hemp and hay worth five shillings.[16]

Besides the clayland parishes of Kesteven, there was a second group of villages situated on the clays, which possessed large tracts of fen common. In certain respects their farming arrangements were akin to those of the clayland parishes. In other ways, however, they resembled the fen villages of Holland. They had open fields, which the parishes of Holland either never had, or had long ago abandoned, and they still kept a high proportion of their cultivated land under crops. In Heckington, the average on seven farms was 53 per cent, whereas in Holland most manors appear to have had between 20 and 40 per cent of their land in arable. But the fen common in Kesteven amounted to thousands of acres as it did in Holland. Heckington manor had 2,330 acres, the manor of East and West Deeping ten thousand acres. Instead of a stinted pasture which was the lot of most Kesteven peasants, the inhabitants of the fen had common for all their stock without restriction.[17] In consequence they were disposed to be graziers.

The pre-eminence of cattle rearing and more particularly fattening is well illustrated in depositions taken in Charles I's reign concerning

---

[16] LRO Probate Inventories, 80. 16; 81. 449.
[17] PRO E 134, 9 Chas. I, Easter 34; E317, Lincs., 15; Joan Thirsk, *op. cit.*, pp. 22–3. Generally speaking, the Car Dike was the boundary between the cultivated land and the fen common in Kesteven.

the use of the common pastures of Heckington. The commons amounted to 2,330 acres. It was evidently reasonably good quality grazing, for two-thirds of it were estimated to be worth ten shillings an acre, and the wetter third five shillings an acre. The manorial lord had the usual brovage rights, which permitted him to take in as many strangers' cattle as he liked from May Day to Martinmas, a right of which he took full advantage. The commoners had unstinted rights, of which some also took full advantage. Mary Jenkinson testified personally that when she lived in the village in the 1590's she had been in the habit of taking into the fen sixty cows, eight oxen, twenty young beasts, thirty horses and a thousand sheep. Yet Mary Jenkinson was only one of a hundred toft-owners with the same rights, and if they had not the same resources, they were not above taking in the stock of outsiders under cover of their own.[18]

The main emphasis of husbandry in the Kesteven fen was on the rearing and fattening of cattle and sheep. Meat, wool, and hides were the principal sources of the farmer's income. We catch a glimpse of the flourishing local market for some of these commodities in the inventory of property of Thomas Wright of Ruskington, who died in 1562 leaving eighteen cattle, four horses, two hundred sheep and some pigs. He had owing to him £5 6s. 8d. for four bullocks, 36s. 8d. for a mare and foal, £3 9s. 2d. for a horse, 33s. 4d. for a bay nag, 33s. 4d. for a steer, 2s. 8d. for three calfskins, 5s. 6d. for another six calf skins, 26s. 8d. for sheepskins, and 22s. for six dog skins. His clients and debtors lived all around him, at Anwick and Roxholm, at Navenby, Heighington, Billinghay, Howell, Donington and Quadring and on the other side of the heath at Norton Disney and Bassingham. At the same time, of course, much of the produce of the claylands went considerably further afield than this. In Henry VIII's reign, Robert Thurlebecke of Walcot was sending his wool to Halifax; a merchant of the Staple at Calais was arranging to receive Kesteven wool shipped via Boston.[19]

Like the parishes of Holland, the whole of the Kesteven fenland was involved in the drainage schemes sponsored by James I and Charles I. For nearly a generation, its economy was disrupted, its routine of life and work disturbed by the intrusion of engineers and adventurers, draining and appropriating a large part of the land. The first district to be affected weas the southernmost fen between Bourne and Crowland, where drainage was begun late in Elizabeth's reign

---

[18] PRO E 134, 9 Chas. I, Easter 34; C 2. Jas. I, T11/32.
[19] LRO Probate Inventory 40, 213; PRO C 1, 912, 29; C 1, 241, 66.

under Captain Thomas Lovell. Lovell's efforts were declared inadequate in the next reign, and the work was resumed in 1619 by Sir William Ayloffe and Anthony Thomas. The drainage of the fen lying immediately to the north, extending from South Kyme to Morton, was undertaken by the Earl of Lindsey between 1635 and 1636. This fen was always known as the Lindsey Level. The parishes stretching along the Witham from Lincoln to South Kyme were spared a similar disorganisation of their life and husbandry, but were required to contribute to schemes for the improvement of the Witham channel.

None of the engineering operations sponsored by the Crown were carried through without hostile interference by the inhabitants. It was not the fact of drainage which kindled indignation so much as the method by which it was initiated and paid for. Outsiders, with little or no knowledge of the fen or the changes which it underwent through the seasons, laying out dikes as and where they pleased, altering the condition of the land, sometimes for better, sometimes for worse, and then appropriating two-thirds of the commons for themselves and the Crown, were unlikely to receive a warm welcome from peasants who had hitherto relied on the fen commons as one of the principal pillars of their husbandry. A petition from the county of Lincoln in 1641 summed up the inhabitants' point of view in these words. 'They (the drainers) take the one half of our common and fen grounds for supposed draining the rest, which they make and leave much worse than they found it, and yet expect melioration from our severals. . . . If we proceed at law for trial of our titles, we are sued, pursevanted, imprisoned and are ordered by the Lords of the Council not to proceed except at the Council Board or before the Commissioners of Sewers.'[20]

Captain Thomas Lovell was the first to taste the bitterness of local opposition in 1598. His account of his experience differed hardly at all from that of his successors a generation later. Opposition was of two kinds. It began with 'cavills and exceptions'—disputes by the commoners on points of law—about boundaries and common rights. These delayed, but did not halt operations. When once they were settled, opposition took the sharper form of 'open tumults and violence,' often encouraged, or at least not hindered, by the local justices of the peace.[21] In the early summer of 1602, men and women living in the neighbourhood of Deeping Fen took up arms against Lovell and threw down dikes, finding an unexpected friend in Mr.

[20] CSPD, 1640-41, p. 592.
[21] PRO SP 14, 8, no. 84.

Lacy, a justice of the peace living at Deeping St. James, who refused to assist in indicting the rioters.[22]

When the second drainage of Deeping fen was carried out in James I's reign, the drainers and the Crown managed to take possession of their share of the common in time to enjoy it for a few years before the Civil War broke out. In the Lindsey Level, on the other hand, the partition of the commons was still being contested by the inhabitants on the eve of the war. The Earl of Lindsey had been promised 14,000 acres when the drainage was complete. At the partition of the commons, however, the Earl of Lincoln, who was lord of Aslackby, Pointon, Billingborough, Horbling and Swaton, complained that the part allotted to him and his tenants 'is upon every flood sooner, longer, and deeper surrounded than heretofore within any man's memory.' The local population made their views even clearer by throwing down banks, destroying crops, and pulling down the houses on the drainers' allotments.[23] When the Civil War broke out, this private war was still in progress, and the peasants living in the Lindsey Level found themselves the leaders of a much wider and yet spontaneous movement to eject the drainers and their tenants from every fen in Lincolnshire. The inhabitants of Little Hale and Horbling took possession of their common in March 1642. By May, 1642 the Earl of Lindsey and other participants had been completely driven out of the Level. The Crown was dispossessed of its share at the same time.[24] The drained lands were turned once more into common pastures and remained so at least until the Restoration in 1660. Most of them, indeed, remained common until the second half of the eighteenth century, when drainage schemes on an entirely new and more acceptable financial basis were introduced hand in hand with enclosure by Parliamentary act.

It has been customary for writers on the drainage of the fen, following the lead of William Dugdale, to deplore the wilful destruction of the dikes by the inhabitants, and to blame upon them the postponement of the drainage for another century and a half. This is a view of the facts, seen in the light of after-events, not in the light of conditions before the drainage began. Ultimately it was necessary and inevitable that the fen should be properly drained. But at the beginning of the seventeenth century, the husbandry of the fen was so well adjusted to the natural conditions that even this winter flooding

[22] *Hist. MSS. Comm., Hatfield MSS.* part 12, pp. 177–80.
[23] *Hist. MSS. Comm., Report IV*, p. 70; CSPD 1640–41, p. 446.
[24] *Hist. MSS. Comm., Report V*, pp. 24, 22; PRO LR2, 287, ff. 1–13.

of the fen represented not loss but gain to the inhabitants—gain in the increase of fish and fowl, and gain manifest in the summer time when the fen was found to bear a richer harvest of hay and grazing than any that the dry pastures of the uplands could show.

A contemporary writer who enumerated the advantages of draining, and tried to dispose of the arguments of his opponents unwittingly showed how much there was to be said for leaving the fen as it was.[25] Apart from the fact that the drainage could not be paid for without depriving the fenlanders of a large share of their commons, it threatened to deprive them also of some valuable natural resources: sedge and turf for fuel, and thack and reed for roofing. It was a matter for serious doubt whether the ordinary commoner would gain as much as he lost by the drainage. One thing was certain, the change could not be carried out without disturbing his routine, and indeed changing the whole balance of his husbandry.

The distinguishing characteristic of farming in the parishes situated on the limestone heath was the predominance of sheep. Husbandry was centred upon the production of good quality wool, which was highly esteemed by the East Anglian clothier. Large areas of the heath were taken up with sheep walks, and although these walks were condemned in the sixteenth century for the crime of devouring villages, they had also been responsible at an earlier date for the birth of some of Kesteven's smaller hamlets. Such, indeed, was the origin of Aunby, a small settlement at the southernmost end of Kesteven, first referred to in written records in the early fourteenth century. A document of Charles I's reign tells us that 'the village of Aunby was first constituted from the ancient use of pasture for sheep, beasts, and a warren of conies, with a shepherd's and warrener's lodge only thereon.' It was later 'broken up for corn, and used in tillage and building of houses fit for husbandry and other necessaries there convenient,' at which time the inhabitants of Holywell, the parent village, and Aunby were 'the first planters, tenants and occupiers thereof.'[26] Aunby was not unusual in its origin. There is no doubt that many more villages grew up in the same way, starting as shepherds' dwellings on summer pastures, and later emerging as self-contained communities with their own field systems. Place names are a useful clue to their origin on the marshland coast of Lincolnshire. But in this case, it is the geographical situation of Aunby which is the tell-tale. Aunby lies on a lonely side-road, on the extreme edge of the

[25] PRO SP 16, 339, no. 27 (1636?).
[26] LRO. H 54/43.

parish. The lane going down to Aunby leads nowhere except to a track which passes over the hill on a straight course for Holywell.

In the sixteenth century, population was more densely settled on the steep western scarp of the heath, where the parishes extend into the clay than in the smaller and more narrowly confined parishes of the eastern slope. Compared with the rest of Kesteven, however, the whole of the heathland was a thinly settled district, with average or less than average population densities—the kind of country which Lord Harley, seeing it in 1723, thought very fine for hunting.[27]

Sparseness of settlement was reflected in the size of farms and the social composition of the population. In the first place, although it is difficult to find documentary material about a region where neither the Crown nor the Church held much property, the probate inventories of peasants living in the district suggest that the average farm was larger than that found in the clay or fen lowlands. The average amount of land sown with crops each year was 26 acres, whereas the fen farmer of Holland had eight acres and the Kesteven clayland farmer had twenty. This result is not surprising since the limestone was the least fertile of the three soils. The harvest per acre was smaller and there was little competition for land. In the second place, the villages on the heath were usually smaller than those of the clay. In Beltisloe wapentake, which includes mostly limestone parishes, the villages varied in size in the mid-sixteenth century from twelve to forty families. The average was 26 families. In Aveland wapentake, which lies on clay, the size varied between seventeen and sixty-five families, the average village having thirty-seven families. Thirdly the limestone villages were more likely than the clayland villages to have a resident squire who was conspicuously richer than the rest of the population. Roughly one in four villages in Beltisloe had a subsidy payer whose goods or land were valued at £40 p.a. or more. In the twenty-two villages of Aveland wapentake (excluding the market town of Bourne) only about one in ten could boast an inhabitant of equivalent wealth. Finally, the proportion of poorest taxpayers, comprising mostly labourers paying on their wages, was lower on the limestone than on the clay. Thirty-nine per cent of the taxpayers of Beltisloe were wage labourers, whereas in the claylands of Aveland the proportion was $45\frac{1}{2}$ per cent. This evidence strengthens conclusions reached above that land was more plentiful in the upland parishes than in the lowlands. Fewer people, in

[27] *Hist. MSS. Comm.*, Portland, vol. 6, p. 84.

consequence, had to supplement their income from their holdings by working for wages as well.[28]

Husbandry in the limestone villages was carried on within the framework of the ordinary open-field system. Parishes which extended from the top of the cliff westward into the clays held to a fairly uniform pattern in the disposition of their arable, meadow and pasture. The arable was usually situated in between the lowest clays and the summit of the ridge, and was divided into two parts, known as the Lowfields and the Highfields. The meadow and some of the pastures lay on the lowest and coldest clay, the rest of the pasture, mainly for sheep, lay on the top of the heath.[29] In 1562 William Barton of Fulbeck had barley growing 'on the heath,' presumably in the Highfield, and 'other barley,' presumably in the Lowfield. Edward Thorpe of Coleby, who died in 1592, had his cultivated land in Coleby on the side of the hill, and his meadow in Bassingham in the clay vale. A farm in Navenby contained arable land in North High Field, Middle High Field, and South High Field, two roads up the side of the cliff making the obvious dividing line between each field. The leys and the meadow were in the two Lowfields, North Low Field and South Low Field, divided by a single road. The meadow in these fields lay along one bank of the River Brant, which is the western boundary of the parish.[30]

The low inherent fertility of the soil dictated crop specialisation on the limestone. Barley was much the largest crop, and occupied 53 per cent of the sown area of the average farm. Peas took up 25 per cent, wheat ten per cent, rye six per cent and oats six per cent. Pulses were a less important fodder crop than in the claylands where the soil was better suited to their growth. But to compensate oats were given a larger place, and in the seventeenth century lentils were occasionally grown. The principal difference between the uplands and lowlands, however, lay in the proportion of land given to wheat and barley, of which soil was the determinant. It enabled the clayland peasant to give 21 per cent of his land to wheat where the heath peasant was wiser to restrict his wheat to ten per cent of his sown land and devote more to barley.[31]

This evidence of crop selection is taken from farms of greatly

[28] LRO Miscellaneous Probate Inventories; British Museum, Harleian MS. 618; PRO E 179, 136, 333; 346.
[29] See, for example, evidence submitted by Susanna Ladington concerning the cultivation of her farm at Fulbeck—PRO E 134, 12 Chas. II, Mich. 60.
[30] LRO Probate Inventories, 40, 217; 82, 284; Ancaster 2, 4, 7.
[31] LRO Miscellaneous Probate Inventories.

varying sizes. On closer analysis, it becomes apparent that the system differed somewhat between large and small farms. The larger the farm the more ground was given to peas. Thomas Paychett of Normanton, for example, who had 47 acres under crops in 1562 gave 34 per cent to peas, whereas William Lyon with a small holding of $9\frac{1}{2}$ acres in 1534 allotted to peas the average proportion of 26 per cent. The account book of Sir John and Thomas Hatcher, who farmed at Careby in the reigns of James I and Charles I and kept an account of crops grown for fifteen years between 1625 and 1639, also illustrates the tendency of large farms to divide the spring-sown land more equally between peas and barley. In 1625 the Hatchers gave $17\frac{1}{2}$ per cent of their sown land to wheat and rye, 34 per cent to barley, 36 per cent to peas and 12 per cent to oats. That year they had $74\frac{1}{2}$ acres under crops. In 1629 when the total land under the plough was $91\frac{1}{2}$ acres, 42 per cent was given to barley, 16 per cent to wheat and rye, and $41\frac{1}{2}$ per cent to peas and oats.[32]

One of John Leland's few comments on the Kesteven countryside, when he visited it in about 1538, concerned the large flocks of sheep on the Lincoln heath. It went to the heart of the matter, for the mainstay of animal husbandry in the upland parishes was sheep. Bishop Sanderson's notes on Welby in the mid-seventeenth century might equally well have been applied to any one of the villages in this region, except that few were as completely destitute of meadow ground. "A barren dry heathy soil,' he wrote, 'but by the industry of the inhabitants it beareth good corn, and the soil is sound for sheep, which they summer and take the wool, and then sell them off against the winter, for there is no meadow ground, but the inhabitants seek abroad for hay into other towns about.' The hillside pastures were set aside as sheepwalks during the day, and the sheep were folded at night on the arable fields. At Aunby, the hamlet which originated among the sheep pastures of Holywell, there was still an extensive sheep walk at the beginning of the seventeenth century. The demesnes of Edenham manor in 1647 included a Great Sheep Walk of 166 acres.[33]

The average sheep flock on the limestone numbered 34 sheep in the sixteenth century, and only about one in four of the peasants who left property by will at death, had none at all. The reasonably well-to-do yeomen like Thomas Heachyll of Normanton, who died in 1591, had as many as four hundred, while gentlemen farmers like Thomas Cony

[32] LRO Probate Inventories, 40, 191; 5, 78; LRO Holywell 97, 22, 1.
[33] *Leland's Itinerary in England*, ed. L. Toulmin Smith, part I, p. 28; LRO Monson VII, 43, f.834; LRO Holywell 54, 4; 7; 2 Ancaster 4, 4.

of Bassingthorpe and John and Thomas Hatcher of Careby had over a thousand.[34]

From the account book of John and Thomas Hatcher of Careby,[35] a picture emerges of the heathland economy in the early seventeenth century. Owner of the whole town of Careby, Sir John Hatcher was presented to the enclosure commissioners in 1607 for decaying four farmhouses and converting eighty acres of arable to pasture. His account book confirms that his principal interest was sheep, for the sale of wool in autumn for a sum of between £150 and £200 constituted his largest single market transaction each year. Always it was sold at one deal, usually to Mr. Reynolds of Colchester, who doubtless applied it to the manufacture of bays and says for which that town was famous. Once, however, the wool clip was bought by John Ruggett of Sudbury, the chief centre of the cloth industry in Suffolk, and another year it was taken up by Robert Mawley of Oundle, Northamptonshire.

While Hatcher's most distant contact was the wool merchant of Essex, his purchases and sales of sheep, cattle, and horses show that there was not a market of importance within a radius of forty miles of his home which he failed to attend. In May each year, he or his son went to Newark Fair to buy oxen and fat cattle. In June they went to Rothwell Fair, just beyond Kettering, to buy coach horses, and in August to Corby to buy and sell dairy cattle. In September they were at Waltham for steers, cows, and calves. All the year round they were visiting the Stamford markets, buying and selling wethers and oxen, and laying in a store of groceries, hemp, cheese and cloth.

Stourbridge and Peterborough Fairs in September were the occasion for buying further household stores—hops, tar, sack cloth, more cheese, and onions for which the fenland was particularly noted. Boston supplied the household with groceries, olives, fish, salt, and wine, and sometimes hempseed. Other markets were patronised only occasionally. Once Thomas Hatcher went to Stow Green and bought a couple of fat steers, and two kine; once to Spilsby to buy ten steers; once to Grantham for bullocks, and once to Market Harborough Fair for a bull and twelve heifers. He went to Nottingham in June, 1638 and bought eight bullocks, to Melton Mowbray the same year for a bay gelding, and later in 1638 to Fotheringhay to sell it, or another like it. As his account book shows the cattle markets which he favoured were usually within reasonable

[34] LRO Probate Inventories 82, 248; *Lincs. N. & Q.*, I, pp. 114–6; LRO Holywell 97, 22, 1.
[35] Ibid.

distance of his home, either in the same county or in the adjoining ones. But once in 1629 he went as far afield as Derbyshire to buy a young bull.

Most kitchen and household supplies came from local markets, particularly Boston and Stamford. But a regular trip was made to London at least once, if not twice a year, for additional purchases. Usually, Squire Hatcher did not go himself, but sent his servant Bartholomew Davies, who transacted his master's legal business, ordered a suit or a couple of jackets from the tailor for him, bought socks for the children, and spices, currants, raisins, prunes, and sugar for the kitchen.

So much journeying either heightened Thomas Hatcher's appreciation of domestic comfort, or made him increasingly sensitive to the vagaries of contemporary fashion. Whichever the reason his house underwent a number of improvements inside and out. Indoor work involved the transport of wainscots from King's Lynn in 1631. For the making of an orchard in the same year, trees were brought from Apethorpe in Northamptonshire, and from Greatford in the fens near Stamford. A mason worked some stone steps leading into the orchard, and in April the ground of the orchard was levelled. The next year more trees were brought from Apethorpe: four apricots, two nectarines, together with peach, cherry and plum trees.

The modern map still bears traces of the forest which once covered the southern portion of Kesteven, and gave to the division a name which means 'district in the wood.' It did not accurately describe the landscape of the whole. In the same way, the later fame of Kesteven as a centre of noble parks and country seats was derived from the country houses which adorned only one portion of the administrative district, namely the southern heathland. The variety of the landscape of Kesteven has been obscured by the prominence of its limestone backbone, forming a steep ridge in the north, and dissolving into undulating hills in the south. The history of Kesteven in the sixteenth century suggests that, from the farming point of view at least, it was not one region but three. The mixed farming of the clay vales, the mainly pastoral husbandry of the fens, the sheep and barley farming of the heath each contributed a different group of commodities to the national larder. There are hints too of differences in the size, class composition, and wealth of the communities inhabiting the three regions. But it is impossible to establish these with any certainty until a more detailed study has been done of its earlier settlement history. Place names alone are proof that certain aspects of regional diversity in Kesteven are as old as recorded history.

X

THE ISLE OF AXHOLME BEFORE VERMUYDEN

THE Isle of Axholme lies in the extreme north-western corner of Lincolnshire, separated from that county by the river Trent, and from Nottinghamshire and Yorkshire by the former channels of the Idle, the Torne, and the Don. Once one of the natural regions of England with an economy distinct from that of its neighbours, it retains to this day its island situation, and something of the insularity which marked its former way of life.

The isle covers an area of 51,104 acres, and until the nineteenth century contained nine parishes, of which three, Belton, Epworth, and Haxey, each measured more than eight thousand acres, and together encompassed more than half the island. Large parishes denote a sparse population in the early days of settlement. The land was unattractive to the farmer, for much of it was permanently inundated, and all of it exposed to the floodwaters of the Humber, the Trent, and smaller rivers. The island was not densely settled at the beginning, therefore, but served the invaders as a corridor to the Midlands. First the Danes and then the Normans contributed vernacular elements to make up its modern name.[1]

Scant attention has hitherto been paid to the farming history of the island before the drainage operations of the seventeenth century. Vermuyden has held the centre of the stage ever since Dugdale in his *History of Imbanking and Draining* described his efforts at draining Hatfield Chase and the flooded parts of Axholme, and deplored the opposition he encountered from the islanders.[2] Dugdale was echoing the official view of an obstinate, ignorant peasantry, clinging to a miserable life because they were incapable of grasping the superior

[1] According to Ekwall, the meaning of the name Axholme is 'the home or island of Haxey', Haxey being a village in Axholme, meaning perhaps 'Haks island'. The Normans added the synonym 'isle'. The result was 'Isle of Axeyholme', later contracted to Isle of Axholme. E. Ekwall, *Concise Oxford Dictionary of English Place Names.*

[2] W. Dugdale, *The History of Imbanking and Draining* . . , 1662, p. 145.

benefits of drainage. The same story has been told with additional detail many times since. Writers have admitted that Vermuyden made mistakes. George Dunston went so far as to say that 'while he (Vermuyden) effectively drained Hatfield and Thorne, he made the condition of the Islanders considerably worse than before.'[3] But no one has yet attempted to see the project in its contemporary setting, as a scheme summarily embarked upon, without much prior investigation into the islanders' old way of life, or consideration of its merits.

It is the purpose of this article to examine farming practice in the Isle of Axholme in the sixteenth and early seventeenth centuries, in order to judge the drainage project from the point of view of the inhabitants. Seen in this way, Vermuyden's work appears not as an attempt to establish a system of husbandry where none had been before, but to substitute one economy for another. The old economy was pastoral, the new one arable. We can look back on the controversy three hundred years later and see the triumph of Vermuyden's plans. The island was effectively drained, and nowadays cereals, roots, and green vegetables are its principal crops. But long before Vermuyden's day, the islanders had evolved a system of husbandry which had come to terms with nature, and made good use of the existing resources. The principal produce of the isle was meat, dairy produce, leather, wheat, and hemp—commodities for which there was a steady demand in sixteenth-century England. Vermuyden promised to make the fen fertile for rape and corn, apparently unaware that the old husbandry could fully justify itself on economic grounds. His struggle with the islanders was not, therefore a struggle to create prosperity in place of poverty; its object was to substitute a new economy for the traditional one.

Axholme can best be described as a lop-sided version of the shape of England and Wales.[4] A central ridge with a maximum height of 133 feet runs the length of the island from north to south, occupies about one-quarter of the total area, and accommodates the principal townships of Crowle, Belton, Epworth, and Haxey, as well as a number of hamlets. The market towns were Crowle and Epworth, but

---

[3] G. Dunston, *The Rivers of Axholme*, p. 27. This book contains the best account of the condition of the island before and during the drainage operations. It omits, as does this article also, any account of Vermuyden's work in Hatfield Chase. Although the drainage of Hatfield Chase and the fens of Axholme was one scheme, it is probable that the condition of each before the drainage was different. Even so, the oft-repeated statement that Hatfield Chase was a useless waste land needs to be tested by the facts, and a fresh study of the sources seems desirable.

[4] See map on p. 152.

all four main centres of population were comparatively large. In 1603 over 150 families lived in each parish.[5]

Originally, the whole of the island was comprised within the ancient manor of Epworth and its members. In the seventeenth century one of these was severed from it, when Crowle manor, which occupied the northern quarter, was conveyed by Charles I to the City of London as part of the Ditchfield grant.[6] The rest, with the exception of some small estates,[7] remained the property of the Crown. It comprised the manor of Epworth, which stretched from Althorpe and Belton south as far as Burnham, and the manor of Westwood, another member of Epworth, which stretched from Burnham to the southern boundary.

By the sixteenth century the Isle of Axholme had a large population of small peasants. More than a quarter of the tenants of Westwood manor had holdings of one acre and less, and over half (54 per cent) had five acres or less.[8] Arthur Young's description of conditions in his day would have been equally appropriate two hundred years before. Farms, he said, were small, and amounted often to no more than four or five acres, while twenty acres supported a family very well because of the exceptional fertility of the land. The very poorest cottagers were proprietors of farms, and though 'poor respecting money,' were 'very happy respecting their mode of existence.'[9]

The arable land of the townships of Axholme lay on the higher ground of the central ridge. An Elizabethan map of part of the isle south of Haxey shows that the common fields lay within the triangle formed by the villages of Epworth, Haxey, and Owston, with no

[5] In 1603 Belton and Haxey parishes each had 700 communicants (approx. 210 families), Crowle 740 communicants (approx. 222 families), and Epworth 500 communicants (approx. 150 families). *The State of the Church*, ed. C. W. Foster, Lincoln Record Society, XXIII, 1926, pp. 340–51.

[6] W. Peck, *A Topographical Account of the Isle of Axholme*, 1815, Appendix No. 3. The Ditchfield grant was crown land conveyed to the City of London by Charles I in 1628 in satisfaction of two loans earlier made to him by the Corporation of London. For details, see R. Ashton, *The Crown and the Money Market, 1603–1640*, Oxford, 1960, pp. 132 sqq. Crowle manor was re-sold to Sir Gervase Elwes, Jeremiah Elwes, and Nicholas Hamerton.

[7] There are references to Haxey Hall Garth manor and Ancowe manor in a survey of 1607. These may be the 'smaller properties' referred to by Dunston, and said to have developed in the sixteenth century under crown ownership and to have been subsequently enfranchised. PRO LR 2, 256, f. 194; G. Dunston, *op. cit.*, p. 16.

[8] PRO LR 2, 256, f. 52 et seq. The first page of this survey is missing, but since the whole covers over 150 pages, the figures are not seriously defective.

[9] Arthur Young, *General View of the Agriculture of the County of Lincoln*, 1799, p. 17.

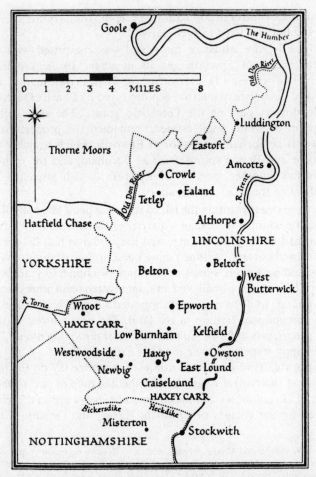

common pasture to separate them. Haxey fields abutted on the fields
of Burnham and Craiselound, Burnham fields on those of East
Lound and Owston, Owston fields on those of Kelfield and Kinnard's
Ferry. Many farmers held land in more than one village, but they did
not necessarily walk long distances between the different parts of
their holdings.[10]

The soil on the higher ground of Axholme was renowned for its
fertility long before Arthur Young proclaimed it 'among the finest in
England.' John Leland over two centuries earlier deemed it 'meatly
high ground, fertile of pasture, and corne,' and this view was

[10] PRO MPB 16; LR 2, 256, f. 52 et seq.

confirmed in more precise terms by Charles I's surveyors. The soil in the common fields of Epworth was said to be of two kinds. The major part lying nearest the town was a black, sandy ground, worth sixteen shillings an acre, the rest a stiff clay worth twelve shillings an acre. The richer soil was sown with hemp one year, barley the next, hemp the next, and rye the next, apparently without any fallows. At Crowle and Eastoft, on the other hand, there is evidence that the common fields were fallowed every fourth year, and this, taken together with the fact that in Westwood manor a balanced farm holding was dispersed in four fields, suggests that a four-course rotation, including one fallow, was the alternative system, if not the more usual one.[11] Certain it is that the arable land was more than usually fertile, and was made to bear as many crops as possible.

By the 1630's the enclosed demesne lands of Epworth manor were managed on a different system, eliminating the need for fallows altogether. A scheme of alternate husbandry was in operation, the tenants dividing their closes into three parts, and using them alternately for hay, grazing, and crops. The estate amounted to roughly 722 acres. In 1633, 56 per cent of the whole was subject to this alternative husbandry, and was classified as arable, meadow, and pasture. Twenty-two per cent was pasture, twenty per cent meadow, and only two per cent strictly arable.

This system of land use was frowned on by John Hynde, the surveyor of the manor, who argued that the land had originally been used for pasture and meadow, and that, since the soil was of the stiff clay kind, ploughing would quickly impoverish it. His reasoning was faulty, but since it would have been difficult with the implements then available to produce as good grassland after ploughing as before, he was probably right. At any rate, by 1650 his words had produced their effect. The land classified as arable, meadow, and pasture had fallen from 56 to 32 per cent, the arable area had increased from two to 31 per cent, and the pasture from 22 to 33 per cent. One of the leases contained a clause prohibiting the tenant from ploughing up meadow and ancient pasture.[12]

The holdings of manorial tenants in Axholme lay for the most part in strips in the open fields, and judging by Westwood manor, which comprised roughly one-quarter of the isle, included a high proportion

---

[11] Arthur Young, *op. cit.*, p. 10; G. Dunston, *op. cit.*, p. 18; PRO E 315, 390, f. 3/v; E 134, 13 Eliz., Easter 5; LR 2, 256, f. 52 et seq. The court roll of Crowle manor for 1381 contains the order for the fallowing of a quarter of the common fields every year. Lincoln Record Office (= LRO), Crowle Manor, 1, 34, 4.

[12] PRO E 315, 390, f. 37v.; E 317, Lincs. 16.

of arable. In 1607, Westwood had sixty per cent of its cultivated land under the plough, thirteen per cent meadow, ten per cent pasture, and ten per cent of enclosed ground. Four and a half per cent was described as arable, meadow, and pasture, and was probably used in the same way as the demesne land of Epworth manor, while the rest consisted of hempland, and land of unspecified use. Compared with the figures of land use in the Holland fenland, it is clear that the peasants of Westwood, and probably of Axholme as a whole, had a much higher proportion of their village lands under crops than the farmers of Holland.[13] At the same time, the economy of both was pastoral, for the village lands in both regions were only a fraction of the total land. Westwood manor was typical of Axholme estates in having only about 1,500 acres under cultivation, while its common, in which the tenants shared pasture rights with the tenants of Epworth manor, amounted to 14,000 acres.

Although the surveyors of Epworth spoke only of hemp, barley, and rye growing in the fields, these were not the only crops, nor even the most important ones. Peas and beans, oats, and wheat were grown as well as flax.[14] The probate inventories show that wheat occupied nearly three times as much ground as rye, and peas rather more than twice as much ground as hemp. Barley was the biggest crop, however, as it was in all other regions of Lincolnshire apart from the marshland, and occupied one-third of the sown area each year. Wheat occupied over a quarter of the sown area (28.4 per cent), and peas rather less than a fifth (18.8 per cent). Hemp occupied 8.4 per cent and rye 10.7 per cent. Oats and flax lay in store, but in the inventories of property used here are not found growing in the fields. They were probably less usual crops and were grown in small quantities.[15]

In the choice of crops there were significant differences between Axholme and the fenland of Holland. Not only was the arable acreage in Axholme relatively larger, but the balance struck between spring and winter sown crops was different. The two facts were probably interconnected, for all Lincolnshire farmers in the sixteenth century appear to have regarded the spring crops—barley and

[13] The arable amounted to between 40 and 42 per cent of the land of two manors in Skirbeck wapentake in Holland, and between 4 and 25 per cent in six manors in Elloe. Joan Thirsk, *Fenland Farming in the Sixteenth Century*, Occasional Paper No. 3, Department of English Local History, University College, Leicester, pp. 22–3. Strip cultivation continues at Epworth to this day.

[14] PRO E 134, 13 Eliz., Easter 5.

[15] LRO Probate inventories.

pulses—as the essential ones no matter what the size of their holdings. If more land was available for crops in one region than in another, then the less important crops, wheat and rye, were given a larger place. Hence more ground was given to winter corn in Axholme than in Holland. Three times as much wheat was grown, and four and a half times as much rye. A reduced acreage of barley (33.4 per cent in Axholme compared with 54 per cent in Holland), and of beans and peas (18.8 per cent in Axholme compared with 28.6 per cent in Holland) compensated for the larger acreage of wheat and rye. There was a much closer resemblance between the crops of Axholme and those of the marshland clays of Lincolnshire, for almost the same proportion of winter corn and barley was grown. Here the chief difference lay in the fact that Axholme grew hemp in quantity, while the marshland grew very little. The acreage devoted wholly to pulses in the marshland was divided in Axholme between hemp and peas.

The importance of hemp and flax is heavily underlined in the probate inventories. They were not grown as cash crops for direct sale, but laid the foundations of a comparatively large-scale domestic industry of spinning and weaving, which was of exceptional importance in the fen regions of Lincolnshire. Whereas few Axholme peasants had any wool in their possession, and less than one in five kept any sheep, hardly a single inventory has been found which does not mention hemp, and sometimes flax, together with the goods made from them. John Parish of Beltoft, who died in 1590, left linen cloth, femble, and harden cloth worth £3 5s. 4d., femble yarn and harden yarn worth ten shillings, heckled line and femble worth two shillings and sixpence, braked hemp worth six shillings and eightpence, and hemp and linseed worth ten shillings. John Farre of Epworth died a year later, and left sacks and sack yarn worth 26s. 8d., and hemp on the ground worth £3. John Harrison of Newbig left two acres of hemp, and forty yards of sack cloth worth 52s. Robert Pettinger of Haxey parish had hemp seed worth 13s. 4d. and three stones of hemp worth six shillings. John Pettinger of East Lound had nineteen yards of linen cloth, twenty-two yards of femble cloth, twenty-six yards of harden, pilled hemp and braked hemp, hemp ground and hemp seed, sack cloth and yarn.[16] These are random examples typical of the rest. They show that the flourishing sack- and canvas-making industry of Axholme in the nineteenth century had a long history behind it. To

[16] LRO Probate inventories, 80, 61; 81, 481, 448;80, 5, 34. Line is flax; femble = the female plant of the hemp; harden = a coarse hempen cloth; heckled line = dressed flax; braked hemp = dressed hemp; pilled hemp = stripped hemp.

the average peasant family of the sixteenth century it was a profitable by-employment. To the poor it was one of the principal ways of earning a living. One of the victories won by the inhabitants of Axholme in their prolonged legal battles with Vermuyden was an award in 1636 of £400 for a stock to employ the poor in the making of sack cloth, to compensate them for the loss of fishing and fowling rights.[17]

Meadow land constituted about thirteen per cent of the land of Westwood manor, and judging by the field names and the small size of individual holdings (two or three roods or one or two acres were the usual allotment) lay in strips grouped among the arable fields, wherever water was conveniently handy. Kelfield, for example, had its meadow along the banks of the Trent. Hay was cut in certain parts of the commons as well, and was specially abundant in wet summers. It was also gathered along the banks of the dikes, for a poor man called Bointon had the right to cut hay along the Idle river in return for keeping the banks in repair, and thus gave his name to Bointon Stile.[18]

Outside the ring of townships and arable fields lay extensive common pasture, of which the greater part lay in the western half of the isle. Crowle manor possessed between three and four thousand acres of common. Epworth manor, with its member manor of Westwood, possessed some fourteen thousand acres, roughly half of it lying south and west of Haxey and Owston, the rest north, east, and west of Epworth and Belton. The large commons of Epworth were divided by name into smaller units, but there were no barriers to the commoners' cattle apart from those imposed by the dikes. All the tenants of Epworth manor could graze their stock wherever they liked throughout the common.[19]

The common pasture was intersected by natural creeks and man-made dikes, serving to drain away the surplus water. Burnham Skiers was an example of a natural creek which separated Burnham's open fields from Haxey North Carr. Heckdike was a man-made channel, first mentioned in documents at the end of the thirteenth century, which linked natural creeks in the southern part of Haxey Carr with the river Trent. It was but one of several sewers built to drain the

[17] 'A Brief Account of the Drainage of the Levels of Hatfield Chase and parts adjacent in the counties of York, Lincoln, and Nottingham', by G. Stovin (1752). Printed in *Yorks Archaeolog. Journal*, XXXVII, 1951, pp. 386 ff.

[18] PRO E 134, Supplementary 901, 1D, Lincs.; E 134, 1 & 2 Jas. II, Hilary 25; E 134, 39 Eliz., Easter 14; LR 2, 256, f. 52 et seq.

[19] PRO E 134, Supplementary 9012, ID, Lincs., E 178, 5412.

commons before Vermuyden's day.[20]

Dikes, sewers, and rivers provided waterways all over the isle. The main traffic routes, which linked the western, southern, and eastern boundaries, were the river Idle, Bickersdike, and the river Trent. On these, ships with mast and sail carried passengers, and goods which included flax, hemp, corn, peat, and coal.[21] The dikes and creeks were mostly narrower waterways, leading off into the heart of the isle, and carrying small craft only. In winter the waterways multiplied and widened and provided an excellent system of communications. At the same time they acted as barriers to keep out strangers, and kept the island to some extent cut off from the rest of the world.[22]

From the commons the islanders took turves and wood for fuel and building repairs, sods and clay to manure their arable lands, hay at the right season, and fish and fowl. In Epworth manor, fishing rights in the river Idle were leased to a few individuals. But all tenants and inhabitants of the manor had the right to set bush nets and catch white fish on Wednesdays and Fridays.[23] Most important of all, the commons provided grazing for stock. So great was the feeding capacity of Crowle commons that the village regularly took in stock in summer from other places. Four grassmen, appointed by the townsfolk, supervised the arrangements, and 'tooke as many Cattell of forreyn Townes as they could gett.' The profits—about forty shillings a year—were put to the use of the town.[24]

Much of the commons, of course, lay under water in winter from Martinmas (November 11) till May Day. But this was not all loss. As the inhabitants of Epworth informed the king's commissioners, too late to undo Vermuyden's work, the floods brought with them 'a thick fatt water,' which enriched the ground, and enabled it to support large numbers of cattle, sheep, and pigs in summer. Moreover, although the fen was inundated in winter, there were always portions of the commons which remained dry. Some parts, like Curlehall Wood on Crowle commons, remained dry islands in the midst of water, and had to be reached by boat. Others adjoined the arable fields and were accessible all the year round. By using these

[20] PRO MPB 16; Gover, Mawer, and Stenton, *Place Names of Nottinghamshire*, English Place-Name Society, XVII, 1940, p. 39; PRO E 134, 39 Eliz., Easter 14. Two of the sewers in Haxey Carr were called Queen's Sewers, and were probably constructed in Elizabeth's reign.

[21] PRO E 178, 5412.

[22] The inhabitants claimed that Bickersdike kept out thieves and marauders from the isle until a bridge was built in Elizabeth's reign. See *infra*.

[23] PRO E 134, 1 & 2 Jas. II, Hilary 25.

[24] PRO E 134, Supplementary 901, 1D, Lincs.

dry patches of commons, as well as the grazing in the arable fields and enclosed pastures, the inhabitants of Epworth and Westwood manors kept 12,000 cattle besides sheep and swine during the winter.[25] Similarly, at Crowle the commoners had four hundred acres of 'good and drye pasture' in winter, and were able to keep 'a great Number of great Cattell and shepe goinge in their fennes and Common in Wynter season.' In dry years the grazing at Crowle was adequate. The only time of shortage was in wet years from the beginning of spring until Whitsuntide, when the stock was multiplying and the common was not yet dried out. No one at Crowle, however, had ever been known to farm out his stock in other places for want of grazing.[26]

The area of commons was large, and, as the commoners of Crowle declared, adequate for their needs. But an increase of population in the sixteenth century threatened to produce a pasture shortage in the southern part of Axholme, and gave rise to disputes between the islanders and their neighbours in Nottinghamshire about common rights. A hundred years earlier the farmers of Misterton and Stockwith in Nottinghamshire had taken cattle unchallenged into Haxey Carr.[27] But the population began to grow, and all villages faced the problem of feeding increasing numbers on a fixed amount of land. At Epworth manor one hundred additional cottages were built between about 1590 and 1630. At Misterton thirty new cottages were erected in forty years.[28] More people meant more stock, and a greater demand for pasture. Misterton's cattle began to invade Haxey Carr in large numbers.

Doubts and disagreements arose out of uncertainty about the boundaries of the commons. Haxey Carr had a definite southern boundary—Bickersdike—but Bickersdike was not the county boundary at this point, nor the manorial boundary. A portion of Haxey Carr between Bickersdike and Heckdike lay in Nottinghamshire, and was claimed as common by the inhabitants of Misterton and Stockwith. But they were unable to get to it easily across Bickersdike. They swam their cattle across in summer, and at other times led them the long way round, first into Stockwith and then

[25] PRO E 134, Supplementary 901, 1D, Lincs.; E 134, 1 & 2 Jas. II, Hilary 25; E 178, 5430, 5412.

[26] PRO E 134, Supplementary 901, 1D, Lincs.

[27] Although, according to Thomas Hullam of Nether Burnham, they did it secretly 'for feare of being espyed.' PRO E 134, 39 Eliz., Easter 14.

[28] PRO E 178, 5412; E 134, 39 Eliz., Easter 14. Similarly at Crowle, Tetley, and Ealand there was an increase of forty households in forty years. PRO E 134, 19 Eliz., Hilary 8.

across Bickersdike by the farthing ferry. The ferry was replaced in the 1530's by a bridge, but the long journey into the Carr continued to be a deterrent to its use. The common rights which Misterton claimed, therefore, were not consistently exercised until Elizabeth's reign.

In the late 1570's the farmers of Misterton decided to make access to the Carr easier by building a ford, and a few years later a bridge, across Bickersdike at the nearest point to the village. Thenceforward, nothing prevented them from driving unlimited cattle into the Carr. Sheep and pigs, which had never been taken over from the Nottinghamshire side, were driven across in the morning and taken back at night.

The inhabitants of Haxey complained that their pasture was being overcharged, and started a dispute which raged in the courts for more than thirty years.[29] In 1570 the judges decided that Misterton and Stockwith had pasture rights for all cattle, but were not entitled to put a cattle herd or shepherd in charge of them. The quarrel did not end there, but its later history is of less interest than the information about husbandry already given. The so-called unprofitable fens of Axholme had long been exploited by the inhabitants for grazing and other purposes. So heavy were the demands made on them in summer, indeed, that the floods were essential to enrich them again in winter. Even the land which continued wet in summer was not wasted, but was cut for hay. In short, 'the very lowest ground in the manor of Epworth in the overfluds was usefull to the inhabitants.'[30]

In the light of these facts, it is not difficult to explain why the inhabitants of Axholme fought a bitter struggle against the confiscation of two-thirds of their commons by Vermuyden, his associates, and the Crown. But neither the Dutchmen nor the king and his advisers were sufficiently informed to understand the opposition which they aroused.

The drainage works were begun before the inhabitants of Axholme were given any opportunity to put forward a case for the old husbandry. Vermuyden signed an agreement with Charles I in May 1626, and eighteen months later claimed that his work was done.[31] In

[29] PRO E 178, 2932; E 134, 17 Eliz., Easter 11; E 134, 39 Eliz., Easter 14; J. Korthals-Altes, *Sir Cornelius Vermuyden* . . , 1925, p. 21.

[30] PRO E 134, 1 & 2 Jas. II, Hilary 25. It may be that some of the misconceptions about the fenland have persisted because of an error in interpreting contemporary documents. The crown called the fenland 'unprofitable'. This has been taken to mean that the fen was unprofitable in every sense, when, in fact, the crown was speaking as a landlord only, and complaining that it did not receive any rent for the fenland. It was not concerned with the question whether the fen was profitable to the inhabitants.

[31] L. E. Harris, *Vermuyden and the Fens*, 1953, pp. 47, 49.

fact, this was but the beginning of a long struggle with the inhabitants. By 1629, when the land promised him in payment for his work was being surveyed, the bitter war between them was well under way. The exchequer commissioners, visiting Axholme in the same year to assess the situation at first hand, met an angry, suspicious population, who insisted on accompanying them on their inspection of the drains at Althorpe. 'Their claymours,' they said, 'were soe great, and they soe ready to affirme any thinge to serve their owne desires, some complayning that they should have too much water, others that they should want water, some making one doubt, others moving another as wee were satisfied that wee might not believe any thinge uppon their information but what our owne view did justifye unto us.'[32] Other accounts of the hostility and active opposition of the islanders are familiar enough to require no repetition here. The reasons that lay behind the opposition, however, are little known and deserve a hearing.

In the first place, the tenants were convinced that the king had no power to dispose of their common, since it had been granted to them, exempt from all improvement, by the former owner of the estate, Sir John Mowbray, in 1359. In the second place, the tenants claimed, correctly, that the flood waters, which deposited silt on the commons in winter, were vitally necessary to their husbandry. As they discovered when Vermuyden had finished his work, the 'thick, fatt water' which had enriched their land became a 'thin, hungry, starveing water,' impoverishing the common and rendering it unable to support as many stock as before. In the third place, the islanders found that part of the common was drained so dry by Vermuyden that they were unable to get enough water for their cattle in summer. Even the Exchequer Commissioners admitted that it would have been better had certain drains not been made, and that the tenants would probably have to let the Trent into the commons at their own costs for lack of water.[33] In the fourth place, the islanders claimed that some of the land which had hitherto lain dry during the summer was flooded for the first time owing to Vermuyden's interference. No precise evidence was given to the commissioners on this point, and since there was a difference of opinion among the witnesses, the commissioners paid little attention to it. But engineers who have examined the technical aspect of Vermuyden's operations have accepted the charges as true, and have blamed Vermuyden for failing to construct

[32] PRO E 178, 5412.
[33] PRO E 134, 1 & 2 Jas. II, Hilary 25; E 178, 5430.

a wide enough channel to carry away waters previously diverted into three courses.[34] In his own lifetime, the belief that Vermuyden had made things worse than before clung to him, and prompted at least one joke at his expense.

> '*Banausus.*   I have a rare device to set Dutch windmills
>   Upon *New-market Heath*, and *Salisbury* Plaine,
>   To draine the Fens.
> *Colax.*   The Fens Sir are not there.
> *Banausus.*   But who knowes but they may be?'[35]

In the fifth place, the inhabitants who had rights of fishing and fowling in the waste lost an important source of income by the drainage. The copyholders' fishing rights in Crowle manor alone were valued at £300 a year in 1650, without counting their value to the poor who also relied on fish and fowl for their food. In the sixth place, the river Idle, on which the inhabitants had been accustomed to transport goods, was stopped up and ceased to be navigable.[36] Lastly, and most important of all, the commons were reduced to between a half and a third their former size. The fourteen thousand acres belonging to Epworth manor were reduced to 5,960 acres, and Crowle common of between three and four thousand acres was reduced to 1,814 acres.[37] Since Vermuyden's drainage project had been loudly proclaimed as a measure for making the fen more profitable than ever before, the islanders did not expect to have to reduce the numbers of their stock. Yet this was the almost unavoidable consequence when more than half the commons was taken from them, and the remainder reduced in fertility. The only alternatives were for the inhabitants to lease additional grazing in Yorkshire, or pasture their stock on land formerly kept as meadow, which meant a smaller hay harvest and less fodder for winter feed.[38]

Farming in the Isle of Axholme was not an exact repetition of farming in the fenland of Holland. Fewer cattle and sheep were

---

[34] PRO E 178, 5412; L. E. Harris, *op. cit.*, pp. 49–50; G. Dunston, *op. cit.*, p. 26.

[35] T[homas] R[andolph], *The Muse's Looking Glass*, London, 1643, p. 37.

[36] PRO E 178, 5444; E 134, 1 & 2 Jas. II, Hilary 25; E 178, 5412. Eventually the copyholders with fishing rights were compensated with 123 acres of land, called Fishers' Close.

[37] According to the original agreement with Vermuyden, the drained common was to be divided into three equal parts. One-third was to be given to Vermuyden, one-third to the Crown, and one-third to the inhabitants. In fact the commoners received nearer a half than a third.

[38] PRO E 178, 5430, 5444; E 134, 1 & 2 Jas. II, Hilary 25. To help matters, the remaining commons were divided among the townships in 1631.

reared, and more land was given over to crops, particularly wheat, rye, and hemp. The probate inventories also suggest that Axholme was not as wealthy a region as Holland. At the same time it is clear that the peasants of Axholme had evolved a perfectly satisfactory and profitable farming routine. Their husbandry was adapted to the natural conditions, they turned the seasonal floods to good account, and regarded them as a benefit, not a waste of their land. They had good reason, therefore, to defend their traditional way of life. The Dutchmen disturbed their routine, and ultimately transformed it out of recognition. They drained the land, made mistakes, altered the topography of the island and with it the customary farming arrangements, and then took more than half the land for their trouble. Dugdale wrote with admiration of the rape and corn which was sown in the fen after the drainage. What he did not appreciate was that the islanders did not need rape, and that they already had sufficient land for their corn. What they wanted in the fen was what they already had—grazing.

The charge that the islanders were stubborn and ignorant in opposing the drainage of the fens was made at the time, and is still current. It was a charge that ought with justice to have been made against Crown and Parliament, for they were utterly ignorant of conditions in Axholme before the drainage. Small wonder, indeed, that the islanders answered Parliament's demand for obedience in 1650 by saying it was 'a Parliament of Clouts,' and 'they could make as good a Parliament themselves.'[39]

The drainage schemes of the seventeenth century changed the course of farming history in the fenland, and finally made it the richest arable region of Lincolnshire. But in his lifetime Vermuyden did nothing to prove his contention that the drained fen of Axholme could be made more profitable than the undrained. He proved only that it could be put to a different use.

POSTSCRIPT

For a correction of detail on the map of Axholme, p. 152, demonstrating that Bickersdike and Heckdike were not joined but ran parallel to each other, see Alan Rogers, 'Three Early Maps of the Isle of Axholme', *Midland History*, I, no. 2, autumn 1971, pp. 24–31.

[39] Dugdale, *op. cit.*, p. 147.

XI

HORN AND THORN IN STAFFORDSHIRE: THE ECONOMY OF A PASTORAL COUNTY

'HORN and thorn' in the sixteenth century stood for pasture farming on enclosed farms, and was anathema to social moralists and politicians. Hitherto much land had been cultivated and grazed in common; now it was being enclosed, and some of it converted from cornland to pasture. Grain production fell and animal husbandry increased. Labourers who had had plenty of work while the land was under the plough found themselves unemployed, and were driven to seek a living elsewhere.

Among all the writers denouncing enclosure, Sir Thomas More, who described the sheep eating men, is assuredly the best known. But many other writers wrote with equal passion if not equal grace. In 1604 Francis Trigge, rector of Welbourn, Lincolnshire, published a pamphlet denouncing enclosure on practical and moral grounds. 'I have heard of an old prophecy', he declared, 'that horn and thorn shall make England forlorn.' The horn was the horn of cattle and sheep; the thorn was the hawthorn used to make so many hedges around the new enclosures. The prophecy foretold that enclosures for stock would turn England into a desolate kingdom of paupers.[1]

Whether this was really an ancient prophecy, perhaps heard on men's lips and yet not written down, it is impossible to say, but it expressed a fear that possessed all Tudor politicians and many writers, and persisted at least until the middle of the seventeenth century. The statutes and the pamphlets of the time constantly reiterated the dread of enclosure. Judged by the printed word one would have thought that a spectre stalked the whole kingdom. In reality, it threatened one half of England only—that half, most of it lying in the East Midlands, the south, and the south-east, where corn-growing systems of farming predominated. These were the areas where enclosure, and particularly the transformation of arable land

---

[1] Francis Trigge, *The Humble Petition of Two Sisters: the Church and Commonwealth . . .* , London, 1604, f. D 5.

to pasture, were liable to cause painful social upheaval. In the other half of England horn and thorn—stock and enclosures—were ancient and long-established features of the landscape. But they were evidently far from the mind and experience of anti-enclosure writers, or were dismissed as exceptions to the general rule. This blinkered view of English agriculture has dominated the outlook of historians ever since. We still like to think of England as a country of waving cornfields with no more than the necessary appurtenances of meadow and pasture. In fact, England had two and not one basic farming types—the arable and the pastoral. They were as different as chalk and cheese, and, taking the kingdom as a whole, much the largest acreage was devoted to pastoral activities. Yet the economy of the pastoral regions has been much neglected and misunderstood. The purpose of this paper, therefore, is to explore it more fully, taking Staffordshire as a supremely good illustration of various grass farming systems. In the sixteenth and seventeenth centuries, Staffordshire was mainly given over to animal husbandry, and much of the land was already enclosed. In short, horn and thorn filled the landscape, and yet it was far from being a forlorn county.

The pastoral way of life differed in important respects from that of arable England, and needs to be studied as a quite separate economy. Not only did it have different agricultural objectives—that is obvious —but the routine of daily life on the farm allowed people to pursue other activities as well, so that the sources of livelihood for the family were diverse. In consequence, the population experienced its own cycles of good and bad fortune, that were something other than pale or, should one say, darker shadow copies of life in arable areas. It was not, as so many observers seemed to think, an inferior form of life, similar to the life of the corn-growing regions, but less successful financially, and so supporting a poorer and more miserable people. It was a different life with different standards, which must be judged on their own merits.

The fundamental distinction between the arable and pastoral economies of England was summed up by contemporaries in the descriptive names: champion and woodland. The champion described the corn-growing areas, the woodland described the pastoral regions. Sometimes the woodland was true woodland, as we would expect to see it; sometimes it had been shorn of trees but nevertheless boasted plentiful grazing land and the economy continued pastoral. Francis Trigge described Essex, Hertfordshire, and Devonshire as woodland in this sense.[2]

---

[2] *Ibid.*, f. B1.

An Elizabethan surveyor drew the same distinction between these two kinds of landscape in his description of the Honor of Tutbury in 1558. The Honor spread over the counties of Staffordshire, Derbyshire, and Leicestershire, Derbyshire 'being all champion and very good and beneficial for meadows, pastures, and corn soil, extending from Tutbury to the Peak, in distance 20 miles . . . And on the other side of the river in the county of Stafford for the most part all woodland.'[3] In the Honor of Tutbury, of course, this reference to a woodland zone in Staffordshire meant Needwood Forest, still in 1558 a well-wooded area. But practically the whole of the county would have fitted this technical description. The county had two other forest areas in Kinver and Cannock. It had extensive moorlands in the north-east, which are an extension of the Derbyshire Peak which our Elizabethan surveyor described as having 'good sheep, pasture, and large waste.' In the rest of the county soils varied from light loams to strong clays which no one chose to plough more than necessary. There was land for corn but much more for grass, and the inhabitants grew only enough cereals for their own needs.

Because all these pastoral regions were by ancient tradition grass-growing, their social structure was different from that of what we might call the 'upstart' pasture farming districts, those that had recently been enclosed and turned to grass, and which were so roundly condemned by sixteenth-century commentators. The 'upstart' regions had formerly concentrated on corn growing, and possessed a social structure appropriate to that pursuit. Their populations lived in villages, for arable farming in common fields can only be carried on successfully from a village centre. When, after enclosure, the land was turned over to grass, and depopulation necessarily followed, the old centre of settlement in the parish remained, much shrunken, accommodating no more than one or two farmers, with perhaps a shepherd and a neatherd. Ancient pasture farming townships, on the other hand, with a long tradition in this branch of farming, looked very different. The population lived in many small and scattered places, and not in one village at the heart of the parish. The contrast is immediately noticeable when one looks at the taxation returns of the period. In arable farming counties like Leicestershire and most of Lincolnshire, the population of the parishes usually lived in one main village or in one or two other hamlets. The Hearth Tax return for Staffordshire reveals a very

---

[3] Stebbing Shaw, *History and Antiquities of Burton, Tutbury, and Needwood Forest in the County of Stafford*, Birmingham, 1812, p. 8.

different settlement pattern. The parish entry does not relate to one
village only but is subdivided between a host of small places.
Occasionally, it is impossible to tell from the size and the names of the
townships which is the main settlement in the parish. One expects to
find people living in socially varied communities accommodating all
classes from the squire and better-off yeomen and husbandmen down
to the labourers and the poor. Instead, half the places in Staffordshire
mix all the classes, but the other half keep them severely apart: the
squires and rich farmers live altogether in one place (presumably their
large houses afforded room for living-in servants), while the poor
lived in their own equally exclusive townships. Take, for example, the
parish of Eccleshall in 1666: of 21 separately-taxed places, three—
Slindon, Bromley, and Broughton—were the homes only of the rich;
eight—Cotes, Podmore, Aspley, Pershall, Great and Little Sugnall,
Cold Meece, and Wootton—were the homes only of the poor. Only
half the places in the parish—10 out of 21—mixed the classes. In
Kinver parish, a forest area this time, there were six taxable places:
Dunsley was the home of the well-to-do, Stourton and Halfcot of
none but poor and middling peasants. Again, only three out of six
accommodated all classes. In Needwood Forest there were five
settlements without any well-to-do people in them: Anslow,
Moreton, Stubby Lane, Draycott, and Hanbury-Woodend.[4]

The fact that rich and poor could live apart from one another was
of considerable significance. They were not as economically
dependent on each other as in the arable areas, where the squire
needed agricultural labourers to cultivate his demesne farm and the
cottager with little or no land starved without opportunities for wage
labour. Socially and politically the poor were not as much exposed to
the influence of the rich, and this made for a sturdy spirit of
independence which manifested itself clearly in times of political
unrest or when the economic livelihood of the people was threatened
from Westminster.[5] The rising of the moorlanders on behalf of
Parliament in February 1643 when 'a person of low quality' led his

---

[4] Public Record Office (= PRO) E 179/256/31. I count as rich farmers and gentry
those persons who were taxed on five or more hearths.
[5] The influence of the squire is discussed in C. S. Kenny, *The History of the Law of
Primogeniture in England*, 1878, p. 47. A dominant and resident landowner was the
centre of intelligence, of charity, and of social life, but 'for these advantages there was a
social price to pay. It is as true in the parish as in the nation that a paternal government
makes a childish people. A man whose brothers and neighbours are dependent upon
him is prone to become overbearing whilst the neighbours and even the brothers are
apt to become obsequious.'

neighbours to besiege Stafford is not remarkable in view of the social structure of the region.[6] Better documented is the fierce struggle waged by the inhabitants of Needwood against the sale of the forest under the Commonwealth. Here we see more clearly than usual the independent spirit of a pasture-farming community, organizing a spontaneous protest without waiting upon the leadership of the gentry. Indeed, the gentry living in Needwood were negligible. In 1661 less than one per cent of the forest population lived in houses of five or more hearths, whereas in the Trent-Thame valley the proportion was nearly five per cent. Sixty-eight per cent of the forest's population were taxpayers living in simple one-hearth houses or were too poor to pay tax at all. The majority of the rest—20 per cent—lived in 2-hearth houses. Clearly it was not a wealthy community, and since its centres of habitation were dispersed, organized political action cannot have been easy. But when Parliament announced its decision in 1654 to sell Needwood Forest to pay the soldiers of the Parliamentary army an opposition party was quickly formed. A petition with twelve pages of signatures was drawn up, on which were inscribed 834 names. In some places the parson headed the list and this may signify that he was the leader and sponsor of the protest. Alternatively, it may simply mean that the signatures were collected after a church service. In some places the signatories were all literate people and clearly did not represent the whole population. But in Hanbury parish a different spirit ruled. Everybody, literate and illiterate alike, was called out to add his or her name. Whole families assembled, and each of its members, five, six, and eight of the same surname in many cases, signed one after the other. Of the 165 signatures collected in Marchington, 134 were marks, in Marchington Woodlands 85 out of the 119 signatures were marks. These pages of signatures are an impressive, even moving testimony to the staunch community spirit and strong cohesion of the forest inhabitants.[7]

The county gave support to the forest people for its own different, but equally good reasons. The Grand Jury at Quarter Sessions argued that the loss of the foresters' commons would mean not only the impoverishment of the inhabitants of Needwood, but would lay a heavy burden of poor relief on the rest of the county. For as in all other forests 'a multitude of poor . . . lived by help of the said forest.'

---

[6] D. H. Pennington and I. A. Roots (eds.), *The Committee at Stafford, 1643–45*, Staffs. Rec. Soc., Fourth Ser., I, 1957, p. lxii.

[7] PRO SP 18/94, no. 56.

The justices of the peace repeated these arguments and added their own. Apart from the hardship that would be inflicted on the poor, and the injustice of depriving the commoners of their ancient and legitimate rights in the forest, the justices pointed out that the soldiers whose pay arrears were to be paid out of the sale were an army of the whole kingdom and not of Staffordshire only, and it was totally unfair that a few townships should bear the burden while 'many great and rich townships shall not pay or sustain a farthing loss.'[8]

The best friend the foresters had was Zachariah Babington of Curborough, near Lichfield (not, it should be noticed, a resident of the forest), who had useful contacts in high places and through whose advocacy the petition against the sale of Needwood was put before Cromwell himself. Cromwell soothed the petitioners with promises that their claims would be fairly considered, but the plan went forward. In 1656 a treaty to partition the open part of the forest (9,220 acres) was prepared, allotting half to the freeholders in lieu of their rights and interests and assigning the rest to the state. The foresters nevertheless kept up a running battle with the Commonwealth surveyors, who lived in a state of permanent trepidation as they proceeded to stake out the allotments. In May 1657, they appealed for a party of horse to be quartered near them, for without them 'we are neither able to secure the forest from continual depredations nor ourselves at least from interruption—threatened by them whom neither axebearers, keepers, nor woodmote court can restrain or keep under.' Nothing less than a dozen or fourteen horse were necessary 'for aweing and deterring those presumptuous trespassers who proceed with strong resolution in destroying the timber day and night, threatening all who offer to control them and bidding defiance to their authority.'[9]

A series of administrative delays and the Restoration of Charles II saved the forest from enclosure at this time. There were further alarms in the later seventeenth century, but enclosure did not take place until 1801. Nevertheless, it is worth briefly summing up the end of the story, for it has lessons to teach. Enclosure took place at a time of 'enclosing mania' as Sir Oswald Mosley despairingly called it, 'when every spot of ground supposed capable of growing a blade of corn must be converted into tillage.' He was not the only local

[8] PRO SP 18/94, no. 57.

[9] O. Mosley, *History of the Castle, Priory, and Town of Tutbury . . .* , London, 1832, p. 289; Shaw, *op. cit.*, p. 26; PRO SP 18/155, no. 18.

inhabitant desolated by the 'scene of melancholy devastation' which ensued. Francis Noel Clarke Mundy wrote a poem on the Fall of Needwood—a poignant lament for a now 'abused land,' once a 'garden of Nature' and also 'the poor man's friend.' But the tide of public opinion was flowing too hard in favour of agricultural improvement and few people had much sympathy with the forest economy they were destroying. Only the abrupt slope of the land between Hanbury and Marchington Woodlands, which made it nearly inaccessible to the plough, spared the northern part of the forest from destruction. All else was changed.[10]

Was it an improvement? The propagandists on behalf of agricultural progress had no doubts that it was. But as we have seen, lack of sympathy and understanding for the ways of pasture farming communities is a persistent theme in agricultural history. In the mid-eighteenth century, it was necessary to point out to some eager improvers that the farming system in vogue at the time in East Anglia, based on the Norfolk rotation, was not necessarily suitable for the mountains of Wales.[11] Writing of Needwood Forest some thirty years after its destruction, Sir Oswald Mosley saw little gain to set beside the loss. 'Since the enclosure the land has not been found of so good a quality as had been previously imagined, and from the depreciation in the price of agricultural produce, doubts may be reasonably entertained whether it would not have been more beneficial to the proprietors if a greater portion of it had been kept in a state of wood, rather than to have undergone the expensive process of cultivation.'[12] What does the farmer of this land say now, one hundred and fifty years later? The historian sees in this episode yet one more example of how the zealots for turning pasture-farming communities into corn-growers had their way; the highland zone was obliged to conform to the standards of the lowland zone.

There were many complex reasons why arable farming was considered a much superior form of life to pasture farming.[13] But at the most superficial level, it is not difficult to see why curious travellers from the English lowlands felt themselves in an

---

[10] Mosley, *op. cit.*, pp. 292–6, 303–04; Francis N. C. Mundy, *Needwood Forest and the Fall of Needwood, with other Poems*, Derby, 1830, pp. 79, 92. I wish to thank Mrs. Margaret Spufford for making this book known to me.

[11] Eric Jones reviewing Naomi Riches, *The Agricultural Revolution in Norfolk, Agric. Hist. Rev.*, XVI, ii, 1968, p. 168.

[12] Mosley, *op. cit.*, p. 308.

[13] They are discussed in Joan Thirsk (ed.), *Agrarian History of England and Wales, vol. IV, 1500–1640*, 1967, pp. xxxi–xxxv.

uncongenial countryside. There was so little cornland. The centres of population were unpretentious. Above all, perhaps, gentlemen's houses were not conspicuously displayed, partly because they were not prominently sited in the centre of a village, partly because there were fewer of them. Well-to-do yeomen and gentry with houses of five or more hearths represented between $2\frac{1}{2}$ and 6 per cent of the population in the country, depending on the district, whereas in Leicestershire these more substantial dwellings represented between 6 and 8 per cent of the total. Such surface differences caused the smug landowner to treat Staffordshire as a poor relation. We, however, have to seek a more balanced view. The absence of luxury and ostentation merely tells us that the gentry class was small and not evenly distributed over the county. The fact that the industrial revolution started in this kind of countryside—in Staffordshire, among other places—warns us that there was enterprise, ingenuity, and capital hidden away, waiting to be released. One of the questions which taxes economic historians most is how and why the industrial revolution started in England before any other European country. An agricultural historian, viewing the diversity of English agricultural regions and rural communities, wishes to narrow this question further, and ask why the industrial revolution started in the pasture farming regions of England. What pressures and tensions in pasture farming communities compelled men to turn from agriculture to industry, and ultimately from a domestic system of industry to a factory system involving the use of more and more labour-saving machinery. If these questions are to be answered satisfactorily, we must understand the nature of the pastoral economy, and trace its evolution particularly closely in the seventeenth and first half of the eighteenth century.

First, let us look more closely at the farming objectives in Staffordshire in the seventeenth century.

The crown looked to Staffordshire in the seventeenth century to supply oxen and wethers for royal use.[14] Indeed, the county was celebrated for its fine oxen—the black long-horned cattle of the northern counties, good for tallow, hide, and horn, strong in labour and yet good milkers as well.[15] Discerning graziers from as far away as Buckinghamshire came to Staffordshire to buy them.[16] The

[14] Staffordshire Record Office (= SRO), Quarter Sessions: Roll 36, Jas. I, nos. 37, 38; Roll 24, Jas. I, no. 20; Roll 40, Jas. I. nos. 22–3.

[15] Joan Thirsk, *op. cit.*, p. 186.

[16] William Salt Library, D 1734/3/4 Bdle 25 (Anglesey Collection).

meadows along the river Dove were the finest grazing grounds in England, where dairy herds flourished. Uttoxeter was a celebrated market for butter and cheese to which factors from London resorted regularly in the middle-seventeenth century, if not earlier. The conversion of Rolleston on the Dove into a dairying parish was described in detail by Sir Oswald Mosley in his history of Tutbury and its castle, and ascribed to the late sixteenth and early seventeenth centuries. But it is not certain that dairying was altogether new in the district at this time.[17] The sheep of the moorlands were praised for their wool and their ability to thrive on the barrenest soils.[18] Pigs were treated like lords. The hen house and swinescot built at Reynolds Hall (near Walsall) was a building 16 feet by 14 feet, half-timbered with partitions, floored over and planked beneath, with doors and windows—bigger and more comfortable than many a poor man's cottage.[19] But it was not only gentlemen's pigs that were treated so well. The Staffordshire system of pig-feeding was commended as a particularly successful method of teaching pigs clean feeding habits. The feeding troughs were kept separate from the sties and hogyards, and were accessible only through a hole large enough for the pig to get its head and neck through. It could feed from the trough but not put its feet in. Thus economies were achieved in the amount of food required and the dung was properly conserved. Mixed with leaves, straw, weeds, and fern, it made an excellent manure for the ploughland, which needed it badly.[20] Much of the arable was kept in cultivation for only a short period of years, four on the heathy moorland, 8–9 years on clay and lighter loams, and then put down to grass again. The only land subject to a more intensive rotation of two crops and a fallow was land lying in common fields, in other words, the ancient and at one time most fertile corn grounds of the county.[21]

If one attempts to identify the speciality of particular regions of Staffordshire, then clearly the north-eastern moorlands were a sheep-grazing, cattle-rearing countryside. The Dove meadows were the principal dairying area. Needwood and Kinver forests, and Cannock Chase were cattle-rearing, horse-breeding, and pig-fattening areas. The goodly cattle, large and fair spread, of Needwood earned

---

[17] R. Plot, *The Natural History of Staffordshire*, 1686, pp. 107–08; Mosley, *op. cit.*, pp. 163–4.

[18] Plot, *op. cit.*, pp. 109, 257.

[19] William Salt Library (= WSL) D260, Box IV (C).

[20] Walter Blith, *The English Improver Improved*, 1652, pp. 146–7.

[21] Plot, *op. cit.*, pp. 341, 344; WSL D260, Box A (f); PRO E134, 34 Chas. II, Mich. 10.

specially favourable mention from Dr. Robert Plot.[22] Horse breeding
in the forests accounts for the reputation of the horse-fairs at Tutbury
and Penkridge.[23] Forests of oak or beech could always fatten pigs.
Everywhere else in Staffordshire the farming business was stock
breeding and feeding.

The weakness in these systems of husbandry lay in the small
amount of grain grown, and the fact that many people had to depend
on buying in some corn from elsewhere. Most of the surrounding
counties were small corn producers like Staffordshire, Herefordshire
being the only shire renowned as a granary of corn, and south
Warwickshire and Leicestershire perhaps the next best suppliers.
Hence, there were problems in years of poor harvest and the dangers
emerged clearly in a bill proposed to Parliament in 1621 to save the
metal workers in the four counties of Staffordshire, Worcestershire,
Shropshire, and Warwickshire from the conspiracies of middlemen,
who were monopolizing (or engrossing, in contemporary parlance)
the supplies of corn, victuals *and* iron brought into these counties.
Instead of offering cash in exchange for the nails, locks, spurs, bridle
bits, buckles, stirrups and arrowheads they bought in these counties,
merchants were offering iron, corn or other food at enhanced prices.
In years of dearth, Staffordshire people were liable to be held to
ransom by the grain speculators.[24]

Nevertheless, the seventeenth century witnessed heroic efforts on
the part of arable farmers in other counties to produce more cereals
and allay the fears of bread shortage. After 1660 England became a
grain exporter, and from 1673 onwards grain farmers were paid
bounties to encourage them to grow for export. Staffordshire
grassland farmers were no longer living dangerously when they
depended on others to produce the grain they needed for their household bread.

Staffordshire's animal husbandry, however, represented no more
than half the economic life of the county. Pasture farming, carried on
to a large extent on family-size holdings, was not a full time occupation for all members. It left men with time for other employment

[22] Plot, *op. cit.*, p. 107. In the 1740's Richard Wilkes remarked on the surprisingly
large numbers of cows and horses still living in Needwood Forest. WSL R. Wilkes,
Original Collections for the History of Staffordshire, p. 20.

[23] Shaw, *op. cit.*, p. 21; J. C. Tildesley, *A History of Penkridge*, 1886, p. 65 *et seq.*

[24] *Star Chamber Proceedings, Henry VIII and Edward VI*, William Salt Arch. Soc.,
1912, pp. 203–04; *Chancery Proceedings temp. Elizabeth, loc. cit.*, 1926, pp. 91–2; W. K.
Boyd, *Chancery Proceedings temp. Eliz.*, N.S., IX, 1906, pp. 111–13; Notestein, Relf,
and Simpson, *Commons Debates, 1621*, VII, pp. 141–3.

which they could combine with farming. The county was rich in minerals, which gave the first impetus to the metal industries, while wool, flax, and hemp grown in the county gave the first impetus to domestic handicrafts. When once these industries were firmly established, however, the county came to depend on other places for some of its raw materials. In the late 1670's Walsall and Wolverhampton were using sow iron from the Forest of Dean, and by the 1740's Staffordshire was receiving iron ore from Scandinavia. It is unlikely, moreover, that the flax used to weave linen in the county was all home-grown, since large quantities were being imported into Hull from the Baltic and after 1699, when the Trent navigation was improved, it could be brought by river into the county.[25]

Staffordshire holds many secrets which it has not yet yielded up to us on the way the partnership between agriculture and industry developed and shaped a distinctive economy and a distinctive form of family life. During the seventeenth century this partnership was the rule rather than the exception, and only a small central zone of the county does not appear to have pursued industries in conjunction with farming. In Needwood Forest timber alone afforded employment to a multitude of foresters, wood turners, and carpenters, as well as providing bark for the tanning industry. The leather industry was naturally attracted to the county because of the presence of so many stock farmers. Sheep and deer skins, and cattle hides were available in quantity. Leather was needed not only for shoes and gloves, but for miners' protective clothing, and for saddles and harness for all engaged in driving animals, carrying goods, and working the land. The south of the county produced coal and iron to feed the metal industries in the neighbourhood. Here were made small domestic articles in constant demand, locks, door and window handles, and the metal fittings needed for saddles, harness, spurs, stirrups, snaffles, and buckles.[26] A proposal for legislation in 1621 tells us of such a rising demand for these articles that craftsmen were taking on excessive numbers of apprentices.[27] But the size of each enterprise remained small, focussed on the family. Small articles, easily made in modest quantities at a time, but meeting an insistent market demand, fitted conveniently into the weekly routine of the farming-industrial family. On the same basis nailing also flourished

[25] W. H. B. Court, *The Rise of the Midland Industries, 1600–1838*, Oxford, 1938, pp. 81, 44; WSL Wilkes, *Original Collections, op. cit.*, p. 98.
[26] Plot, *op. cit.*, p. 376.
[27] Notestein, Relf, and Simpson, *loc. cit.*

in this district. Sedgley alone was said to have 2,000 nailers working there in 1686. And nailers were among the industrial workers who preserved longest their attachment to land.[28]

Metal workers were a comparatively stable element in the population. Colliers and ironstone miners, on the other hand, were more mobile, erecting in the woodlands—of Cannock, for example—little cottages, roofed with turves, to house men who were here today and gone tomorrow.[29] Kinver forest in the south-west of the county similarly had its share of casual and permanent artisans. It was famous for scythe smiths and other makers of edge tools. But the surnames of the inhabitants of Kingswinford in 1666 afford a glimpse of another group of migratory craftsmen—glassworkers who had been brought into Sussex by Queen Elizabeth a hundred years before, and who had gradually been forced westwards by the shortage of timber. They are known to have settled for a while in Abbots Bromley and Eccleshall, and subsequently came to Stourbridge. In 1666 taxpayers in the parish of Kingswinford included Edward Carey, gentleman, Paul Tyzack, and Paul Hensey, men with surnames that are famous in the history of glass making.[30] There is even a slight trace of copper miners, prospecting in Kinver by the mid-seventeenth century. There lived in Kingswinford, Humphrey Langnure, surely a descendant of the Langnauer family, partners in the Augsburg firm of Haug and Langnauer, which had sent German miners to England in Elizabeth's reign in search of copper in Westmorland, Cumberland, Yorkshire and Lancashire, the west Midlands, the south-west and Wales. But if Kinver forest industries in the later seventeenth century owed something to the skills of foreign craftsmen and miners, English surnames denote a great variety of other occupations connected with timber, tanning, and iron: Bagger, Cartwright, Glover, Wood, and Smith.[31]

In the north-west of the county the pottery industry was firmly established in the neighbourhood of Burslem, exploiting the many different kinds of clay in the locality.[32] For more adventurous, foot-

[28] Plot, *op. cit.*, p. 375; Marie Rowlands, 'The Probate Records of Staffordshire Tradesmen, 1660–1710'. I wish to thank Miss Rowlands for allowing me to see this detailed study of Staffordshire's industrial workers in manuscript.

[29] PRO E 178/4533.

[30] T. Pape, 'The Lorraine Glassmakers in North Staffordshire', Trans. N. Staffs. F.C., LXXXII, 1948, p. 111 *et. seq.* See also W. H. B. Court, *op. cit.*, pp. 120–21.

[31] PRO E 179/256/31; R. H. Tawney and Eileen Power (Eds.), *Tudor Economic Documents*, I, p. 251.

[32] Plot, *op. cit.*, p. 211.

loose young men there was coal and ironstone mining. Mining, indeed, appears in the documents to have been a sort of 'free-for-all' without too much respect for property rights, some participants engaging in it on a highly casual basis. A case heard at Quarter Sessions, arising from the theft of a horse from a Grindon blacksmith, tells us incidentally of the movements of Robert Thorley, a yeoman of Colwich, who on one day was in the company of a Grindon yeoman 'getting of lead ore at Grindon Lowes' and the next day was on the road from Grindon to Fleet Green to fetch a blacksmith to shoe oxen for his father. [33] John Podmore, yeoman, complained of a gang of local men who attacked him and his men when they were working at his coalmine in Brerehurst, near Tunstall in 1608, carrying off his windglass, and preventing him from occupying the mine for a week.[34] John Meare, a collier of Shelton, and Henry Doe started to sink a shaft at Hanley and persuaded Sebastian and Katherine Bery to give them food and lodging on credit until they got coal. For six months this arrangement continued until they owed £3 3s. 5d. But as soon as they had some success, they moved lodgings to the house of another victualler and refused to pay their debts to the Bery family. Moreover, when the Berys secured a justice's order demanding payment, and Mrs. Bery went to the pit to collect it, she had her arm broken for her pains.[35]

In the north-east moorlands the surnames of taxpayers in 1666 tell their own story of lead and ironstone mining and other industrial occupations. Caverswall parish had families by the name of Locker, Coop, Steele, Bloore, Tipper, and Radlock. At Cheadle the surnames mingle agricultural and industrial pursuits. Messrs. Shepherd, Heath, Moore, and Moss, lived alongside Messrs. Slater, Salt, Glover, Leadbitter, and Tipper. It is tempting to see in the prominence of surnames with such obvious local associations a population with weaker migratory inclinations than most. A village in south-eastern England would not yield such a harvest of obviously indigenous occupational surnames. But we know too little about surname history as yet to risk such generalizations.[36]

To all the industries of Staffordshire based upon the presence of minerals and ores in the county we must add domestic handicrafts. The weaving of wool, hemp, and flax and other clothing industries

[33] SRO Quarter Sessions Roll 38, Jas. I, nos. 35, 36.
[34] *Ibid.*, Roll 14, Jas. I, no. 71.
[35] *Ibid.*, Roll 17, Jas. I, no. 51.
[36] PRO E 179/256/31.

were widely diffused in country cottages as well as in the towns. They
brought fame mostly to the towns, however, since it was there that the
goods were assembled for sale. Thus Newcastle was famed for its felt
hats, Tamworth, Burton on Trent, and Newcastle for their wool
cloth.[37]

Even this is not the end of the catalogue of occupations carried on
in conjunction with pasture farming. Stock husbandry, more perhaps
than corn-growing, drives farmers and dealers on to the roads to buy
and sell their wares. Every beast fed on the farm that did not finish up
on the farmer's own table had to be driven along the road by
someone, either when it was bought in or when it was ready for the
market. We catch a glimpse of the itinerant life of stock men in the
testimony of Thomas Tetlow of Chapel-en-le-Frith, Derbyshire,
husbandman, when suspicion fell on him in 1607 of stealing a bay nag
at Grindon in Staffordshire. He was asked to give an account of his
movements between August and December, 1607. He explained that
he was at Chesterfield fair (Derbyshire) in mid-July, a week later he
went to London and drank with Thomas Smith, a drover of Tatenhill,
near Smithfield. Thence he returned to the wakes at Longnor, and
came back to Grindon.[38]

The roads of Staffordshire, in consequence, were thronged with
hungry and thirsty animals and drivers looking for inns and
alehouses. The facilities in the seventeenth century never seemed
adequate to the demand. The inhabitants of Talke-on-the-Hill, for
example, petitioned in 1630 for an additional inn since it was a great
highway from the north to London and the existing inn was of such
high repute that it could not accommodate all the guests that resorted
there. The portway from Newport to Stafford and Coventry was a
great travelled way from Cheshire to London for waggons and
droves, but in 1632 there was no victualling house between
Hednesford and Norton in Staffordshire and Minworth in Warwickshire. An aspirant for a licence lived at Nether Stonnal in Shenston
parish.[39]

It is, of course, true that every county of England yields complaints
at this time of the excessive number of disorderly alehouses, and no
one would want to suggest that Staffordshire was a harder drinking
county than the rest. The increasing number of alehouses was a sign

[37] See, for example, the many weavers in Hanbury and Marchington. Marie
Rowlands, 'Towns in Staffordshire at the End of the Seventeenth Century,' not yet
published.
[38] SRO Quarter Sessions Roll 38, Jas. I, nos. 33, 34, 35, 36.
[39] *Ibid.* Roll 21, Chas. I, no. 22; Roll 73, Jas. I, nos. 45, 46. .

of the increasing scale of internal trade at this time. What is significant is the number of people licensed to keep alehouses and inns who had other occupations as well, and worked as tailors, weavers, shearmen, wheelwrights, husbandmen, shoemakers, dyers, and joiners. In the eyes of the authorities this was not to be encouraged. A petition from the parishioners of Rugeley in James I's reign attributed the increase in the numbers of poor in the parish to the excessive number of alehouses, and went on to complain that many tradesmen became alehouse keepers and, to welcome their customers, kept them company, neglecting their trades and idling their days away until they fell into poverty. But clearly the intention of alehouse keepers who could keep sober was to have two jobs at once.[40]

In short, it was common form in this countryside in the seventeenth century to have two strings to one's bow. This was the period when dual occupations were most happily and profitably combined. It is also true, of course, that a gradual change was under way by the end of the century as men turned over from a dual source of income to one based on industry alone. But the change was slow, for every combination of occupations in Staffordshire was well integrated into a life focussed on the family as a wage-earning unit. The alehouse was not much more than the parlour of the cottage, the forge and the pottery were sheds next door to the cottage, the weaving loom might be in the parlour or chamber or weaving shed. Meat, milk, cheese, and butter were assured by the family cow or cows, the sheep and pigs.[41] There is no need to elaborate on the advantage of this way of life. It was the best insurance that men with almost no savings and certainly no capital resources could have devised. If misfortune attended one activity, there was always the other to fall back on.

The question that follows immediately from this concerns the standard of living enjoyed by the population. Here we must beware of the judgments of outsiders. The writings of curious travellers of the sixteenth and seventeenth centuries are full of distaste for the landscape that we today find most exhilarating and refreshing—the hills, the mountains, the moorlands, the parks, and the woodlands. To men who looked for signs of a bounteous corn harvest which would assure them of bread for the coming year, a green countryside was a barren waste, which filled them with foreboding.[42] A frank admission of the

[40] *Ibid.*, Roll 26, Jas. I, no. 34.
[41] D. M. Smith, 'Industrial Architecture in the Potteries,' N. Staffs. Jl. F.S. 5, 1965, pp. 80–81.
[42] Joan Thirsk, *op. cit.*, pp. xxxiii–xxxv.

errors such prejudices could induce was made by the Reverend George Plaxton, vicar of Sheriff Hales in 1673 and later parson of Kinnersley, just over the border in Shropshire. He lived there for thirty years and came to know the place well, but his first encounter held surprises for him. The town was surrounded by a large morass overflowed in winter; it was impossible to get to the parish on dry arable land. And yet one out of every six of his parishioners was 60 years old and more, and some 85 and 90, and 'at my entrance there, I found neither gentleman nor beggar.' Clearly the inhabitants who survived childhood enjoyed a healthy life and made a good living.

During his incumbency, Plaxton witnessed great improvement of the waste by draining and praised the feeding qualities of the hay, which fed oxen to perfection. 'I have heard some graziers say that they could not by their best upland hay feed an ox so fat as the moor hay would do.'[43] But even before drainage, we can be sure that the moor hay was fully appreciated and exploited by the inhabitants.

Daniel Defoe was infected with the southerner's prejudices, though he had the good sense, as became the son of a meat salesman, to praise the efforts of pasture farmers when he saw their lusty beasts on the way to the butcher. To him we owe one of our rare glimpses of the life of the miner-husbandman in the West Midlands. He was travelling in the Derbyshire Peak, and saw 'the most uncouth spectacle' of a miner clothed in leather, climbing out of one of the lead groves. He was 'lean as a skeleton, pale as a dead corpse, his hair and beard a deep black, his flesh lank, and, as we thought, something of the colour of the lead itself.' He looked like 'an inhabitant of the dark regions.' Defoe's picture is painted in the grimmest colours. But he also came upon a leadmining family at home. They were dwelling in a cave, and again Defoe was horrified. The wife was extremely grateful for the coins that he and his companions dropped into her hand; his account was designed to arouse pity in the reader. And yet it is riddled with contradictions. The five children were plump and fat, the wife was comely. A lean cow grazed at the door, as well as a sow and pigs; one and a half flitches of bacon were hanging inside the cave. A little close of good barley was almost ready to be harvested. Clearly, the family did not want for food. Defoe's party went inside the cave and found 'everything was clean and neat, though mean and ordinary. Two curtains divided the cave into three rooms. There were shelves with earthenware and some pewter and brass.' It all gave 'the appearance

[43] 'Natural Observations . . . by Rev. George Plaxton, communicated by Ralph Thoresby', *Philos. Trans.*, vols. 25 and 26, no. 310, pp. 2418–20.

of substance' and they 'seemed to live very pleasantly'. On enquiry, Defoe learned that the husband earned 5d a day as a leadminer, and the wife washed ore for 3d a day when she was free to work. This way of life was unfamiliar to Defoe, and perhaps by the standards of pasture-farming communities generally this was a poor family. And yet there were advantages which even Defoe could see—a measure of economic independence and contentment, which compared very favourably with what Defoe called 'the dirt and nastiness of the miserable cottages of the poor'—a reference, perhaps, to the poor in the towns or to those dwelling in the corn-growing areas of the countryside, burdened with their large populations of landless labourers.[44]

Defoe's miner was not particularly well paid. A circumstantial report on leadmining at Wirksworth in the Derbyshire Peak in Charles I's reign states that the wages of winders (mostly women and boys) was 18d, 20d, or at most 2s 2d a week, while bearers underground received between 12d and 18d. But there was also a mining aristocracy of highly skilled men working underground who earned 4–5s a week, and even more—5s 6d to 6s 6d.[45] Moreover, it is noticeable that their wage was a weekly and not a daily rate as in agriculture. It is true that the money value at the highest rate of pay appears low by farming standards. For a farm labourer in southern England, a wage of one shilling a day without allowance for meat and drink was usual by 1640. But we do not know what the perquisites were in either case, the hours of work in the mines, or the number of weeks worked in the year. Once again it becomes clear that the two ways of life are not easily compared.

What of the condition of other industrial workers? A much-quoted pamphlet, published in 1713, on the life of the Wednesbury nailers, conjures up another picture of industrial poverty. Nailers, it declared, worked from 4 o'clock on Monday morning until late on Saturday to earn three shillings a week, and frequently this sum was reduced by the bad quality of the iron supplied. The pamphleteer's motives for writing this essay were to improve the ability of the necessitous poor to pay taxes. It does not sound as if he was of their class, or would have received thanks from them had they known of his efforts. Unfortunately, the original pamphlet cannot be traced, and a brief quotation is all we have, cited by a late nineteenth-century

---

[44] Daniel Defoe, *A Tour through England and Wales*, Everyman Edition, II, pp. 161–4.
[45] PRO DL 41/17/19.

writer, F. A. Hackwood, in a book on Wednesbury workshops. It is impossible, therefore, to judge the writer's knowledge of his subject. But Miss Marie Rowlands, who has made a detailed study of the property at death of Staffordshire nailers in the period, 1660–1710, recommends a healthy scepticism towards this kind of melancholy generalization. The inventories of nailers who left goods at death suggest material prosperity, based upon a combination of incomes from nailing, sometimes from lime-digging and coal-mining, but more often than anything else from farming.[46]

Amid this diversity of opinions on the standard of life of the part-time farmer, part-time industrial worker, I am inclined to give most credence to the views of parsons. They lived among their flock and came to know them well. The Reverend George Plaxton is one impressive and reliable witness. The Reverend Richard Baxter is another. Baxter was a fearless Puritan divine, who exerted considerable influence upon state affairs under the Commonwealth. He was well acquainted with the life of ordinary people in Kidderminster, Acton (Middlesex), and Westminster (London). At the end of his life, in 1691, he wrote his last treatise on the poor husbandman—an impassioned appeal to rich landlords to ease the lot of poor farm tenants. His chief concern was for their religious education, but the opportunities for education were intimately linked up with the economies of getting a living, and he was indignant at the burden of rent they paid. Baxter's essay is important in this context because he specifically excluded from his appeal for compassion the men engaged in industry such as 'the nailers, and spurriers, and scythesmiths and swordmakers, and all the rest about Dudley and Stourbridge, Brumicham and Walsall and Wedgbury, and Wolverhampton and all that country'; and he excluded the smiths, joiners, turners, weavers, shoemakers, and tailors who had a small-holding in addition to their trade. In short, his sympathies were aroused for those who depended only on their living from the land, and not for the part-time farmer-industrial workers, who populated the pastoral regions of Staffordshire, Worcestershire, and Warwick-shire.[47]

[46] F. A. Hackwood, *Wednesbury Workshops*, 1889, cited in W. A. S. Hewins, *English Trade and Finance chiefly in the Seventeenth Century*, 1892, p. 17. I wish to thank Miss Rowlands for this reference. She has made a thorough search for the original pamphlet without success.
[47] F. J. Powicke (ed.), *The Reverend Richard Baxter's Last Treatise*, John Rylands Library, 1926, pp. 22–4, 26–7. It is evident that Baxter had a particular landlord or landlords in mind when describing the miserable lot of the husbandman. Indeed, in a

The comparative independence and security of men with an interest in two occupations gave them good reason to work to preserve it. Richard Wilkes, a physician of Willenhall, writing in the 1740's, may not have had first hand evidence of the motives inspiring inventors and innovators forty years before but in his adult life he had many friends of the same kind. The explanation he gives of the economic issues at stake at that time, on the eve of the industrial revolution, commands careful attention. Coal supplies near the surface in south Staffordshire, he explained, were nearing exhaustion. Many thousands of families who lived '*in plenty*' (my italics) upon the coalmining and iron manufacture knew that they would be reduced to want or would have to remove elsewhere if they did not find a way of getting coal at greater depths, in quantity and at reasonable cost. It was for this reason that Thomas Savery's steam engine, the precursor of the more successful engine of Newcomen, was tried out at Wednesbury at the turn of the century. It failed to drain the land and the neighbouring mine, but it was a sign of the practical urgency with which local people regarded the problem. The search for a more successful design of steam engine continued.[48]

Wilkes evidently believed that the industrial population of Staffordshire around 1700 lived in plenty. Perhaps this was no more than guesswork, based on his observations at the time of writing in the 1740's, when the prospects for industrialization were more hopeful. Even so, as a comment on the 1740's this is still a useful, informed observation. But the motives he ascribes to the innovators are entirely credible, for they were no different from those that compelled the inhabitants of Needwood Forest to resist the schemes of Cromwell's Parliament. These were not people who depended on the gentry for their living. They had to look after themselves and make their own livelihood. Is it surprising then that the most substantial achievements in the early stages of the industrial revolution were financed by these small men, building up their savings slowly, experimenting assiduously, spurred on by the most compelling and sober of motives, to ensure a continuing living on their home ground for themselves and their children? The pre-

reference to rack-renting landlords he gives a clue: 'Some great ones that know where I was born may know what I instance in.' *op. cit.*, p. 38.

[48] WSL, SMS 468, Richard Wilkes's Notes for a History of Staffordshire, paper headed 'The Fire or Steam Engine'; Rhys Jenkins, 'Savery, Newcomen, and the Early History of the Steam Engine', *Trans. Newcomen Soc.*, III, 1922–3, p. 96 *et. seq.*; R. A. Mott, 'The Newcomen Engine in the Eighteenth Century', *loc. cit.*, XXXV, 1962–3, p. 70 *et seq.*

conditions for industrialization in the eighteenth century have prompted much discussion and argument, but one of the most powerful was surely the success of the small part-farming, part-industrial family of pastoral England in the seventeenth century.

POSTSCRIPT

The work of Dr. Marie Rowlands, which was in progress when this essay was first written, has now been published: Marie B. Rowlands, *Masters and Men in the West Midland Metalware Trades before the Industrial Revolution*, Manchester Univ. Press, 1975. See also by the same author, 'Society and Industry in the W. Midlands', *Midland History*, IV, i, 1977.

XII

SEVENTEENTH-CENTURY AGRICULTURE AND SOCIAL CHANGE

THIS essay is an attempt to analyse in more detail than hitherto agricultural developments in the seventeenth century, and to present them within a more clearly defined social and geographical framework. The whole century is recognized as a period of economic and political crisis. Agriculturally, this crisis is most readily attributable to the relentlessly falling prices of grain, which posed long-term problems of readjustment to specialized grain growers. But these were only one group among many engaged in agriculture. How did the thousands of farmers who were engaged in other branches of the farming business fare during the seventeenth century? The answer is that some of them met the new circumstances with solutions which were economically successful and far less destructive of the small farmer than those adopted in the specialized corn-growing areas. Thus the farming systems of England became more sharply differentiated economically and socially; and the stage was prepared for changes in the eighteenth century which wrought an agricultural revolution in arable regions and an industrial revolution in pastoral ones.

During the first half of the seventeenth century, fears at the over-production of grain and its low price commanded the forefront of the stage in all government discussions on agriculture, and particularly during the troubled depression years of 1620–4.[1] In fact, these fears were exaggerated and premature, and they turned to alarms at grain shortage between 1630 and 1632 and in the late 1640's. But the idea of giving some financial encouragement to corn growers was being canvassed by the middle of the century—by Henry Robinson[2] in a pamphlet written in 1652 if not earlier—and after the Restoration

[1] W. Notestein, F. H. Relf, and H. Simpson, *Commons Debates, 1621*, 1935, IV, p. 105.
[2] Henry Robinson, *Certain Proposals in Order to the People's Freedom and Accommodation*, 1652.

farmers were constantly urged to export grain overseas so that corn production could be maintained and its price improved. After 1673 farmers received bounties for so doing.[3] This effort to maintain grain prices proved vain, however, and they fell steadily between 1660 and 1750.[4]

But many corn growers were also wool producers, and in this role they also had cause to complain for low wool prices persisted for most of the century. Rising wool prices which had characterized the sixteenth century were at an end by 1603 and a debate on falling prices had begun by 1610. A sharp crisis accompanied the outbreak of the Thirty Years' War, for it abruptly reduced the demand for cloth in Europe, spreading unemployment among the cloth-workers, and quickly reacting upon the wool growers. Thus the shrillest and most alarmist complaints from the countryside in the years 1618–24 came, not surprisingly, from a sheep–corn area, the Lincolnshire wolds, where Sir William Pelham of Brocklesby described small tenants giving up their farms and selling their bed straw for food, eating raw dog flesh and horse flesh for very hunger.[5] It was one of many episodes in the corn–sheep areas which gradually drove the small farmer out of existence.

Grass sheep farmers, however, were almost equally distressed by the cloth crisis, and the complaints of both groups were represented in the report of the Northamptonshire justices of the peace in 1620. Wool, they told the Privy Council, was the chief commodity of the county, yet it would not sell at the lowest price. Compared with this misfortune, the low price of barley was a minor matter; indeed, the latter was rather welcomed since it allayed the discontent of the poor, the 'tumultuacious levelling' of 1607 being still green in the memory.[6]

Low wool prices remained a source of anxiety for the rest of the century. Spanish wool was a strong competitor with English wool both at home and overseas. Yet the government persisted in curtailing the market for English wool by prohibiting exports. After

[3] *Statutes of the Realm*, v, p. 781.

[4] A. H. John, 'The Course of Agricultural Change, 1660–1760', in *Studies in the Industrial Revolution*, ed. L. S. Pressnell, 1960, p. 134 *et seq.*; W. G. Hoskins, 'Harvest Fluctuations and English Economic History, 1620–1759', A.H.R., XVI, i, 1968, graph facing p. 15. But see also M. Flinn, 'Agricultural Productivity and Economic Growth in England, 1700–60: a Comment', *Jnl Econ. Hist.*, XXVI, i, 1966, p. 97, who argues for only a slight secular downward trend in grain prices, 1660–1720.

[5] P. J. Bowden, *The Wool Trade in Tudor and Stuart England*, 1962, p. 186; Joan Thirsk, *English Peasant Farming*, 1957, p. 193.

[6] P.R.O., SP 14/113, no. 21.

the passing of the Irish Cattle Act in 1667, Ireland was forced to turn from cattle to sheep production and her wool also competed successfully against English wool. English wool prices followed a long downward trend after the Restoration, interrupted only during periods of temporary shortage.[7]

Stock farmers and dairymen benefited from a sustained demand for meat and other livestock products which caused prices to maintain a steadier level over the century as a whole.[8] The interests of rearers and graziers were not equally served, however. Already in 1621 the scale of imports of Irish cattle was being criticized as a drain on the bullion reserves of the nation. With butter, they were said to cost £10,000 a year.[9] In the course of the next generation, Irish cattle were increasingly blamed for the stationary or falling level of rents for good grazing land, which seriously hit the incomes of the gentry. Graziers, it was argued, were failing to take up pastures because they were unable to compete with the Irish producers. The remedy adopted at the Restoration was an act in 1663 imposing a duty on imported fat cattle and sheep, followed by the Irish Cattle Act of 1667 which prohibited all livestock imports, both lean and fat, from Ireland. This greatly diminished the supplies of lean stock in England and had the effect of driving up the prices of store animals, greatly to the profit of the rearers of cattle in highland England, Wales, and Scotland. Counties like Devon, Lancashire, and Northumberland benefited at the expense of the graziers of the Midlands and the south who had to pay higher prices for lean stock than ever before.[10] Thus for a time the profits of meat production were redistributed in favour of the highland rearers at the expense of the lowland graziers. The vociferous complaints against the Irish Cattle Act did not die away until the early 1680's, when in fresh discussions on the merits of the act none could be found to support its repeal.[11] Yet there is no evidence that Midland graziers found the going easier.[12] Around

[7] Bowden, *op. cit.*, pp. 46–8, 213–17, 230; P.R.O., SP 29/176, no. 130; CSPD 1673–5, pp. 169–70; Bodleian MS. Top. Kent, A i, fol. 26; John, *op. cit.*, p. 142.
[8] *Ibid.*
[9] Notestein, Relf, and Simpson, *op. cit.*, IV, p. 105.
[10] P.R.O., SP 29/176, no. 130; Bodleian MS. Top. Kent, A i, fol. 26; Roger Coke, *A Discourse of Trade*, 1670, p. 33; 'The Grand Concern of England Explained. . .', 1673, *Harl. Misc.*, 1746, VIII, p. 534.
[11] John Houghton, *A Collection for the Improvement of Husbandry and Trade*, ed. R. Bradley, 1727, II, p. 3.
[12] Tenants were extremely reluctant to take up land at Ashby de la Zouch, Leics., a grazing parish on the Hastings family estates, in the years 1685–9. I owe this information to the kindness of Mr Christopher Moxon.

London, however, specialized fattening procedures were evidently producing substantial profits: for example, bullocks which were bought up, stall fed for a year in the Home Counties, and sold fat were yielding high returns while calf fattening was a remunerative speciality in Suffolk and Essex.[13]

Prices of dairy produce, like those of meat, also held up better than grain. In the middle of the century, Sir Richard Weston confidently maintained that the produce of meadows, namely, butter, cheese, tallow, hides, beef, and wool, were all of greater value than corn.[14] But the dairymen were not unaffected by short-term difficulties. From East Anglia they were unable to get their produce away to London by coastal vessels in 1630 because of the Dunkirk privateers preying on the east coast.[15] The Irish Cattle Act in 1667 caused Irish farmers to turn from cattle production for the English market to dairying whereby they captured English markets for dairy produce in Flanders, France, Portugal, and Spain.[16] This development injured the dairy producers of the south and east and, according to J. H. Clapham, killed England's export trade in butter.[17] Nevertheless, butter and cheese were easily transported inland, the home demand was insistent, and prices remained stable after 1665.[18] Moreover, in the neighbourhood of towns, and particularly in London, milk sales rose markedly as increasing numbers of pedlars hawked it through the streets. A London milkwoman in the 1690's sold on average sixteen pints of milk a week to each of her customers.[19]

These brief remarks do no more than draw attention to some facets of agricultural development which come to light in contemporary pamphlets, newspapers, and Parliamentary debates. But they are valuable in directing attention at branches of the farming business other than corn growing: each farming type had its own chronology of crises; each crisis threw up different problems for different specialists. Thus, legislation on Irish cattle imports exerted different effects on the rearers of stock (primarily a business of the highland zone of England) and on the graziers (mostly based on the Midlands and south); the evident difficulties of corn producers in selling grain in a saturated market implies differences between the fortunes of

[13] Houghton, *op. cit.*, I, pp. 285, 297, 300.
[14] Samuel Hartlib, *His Legacie*, 1651, p. 49.
[15] P.R.O., SP 16/162, no. 41.
[16] Coke, *op. cit.*, p. 34.
[17] J. H. Clapham, *A Concise Economic History of Britain*, 1957, p. 285.
[18] John, *op. cit.*, p. 144.
[19] Houghton, *op. cit.*, I, p. 410.

farmers cultivating high-grade crops on the most fertile soils and of those producing inferior qualities of grain on the less fertile ones; the hazards of war and changes of policy towards Irish food imports damaged the dairymen of East Anglia and the south at one moment and the West Midlands dairymen at another.[20] And throughout the century it is evident that farmers near towns had a more buoyant market than those at a distance. In short, we can discern differences in the nature and gravity of the seventeenth-century crisis based on geography and farming types.

These, however, are not the only means to a more refined analysis of seventeenth-century agricultural trends. Given the predominance of large farmers in the specialized corn-growing areas and the numerical preponderance of small farmers in the pastoral districts, the geographical differences clearly carry social implications as well. And wider perspectives open up when we consider the contemporary literature on agriculture, offering advice to farmers facing the economic problems of their time. Some suggestions, like the growing of vegetables, were immediately within the grasp of the small farmers with little or no capital; others, like the watering of meadows, lay only within the grasp of the rich gentleman or yeoman who could afford to wait years for the full return on his investment. To separate the factors which facilitated agricultural improvements in some places and obstructed them in others, and to measure the ramified consequences of this uneven development, is a complex and ambitious undertaking, especially since farming systems were so numerous and varied. Yet we know that in the end the choices made by different types of farmers shaped conditions in the eighteenth century for an industrial revolution in pastoral areas and an agricultural revolution in arable ones. Thus, as a first step, it should not be impossible to separate, if only in a generalized way, the social and technical factors which changed the structure of English farming regions between 1600 and 1700 and set certain rural communities on paths which diverged ever more sharply after 1750. This should clear the way for local studies which can probe the problem more deeply,

---

[20] One of the arguments against the Irish Cattle Act was that much pasture had been turned from breeding to dairying purposes before the Irish Cattle Act and such land was now being hit by the competition of Irish butter. I assume that this is a reference to lands in the West Midlands, where there is positive evidence of this change of farming system. That Irish butter and cheese were the cause of the low prices of the English product was, however, contested by Houghton. John Houghton, *A Collection of Letters for the Improvement of Husbandry and Trade*, 1681, no. 9, 19 Oct. 1682, p. 87.

and in due course make possible a more far-reaching comparative analysis.

Specialist corn growers have received most attention from historians because their history is among the best documented and lends itself most readily to generalization. Moreover, bread was a staple food and so bread producers have always been regarded as the central pillar of the farming structure. The growers of high-quality grains for food and drink were found on the wolds and downlands, on the loams and brecks of East Anglia, and in the vales and lowland plains. The life of such communities was centred upon villages which are also deemed typical of the English rural scene. Presided over by the squire, all classes—yeomen, husbandmen, cottagers, labourers, and paupers—were represented in the one community. By the sixteenth or seventeenth centuries, such villages usually lacked any considerable reserves of waste land waiting to be brought into cultivation and so increased production was possible only by intensifying cultivation on the existing land.[21] Much ingenuity was shown in achieving this. A steady increase took place in the proportion of land given to fodder crops, which fed more stock which manured the land more effectively, and so produced more corn. The Lincolnshire hills and vales yield plentiful evidence of this development.[22] In the common fields of Oxfordshire the self-sown leys which were used to feed more stock in the 1630's gave way in the second half of the century to deliberately sown grasses such as rye grass, trefoil, lucerne, clover, and particularly sainfoin.[23] Somewhere between 1650, when Sir Richard Weston wrote his propaganda in favour of clover, and 1662 the price of seed fell from 2s. a pound to 7d. Men had learned to thresh the seed for themselves and no longer relied entirely on Dutch imports. Thus clover became a practical proposition, which Andrew Yarranton could with some assurance recommend to West Midlands farmers below the rank of rich gentlemen and yeomen. For this reason, clover spread more widely after the 1660's.[24] At the same

[21] A more detailed analysis is contained in Joan Thirsk, ed., *The Agrarian History of England and Wales, IV*, 1500–1640, (henceforth A.H.E.W. IV), 1967, pp. 1–112. Cf. also E. L. Jones, *Agriculture and Economic Growth in England, 1650–1815*, 1967, pp. 154 *et seq.*

[22] Thirsk, *English Peasant Farming*, p. 192.

[23] Michael Havinden, 'Agricultural Progress in Open-Field Oxfordshire', A.H.R., IX, ii, 1961, pp. 74–7.

[24] *Andrew Yarranton, The Improvement Improved. A Second Edition of the Great Improvement of Lands by Clover*, 1663, pp. 4, 44, 31; P. E. Dove, *Account of Andrew Yarranton. The Founder of English Political Economy*, 1854, p. 8; Bodleian MS. Aubrey 2, fol. 152; G. E. Fussell, 'Adventures with Clover', *Agriculture*, LXII, no. 7, 1955, p. 343. The quality of the imported seed in the 1650's was very variable and Walter

time, turnips, which were first popularized as a field crop in Norfolk and Suffolk by the Flemish aliens in the early seventeenth century, were grown more freely on the lighter loams by the middle decades, and, like clover, they improved the performance of the livestock side of arable farming and so indirectly the corn yield.[25]

Meanwhile a search was under way for better varieties of seed that would yield heavier crops of corn. We probably do not know one-tenth of the experiments that were going on. Robert Plot wrote of more productive strains of wheat and barley which were cultivated in Oxfordshire and slowly, too slowly for his taste, spread to other counties in the course of the seventeenth century.[26] It is pure luck that Plot happened to record these facts; they must represent a minute proportion of new strains of traditional crops being exploited at this time in the arable centres of England.

The main improvements listed in reply to the questionnaire put out by the Royal Society in 1664 described better rotations in the arable fields, more generous use of fertilizers on the arable, more use of the sheepfold as a fertilizer, and the careful choice of seed. Questions were put about meadows and pastures but the answers that have survived were brief, and only enumerated the traditional remedies for poor quality grass.[27] Nevertheless, it was in these corn-growing areas that the watering of meadows took hold in the 1630's, spreading through Wiltshire, Berkshire, Dorset, Hampshire, and later into the Midlands.[28] Like so many of the innovations in corn-growing regions, it is associated with substantial farmers and the owners of great estates. The first watering of meadows by artificial dykes had been devised by Rowland Vaughan, a substantial gentleman farmer living in the Golden Valley of Herefordshire. The digging of the trenches for watering cost him many hundred pounds and it is not surprising that he could not persuade others in the valley to follow his

Blith urged growers to send a reliable man to the Low Countries to buy it, another impracticable suggestion to the small farmer. W. Blith, *The English Improver Improved*, 1652 edn, p. 179.

[25] E. Kerridge, *The Agricultural Revolution*, 1967, pp. 270–6.

[26] Thirsk, A.H.E.W. IV, p. 168. It is perhaps significant that the early ripening variety of barley used in Oxfordshire which could be sown and returned to the barn in nine or ten weeks—ideal in wet and backward springs—had been introduced to Oxfordshire from Patney in Wiltshire, which was an estate belonging to the Earl of Craven. R. Plot, *The Natural History of Oxfordshire*, 1676, pp. 152–3; Bodleian MS. Aubrey 2, fol. 84.

[27] Royal Society, Georgical Enquiries, Classified Papers, x(3).

[28] E. Kerridge, 'The Sheepfold in Wiltshire and the Floating of the Water Meadows', *Econ. Hist. Rev.*, 2nd ser., VI, 1954, pp. 286–9; *idem. Agricultural Revolution*, pp. 266–7.

example. His description of his neighbours makes it clear that he lived among small dairymen who were busy with their cheese and butter making from May to July and wove hemp and flax in winter. They could not have afforded such expensive innovations.[29] Hence the idea was taken up among wealthier farmers in the corn-growing regions, on the chalk downlands of Salisbury plain where the Earl of Pembroke owned estates, and subsequently in other counties further east. Sir Richard Weston adopted the idea on his lands in Surrey and spent £1,500 on it, not to mention the costs of litigation with his neighbours who claimed damage to their lands by flooding.[30] In Wiltshire Dr Kerridge has found manor courts agreeing upon co-operative schemes for watering their meadows. But since it remains doubtful how many small husbandmen could have afforded to be involved in such a costly enterprise, it may be that by this time such Wiltshire villages had already succeeded in driving out the small occupier. This would be consonant with Dr Kerridge's general observation that by 1657 the watering of meadows 'was normal amongst gentlemen farmers and cultivating land owners.'[31]

Zeal for experiments together with the capital to back them were conspicuous among substantial yeomen and gentry on the most fertile cornlands of the kingdom, and it is no accident that the two outstanding farm account books that have survived from the seventeenth century were written by men farming lands in these districts: Robert Loder at Harwell on the Berkshire downs, and Henry Best at Elmswell on the Yorkshire wolds.[32] The agricultural revolution of the eighteenth century was likewise publicized by the same class of men farming similar soils. Jethro Tull's *Horse-Hoeing Husbandry* emerged from experience of farming in Berkshire at Crowmarsh Gifford (on the Thames near Wallingford)—superb corn-growing country, producing grain for the London market. After his book was published, Tull moved to a hill farm on the chalk downlands between Berkshire and Wiltshire—an arable, sheep–corn area. Turnip Townshend was similarly concerned with the improvement of potential arable land at Rainham, near Fakenham, on the brecklands of Norfolk, which when consolidated by sheep and improved by their manure became fertile granaries of corn.

[29] E. B. Wood, ed., *Rowland Vaughan, His Booke*, 1897, pp. 30–1.
[30] P.R.O., E 178/5669.
[31] Kerridge, *Agricultural Revolution*, pp. 254, 262 *et seq.*
[32] G. E. Fussell, ed., *Robert Loder's Farm Accounts, 1610–20*, Camden Soc., 3rd ser., LIII, 1936; C. B. Robinson, ed., *Rural Economy in Yorkshire in 1641*, Surtees Soc., XXXIII, 1857.

Considerably later in the eighteenth century Thomas Coke worked on the same principles in the same countryside.[33]

The logic in this enthusiasm for more intensive arable farming in a period of stagnating prices lay—for farmers on the light lands of the downs and wolds and brecklands, at least—in technical necessity. The sheep–corn system was ideal on these soils and no other commended itself as a substitute. The readiest solution to falling profits, namely, more intensive and more efficient production of the same commodities, was well within the capacity of the large farmer. The consolidation and enclosure of land and the engrossing of farms were all means to this end. Moreover, by growing more fodder crops, more sheep could be kept on the hills and more cattle in the vales, and thus the sources of income were diversified. In certain geographical situations, other solutions, involving the use of more distant grazing lands as a supplement to the resources of the hill farms, were favoured. Gentlemen farmers on the Lincolnshire wolds and the Kesteven heath rented marshland and fenland to fatten cattle which they could not finish on their home pastures. This practice continued throughout the seventeenth century and only slackened off in the eighteenth when hill farmers recognized the value of growing turnips at home for stock feeding. The renting of these distant pastures was not within the means of the small husbandman.[34]

In the clay vales farmers had more alternative choices in the changing economic circumstances of the seventeenth century. They were not inescapably tied to corn growing, but could enclose their land and turn it to grass. On heavy soils this was an attractive solution, particularly as it solved the problem posed by high wages, of which lowland farmers generally complained in the second half of the seventeenth century.[35] 'Pasturage is more profitable than tillage,' wrote one pamphleteer in 1654, 'why should they (i.e. the enclosing farmers) not have liberty to lay down their arable land for grass.'[36] In fact, they continued to do just this in many parts of the East Midlands —in Leicestershire, Northamptonshire, and north Buckinghamshire. It is roughly estimated that nearly a quarter of Leicestershire was enclosed in the seventeenth century.[37] The pamphlet controversy for

[33] Lord Ernle, *English Farming Past and Present*, 1936 edn, pp. 170, 173–4, 218.
[34] Thirsk, *English Peasant Farming*, pp. 176–7.
[35] Coke, *op. cit.*, p. 15; Bodleian MS. Top. Kent, AI, fol. 26; *Plain English in a Familiar Conference betwixt three Friends, Rusticus, Civis, and Veridicus, concerning the Deadness of our Markets*, 1673, p. 6.
[36] *Considerations concerning Common Fields*, 1654, p. 21.
[37] *Leics. V.C.H.*, II, pp. 204, 223.

and against enclosure between two Leicestershire parsons, John Moore and Joseph Lee, in 1653–4 seems something of an anachronism in seventeenth-century England—for public opinion was generally moving in favour of enclosure so long as it safeguarded the interests of the poor commoners—yet it did not appear so in the East Midlands; here enclosure was still a lively present issue.[38]

There is general agreement among those who have worked on particular parishes and estates in the arable districts of England that these economic changes caused land to become more and more concentrated in the hands of the larger farmers. A. H. Johnson who many years ago sought to explain the decline of the small landowners found evidence for it between the sixteenth and the mid-eighteenth centuries, and more particularly between 1688 and 1750, in Oxfordshire parishes generally, and on various estates in Norfolk, Sussex, Kent, Wiltshire, the Isle of Wight, and Leicestershire.[39] It is noticeable that his evidence was drawn from the best corn-growing regions. His comparisons were of a rough and ready kind, but the difficulties in estimating changes in the number of owner-occupiers during the seventeenth century have discouraged others from attempting other large comparisons. Most modest examples from single parishes, however, have shown the same trends.

At Sherington in Buckinghamshire, for example, modest freeholders who had been gaining ground in the late sixteenth century when manorial lords sold out their interests, and who continued to flourish until the 1660's, were driven out by indebtedness between 1660 and 1710. The engrossing of holdings proceeded apace and many merchants and town dwellers became owners.[40] At Chippenham in Cambridgeshire, where the common fields were not enclosed until 1791, large farms nevertheless grew at the expense of the rest during the seventeenth century. Circumstances in this case suggest that it was not always debt that drove men to sell. Rents were falling, and the weight of taxation borne by owners of land was rising. Since there were sound arguments for becoming a tenant rather than an owner in the second half of the seventeenth century, the three

---

[38] John Moore, *The Crying Sin of England of not caring for the Poor*, 1653; *idem, A Scripture Word against Inclosure. . .* , 1656; *idem, A Reply to a Pamphlet entitled Considerations. . .* , 1656; *Considerations concerning Common Fields*, 1654; J. Lee, *Vindication of a Regulated Inclosure*, 1656; *A Vindication of the Considerations concerning Common Fields and Inclosures. . .* , 1656. See also W. E. Tate, *The English Village Community. . .* , 1967, p. 77.
[39] A. H. Johnson, *The Disappearance of the Small Landowner*, 1963 edn, pp. 132–8.
[40] A. C. Chibnall, *Sherington.. Fiefs and Fields of a Buckinghamshire Village*, 1965; Margaret Spufford, reviewing the above in A.H.R., 16, i, 1968, p. 72.

Chippenham farmers who sold out farms of between 120 and 155 acres apiece in 1696 to enable the lord to create a park may have made their choice deliberately and willingly.[41]

Some gentle propaganda in favour of small farms began to flow in the late 60's and early 70's from people familiar with conditions in the lowland zone, who viewed with increasing anxiety the fall of rents. Sir Thomas Culpeper, junior, in the preface which he wrote in 1668 to his father's *Tract against the High Rate of Usury* described the increase of large farms as more appropriate to New England than Old England, and mourned the diminution of small ones. Carew Reynel believed that 'the smaller estates the land is divided into the better for the nation, the more are maintained, and the land better husbanded.'[42]

The decline of the small landowner in the seventeenth century, then, was a feature of specialized arable regions, and also of vale lands newly enclosed for pasture, not, as we shall see presently, of traditional pasture-farming districts. The smaller farmer was being driven out by a combination of factors, notably the technical economies possible in large-scale cereal production, or in conversions to pasture, sluggish grain prices, and the high cost and quantity of labour in corn growing. Capital was essential both to the farmers who chose to intensify grain production and to those who chose to turn over entirely to grazing. Not surprisingly, it was from among these farmers, and not from the ancient pasture-farming communities, that the livestock improvers like Robert Bakewell and the Culley brothers emerged in the eighteenth century.[43] They had been nurtured in communities so structured as to promote the interests of the thrusting and ambitious improver.

This generalized conspectus of arable-farming regions in the seventeenth century takes its guide lines from the examples of the best corn-growing lands and the most ordered village communities. It

[41] Margaret Spufford, *A Cambridgeshire Community, Chippenham from Settlement to Enclosure*, Leics. University, Dept. of English Local History, Occasional Paper, no. 20, 1965, pp. 45–6, 48–9. For evidence of the continued decline of the small farmer in the first half of the eighteenth century, see G. E. Mingay, 'The Size of Farms in the Eighteenth Century', *Econ. Hist. Rev.*, 2nd ser., xiv, 1962, pp. 481–4. *Cf.* also the statement of William Ellis that it is doubtful 'whether since the early part of the eighteenth century it has profited the man of middle acres to own the land he farms.' Cited in Charles Wilson, *England's Apprenticeship*, 1965, p. 252. See also H. J. Habakkuk, 'La Disparition du paysan anglais', *Annales E.S.C.*, 20e année, 1965, no. 4, pp. 649–63.

[42] Culpeper, Preface to the 1st edn, 1668; Carew Reynel, *The True English Interest*, 1674, p. 20.

[43] H. C. Pawson, *Robert Bakewell*, 1957, pp. 18 *et seq.*; D. J. Rowe, 'The Culleys—Northumberland Farmers, 1767–1813', A.H.R., 19,ii, 1971, pp. 156–74.

omits certain variants: these were the villages with less fertile soils which continued under arable cultivation without yielding great rewards to their cultivators; crops other than corn could quickly win general favour if they prospered in the environment. The variant villages, socially speaking, were those which lacked the controlling influence of a squire, either because the ownership of land was divided among several lords of almost equal status, or because the village entirely lacked a lord (this could occur if the manorial rights were sold up and the manorial courts ceased to be held), or because the manorial lord allowed things to slide through sheer negligence. Many such communities maintained a strong freeholder class, which ruled the village when necessary, but which failed, often from self interest, to check the influx of immigrant cottagers and squatters. These became the 'open' villages of the eighteenth century, providing much-needed casual labour for the farmers in the 'closed' villages roundabout. Wigston Magna, Leicestershire, is one such example: it solved the problem of employment for its inhabitants by turning to framework knitting, which was already entrenched in forest areas nearby, and which spread in the second half of the seventeenth century into the almost equally congenial environment afforded by such 'open' villages.[44] Industries, however, were not the only solution to the problem of employment in such communities. Another solution lay in the cultivation of special, labour-intensive crops.

Pamphlet literature during the seventeenth century recommended with growing conviction and growing precision the cultivation of specialized cash crops, commanding a high and profitable price at the markets. These were fruit and vegetables; herbs and spices for cooking and medicinal purposes, such as saffron, caraway, mustard, and liquorice; industrial dyes such as woad, weld, madder, and safflower; flax and hemp for cloth weaving; mulberries for feeding silkworms; and teasels which were used for brushing up the nap of cloth and were considerably cheaper than wire cards. The first exhortations to grow these crops were made by men who had travelled in European countries, particularly Flanders and France, and drew object lessons from their observations. Some were cloth merchants who readily saw the commercial advantages of producing flax, hemp, and dyes at home instead of importing them; others were gentlemen who collected unusual plants and foods for their gardens and dining tables and either bought them from special importers in

---

[44] W. G. Hoskins, *The Midland Peasant*, 1957, pp. 97–110, 228.

London or sent their gardeners abroad to collect them.[45]

The lessons were only slowly driven home. When the example of the Dutch was preached to Englishmen in the early 1620's as a model to be copied for alleviating the economic crisis, the cultivation of flax, hemp, and tobacco at home were principally commended as a means of saving on foreign imports. The obvious remedies for the sick economy at that time seemed to lie in increasing the volume of trade and improving the money supply.[46] By the middle of the century, however, proposals for overcoming a new and even deeper depression were far more broadly conceived, and gave a prominent place to schemes for the diversification of agriculture. The need to provide more employment for the poor loomed large, and, with this objective in mind, political writers set great store by labour-demanding crops which would increase work on the land and indirectly in industry. Thus Henry Robinson's pamphlet in 1652 entitled *Certain Proposals in order to the People's Freedom and Accommodation* wished to foster weaving industries of silk, cotton, hemp, and flax as well as wool, and to grow most of these fibres at home. To provide additional land for them he urged the more productive use of wastes, which meant, of course, enclosure as a first step. But so long as the commoners' interests were protected, Robinson believed this to be a desirable improvement.[47] These two arguments in combination became standard among writers on the economy during the Interregnum and for the rest of the century. Flax and hemp would increase the variety and quantity of domestic handicrafts; dye crops required much hand labour and would also save the cost of imported dyes; vegetables and fruit used land and labour intensively, were in great demand, and extremely profitable. Changes in dietary habits had occurred during the civil wars and people now ate only one main meal a day, consuming less meat and eating more fruit and vegetables.[48] Sales in towns were brisk: Londoners of all

[45] Mea Allan, *The Tradescants, their Plants, Gardens, and Museum, 1570–1663*, 1964, *passim*. See also *infra*, p. 197.

[46] Thomas Mun, *England's Treasure by Foreign Trade* in J. R. McCulloch, *Early English Tracts on Commerce*, 1952, pp. 115 *et seq*. It was published in 1664 but was written in 1623. B. Supple, 'Thomas Mun and the Commercial Crisis, 1623', B.I.H.R., XXVII, 1954, pp. 91–4.

[47] Some of the same ideas occur in the earlier pamphlets by Henry Robinson, namely, *England's Safety in Trade's Increase*, 1641, and *Brief Considerations concerning the Advancement of Trade and Navigation*, 1649. See also William Goffe, 'How to Advance the Trade of the Nation and Employ the Poor', *Harl. Misc.*, VI, pp. 385–9.

[48] Sir William Coventry, 'Essay concerning the Decay of Rents and their Remedies', 1670, Brit. Mus., Sloane MS. 3828, fols. 205–10. See also 'The Grand Concern of

classes bought fruit from pedlars and munched it in the streets—like goats, the Venetian Busino remarked unkindly.[49]

The literature advocating these crops was voluminous after 1650 and cannot be recited in detail. But two editions of Walter Blith's textbook on husbandry serve as signposts to the success of the propaganda. In 1649 Blith published *The English Improver or a New Survey of Husbandry*, and enumerated 'six pieces of improvement.' These were (i) the floating and watering of land, (ii) the draining of fens, bogs, and marshland, (iii) the ploughing of old pasture, and enclosure without depopulation, (iv) the careful use of manures appropriate to different soils, (v) the planting of woods, and (vi) the more modest improvement of lands presenting special problems. In 1652 the new edition of this work, entitled *The English Improver Improved*, contained the same recommendations but added 'six newer pieces of improvement.' These were (i) the growing of clover, sainfoin, and lucerne, (ii) the correct use of ploughs appropriate to different soils, (iii) the planting of weld, woad, and madder, (iv) the planting of hops, saffron, and liquorice, (v) the cultivation of rape, coleseed, hemp, and flax, and (vi) the planting of orchard and garden fruits. In the revised text Blith implied that some at least of these new crops had only just been brought to his notice, perhaps, we may guess, as a result of comments by readers of the first edition. Of weld, he wrote with a trace of pique, 'it is my desire to make public whatever comes under my experience, yet this hath been used this many years by many private gentlemen in divers parts but not discovered for public practice. . . I fear men's spirits are strangely private that have made excellent experiments and yet will not communicate.'[50]

Where and by whom were these crops adopted and how did they relieve the problems of corn-growing communities in the seventeenth century? The dye crops, vegetables, fruits, herbs, and spices were all taken up with alacrity in arable areas. For technical reasons, the dye crops did not generally commend themselves to small growers, and, except in market gardens, were cultivated by more substantial farmers with capital, and even by adventurers who moved around the country renting land for short periods at high prices.[51] Madder, for example, took three years to mature and yield its first crop.

Continued
England explained', 1673, *Harl. Misc.*, VIII, 1746, p. 544, referring to the 'leaving off eating of suppers.'

[49] Ronald Webber, *The Early Horticulturists*, 1968, p. 41.

[50] Walter Blith, *The English Improver, or a New Survey of Husbandry*, 1649, title page; *idem, The English Improver Improved*, 1652, pp. 224–5.

[51] Kerridge, *Agricultural Revolution*, 1967, pp. 194, 210–11.

Moreover, the best plants had to be brought from Zealand or at least bought in London from an importer. After three years of waiting, the grower preferably needed access to a madder mill for drying and pounding, although as an alternative he could employ women and children to do the job by hand during the winter. At all events, he faced strong competition from the Dutch product, for Zealand madder was noted for its high quality and was imported in quantity. Nevertheless, if successful, madder could yield a profit of £300 an acre after three years, and £160 for an indifferent crop.[52]

The early attempts at madder growing in England are associated with a London dyer, Mr Minne, who evidently had the capital to invest in a long-term project. Around 1620 he sent George Bedford to study its secrets in the Netherlands and spent £1,000 in nine years keeping him there. When Bedford returned with some plants, he tried to grow them in Romney Marsh, a significant choice of district, for it was a happy hunting ground for outsiders who leased land in the seventeenth century and did not reside there.[53] Another adventurer with madder was Sir Nicholas Crisp who set up a madder plantation at Deptford. Later in the century it was grown for a short while near Wisbech, but since Wisbech lies on the edge of the Bedford level, we may fairly suspect that this was an enterprise promoted not by traditional fen peasants but by some of the big farmers who came into the Level after drainage and took up large tracts of land as a speculative venture.[54] The only madder growing which was carried on on a small scale occurred in market gardens around towns and mainly around cloth-working centres. Growers cultivated vegetables such as cabbage, kidney beans, radishes, onions, and herbs between the madder plants to yield a harvest in the years before the madder was ready, and since both kinds of plants needed continuous weeding, this system worked well.[55]

Woad was another dye which required capital and had to be grown on a large scale if it was to yield the best profit. 'Experiments of a little parcel,' wrote Walter Blith, were useless; one must grow enough to keep at least one mill at work. It also made heavy demands on labour during the summer for two weedings and at least two cuttings in mid-June and mid-July. Thus clothiers disliked it because it made labour

[52] Philip Miller, *The Method of Cultivating Madder*, 1758, *passim*; J. Mortimer, *The Whole Art of Husbandry*, 1707, pp. 123 *et seq.*; Blith, 1653 edn., *op. cit.*, p. 235.
[53] P.R.O., SP 16/164, nos. 53 & 53, I-III; L. B. Larking, *Proceedings principally in the County of Kent. . .* , Camden Soc., 1862, pp. 54-5.
[54] Blith, 1652, *op. cit.*, p. 235; Houghton, ed. Bradley, *op. cit.*, II, p. 372.
[55] W. Coles, *Adam in Eden*, 1657, pp. 584-5; Blith, 1652, *op. cit.*, p. 233.

short for spinning in summer. It was therefore not well suited to
pastoral areas where the cloth industry was entrenched, and much
better suited to arable-farming systems where a summer supply of
casual labour was already at hand. In these conditions it was one of
the most rewarding crops of any. 'The best estates that hath been got
in all our rich upland countries,' maintained Walter Blith, 'have been
got by it (i.e. woad).' By this he meant estates in the Midland counties
of Northamptonshire, Leicestershire, Rutland, Felden Warwickshire, Oxfordshire, parts of Worcestershire, and Gloucestershire, and
in Bedfordshire and Buckinghamshire where woad was incorporated
in a system of alternate husbandry, being a good first crop when
pasture was being broken up for corn. Its other home was in gardens
particularly around cloth towns such as Godalming, Farnham, and
Winchester.[56]

A dye crop which found a congenial home on upland arable farms
was weld, producing a bright yellow dye. It prospered on chalky
barren hillsides wherever the soil was warm and dry. Thus it was
widely grown on the downlands around Canterbury and Wye where
it was inserted into the arable rotation, being sown in with barley or
oats one year for a harvest the following year. It did not call for much
cultivation while growing, though it was a 'ticklish vegetable' prone
to blasting and to other accidents if bad weather damaged it in spring.
When harvested the stalks simply had to be dried and some of the
seed shaken out for the next year's crop. It was a plant which
diversified the interests of sheep-corn farmers without posing any
special problems of cultivation and harvesting.[57]

A new dye crop which gained ground notably in the 1660's and
1670's was safflower or bastard saffron. It yielded a reddish pink dye
and was much in demand from the silk dyers, who had hitherto
obtained the bulk of their supplies from around Strasbourg in
Germany. It was an indigenous English plant but it began to be
grown more deliberately around London, in Gloucestershire, and in
Oxfordshire in an effort to undercut the price of the imported article.
Successul growers found it extremely profitable, yielding clear gains

[56] P.R.O., SP 14/113, no. 21; Blith, 1652, *op. cit.*, pp. 226–7, 230; L. Meager, *The
Mystery of Husbandry. . .* , 1697, p. 106; Guildford Muniment Room, Loseley MS.,
1965; 1966, 1–4; Hants. County Record Office, 1583, B. I owe this reference to Miss
Adrienne Batchelor.
[57] John Banister, *Synopsis of Husbandry*, 1799, pp. 197–202. This is the most
circumstantial account of weld growing known to me. I wish to thank Dr Dennis
Baker for the reference. See also Blith, 1652, *op. cit.*, pp. 222–5; Houghton, ed. Bradley,
op. cit., II, p. 459; Mortimer, *op. cit.*, p. 127.

of £20–£30 per acre in a year; its only disadvantage was that it was harvested at the same time as wheat. Thus it is not clear whether it was adopted by pasture farmers or was taken up by arable farmers with unusually ample supplies of casual labour during the summer.[58]

Saffron was a traditional English crop which feared no competitors. It was deemed far superior in quality to any of foreign origin. Its chief use was medicinal, demand was high, and it commanded good prices. It was grown in arable fields, even in common fields, in Suffolk, Essex, and Cambridgeshire, and also in Herefordshire. It called for much hand labour, first in setting the bulbs in trenches, and then in gathering the saffron every morning for about a month in summer. Clear profit ranged from £3 10s. to over £30 an acre.[59]

Another special crop was liquorice which was grown around towns where plenty of dung was available. Since it stayed in the ground for three summers before the roots grew to any size, vegetables such as onions, leeks, and lettuces were cultivated in between. It was grown in quantity around London, at Godalming in Surrey, at Pontefract in Yorkshire, and around Worksop in Nottinghamshire. In the words of John Parkinson, the herbalist, writing in 1640 it 'is much used nowadays to be planted in great quantity even to fill many acres of ground, whereof riseth a great deal of profit to those that know how to order it and have fit grounds for it to thrive in.' At the end of the century profits of £50–£100 an acre were quoted in exceptional cases.[60]

Market gardeners have already appeared in this account as growers of dyes and medicinal crops. But vegetables and fruit were their main livelihood and contemporary descriptions leave no doubt of the remarkable success of this specialized branch of farming. Vegetable seeds were cheaply and easily bought from seedsmen in London and other towns and from country innkeepers.[61] The land required was

---

[58] Houghton, ed. Bradley, *op. cit.*, III, pp. 354–5; IV, p. 361; Hist. MSS. Comm., IX, *House of Lords MSS.*, p. 28; Carew Reynel, *op. cit.*, p. 87. A petition against a duty on safflower *c.* 1670 says that not more than 2,000 lb. were then grown in England compared with 600 cwt which was imported from Germany. This was in the early days of its commercial cultivation in England. *CSPD 1660–85, Addenda*, p. 505.

[59] W. Coles, *The Art of Simpling*, 1656, p. 51; *idem, Adam in Eden*, p. 172; Houghton, ed. Bradley, *op. cit.*, II, pp. 331–2; IV, pp. 283–7; Blith, 1652, *op. cit.*, p. 244; Mortimer, *op. cit.*, pp. 129–30.

[60] Blith, 1652, *op. cit.*, pp. 246–8; Houghton, ed. Bradley, *op. cit.*, IV, pp. 41–3; Mortimer, *op. cit.*, pp. 127–9; John Parkinson, *Paradisi in Sole*, 1656, p. 472.

[61] P.R.O., SP 46/100, fol. 242, lists an order for vegetable seeds, 1656(?); 1½ lb. of best onion seed cost 5s., ½ lb. lettuce seed 2s., and ¼ peck of radish seed 2s.

small, and every foot was profitably used; fruit trees separated the beds of vegetables. The towns which devoured the produce readily supplied dung for the next season's crops. In short, horticulture was ideally suited to small peasants with little land, no capital, but plenty of family labour, and with easy access to a town. Good market-garden land fetched high rents, but vegetables could be grown on poorer land, richly dunged, and were sown on many strips in common fields. While good-quality produce fetched handsome prices, better returns still came from the cultivation of vegetables for seed.[62] Four or five acres of land used in this way, declared John Houghton, would sometimes maintain a family better and employ more labourers than fifty acres of other land. £100 from an acre was thought a not impossible return.[63]

The prosperity of the market gardeners along Thames-side is well known but they also throve in many other districts of the Home Counties and, indeed, all over southern England in the neighbourhood of busy towns. Tewkesbury, for example, produced excellent carrots which were distributed to markets via the Avon and the Severn. In Surrey the gardeners were clustered on the Lower Greensand, on the Bagshot Beds, and on alluvial soils in the valleys of the rivers Mole and Wey. In consequence, the whole county was especially renowned for its 'gardening profit,' a reputation which is reflected in numerous tithe disputes relating to vegetables and also to hops, the latter being extensively grown around Godalming and Farnham. A dispute in 1687 at Farnham listed twenty-two people in the parish growing hops and this did not claim to be a complete list. Witnesses alleged that there were forty owners or occupiers of land planted with hops and that they covered between 250 and 300 acres of land. The tithe owners evidently shared handsomely in the benefits for the tithe of $6\frac{1}{2}$ acres of hops was said to be valued at £15.[64]

Books on horticulture found a ready sale in the second half of the seventeenth century. French works were translated into English and Englishmen wrote their own handbooks, 'wrung out of the earth' as one reviewer put it. The work to which this description was

[62] The Venetian Busino said that gravelly land around London was dug out to about 6–7 feet and filled up with the filth of the city, so making it very fertile for garden crops. Webber, *op. cit.*, p. 51; Mortimer, *op. cit.*, p. 146.

[63] John Houghton, *England's Great Happiness or a Dialogue between Content and Complaint*, 1677, p. 12; Blith, 1652, *op. cit.*, p. 261; *Philos. Trans.*, X-XII, no. 116, p. 363.

[64] *Philos. Trans.*, X-XII, no. 131, p. 796; no. 136, p. 922; Hist. MSS. Comm., *Portland II*, p. 30; P.R.O., E 134, 33 & 34 Chas. II, Hil. 26; 13 & 14 Chas. II, Hil. 7; 21 Chas II, Trin. 7; 3 Jas. II, Easter 2.

particularly applied was *The Garden of England* by Sir Hugh Platt, which incorporated much that he had learned by diligent correspondence and assiduous visits to gardeners around London. Clubs of experts were formed in London, where men received the latest information from other parts of the country and from Europe, and being 'apt to essay novelties and rarities' they turned this knowledge to good account.[65]

The intensity of cultivation in the best organized market gardens is illustrated in the probate inventory of Robert Gascoine, a gardener of St Martin in the Fields, who died in February 1718. He had row upon row of cauliflower and cabbage plants—1,000 plants were set in two banks three rows wide—radishes, carrots, colewort, young lettuce, asparagus, onions, spinach, and artichokes, while fruit trees lined the palings between the beds. Forty rods of asparagus were of the first year's planting, 124 rods were one year old, and 32 rods were ready for cutting, with colewort in the alleys between. In addition other beds of asparagus and lettuce were being forced under glass. The surname of this gardener strongly suggests a French immigrant, but if his expertise and the scale of his enterprise placed him in the first rank of market gardeners, he was not alone. Other gardeners' inventories show the same system in operation, their crops being sometimes more specialized and sometimes less. John Lee of St Martin in the Fields, dying in July 1684, had specialized in asparagus and cucumber as well as growing cherry and other fruit trees between the beds. Curtis Akers of Chelsea in April 1686 was growing herbs, asparagus, carrots, parsnips, and beans. Another gardener in St Martin in the Fields in February 1682 grew only asparagus.[66]

This evidence does not give any clue to the total volume of production, nor can we compare the value of vegetables, fruit, and other special crops with the grain, meat, and dairy produce sent to the market by other farmers.[67] But the weight of contemporary comment leaves no doubt that specialists in these branches of farming weathered the crisis of the seventeenth century with ease. By 1670 Sir William Coventry put the argument in their favour in the simplest

---

[65] See bibliography in Webber, *op. cit.*; *Philos. Trans.*, x-xii, pp. 303, 373–4, 922.

[66] Middlesex County Record Office, MI, 1718/10; 1684/93; 1686/36; 1682/18.

[67] Gregory King's estimates help us to make some guesses. He estimated the value of hemp, flax, woad, saffron, and dyes at £1,000,000, and the produce of arable land (grains and legumes) at £10,000,000. Vegetables, fruits and garden stuff were valued at £1,200,000. George E. Barnett, ed., *Two Tracts by Gregory King*, 1936, p. 36; J. Thirsk, *Economic Policy and Projects*, 1978, p. 177.

cash terms: corn and cattle were being produced to excess and the population was not increasing rapidly enough to consume it all. The solutions to this dilemma were to sell the surplus abroad (corn bounties, in fact, followed soon afterwards), or to increase the population consuming it at home, or to divert land from corn and meat to the growing of other crops, the ones which he most favoured being wood, flax, and hemp.[68] Farming textbooks in the second half of the seventeenth century consistently gave specialized cash crops their full share of space and added circumstantial details on yields, labour costs, and the net profit. The correspondence columns of John Houghton's weekly journal, *A Collection for the Improvement of Husbandry and Trade*, contained frequent homilies on their advantages; and the current market prices of saffron, caraway seed, linseed, and mustard were quoted regularly between 1649 and 1697.[69]

Except for hemp and flax, which are dealt with below in the account of pasture-farming regions, all these specialized crops were the produce of arable farming regions. As we have seen, some were taken up by the market gardeners and other small growers, others were adopted by wealthier and bolder spirits who were prepared to invest capital and take risks, and were assured of adequate casual labour in busy seasons. Such pools of labour were most readily at hand in 'open' villages and it was doubtless in the neighbourhood of such communities that the most successful enterprises were established and maintained.

Further work will undoubtedly yield instructive illustrations of the association between labour-intensive crops and over-populous villages in arable regions. An example from a town in Gloucester-shire, however, gives a vivid example of this association, arising through unusual circumstances in a pastoral area. 'Open' communities were not, of course, confined to arable districts; but their labour problems stood out most conspicuously in the latter case because they contrasted strongly with the 'closed' villages round about and because the two types complemented each other economically. There were 'open' villages in pastoral regions, but, as we shall see below, they did not present employment problems that were any different in kind from those of all other pastoral communities. Underemployment was common to them all.

[68] Brit. Mus., Sloane MS. 3828, fols. 205–10.
[69] The value of these crops in relieving poverty among the increasing population of the Netherlands is discussed in B. H. Slicher van Bath, 'Historical Demography and the Social and Economic Development of the Netherlands', *Daedalus*, Spring 1968, pp. 612, 614.

Winchcombe was a market town in the pastoral vale of Gloucester. Its markets had fallen into decay, and it may thus be presumed to have had an economy that was hardly different from that of a village, though its population was larger. Tobacco growing took firm hold, as it did in many other villages in Worcestershire and Gloucestershire. Moreover, the lord of the manor failed to hold any courts or to enforce the bylaws, and uncontrolled immigration into Winchcombe followed. Single family houses were divided into tenements to accommodate two, three, and four families. The houses fell into disrepair and were in danger of falling into the street. Lodgers and beggars thronged the place: according to the poor law overseers there were twenty households of paupers begging for alms for every household able to bestow them. The lord of the manor attempted to remedy this state of affairs in 1638 by imposing entry fines for the first time in many years, and met with indignant resistance from his tenants. The dispute of 1638 was thus concerned with an inquiry into the customs of Winchcombe. 'Hath not the neglect of executing the orders and bylaws upon offenders much encouraged the people there to become careless of offending in taking in of inmates and undertenants?' asked the Exchequer commissioners. This was clearly one of the causes of the trouble. But it is impossible for us not to see some association between tobacco growing and the inordinate growth of Winchcombe's population. The lord of the manor had neglected to control movement into the town. The trade of the market was declining. Tobacco was a labour-intensive crop which offered work and cash to all comers. People had crowded into Winchcombe for cheap accommodation and jobs, and the prohibition on the growing of tobacco after 1619 had not noticeably detracted from its popularity. The planters paid fines and later excise and continued to grow it. In 1652 an Act prohibited tobacco growing afresh, but it was followed by yet another in 1653 allowing offenders to pay excise and quietly harvest their crops. Not so in 1654. The Council of State took the legislation more seriously this time and sent soldiers to destroy the crop. Winchcombe people raised three hundred armed horse and foot to resist the attack, declaring that they were bred to the trade, and 'if they lose it they will lose their lives.' Signatories to a petition to Cromwell from Winchcombe tobacco growers numbered 110 persons.[70]

[70] P.R.O., E 134, 14 Chas. I, Mich. 31; SP 25, I, 75, pp. 374–5, 409; SP 18, 72, no. 65; R. Steele, *A Bibliography of Royal Proclamations of the Tudor and Stuart Sovereigns*, p. 150, 30 Dec. 1619, gives the first proclamation banning tobacco growing throughout England and Wales.

Tobacco growing was not stamped out until the late 1670's. Winch-combe was left in a pitiful plight, overpopulated and without adequate work. Its inhabitants subsequently resorted to stocking knitting. A visitor passing through the town in 1678 remarked upon the sight of the women folk carrying their puddings and bread to the common bakehouse, smoking and knitting as they went.[71]

In this account of arable-farming systems in the seventeenth century, three main streams of development may be discerned. On the best corn-growing lands, the large farmers prospered, offsetting the fall of grain prices by growing more grain with greater efficiency and driving out the small growers. In the vales, events followed the same course, except that in some places arable farms were converted to pasture for feeding cattle and keeping sheep. The work that was provided for the agricultural labourer was little enough on pasture farms[72] and liable to sudden interruption on arable ones. On suitable land less fertile for corn, special cash crops were grown by men with capital who could rely on the plentiful supply of casual labour from 'open' villages. However, the Diggers in Surrey, Kent, Northampton-shire, and Buckinghamshire who dug up the commons in 1649 during deep economic depression expressed the resentment of many poor labourers in arable areas when misfortune hit their employers and left them both landless and workless.[73] As for the small farmer in arable areas, he had little hope of survival, except in those districts which were suited to market gardening. Here, indeed, he had positive advantages over his richer and larger competitor.

It remains for us to consider how the peasantry fared in pastoral regions. The pasture-farming regions present a different set of social and geographical circumstances. Grass growing was the primary objective of all farmers but their ultimate goals were varied, and may be broadly grouped under four headings: in the mountains and moor-lands of northern England and on the moorlands of the south-west, cattle and sheep were reared; in the vales of the West Midlands and in other areas where the heavy soils lay under permanent grass, dairying was one speciality, rearing and fattening, sometimes in combination,

---

[71] Hist. MSS. Comm., *Portland II*, p. 303.

[72] A good example of a corn-growing village which was converted to pasture is the Verney family's home at Claydon, Bucks. It was a 'closed' village in which the rich farmers were graziers and the poor were dairymen. The surplus population which could not find work in the parish or in neighbouring ones drifted to London. I wish to thank Dr John Broad for this information.

[73] Brit. Mus., Thomason Tracts, E 669 f 15 (21) and (23); Keith Thomas, 'Another Digger Broadside', *Past and Present*, 42, 1969, pp. 57–68.

were the others. In forest areas horse breeding and pig fattening played an important role alongside stock keeping; in the fenlands of eastern England and the Somerset Level stock enterprises were mixed.[74]

Pasture farmers lived in isolated farms and hamlets as well as in villages, and the population was thus more widely scattered than in the arable lowlands. Manorial courts could not exercise close surveillance over their tenants, and tenants generally held their land by freer tenures. In many of these dispersed centres of settlement, moreover, it is noticeable that the population consisted of one class only; the poor and the rich did not always live cheek by jowl, as in the nucleated villages. In Staffordshire, for example, it is remarkable how many hamlets recorded in the Hearth Tax Return of 1666 consisted either of the rich or of the poor but not of both. In fact in many parishes, some of which had ten or fourteen separate settlements, it was usual to find that half the townships mixed the classes, while in the other half they lived firmly segregated. All in all, the inhabitants enjoyed much greater freedom and this bred in them a fiery spirit of independence, which armed them for struggle. As one nineteenth-century writer expressed it, when comparing this life favourably with that of the inhabitants of the squire's village, 'a dominant and resident landowner was the centre of intelligence, of charity, and of social life,' but for these advantages there was a social price to pay. 'It is as true in the parish as in the nation that a paternal government makes a childish people. A man whose brothers and neighbours are dependent upon him is prone to become overbearing whilst the neighbours and even the brothers are apt to become obsequious.' There was little danger of this in the pastoral districts of the kingdom.[75]

The seventeenth century was a testing time for pasture farmers living in fens and forests. Strife and controversy had surrounded enclosure and engrossing in the arable regions for more than a hundred years. Now the pastoral areas came under attack from the agricultural improvers. 'Improvement of the wastes and forests' became the slogan of the age. The Crown led the way in the early decades of the century with its schemes for the drainage of the fens and disafforestation of the forests, in both of which countrysides it had considerable landed interests. The principal investors in, and beneficiaries from, its schemes were members of the court circle, nobility and gentry, as well as the drainers and their friends. The

---

[74] These farming types are mapped in Thirsk, A.H.E.W. IV, p. 4.
[75] See Chapter XI above, pp. 166–7.

native peasantry had nothing to gain and much to lose by their designs, for in both forests and fens they were intended to turn pastoral economies into arable ones, and would inevitably have altered the structure of the local communities. The agricultural system in pastoral areas prospered on the basis of certain well-defined conditions. Society was dominated by family farmers; the economy depended on imports of corn from other districts, the use of spacious commons for feeding stock, and the availability of supplementary work in industries of many kinds. The drainers in the fens and the improvers disafforesting the forests did not fully appreciate that the destruction of the old economies meant the destruction of their societies as well; the inhabitants, on the other hand, perceived this instinctively. Most of the riots in the years before the civil war (though not the Midland Revolt of 1607) broke out in pastoral and forest areas, threatened by changes which undermined their whole way of life. The worst outbreaks occurred in the years 1629–32, when the three pillars of the economy—imported corn, spacious commons, and domestic industries—threatened to crumble simultaneously. First bad weather hit the pasture farmers, creating a shortage of hay and cattle feed, and spreading cattle murrain among their herds. Then it spoiled the corn harvests in 1630 and 1632 and made it impossible for some pastoral communities to buy corn at any price. Plague took hold in 1631. And acute unemployment hit the domestic, and particularly the cloth, industries. 'Want of work,' bad weather, and the intrusions of drainers and improvers hit the pastoral areas with unprecedented harshness. Hence the many riots in the pastoral and forest districts of Wiltshire, Dorset, Hampshire, Gloucestershire, Worcestershire, and Rutland.[76]

The conviction that improvement of the wastes and forests was the first priority in agriculture persisted if anything more strongly during the Interregnum than under the early Stuarts.[77] The only difference was that writers hedged their recommendations about with safeguards for the commoners. 'Improvement' had become a dirty word. 'Scarce anyone,' wrote John Houghton later on recalling these years,

[76] H. C. Darby, *The Draining of the Fens*, 2nd edn., 1968, pp. 49–58; P.R.O., SP 16, 185, nos. 2; Acts of the Privy Council, 1630–31, nos. 329, 330, 536, 646, 816, 818, 835, 855, 1041, 1057, 1129, 1130, 1156, 1158, 1165. See also E. Kerridge, 'The Revolts in Wiltshire against Charles I', *Wilts. Arch. and Nat. Hist. Mag.*, LVII, 1958–9, pp. 64–75.

[77] For three examples of reports and tracts on this subject, see SP 18/69, no. 6 ('Proposals by Dr John Parker and Edward Cressett for best Improvement of the Forests', 1654); Silvanus Taylor, *Common Good or the Improvement of Commons, Forests, and Chases. . .*, 1652; Appendix to Blith, 1652, *op. cit.*, pp. 263 *et seq.*, entitled 'A Remonstrance . . . for regulating Forests, Wastes or Commons. . .'

'durst offer for improvements lest he should be called a Projector as if he came from the fens to borrow 5s. to purchase £5,000 yearly, so averse were our English then from all care of improvements.'[78] The angry commoners instilled a fear which lingered well beyond Houghton's time. It still permeated the atmosphere of debates in the House of Lords on the draining of the fens in 1701 and 1711. The plan to enclose and drain was called 'the most arbitrary proceeding in the world. It invades the properties of thousands of people.'[79]

The vision which inspired would-be improvers of forests, fens, and chases during the Interregnum was the prospect of increasing employment. One-fifth more people, argued Silvanus Taylor, might be fed if waste lands were enclosed. But he did not plan or predict the class structure of such communities. The experiments which were brought to conclusion in the fens created large farms running into hundreds of acres, occupied by strangers rather than local inhabitants, including many Dutchmen.[80] Thus the crisis of the seventeenth century in these regions was created by short-sighted planners with an obsessive predilection for corn-growing economies, blind to the looming economic difficulties of corn growers elsewhere, and wilfully ignoring the fact that corn-growing systems fostered large farms far more successfully than they sustained small peasants. Their schemes were designed to create class-divided communities of the lowland kind with their due proportion of yeomen, husbandmen, labourers, and paupers, presided over by an affluent gentleman. Fortunately, they did not succeed in moulding much of pastoral England in the image of the arable lowlands.

Outside these disturbed areas, agricultural improvements by pasture farmers were necessarily made at modest cost, did not generally disturb neighbours, and thus leave less trace in our records. The social obstacles to expensive capital improvements have already been illustrated in the experiences of Rowland Vaughan who devised the scheme for watering meadows in the Golden Valley of Hereford-shire. He cheerfully spent large sums in order to get his young lambs ready for the butcher a month before his competitors. His

---

[78] J. Houghton, *A Collection for Improvement of Husbandry and Trade*, 1692, p. 76.

[79] Thirsk, *English Peasant Farming*, pp. 126–7.

[80] P.R.O., SP 46/88, fols. 173 *et seq.*, illustrate the experiences of Rumbold Jacobson, merchant of London and lessee of 428 acres of Hatfield Chase, *c*. 1640–1. The report in 1654 by Parker and Cressett (see above, p. 206, n. 77), discussing the possibility of improving the forests by leasing out large portions, assumed that the commoners would not take up such leases out of hostility to the whole project, while 'others will be very tender of disgusting their neighbours the commoners in hiring it from them.' P.R.O., SP 18, 69, no. 6.

neighbours, on the other hand, who were family farmers, dairying in the summer and weaving hemp and flax in the winter, pursued another course of life altogether.[81]

Despite the difficulties, described by Andrew Yarranton, in spreading innovations among farmers without much spare cash for experiments that could easily fail, stock in pasture-farming areas benefited from the ley grasses that were improving the feed of animals in arable areas. In general, however, they continued to be fed mainly on grass and hay, though care was devoted to the improvement of the herbage by careful grazing, frequent cutting down of thistles, rushes, etc., and by the application of dung, lime, potash, and ashes, and by drainage with open or covered drains. These measures, which feature prominently in the replies to the Georgical inquiries in 1664, were all traditional, but they nevertheless produced substantial improvements in the feeding capacity of pastures. Walter Blith in 1652 particularly extolled the efforts of farmers in the woodland parts, 'as in Worcestershire, Warwickshire, Staffordshire, Shropshire, and Wales-ward and northward,' in improving their coarse lands by these traditional methods. He judged the land to be as highly improved as many parts of the fielden country *and fuller of wealthier inhabitants.*[82]

Little evidence survives concerning the selection and care of stock; but the social structure of pastoral communities affords part of the explanation. They did not produce men who kept accounts or had the flair for publicly advertising their achievements. Samuel Hartlib complained in 1651 that 'we advance not the best species,' but it is not clear which farmers he had in mind; and he did single out for measured praise the pasture farmers of Lancashire and some other northern counties, who 'are a little careful in these particulars.'[83] What is clear is that the pastoral regions, as the main breeding centres for stock, had been responsible for developing a remarkable number of different breeds of cattle, sheep, and horses, which were adapted to suit different environments. If a man changed the environment by improving his land, then he could change the breed of his animals, as farmers of enclosed pastures in the sixteenth century evidently changed the breeds of sheep which they kept.

[81] See *supra*, pp. 189–90.
[82] Royal Society, Georgical Enquiries, Classified Papers, x(3), *passim*. These reports are summarized in R. V. Lennard, 'English Agriculture under Charles II. . . ', *Econ. Hist. Rev.*, IV, 1932–4, pp. 23–45; Blith, 1652, *op. cit.*, p. 38, my italics.
[83] Samuel Hartlib, *His Legacie*, 1651, p. 96. These remarks were made with particular reference to dairy cattle.

If we look in vain for spectacular innovations and the willingness to invest capital such as that which possessed corn growers like Henry Best, Jethro Tull, and others, this does not mean that the populations of pastoral areas were living in a derelict and miserable backwater, outside the main stream of enterprise. Traditionally, pastoral areas were the abode of small family farmers and their way of life suited their environment. The common pastures were a community asset available to all, and many farming systems, like dairying and pig keeping, required small capital. But another key to the success of this way of life, which enabled men to weather successfully the seventeenth-century crisis, was the many additional opportunities for earning a living. Some simply involved exploiting the diversity of natural resources: fishing, fowling, cutting reeds for thatching and for fuel in the fens; timber felling and the manufacture of woodware in the forests. Mining offered work in some areas; in others there were domestic industries such as potting, nail making, metal working, lace making, stocking knitting, and the weaving of woollen, linen, and hempen cloth. In some districts the growth of flax and hemp weaving was facilitated by larger imports of the raw material from the Baltic which was more widely distributed inland as rivers were improved. Nidderdale in West Yorkshire and parts of Derbyshire, for example, enjoyed an easy link with the port of Hull.[84] In other counties the domestic weaving of hemp and flax went hand in hand with an increase in the cultivation of these crops. Some of the propaganda in favour of growing them was directed at counties lacking adequate domestic industries, such as Leicestershire, Northamptonshire, and Oxfordshire.[85] In fact, however, it was in pastoral areas where handicraft industries were already well established that it spread most successfully, particularly in the West Midlands, in parts of Herefordshire, Worcestershire, Warwickshire, Nottinghamshire, Derbyshire, and Staffordshire.[86] Staffordshire, indeed, was described by Robert Sharrock as exemplary in its system of growing these two crops; and it seems legitimate to argue from the increasing references in this county to tithes of hemp and flax in the later seventeenth and early eighteenth centuries that production was expanding.[87] Other pastoral

---

[84] Bernard Jennings, ed., *A History of Nidderdale*, 1967, pp. 171–2, 176.

[85] P. E. Dove, *Account of Andrew Yarranton, the Founder of English Political Economy*, 1854, p. 44.

[86] Blith, 1652, *op. cit.*, p. 254.

[87] Robert Sharrock, *An Improvement to the Art of Gardening*, 1694, pp. 43–4. The evidence for larger crops of hemp and flax comes from the glebe terriers of Staffordshire which refer with increasing frequency, 1698–1735, to tithes of hemp and flax in

areas which grew flax and hemp were the marshlands of Thames-side in Essex and Kent, the fens of eastern England and the Somerset Level, parts of Dorset, the Weald of Kent around Maidstone, which was the renowned thread-making centre of the kingdom, and the forests of Northamptonshire. When Sir Richard Weston came back from the Netherlands urging flax growing, he recommended experiments in St Leonards Forest in Sussex.[88] Like the industrial crops which flourished in arable regions, hemp and flax were universally regarded as profitable ventures: some hemp and flax ground was rented for £3 an acre, labour costs added another £2 or £3, but the crop was worth £10–12. Thus profits were in the region of £5–6 an acre.[89]

In pastoral regions farming combined with industrial employment was almost common form. The combination was well integrated into a life focused on the family as the wage-earning group. The nailer's forge and the pottery were sheds next door to the farmhouse, while the weaving loom might be in the parlour or chamber or in a separate weaving shed.[90] A rare glimpse of the detailed programme of daily life is offered in the diary of a farmer-weaver in 1782–3 who worked out of doors one day till three o'clock and then wove two yards of cloth before sunset. On wet days he might weave eight and a half to nine yards. One Christmas eve he wove two yards before 11 a.m. and spent the rest of the day doing winter jobs around the house and midden. In addition, he had occasional work on other people's farms, hauling timber, preparing a calf stall, fetching and carrying with his own horse and cart, and picking cherries.[91] The variety of work compensated for the absence of some material comforts. Indeed, the use of the term 'by-employments' for the industrial occupations of pasture farmers may convey a false impression. They were not accidental or subsidiary, secondary, or a miserable makeshift. They were an integral part of the pastoral way of life. They remain so in many pastoral regions of England, though the numbers of people so

Continued

the parishes of the county. I wish to thank Dr Eric Evans for assembling this evidence for me and allowing me to use it here.

[88] Blith, 1652, *op. cit.*, pp. 251, 254; Michael Williams, 'The Draining and Reclamation of Meare Pool, Somerset', Thirteenth Annual Report, Somerset River Board, 1962–3, Bridgwater, 1963, p. 1; Thirsk, A.H.E.W. IV, p. 13; Richard Weston, *Discourse of Husbandry used in Brabant and Flanders*, 2nd edn, ed. Samuel Hartlib, 1652, p. 18.

[89] Hartlib, *His Legacie*, pp. 40–1; Houghton, ed. Bradley, *op. cit.*, II, p. 389.

[90] Cf. Marie B. Rowlands, 'Industry and Social Change in Staffordshire, 1660–1760', *Trans. Lichfield & S. Staffs. Arch. & Hist. Soc.*, IX, 1967–8, p. 39.

[91] Quoted by Edward Thompson in 'Time, Work-Discipline, and Industrial Capitalism', *Past and Present*, 38, pp. 71–2.

occupied form such a small proportion of the total population that they are not seriously considered.[92] But in countries where peasant-workers still represent a much larger slice of the population, this way of life is recognized and studied as a permanent social and economic phenomenon with merits of its own. In Poland, for example, it is agreed that the family budget of the peasant-worker at the present time is decidedly larger than that of the farmer of a medium-sized holding with only his land to support him.[93] In England today it is reasonable to regard the peasant-worker as a negligible element in rural society, but not so in the seventeenth century. Indeed, we may guess that such farmers must have comprised somewhere near half the farming population of the kingdom. The economy and fortunes of this group deserve more attention than has yet been given to them for theirs is a different story with a different chronology from that of the small owner-occupier and small tenant in arable regions.

It is too early to make dogmatic generalized statements about the economic fortunes of traditional pasture-farming areas in the seventeenth century or about the size of their populations. But there are suggestive clues to some economic trends. Multiple sources of income attracted immigrants to the pastoral areas. Numerous contemporaries remarked (usually with disapproval) on this migration, particularly into the forests and fens of the Midland, southern, and eastern counties. Against this background the Act of Settlement in 1662 takes on a special significance. Its preamble refers to the movement of people from parish to parish 'to settle themselves where there is the best stock, the largest commons or wastes to build cottages, and the most woods for them to burn and destroy.' Roger Coke, writing eight years after the passing of this Act, believed it to be without effect: squatters on the waste were increasing daily.[94]

In some places we can measure a substantial growth of population at least until the Act of Settlement. In others it continued into the early eighteenth century. In part of the Lincolnshire fenland, for example, numbers almost doubled between 1563 and 1723, whereas in arable parts of the same county the population at these two dates was more or less the same. Warwickshire figures of average populations in arable and forest areas do not illustrate growth rates but they

---

[92] They represented 11.2 per cent of the total number of occupiers of land in England and Wales in the National Farm Survey of 1941-3.

[93] Władisław Adamski, 'Investigations on Off-Farm Income in Poland', summary of a paper read to a seminar at Birmingham University on Peasant Farming in Europe, March 1968.

[94] Thirsk, A.H.E.W. IV, pp. 409–12; Coke, *op. cit.*, p. 16.

do demonstrate the larger populations living in the forests: the average size of communities in old enclosed arable parishes in 1663 was 46 households, in unenclosed arable parishes 54 households, and in pastoral (Arden) parishes 120 households.[95]

Professor Everitt's comparison of labourers with less than an acre of land in the period 1500–1640 shows a considerably higher proportion in fielden parishes (72 per cent) than in fell parishes (65 per cent) or forest parishes (44 per cent), and of course, in fell and forest regions the common rights that went with land were much more valuable.[96] Among the more substantial peasants an increase, rather than a decrease, took place in the number of landholders in the course of the seventeenth century. In the forest of Pendle, Lancashire, for example, the number of medium and small copyholders increased markedly. In four stock-rearing communities in Pendle the 55 copyholders in 1608 more than doubled to 129 in 1662.[97] In Nidderdale, Yorkshire, a noticeable decline in the average size of farms had taken place by the late seventeenth century.[98] In Rossendale, Lancashire, 72 copyholders in 1507 had increased to 200 by 1608 and to 314 by 1662. The increase was partly brought about by the enclosure of waste land, partly by the subdivision of existing farms. Land was being distributed among more and more people (engrossing was practically unknown), and the process was not reversed in Rossendale even in the eighteenth and nineteenth centuries. After the introduction of cotton manufacture, holdings became more, and not less, minutely subdivided. A rough calculation suggests that the proportion of holdings of less than fifteen acres was two-fifths in the seventeenth and two-thirds in the nineteenth century.[99]

In other pastoral areas comparisons over time are not possible, but it is clear that at the time of the Parliamentary enclosures many pastoral parishes still had a remarkable number of small proprietors. At Foleshill in Arden, Warwickshire, in 1775 794 acres were divided between 107 different proprietors. In the fenland of Holland, Lincolnshire, Gosberton had 160 landowners in 1798, Quadring over

---

[95] Thirsk, *English Peasant Farming*, pp. 141, 168–70; J. M. Martin, 'The Parliamentary Enclosure Movement and Rural Society in Warwickshire', A.H.R., XV, i, p. 20.

[96] Thirsk, A.H.E.W. IV, pp. 400–6.

[97] Mary Brigg, 'The Forest of Pendle in the Seventeenth Century', *Trans. Lancs. and Cheshire Hist. Soc.*, CXIII, p. 72.

[98] Jennings, ed., *op. cit.*, pp. 147, 171–2.

[99] G. H. Tupling, *The Economic History of Rossendale*, Chetham Soc., n.s., 86, 1927, pp. 76, 235, 95, 227–9.

150. Small peasants were not noticeably losing their hold on the land, and in some places they were strengthening it in the sense that more people were acquiring a small stake in the soil.[100]

Most writers in the second half of the seventeenth century explicitly or implicitly held the belief that pasture farming was more profitable than corn growing. Charles Davenant, using Gregory King's figures on land use and yields, offered the opinion in 1699 that 'it seems more to the national interest of England to employ its land to the breeding and feeding of cattle than to the produce of corn.[101] This general supposition invites belief because it accords with the general trend in agriculture throughout western Europe between 1650 and 1750.[102]

In England pasture farmers enjoyed an assured and relatively stable market for their produce, and solved the problem created by the dwindling size of their holdings by undertaking more industrial employment. These developments caused some writers to press the novel argument that pasture farming supported a larger population than corn. Reckoning in the work created by crops like wool, hemp, and flax, it was plausible. A Gloucestershire agriculturist who had promoted hemp and flax growing argued the case from his own practical experience. He calculated that forty acres of flax would employ more than 800 people for a year, and, even allowing a wage bill of 8d. a day for 300 men, 6d. a day for 300 women, and 3d. a day for 200 young people, it would still yield more profit to the sower than 160 acres of corn or grass.[103] Sir Richard Weston claimed that one acre of flax was worth four to five acres of corn; and to prove that pastoral regions generally provided more work than corn lands he turned to the examples of Normandy, Picardy, and Lombardy in France, Holland, Friesland, Zeeland, and Flanders — all pastoral regions which, he claimed, were the most populous places in Europe. Dairy farms occupying 100 acres of land employed many more hands than 100 acres of the best corn land; even sheep keeping, while it depopulated the countryside, nevertheless kept a great many people

[100] J. M. Martin, 'Warwickshire and the Parliamentary Enclosure Movement', Birmingham University Ph.D. thesis, 1965, pp. 80–1; David Grigg, *The Agricultural Revolution in South Lincolnshire*, 1966, p. 84. Cf. the saying that the Isle of Axholme had so many freeholders that whoever got the Isle could get the county. Francis Hill, *Georgian Lincoln*, p. 30.

[101] Charles Davenant, *An Essay upon the Probable Methods of Making a People Gainers in the Balance of Trade*, 1699, pp. 88–9.

[102] B. H. Slicher van Bath, *The Agrarian History of Western Europe, A.D. 500–1850*, 1963, pp. 206–17.

[103] P.R.O., SP 14/180, no. 79.

in working the wool into cloth.[104] John Houghton in 1692 argued along the same lines. Did not the wool and skins produced by an acre of pasture create greater employment than tillage? He had made some calculations and promised some time to print them.[105]

While the evidence is circumstantial and fragmentary it seems reasonable to suggest that the pasture-farming regions of the kingdom in the seventeenth century presented a picture of greater economic prosperity for larger numbers of people than the arable regions. The rebuilding of peasant houses in the north and west which took place generally after the Civil War period may perhaps be deemed a further reflection of this prosperity.[106]

The merits of the dual economy of pastoral regions were frequently misunderstood. Defoe gives us one of the few portraits of the farmer-leadminer's life in the Derbyshire Peak. The sight of a family living in a cave with little ready cash filled him with horror. The wife was inordinately grateful when he and his friends tipped the loose change from their purses into her hand. And yet he had to admit that the cave was clean though simple; the children were very bonny, the wife was comely. A close of corn at the door was ready to be harvested. A cow, thin though it was, grazed at hand and pigs rooted about nearby. Bacon hung in the roof. The husband worked in the mines, and when the wife was free, she washed ore.[107] This was clearly a poor family by the standards of pasture-farming communities generally, but it was not the abject hopeless poverty of landless, and frequently workless, labourers who formed a growing proportion (at least a third and more) of the population of arable villages in the lowlands.

The most sympathetic and understanding observer of this economy in the later seventeenth century, however, was the Puritan divine, Richard Baxter. Indeed, he is an explicit exponent of the more general argument advanced in the paper. In 1691 he wrote his last treatise, *The Poor Husbandman's Advocate to Rich Racking Landlords*. Baxter came from Kidderminster in Worcestershire, a thickly populated region of peasant workers of every kind, metal workers, nailers, potters, miners, leather workers, and glass workers. He had also lived in and around London, in Westminster, and in Acton, Middlesex. His plea to landlords to show generosity to husbandmen

[104] Hartlib, *His Legacie*, pp. 55–6. Hartlib listed the commodities got from cattle (meaning cattle and sheep) as cloth, stuffs, stockings, butter, cheese, hides, shoes, and tallow.

[105] Houghton, ed. Bradley, *op. cit.*, I, p. 49.

[106] M. W. Barley, *The English Farmhouse and Cottage*, 1961, pp. 227, 230, 236, 244.

[107] D. Defoe, *A Tour through England and Wales*, Everyman edn, II, pp. 161–3.

was not a petition on behalf of all husbandmen, but only on behalf of what he called the racked poor; *not*, he observed, the market gardeners of the Home Counties who, though they paid double rent for their grounds, had a treble opportunity to improve them. (These are some of our arable farmers producing labour demanding crops.) 'Nor do I speak of those tenants that have some small tenement of £5 or £10 per annum and have besides a trade which doth maintain them.' He instanced here weavers, butchers, tailors, joiners, and carpenters. Elsewhere he spoke of the comparative security of life of the nailers, spurriers, swordsmiths, scythesmiths, and sword makers around Dudley, Stourbridge, Birmingham, Walsall, Wednesbury, and Wolverhampton. In short, his was an impassioned plea not for peasant-workers in pasture-farming regions, or for arable farmers growing special cash crops, but for the poor husbandmen in the traditional corn-growing districts, whence the small landowners were fast disappearing, and whence, in his view, small tenants were also being driven by rack-renting landlords.[108]

One of the questions that follows from this analysis of social and economic trends in the seventeenth-century countryside is how and why the dual economies in pastoral regions stimulated technical innovation in industry. It is plainly anomalous to expect agricultural innovations of an expensive kind from these regions. The pressure upon industry seems to derive from the very success of the dual economy. As the market for industrial goods expanded, it met labour shortages which peasant workers could not, or would not, satisfy, and which are reflected in the rapid rise in textile wages in the first half of the eighteenth century.[109] For peasant workers to turn wholly to industry meant surrendering their hold on the land and surrendering, moreover, a life of varied labour as well as independence.[110] The advantage to the national economy of factory-based industries may seem clear enough if we take a sternly economic view excluding other considerations, but it was purchased at the price

---

[108] F. J. Powicke, ed., *The Reverend Richard Baxter's Last Treatise*, John Rylands Library Publication, 1926, pp. 25–8.

[109] Professor Crouzet suggests in a recent essay that one of the two most powerful stimuli to technical innovation was the shortage of labour in the handicraft industries of S. Lancs., Yorks., the Midlands, and in the metal-working industries of the Black Country. F. Crouzet, 'Angleterre et France au XVIIIe siècle. Essai d'analyse comparée de deux croissances économiques', *Annales E.S.C.*, 21e année, no. 2, 1966, pp. 286–7. See also E. W. Gilboy, *Wages in Eighteenth-Century England*, 1934, pp. 191 *et seq.*

[110] This is the view of Gilboy, *op. cit.*, p. 143, and is supported by other authorities there cited. See also Crouzet, *op. cit.*, p. 288; N. J. Smelser, *Social Change in the Industrial Revolution*, 1959, p. 77.

of a traditional, and in many respects congenial, life centred upon a smallholding of land, with its industrial annexe. Throughout the seventeenth century, at least, the economics of smallholdings in pastoral regions were not such as to drive the peasant worker from the land.

Phyllis Deane has recently described in general terms the causes of the industrial and agricultural revolutions. She concluded with certain misgivings about generalizations on a national scale. 'The national economy is not always the most convenient unit of economic analysis. The effect of regional variations in economic conditions is that statistics relating to a particular area may give no indication of the comparable movements for the nation as a whole, and that the national aggregates may obscure the trends for regions in which the significant changes are taking place. An attempt to assess the quality and rate of economic change at the national level may not lead to meaningful results whether we are looking for the significant continuities or for the significant discontinuities of history.'[111] These reflections justify a first attempt at illuminating 'the trends for regions in which the significant changes are taking place.' It carries the story only to the end of the seventeenth century. To disentangle regional trends from national aggregates, more detailed local studies are needed which will trace developments in the seventeenth century more precisely and, more important, in the early eighteenth century when a further shift of emphasis took place in the economies of both pastoral and arable regions and the ground was finally prepared for two separate revolutions after 1750.

[111] Phyllis Deane, *The First Industrial Revolution*, 1965, pp. 17–18.

XIII

INDUSTRIES IN THE COUNTRYSIDE

In 1634 William White, William Steventon, and John Perkins, gentlemen, were plaintiffs in a suit filed in the Court of Exchequer against William and Oliver Trotter, Richard Haygarth, Henry Mason and seven others. It concerned the customs of the lordship of Dent, a manor in the west Yorkshire dales which embraced Dentdale and Garsdale. In consequence, justices were appointed to make personal investigation, and at the free school in Dent on a wintry day in the middle of January questions were put to the oldest inhabitants with the longest memories. Edward Lande, an octogenarian of Dent, declared that if a customary tenant died seised of a tenement without having devised or disposed of it by will, then it descended 'to all his sons equally to be divided amongst them.' And, he added, 'by reason of such division of tenements, the tenants are much increased in number more than they were, and the tenements become so small in quantity that many of them are not above three or four acres apiece and generally nor above eight or nine acres so that they could not maintain their families were it not by their industry in knitting coarse stockings.'[1]

Here is an illuminating contemporary explanation for the rise of a local handicraft industry. It does not attribute it to the energies of an entrepreneur, or to the ease with which supplies of wool could be procured locally, or to any compelling market demands, but to the special social and economic circumstances of the inhabitants of Garsdale and Dentdale, which compelled them to seek some employment in addition to their farming. It suggests that in other districts where rural industries are known to have played an important part in augmenting farm incomes, it would be rewarding to consider the agricultural and social situation in which they began.

Such an analysis is, of course, beset with pitfalls. There is no certainty or finality in any explanation for the growth of a rural industry in one district rather than another. Its location may seem logical enough if it uses raw materials which are available in the

[1] Public Record Office (= PRO) E 134, 10–11 Chas. I, Hil. 22.

district. But many rural industries have achieved national importance which do not fit into this category. It is usual, for example, to attribute the cloth industries of the West country, of Kent, and of Suffolk, to the availability of certain natural resources necessary for the making of cloth, namely, a local supply of wool, a plentiful supply of water, the existence of local seams of fuller's earth, and good communications with markets and ports. None of these reasons is completely satisfying. As Thomas Fuller observed in the mid-seventeenth century, local wool did not make a cloth industry. Counties like Leicestershire, Lincolnshire, Northamptonshire and Cambridgeshire, which had 'most of wool, have least of clothing therein'. The wool was usually available in a neighbouring farming region, but not in the region where the industry was situated. The clothiers of the Weald of Kent could procure wool from the fat sheep of the Romney Marshes or from the sheep on the Downs, but in the Weald itself, in the words of a fourteenth-century commentator, 'there is not an abundant growth of wools.' The Wiltshire industry could obtain its wool from the Cotswold hills and from Salisbury Plain, but much of the industry was concentrated in north-west Wiltshire where wool was among the least important products of the farm. The clothiers of central Suffolk could have bought some of their wool in east or west Suffolk but seem, in fact, to have relied on the wools of the Midland counties, particularly Leicestershire, Lincolnshire, Northamptonshire and Cambridgeshire. As wool was so easily transported, and since also it is doubtful whether there was any corner of England which did not have a wool-producing area in the vicinity, it can never have been the factor which made or marred a nascent industry.[2]

Local seams of fuller's earth were evidently no more vital to a cloth industry than wool, for the East Anglian cloth centres relied on supplies from Kent. Nor was a convenient local port essential since the West country cloth merchants in the Tudor period managed without undue inconvenience to carry their burdens by road to Blackwell Hall in London. Water was essential for the fulling process, but water alone did not make a cloth centre, or the embryonic industry of Hertfordshire in the early fifteenth century would not have died a mysterious death in the early sixteenth. It may be argued,

---

[2] Thos. Fuller, *The Church History of Britain* (1845), II, p. 287; Robert Furley; *A History of the Weald of Kent*, II part I, p. 336; *V. C. H. Wiltshire*, IV, p. 44; J. E. Pilgrim, *The Cloth Industry in Essex and Suffolk, 1558–1640*, unpublished M.A. thesis, London University, 1939, p. 2.

of course, that the location of a handicraft industry can be an accident due to the enterprise of a single individual. It is not difficult to find both abortive and successful examples in the better-documented eighteenth and nineteenth centuries. But even in these instances it is impossible to dissociate their survival from their success in procuring and organizing an adequate labour force, and we are once more brought up against the question of the social and economic environment. Finally, since the geographers are permitted to enumerate the circumstances favouring the growth of a market town or port without claiming that these were the chief or only determinants, it seems reasonable (with encouragement from the inhabitants of Dentdale) to seek in an analysis of the farming economy and, more particularly, the social structure of the local community some of the circumstances which favoured the growth of rural industries in one region rather than another.[3]

It is impossible in a brief essay to consider all the country industries which flourished in England in the fifteenth to seventeenth centuries. Nor is there enough information about local economies to permit such a prodigious task to be undertaken here and now. Attention will therefore be given only to those industries which were carried on in conjunction with farming, and which catered for a national rather than a local market. But such a definition embraces the extractive industries, whose location was determined by the presence of minerals in the ground. In these mineral-yielding areas, industry and agriculture were ancient bedfellows, and in most places it is doubtful whether the beginnings of settled agriculture preceded or followed the mining for tin, lead, copper, iron, stone, and chalk. There is, therefore, no need to seek for pre-disposing social and economic circumstances to account for the rise of the industry. This is not to deny, however, that many interesting problems concerning these regions await investigation. The historian cannot fail to ponder how the resources of families were disposed in such communities to enable the two occupations to be dovetailed together. In general, mineral production was concentrated in the western half of England where much of the farming was pastoral, and since it required less labour than arable farming, it left the householder free to engage in mining while his family attended to the land and the animals. In this way, the mining-farming family made a success of the two occupations. But what of the social conflicts and economic problems that must have

[3] *Cal. S.P Dom. 1623–5*, p. 216; *V.C.H. Hertfordshire*, IV, p. 210.

developed as populations grew and an increasing number of workers took to mining without farming? Over England as a whole there is no doubt that the mining-farming communities were large and frequently populous. A description of Derbyshire by the local justices of the peace in 1620 affords one example of a country where, already it seems, the farmers were in danger of being outnumbered by the industrial workers. 'Many thousands live in work at lead mines, coal mines, stone pits, and iron works.' 'The hardcorn gotten therein will not serve above the one half of the people that live in it, a great part of our county bearing nothing but oats.' Hence, the population was heavily dependent for its food on Danzig rye brought from Hull via the Trent.[4]

These and other problems of rural-industrial communities deserve proper study in any complete account of industries in the countryside. Here they are omitted in order that attention may be given to the handicraft industries which developed within communities already engaged in farming. Of these, the Wiltshire cloth industry was more ancient than any and grew to maturity earlier than any other. Its geographical and economic situation furnishes an apt illustration of some general propositions which can be tested elsewhere.

The first signs of a cloth-making industry in the countryside, supplying a national market, date from the second half of the fourteenth century. Before that clothmaking had been an industry of the towns like Marlborough and Salisbury. But when once the fulling mill began to drive the industry to the banks of fast running streams and so into the countryside, the villages immediately in the vicinity of the old cloth towns, in the Kennet valley around Marlborough and in the Wylye and Nadder valleys around Salisbury, began to attract a population of weavers, dyers, and fullers. When the industry began to expand and to serve a national market, in the late fourteenth century, a larger labour force had to be found, and at this point new rural centres, not nurtured by the old cloth towns, began to emerge—in the north-western sector of the county, between Malmesbury and Westbury, a region given over to the small pasture farms of cheese-making dairymen, and in the south-western corner around Mere, in the country of small butter-making farms. Wiltshire had two main

---

[4] G. R. Lewis, *The Stannaries*, pp. 185–7; PRO SP 14/113, no. 17. For earlier examples of economic conflict, *see* H.P.R. Finberg, *Tavistock Abbey*, pp. 177–8. For a map of areas of mineral production in the fourteenth century, see H.C. Darby, *An Historical Geography of England before A.D. 1800*, p. 257.

types of farming. The dairy farms lay in country that was early enclosed, while a sheep-corn husbandry sustained the chalk and lime-stone lands of Salisbury Plain and the Cotswolds, and kept many of the fields and commons open until the end of the eighteenth century. Owing to the paucity of documents in the Middle Ages, the sharp contrast between the two types of farming is not visible until the sixteenth century. But distinctions so fundamental are not made overnight. It is certain that they were of long standing, and later gave a very different character to the agricultural revolution in each region in the eighteenth and nineteenth centuries. The contrast has been summarized thus:—'the inclosed, non-manorial countries—the cheese and butter countries—were the lands of family farmers and self-employed persons, while the manorialized, champion, sheep-and-corn countries—the chalk, Cotswold, and Corallian countries—were the main field for the development of agrarian capitalism and for the agricultural revolution'.[5]

The identity of the clothing and dairying regions in the west country did not escape the notice of Daniel Defoe. The logical sequence of his remarks, describing first the cloth industry and then the dairying in the same region, is somewhat obscured by his liking for digressions. But in fact his observation is precise. In the area enclosed between the towns of Bristol, Sherborne, Devizes, and Cirencester, in a district spreading through part of Wiltshire, Somerset, and Gloucestershire, Defoe found a flourishing cloth industry *and* 'large feeding farms which we call dairies' where cheese was made and pigs fattened on the waste products.[6]

In this Defoe saw no sociological significance. But it may be more than a coincidence that exactly the same type of farming should characterize the area of Suffolk in which its cloth industry lay. Here the speciality was coloured cloth for which demand was at its height in the late fifteenth and early sixteenth centuries. Apart from a few scattered centres further north and east where a different cloth, called kersey, was made, the industry was centred upon the southern portion of central Suffolk in and around Sudbury. The farming region of central Suffolk which covers some two-thirds of the county is traditionally known as the wood-pasture region—the region of dairy farms exporting cheese and butter to London in large quantity

[5] E. Carus-Wilson, 'The Woollen Industry before 1550,' *V.C.H. Wilts.*, IV, p. 115 *et seq*; E. Kerridge, 'Agriculture, 1500–1793', *ibid.*, p. 43 *et seq.*
[6] Daniel Defoe, *A Tour through the whole island of Great Britain*, ed. G. D. H. Cole (1927), II, pp. 280, 284–5.

in the sixteenth century. It was old-enclosed country, possibly it had never been open, but had been cleared of woodland and the land henceforth held in severalty. The other farming regions of Suffolk consisted of a small area of fenland in the north-west corner of the county, and two strips of sand and breckland lying to east and west of the wood-pasture region, where sheep-folding and barley production kept the land fertile and yielded wool for the clothier. But the sand lands had no cloth industry. The economies of the wood pasture region and the eastern and western sands were succinctly described by the local justices of the peace in 1622. 'Our county consists of two several conditions of soil, the one champion, which yields for the most part sheep and some corn; the other enclosed pasture grounds employed most to grazing and dairy, so as the champion doth not only serve itself with corn but is forced continually to supply the woodland especially in wet and cold years.'[7]

The situation of the Suffolk cloth industry was remarkably similar to that of Wiltshire except in one respect. It did not spread throughout Suffolk's wood-pasture region, but was concentrated at the southern end. This may be due entirely to the network of rivers in the southern half of the county emptying fast-flowing waters into the estuaries of the Stour, the Orwell, and the Deben, and so far superior to the slow-moving waters of the river Waveney on the northern border of the county. But consideration must be given to some of the social factors which may have affected central Suffolk unevenly. Unfortunately, Suffolk is a problem county where it is easier to pose questions than to answer them. Its settlement history, for example, is impossible to unravel without a study of its place names, and this is only the first difficulty in the way of understanding the social organization of central Suffolk. But if the inhabitants of Dentdale were correct in implying that large populations could sometimes attract industries to them, then we must consider the possibility that the clothing district of Suffolk, which was more thinly settled than north Suffolk in Domesday times, had grown more populous by the fourteenth century, and posed problems of unemployment and over-population which industries alone could solve. Had its land proved specially attractive to immigrants in the Middle Ages, or did its natives, for some reason inherent in their own social institutions, produce and support larger families than elsewhere? Neither of these questions can be satisfactorily answered at present, but since they concern a problem of general importance to the study of all rural

[7]   J. E. Pilgrim, *op. cit.*, *passim*; PRO SP 14/128, no. 65.

industries—namely the causes of differential rates of population growth—it is worth pausing to discuss them. The manorial organization of central Suffolk was weak. Its manors were small, and frequently consisted of little more than a demesne farm with two or three small holdings. A weak manorial framework could and did permit an unusually rapid growth of population through immigration in regions where there was land to attract the landless.[8] Since by the sixteenth century parts of central Suffolk were suffering a distinct shortage of commons and waste, earlier migration to the district for lack of any strong manorial control is a factor to be reckoned with. The second possibility is that local customs of inheritance had contributed to the large populations. In the fen villages of Lincolnshire, the custom of partible inheritance, by providing all the male children with a portion of the paternal land, is known to have played a decisive part in the growth of large village communities.[9] Partible inheritance was practised in Suffolk, though no one has yet defined the districts in which it was most commonly found. The custom of Borough English was also well known in Suffolk and seems to have been widespread in the northern half of central Suffolk and in the south-east coastal area. It is usual to assume that this custom had the same effect as the rule of primogeniture in keeping one male member on the family holding and sending the others away. But, in fact, no assumptions concerning the effects of Borough English can yet safely be made, for there is reason to suspect that when the youngest son inherited the residue of his father's estate, his older brothers had often already received their share. If this were generally true, Borough English may have differed little from partible inheritance in its effect on the ownership of land, and the two customs, working their effects in certain districts while the rule of primogeniture governed others. may have had significant consequences for the uneven distribution of population in the county as a whole.[10]

[8] *V.C.H. Suffolk*, I, pp. 633, 640; cf. R. H. Hilton, *Social Structure of Rural Warwickshire in the Middle Ages*, Dugdale Soc. Occ. Paper, no. 9, pp. 10–15.

[9] H. E. Hallam, 'Some thirteenth century censuses'. *Econ. Hist. Rev.*, 2nd Ser., X, no. 3 (1958), p. 340 *et seq*. This article suggests not only that partible inheritance caused young people to stay in their native places because they had land to inherit, but also that they married younger and had more children. *See* pp. 354, 355.

[10] Some Suffolk examples of partible inheritance are listed in G. C. Homans, *English Villagers in the Thirteenth Century*, p. 428, note 16. On Borough English, *see* the inconclusive account in Thomas Robinson, *The Common Law of Kent with an appendix concerning Borough English* (1822), pp. 386, 389, and G. R. Corner, 'On the Custom of Borough English', *Proc. Suffolk Inst. of Archaeology*, II, pp. 227–41. I wish to thank Mr Norman Scarfe for a map of places in Suffolk where Borough English was the custom.

We can do no more than speculate on the effects both of immigration and of native inheritance customs. And local historians may well prove these factors to be irrelevant in Suffolk. But they may not be irrelevant in all industrial areas, and they require careful consideration before we accept a purely geographical explanation for the location of industries in the countryside. In some of the districts to be discussed below, in the moorland and fenland regions, with their ample common rights, and in woodland regions with their stores of timber, contemporaries deplored immigration. In at least four out of the six districts examined here, partible inheritance is known to have been practised, and in one of these it was declared to be the cause of overpopulation. Its influence cannot summarily be dismissed. In the first place, local studies show that partible inheritance was a far more widespread manorial custom than the nineteenth-century writers on gavelkind believed. Secondly, the extent to which it persisted among freeholders who could alienate their land, and among customary tenants who claimed a tenure almost as secure as a freeholder, is unknown. Despite the lawyers' insistence that the rule of primogeniture became almost universal after the thirteenth century, a small sample of early Tudor wills from Bedfordshire, a county where there is no reason to suspect the survival of partible inheritance as a strong manorial custom, shows how often men still shared their land among all, or some, of their sons.[11] Thirdly, the rule of primogeniture is a most unnatural law to inflict upon a parent. Was it perhaps not until the sixteenth century, when primogeniture became the law of Wales, when much Kent land was disgavelled piecemeal, and private agreements were reached within manors to discontinue the practice of gavelkind, that it became the almost universal rule on small estates? In our present state of ignorance, it is a reasonable hypothesis, and a reasonable argument for considering inheritance customs among the causes of the uneven rate of population growth in different districts.

For Kent there is somewhat more information about the social composition of its population than for Suffolk, but rather less about the cloth industry. The lawyers accepted the view that all land in Kent was subject to gavelkind unless the contrary was proved. Since this custom tended to keep people in their native places, it gave rise to large and immobile populations. But in Kent they were not evenly distributed throughout the county. In the mid-sixteenth century the

[11] Ed. A. F. Cirket, *English Wills, 1498–1526*, Beds. Hist. Rec. Soc., XXXVII. Of 69 wills containing bequests of land, only 40% insist that, after the death of the wife, all land shall descend to the eldest son. The remainder divide the land between some or all the children.

Wealden parishes had much larger populations, and by the end of the eighteenth century, its farms were noticeably smaller than in east Kent.[12] A second factor contributing to this uneven development must, therefore, be considered, namely the existence in the Weald of forest resources which yielded men a living from occupations other than farming, such as timber-felling and carpentry, wood-turning, charcoal-burning, and iron-smelting. In the fourteenth and fifteenth centuries, yet another industry was established in the Weald, that of clothmaking. It was important in towns such as Canterbury and Maidstone, but the rural industry was situated in the Wealden parishes of Cranbrook, Goudhurst, Tenterden, Hawkhurst, Headcorn and the neighbourhood. Supplies of fullers' earth were found locally, and the narrow valleys enabled the streams to be pent up by dams, and so to drive the fulling mills.[13]

The Weald was ancient woodland where much settlement consisted of hamlets and scattered farms. Some of these did not come into existence until the twelfth and thirteen centuries, and all were probably enclosed from the beginning. If we may again assume that the farming of the sixteenth century had a long tradition behind it, it consisted in the breeding and fattening of cattle with some dairying. This was in marked contrast to the mainly arable, corn-growing, and corn-exporting, region of east Kent.[14] Most probate inventories of Wealden farmers in the early seventeenth century mention a milk-

[12] William Holdsworth, *History of English Law*, III, p. 262. For the sixteenth-century population of Kent, see British Museum (= BM) Harleian MS 594. This census of 1563 covers the diocese of Canterbury only (the return for the diocese of Rochester is missing), but it is enough to show how much larger were the populations of the Wealden parishes than those in the rest of Kent. The usual population of a Kent parish was something less than sixty families. For example, 22 out of 26 parishes in Sittingbourne deanery had less than sixty households, and 14 (53%) had less than 30. But in the Charing deanery, which includes most of the Wealden parishes associated with the cloth industry, only 6, out of 24 parishes had less than 60 families, and only 2 out of 24 (8%) had less than 30 families. The larger size of the Wealden parishes does not invalidate this comparison because they all contained great areas of woodland, parks, and commons. On the size of farms in the eighteenth century, see John Boys, *General View of the Agriculture of the county of Kent* (1813), p. 3, footnote.

[13] Robert Furley, *op. cit.*, II, part I, pp. 325, 329–31; *V.C.H. Kent*, III, p. 403 *et seq.*; E. Straker, *Wealden Iron*, p. 264 *et seq.* For a valuable and suggestive comparative study of the forest areas of Northamptonshire, where populations were large, the commons attracted immigrants, the custom of inheritance was a form of Borough English, and a weaving industry developed in the later eighteenth century, *see* P. A. J. Pettit, *The Royal Forests of Northamptonshire*, Northants. Record Soc., XXIII, 1968.

[14] PRO SP 14/112, no. 12; Kent County Archives (= KCA) Probate inventories, *passim*.

house and stores of cheese and butter, and the clothiers seem to have dealt in both wool and cheese. William Hugget of Pluckley, clothier, had 264 lbs of cheese in his house in 1614 as well as 568 quarters of wool together with cloth and dyestuffs. John Mills of Smarden, clothier, had thirteen cheeses weighing 100 lbs as well as eleven quarters of wool. Were these clothiers adapting their business to the needs of their clients and selling them wool in exchange for their cheese? It is a reasonable guess. But it would be inaccurate to describe the Weald as a mainly dairying region in the early seventeenth century. Much effort was being directed by that time towards the rearing and fattening of cattle and sheep. A single probate inventory will illustrate the point. Isaac Hunt of Woodchurch had four swine, six geese, three hens, two kine and two heifers, four 2-yearling steers, three twelve-monthings, 31 fattening sheep and 22 others, three mares and a colt, and 27 acres of grass. His storehouse contained three flitches of bacon, 24 lbs of hempyarn, three gallons of butter, and ten cheeses. He had a milkhouse, the usual farm accommodation of a modest yeoman, and a shop. He was evidently something of a dairyman but he fattened sheep and cattle as well. The Weald by this time was an important supplier of London's meat and its grazing interests were implied by Gervase Markham in the remark that the improved soils could produce 'a very good and sweet pasture . . . profitable both for sheep and bullocks.'[15] In short, it was again in a populous pastoral area where breeding and some dairying were combined with fattening, where farms were small and enclosed, that the Kent cloth industry lived and died.

The last centre of the cloth industry to be considered here is that of Westmorland. Its centre was Kendal, which was already famous for its cloth at the end of the fourteenth century. The industry did not spread into the countryside until the fifteenth century when it assumed great local importance. By the beginning of the Tudor period there were eighteen fulling mills in the parish of Grasmere alone. The industry died a mysterious death in Elizabeth's reign as did the Kent cloth industry in the seventeenth century. A full inquest has not yet been held though two causes of death have been put forward, that Kendal cloth fell out of favour with the London tradesman, and that plague decimated the population in the 1570's and 1590's.[16] The first explanation seems inadequate by itself while

---

[15] KCA PRC 28/5 & 8; Gervase Markham, *The Inrichment of the Weald of Kent* (1625), p. 13.
[16] M. L. Armitt, 'Fullers and freeholders of the parish of Grasmere', *Trans. Cumb. &*

the second is demonstrably incorrect. Nevertheless, the plague in these two decades did reveal the precarious balance of the farming economy of the region which had caused the cloth industry to play such an important rôle in supplementing incomes.

Westmorland is a small county of which half comprises mountain and moorland. Its farming consisted in the breeding of cattle for sale to lowland farmers and in sheep-keeping for the sake of the wool. The cornland was meagre—the farmer was fortunate who had twelve acres to sow each spring, and on this he grew mostly oats, with a certain amount of bigg and March wheat and rye. Meadow, pasture, and moorland grazings were plentiful. In the early nineteenth century Westmorland butter had a high reputation for quality, but there is no sign that dairying served more than domestic needs in the sixteenth century.[17] In short, this was a county of pasture farms which, though small, had appurtenant common rights on extensive moorlands. The most remarkable feature of Westmorland, however, was the very large populations which it supported in its narrow valleys. A number of rural parishes had between two and three hundred families apiece, which may be compared with a normal average of thirty to sixty families for Kent parishes and between one and two hundred families for the more thickly settled Weald parishes. It is true that the fell parishes were vast but they consisted mostly of moorland and had a comparatively narrow strip of valley land. Yet the parish of Orton had 211 households in 1563, and a survey of the manor in 1589 describes many recent improvements of land and newly-built cottages suggesting a continuously growing population. Grasmere accommodated 186 families, Ravenstonedale next door had 116 families, Kirkby Stephen 300 and Wharton 284 families. Considering that Westmorland was so barren and rugged, it was extraordinarily populous, and we may well accept the substantial truth of the statement of the Westmorland justices in 1622 that 'the smallness, barrenness, and the multitude of inhabitants in the habitable places of this country is such and so far incomparable to the other counties of this kingdom.'[18]

Westm. Antiq. & Archaeolog. Soc., N.S. VIII (1908), pp. 195–8.

[17] Cumberland Record Office, Carlisle, and Lancs. Record Office, Preston, probate inventories, *passim*; F. W. Garnett, *Westmorland Agriculture, 1800–1900*, p. 137. Twelve acres represents statute measure. The local measure, as it appears in the probate inventories, was eight acres.

[18] BM Harleian MS. 594; Cumberland Record Office, 1589 Survey of the Lands of Leonard Dacre, attained; PRO SP 14/131, no. 25.

The paradox has to be explained. The valleys in the fells were thickly populated and yet their farming economy was ever tilted on the verge of a crisis. It was not properly self-sufficient in corn. The climate made every harvest more than ordinarily hazardous, and the cornland was in any case limited. A crisis of famine and consequent plague could easily be precipitated by a harvest failure. The justices of the peace who remarked upon the large populations of Westmorland in 1622 were explaining the gravity of a crisis caused by the scarcity of bread. The harvest failure of 1597 had brought just such another disaster affecting all four northern counties. In vivid language the bishop of Durham described to Lord Burghley how 'in the bishopric of Durham five hundred ploughs have decayed in a few years and corn has to be fetched from Newcastle, whereby the plague is spread in the northern counties. . . . Of eight thousand acres lately in tillage, now not eight score are tilled; those who sold corn have to buy . . . tenants cannot pay their rents.'[19]

Farming was precarious, but it was not precarious enough to drive people from the narrow congested valleys of the fells. Two reasons suggest themselves. Meadow and pasture were plentiful for the keeping of cattle and sheep. A man who looked naturally to the land for his living could count himself a king of infinite space if he had no more than a small piece of arable and unstinted common rights. In the seventeenth and eighteenth centuries, writers viewing the agrarian problem of the Midlands bewailed the attractions of open commons to migrant paupers seeking a corner of land on which to settle.[20] By that date, people were perambulating the Midlands in search of a somewhat rare commodity. But in the pastoral regions of England, open commons were not scarce. They might now attract migrants from elsewhere, but for centuries before this they had held out an encouraging hand to the young, and had kept the children in their native places to marry, earn a living, rear their children, and die. The wide moorlands bred contentment because they offered a satisfactory living, and this in turn kept people at home and fostered what outsiders regarded as clannishness. If it is legitimate to see in some more isolated modern communities a pale reflection of the traditions and attitudes of the past, then we may suspect that the strong ties of

[19] Quoted in Henry Barnes, 'Visitations of the plague in Cumberland and Westmorland', *Trans. Cumb. & Westm. Antiq. & Archaeolog. Soc.*, XI, 1891, pp. 178–9. Similar shortages in the 19th century were mentioned by F. W. Garnett, *op. cit.*, p. 19.

[20] See, for example, Samuel Hartlib's remark—'There are fewest poor where there are fewest commons'. *Samuel Hartlib, his Legacie*, 1652, p. 42.

family unity, which even now keep young men and young women in the fells on the farms of their fathers till long after others of their generation have married and moved away, were bonds of iron three or four hundred years ago. The family was and is the working unit, all joining in the running of the farm, all accepting without question the fact that the family holding would provide for them all or else that the family's savings would go to buy a lease or an interest in land nearby. The custom of partible inheritance fosters this attitude, and its survival among a small number of families in Gosforth in Cumberland to this day suggests that it was once more common in the northern fells.[21] Hence, a society which does not drive its children away to earn their living elsewhere, which pursues a pastoral economy that is not greedy of land, that does not compel men to enclose every rod in the quest for survival and profit, such a society may well breed large populations and create for itself an increasing problem of feeding them. For these people did not live in paradise. Some of their herds and the flocks which they grazed on the fells in summer had to be found fodder and shelter in winter, and this the narrow valleys could not always fully provide. Many fell communities supplemented their farming incomes by iron-mining, lead-mining, stone, and slate quarrying. Others were not so advantageously placed but they had the labour force to engage in rural handicrafts if the opportunity occurred. Nowadays they cater for the holidaymaker.[22]

Another society of small peasant farmers possessing some of the features common to fell communities existed in the Lincolnshire fens. Farmers were engaged in rearing cattle and some sheep, fattening beef and mutton, breeding horses and keeping geese. It was another area where the commons were large and unstinted and where common rights included not only grazing rights but generous allotments of peat, sedge, willows, and the right to catch fish and fowl. The community had enough resources to support a custom of partible inheritance, and in the Middle Ages, when this custom was practised in some villages, there is persuasive evidence to show that populations grew faster than in villages where primogeniture was the rule. It is not certain how long this custom survived, but, even in the

---

[21] W. M. Williams, *The Sociology of an English Village: Gosforth*, pp. 37–55.
[22] When the cloth industry ceased, it seems to have been replaced by stocking-knitting. The first evidence which I have found in Westmorland dates from the 1690's. It persisted longest in the Orton, Ravenstonedale, Kirkby Stephen district. F. W. Garnett, *op. cit.*, p. 4.

seventeenth century, the population of Elloe wapentake, which had the largest amount of open commons in the Lincolnshire fenland, whether through immigration or by its own efforts, grew at a far greater rate than that of the rest of Lincolnshire.[23]

In such circumstances, we can understand why the weaving of hemp, flax, and wool was a by-employment in many fen households. It is unlikely that this industry met a national demand, and since it did not compete in the export market, it does not receive attention in public records. But if one compares the personal property of Suffolk farmers, who grew hemp in quantity but wove none of it, with the fen farmers who grew it, processed it, wove it, and had many yards of cloth in store, it is reasonable to rank this industry as a handicraft serving more than merely domestic needs, and supplementing the resources of yet another populous pasture-farming community.[24]

Finally, we may return again to the hand-knitting industry of Dentdale and Garsdale, and summarize briefly certain known facts about its farming and its industry. Gavelkind inheritance, aggravated no doubt by the general rise of population in the sixteenth century, caused its population to outgrow the resources of the land. This seems credible in view of the fact that the parish of Sedbergh had a population of 663 families in 1563: 346 in the town of Sedbergh, 251 in Dentdale and 66 families in Garsdale. The husbandry of Dentdale and Garsdale was devoted to rearing and dairying. Wensleydale cheese achieved its greatest reputation in a later age, but it was already marketed in the sixteenth century. Hand-knitting became an important local industry in the Tudor period, and from then until the nineteenth century, Dentdale was considered to be the principal home of the knitters. Now, in the mid-twentieth century, the small dairy farmers of the dales still pose economic problems to the agricultural economists who wish to see the land yield something more than subsistence to its occupiers.[25]

[23] Joan Thirsk, *English Peasant Farming*, pp. 28–31, 140–41; H. E. Hallam, *op. cit.*, p. 361.

[24] More domestic weaving of flax, hemp, and wool seems to have been carried on in the whole county of Lincolnshire than in many other counties. Therefore, it is difficult to gauge the relative importance of the industry in the different regions. But insofar as it is possible to measure it by reference to the probate inventories, I believe that it was economically more important in the fens of Holland than elsewhere, though the fens also had other by-employments such as rush-plaiting. In the Isle of Axholme the by-employment was undoubtedly sack-cloth weaving.

[25] BM Harleian MS. 594; Leeds Central Library, Archives Dept., and Lancs. Record Office, probate inventories, *passim*; Marie Hartley and Joan Ingilby, *The Old Hand-knitters of the Dales* (1951), p. 7 *et seq.*; W. Patterson, 'The New Pennine Dairy Farming', *Agriculture*, LXVI, no. 8, pp. 340–42.

It is not the intention of this essay to propound a theory for the situation of rural handicraft industries which can be applied mechanically to them all, but to enumerate some of the common factors which seem to be present in a number of semi-farming, semi-industrial communities, and to suggest that attention be paid to them in any future study of rural industries such as lace-making, hat-making, glove-making, and basket-making, which are not mentioned here. The common factors seem to be these: a populous community of small farmers, often mainly freeholders (as in Suffolk) or customary tenants with a tenure almost as good as a freehold (as in the Yorkshire dales), pursuing a pastoral economy. This may rest upon dairying in which case the farms are usually early enclosed, and manorial organisation and cooperative farming, in consequence, are weak or non-existent. Or it may rest upon breeding and rearing on generous pasture commons, where there is no practical incentive to enclose, where the arable land is meagre, and where again there is no strong framework of open fields and cooperative husbandry. In the rearing districts the resources of the land (particularly the generous commons) are sufficient to support, and do support, a custom of gavelkind. In the dairying regions the same custom cannot certainly be held responsible for the large populations. Underlying all this, we may see a certain logic sometimes in the way these common factors are linked together. Some of the land best suited to pasture was not cleared of woodland until a comparatively late stage in local settlement history. It was likely to be immediately enclosed. It was likely to give rise to a community of independent farmers who recognized not the hamlet or the village, but the family, as the cooperative working unit. If the land was suitable for dairying, it had enough water to support a cloth industry too. In a less hospitable countryside, where there were wide moorlands or large fenland commons, and little suitable cornland, the husbandry was bound to consist in rearing and sheep-keeping. The commons attracted landless youths. The farming required less labour than a corn-growing farm and left men time to engage in a subsidiary occupation.

Perhaps, indeed, the intelligent globe-trotters of Tudor and Stuart England took for granted some of the propositions which we, who are far removed from them in time and experience, have painfully to prove. The phrase 'scratch a weaver and find a parcener' sums up that part of this argument which is concerned with the effects of gavelkind, and says as much as the handknitters of Dentdale. The Somerset J.P's who summarized in a sentence the economy of four hundreds of Somerset seem to be describing just the landscape in which handicraft industries could flourish: 'The country, a great part of it being forest and woodlands and the rest very barren for corn ... the people of the country (for the most part) being occupied about the trade of clothmaking, spinning, weaving, and tucking.' The inhabitants of Hertfordshire, resisting an attempt by the Crown in James I's reign to establish the New Draperies in their county, described, on the other hand, the kind of landscape which could not support a handicraft industry—a corn-growing region which gave full employment to all. 'The county of Hertford doth consist for the most part of tillage ... it has better means to set the poor children on work without this new invention than some other counties, viz. by employing the female children in picking of their wheat a great part of the year and the male children by straining before their ploughs in seedtime and other necessary occasions of husbandry.' Does this, indeed, help to explain the strange death of clothmaking in Hertfordshire? It appeared in the fifteenth century in just the area where one would want to place it, east of Royston, Buntingford and Ware in a district much of which was not cleared of woodland before the twelfth century, where the land was immediately enclosed, and a landscape of hamlets and isolated farms took shape. The rivers would have yielded more than enough water for the cloth industry, but instead other influences were at work, and it became a corn county. And the cloth industry disappeared[26] in the early sixteenth century when in other places it was at the height of its prosperity.

There seems to be enough positive evidence to support the proposition that the location of handicraft industries is not altogether haphazard, but is associated with certain types of farming community and certain kinds of social organization. One could go further and suggest that the period in which these industries arose in different districts deserves scrutiny. Professor Malowist has recently remarked upon the simultaneous rise of the cloth industry in the fourteenth and fifteenth centuries and the crisis in agriculture.[27] This phenomenon is not peculiar to England but is found in the Low Countries, southern Germany, and Italy. One could reasonably postulate some association between the rise of population and

[26] PRO SP 14/144, no. 24; SP 14/96, no. 39; *V.C.H. Herts.*, IV, pp. 210, 249.

[27] 'It seems to me that this fact proves that agriculture did not suffice to give them a living, and this, in turn, may have been the result of the low level of their agricultural efficiency.' M. Malowist, 'The economic and social development of the Baltic countries from the fifteenth to the seventeenth centuries', *Econ. Hist. Rev.*, 2nd Ser., XII, no. 2, p. 178.

pressure on the land in the sixteenth century, and the rise of the handknitting industry in the Yorkshire dales. One might then consider why the framework-knitting industry did not spread into Leicestershire until the later seventeenth century, while cotton and wool manufacture did not take root in the Peak district of Derbyshire until the eighteenth century.[28] But here we must end one discussion, not begin another.[29]

[28] W. G. Hoskins, *The Midland Peasant*, pp. 227–8; Owen Ashmore, 'The early textile industry in North-west Derbyshire', *Derbyshire Miscellany*, no. 9, June 1953, p. 129.

[29] I wish to thank Drs. A. Everitt, H. P. R. Finberg, R. Hilton, W. G. Hoskins and Mr Norman Scarfe for their helpful criticism of this paper.

XIV

THE FANTASTICAL FOLLY OF FASHION: THE ENGLISH STOCKING KNITTING INDUSTRY, 1500–1700

> The phantastical folly of our nation (even from the courtier to the carter) is such that no form of apparel liketh us longer than the first garment is in the wearing, if it continue so long . . . (William Harrison, 1577)

Fashion is accorded a lowly place by economic historians when they account for the rise of the clothing industries and the changing direction of their trade. They prefer to look for sterner economic explanations, such as the debasement of the coinage, war, new customs tariffs, and occasionally bad (or good) craftsmanship. Thus they turn their back on the evidence of contemporaries, and on the evidence of their own eyes in the modern world. How would the clothing trades survive on their present scale but for the tyranny of fashion, which now compels all classes to change their style of dress, if not every season, then at least every year? We have seen in the 1960s and '70s teenagers readily falling victim to the persuasive guile of the clothing manufacturers, and creating a booming branch of the industry in consequence. Earlier in this century, when teenagers lacked the necessary cash, salesmen addressed themselves more aggressively to an older and more moneyed age group. In the sixteenth century the most compliant buyers of fashionable clothing were undoubtedly the nobility and gentry. But since in every age fashions beguile all ages and classes in varying degrees, ordinary folk lower down the social scale were susceptible too, and strained their resources to ape their betters. As the proclamation of 1562 bewailed, 'such as be of the meaner sort, and be least able with their livings to maintain the same' felt they must follow the fashion.[1]

Contemporary literature is full of baleful comment upon the dictates of fashion, which first seized the rich in thrall and then their

---

[1] W. Hooper, 'Tudor sumptuary laws', *English Historical Review*, xxx (1915), p. 439.

servants. 'No other nations take such pride in apparel as England',
wrote Philip Stubbs in 1595. Moreover, 'no people in the world are so
curious in new fangles as they of England be'.[2] 'I have known divers
(serving men)', wrote William Vaughan in 1600, 'who would bestow
all the money they had in the world on sumptuous garments. And
when I asked them how they would live hereafter, they would answer:
a good marriage will one day make amends for all.'[3]

The vagaries of fashion disturbed the ultra-sensitive moralists of
the day; but they also disturbed the politicians, for every change of
style in dress had economic consequences, and these could be
damaging to native industries. It was this consideration, together
with the desire to preserve distinctions between social classes, which
explains the sumptuary legislation which flowed in a swelling stream
from 1463 onwards. In the hundred years up to 1550 'excessive
apparel' was controlled by six Acts and two proclamations. In the
next fifty years up to 1600 it required one Act and eight proclamations to order matters; indeed, a remarkable system of surveillance
was called into being in 1566, involving the stationing of four 'sad and
discreet' persons at the gates of the City of London from 7 a.m. to 11
a.m. and from 1 p.m. to 6 p.m. daily, watching for people who might
be wearing prohibited styles of hose.[4] As time went on, the 'pride of
apparel' seemed to grow more rather than less.

Fashion, then, was recognised by contemporaries as a powerful
influence over the clothing industries. This essay deals with one of its
branches, the stocking knitting industry, which may be said to have
owed its existence to a change of fashion in the sixteenth century. It
was a handicraft among local peasant communities before this
period, probably for centuries before, but it developed into an
industry commanding a considerable place in English domestic trade
from the mid-sixteenth century onwards. Its success was almost as
spectacular in its way as that of the New Draperies. It did not play the
same important role in English overseas trade as they did, though a
steady export business was built up, but stockings bulked large in
domestic trade. And, like the weaving of New Draperies, knitting
became an industrial occupation that gave a livelihood, or part of
one, to a large number of country people. Like the New Draperies, it
was a peasant handicraft that was successfully commercialised.

To account for the rise of the stocking knitting industry it is

[2] P. Stubbs, *The Anatomie of Abuses* (1595), pp. 9, 10.
[3] W. Vaughan, *The Golden Grove* (1600), pages not numbered.
[4] Hooper, *op. cit.*, p. 443 and *passim*.

necessary to examine the prevailing fashions in leg wear. Until the Tudor period a single garment that combined breeches and stockings covered the legs of menfolk of all classes and was known as 'hose'. The breeches could be more or less elaborate, sometimes being stuffed out with bulky linings and slashed with 'panes' of different fabric. The stocking part was made separately and then stitched to the breeches; it was made from material cut on the cross and sewn to shape, giving a seam down the back of the leg. The cross grain gave a certain amount of stretch to the material, so that it fitted the legs more closely. If, as occasionally happened, the two parts of the garment were not stitched together, they were joined by bands or cross garters; they were then distinguished by name as 'upper stocks' and 'nether stocks'. If working men did not always wear 'hose' like this, they wore instead what we would nowadays call 'tights'—close fitting stockings with pants attached, worn under a tunic. Women's stockings were made in the same way as men's nether stocks, cut and sewn from woven material bought by the yard, and gartered above the knee.[5]

The fashion began to change in the first half of the sixteenth century under the influence of Italian, Spanish and French styles. The nobility and gentry were the leaders in this respect, introducing styles which they encountered on their travels abroad. Every social commentator had a word for the 'Italianated, Frenchified ... Dutch, and Babilonian' fashions, and among these innovations were knitted stockings.[6] Knitted goods that were attractive and shapely enough to rank as high fashion seem to have been developed in France (especially in Paris) and in Italy (at Florence) during the fifteenth century.[7] Observing the subsequent vogue for knitted stockings in England, the historians of costume have maintained that in this country 'knitting did not become established until the sixteenth century'.[8] This is scarcely credible. The chain mail of medieval armour is, in fact, a knitted garter stitch. Knitted caps are mentioned as a commonplace article of clothing in a statute of 1488, when their price was fixed at 2s 8d.[9] Even though no medieval archaeological sites have yet yielded knitting needles or fragments of knitted fabric, it is difficult to believe that the art of knitting was

[5] C. W. and P. Cunnington, *Handbook of English Costume in the Sixteenth Century* (1970), pp. 32, 35, 37, 205, 116, 95, 180.

[6] Vaughan, *op. cit.*

[7] Cunnington and Cunnington, *op. cit.*, p. 88. This is clearly a subject that requires closer investigation.

[8] *Ibid.*, p. 87.

[9] M. Hartley and J. Ingilby, *The Old Hand-knitters of the Dales* (1969 edition), p. 6.

unknown until the sixteenth, or, at best, the fifteenth century. It is much more likely that it was a peasant handicraft, producing rough, and probably shapeless, though serviceable, clothing, which leaves no trace in our records because it had nothing attractive to offer to merchants in national or international trade.[10] The New Draperies have recently been identified by Professor Coleman as traditional peasant cloths which served purely local needs until they were taken up by merchants in the sixteenth century, when they were urgently seeking cheaper quality goods for an increasingly competitive European market.[11] Professor Miller had already explained the success of English kerseys and coloured cloths in the fourteenth and fifteenth centuries in similar terms; they too were local peasant handicrafts, newly drawn into international commerce.[12] The English stocking knitting industry almost certainly belongs in the same category of an ancient peasant handicraft that was suddenly caught up in the network of national and international trade. How it happened is a tangled story, but its outlines emerge reasonably clearly.

In the early sixteenth century silk knitted stockings were high fashion in court circles in Spain. This fashion was known at the English court, but could hardly as yet be imitated. A pair of Spanish silk stockings was a precious acquisition for Englishmen, and seems, indeed, to have been a privilege of kings alone. Henry VIII always wore cloth hose made from 'ell broad taffety' except when 'by great chance there came a pair of Spanish silk stockings from Spain'. Edward VI became the next proud owner of a pair of long Spanish silk stockings, presented to him by Sir Thomas Gresham.[13] Just how expensive they were we may deduce from an entry in the London port book of 1567–68. Twelve pairs of silk hose were shipped from Malaga to London and valued by the customs officer at nearly £4 a pair. Since such valuations were well below, and sometimes only half, the true value, we may estimate their full worth at something nearer £8 a pair.[14]

---

[10] It is worth noting that when the framework knitters appealed in 1655 for incorporation, they declared that ordinary hand knitting '*for public use*' (my italics) was 'not much more anciently . . . practised in this nation' than framework knitting. They seemed to be making a careful distinction between knitting for private and public use. J. Thirsk and J. P. Cooper (eds.), *Seventeenth-century Economic Documents* (1972), p. 260.

[11] D. C. Coleman, 'An innovation and its diffusion: the "New Draperies" ', *Econ. Hist. Rev.*, 2nd ser., XXII (1969), *passim*.

[12] E. Miller, 'The fortunes of the English textile industry in the thirteenth century', *Econ. Hist. Rev.*, 2nd ser., XVIII (1965), pp. 78–80.

[13] J. Stow, *The Annales or Generall Chronicle of England* (1615), p. 867.

[14] B. Dietz, *The Port and Trade of Early Elizabethan London: Documents*, London

By Elizabeth's reign, however, silk stockings were somewhat less rare, and could be coveted by lesser mortals. In 1560 Mistress Mountague gave Queen Elizabeth a pair of black knit silk stockings, which she had made herself. The Queen was so delighted with their 'pleasant, fine, and delicate' appearance, that henceforth she never wore cloth hose again.[15] In the next two decades foreign, or English-made, silk stockings became more common, and by 1582, when the new Book of Rates was issued, Spanish silk stockings were valued by customs men at only 26s 8d. This means that they were worth perhaps £2 10s or £3, less than half the cost of the samples imported in 1567–68.[16]

Meanwhile stockings knitted from wool were beginning to share some of the favour originally bestowed on knitted silk. Documented references in the early decades of the sixteenth century suggest that knitted stockings were then worn mostly by children and country folk. A pair of knitted hose cost 5d in Nottingham in 1519. A teenage boy's clothing account mentions knit hose in 1530, as does the account of the orphan son of Sir Henry Willoughby in 1550. But in a statute of 1552 knit hose were mentioned in a matter-of-fact way as though they were commonplace.[17] Old-style 'hose', namely breeches and stockings in one piece, were evidently passing out of favour, and although cloth stockings continued to serve their turn for some purposes (soldiers sent to Flanders in 1659 were wearing stockings made of Welsh woven cotton),[18] they were giving way increasingly to knitted stockings. The fact that stockings, when separated from breeches, could be more frequently washed must have counted as an advantage, though we have no evidence that people availed themselves of this opportunity. But when once knitted fabric was given a trial, it quickly showed its superiority over cloth; it fitted tighter, and kept its shape longer, besides, of course, permitting new varieties of design and colour. It is also possible that some special shaping of the knitting round calf and ankle was being practised by the knitters of silk stockings, which was copied by the knitters in wool, and so made for a more stylish garment; but this can only be a matter of speculation.

Record Society (1972), No. 282; T. S. Willan (ed.), *A Tudor Book of Rates* (1962), p. xliv.

[15] Stow, *op. cit.*, p. 867.

[16] Willan, *op. cit.*, p. 33.

[17] *V.C.H. Notts.*, II, p. 352; Cunnington and Cunnington, *op. cit.*, p. 203 n.; Hartley and Ingilby, *op. cit.*, p. 7.

[18] Thirsk and Cooper, *op. cit.*, p. 371.

By 1600 the changing usage of technical terms in the clothing trade points to the conclusion that the old style 'hose' had been superseded. After 1550 the word 'hose' meant breeches only, and legs were covered with 'netherstocks' or 'stockings', which were almost invariably knitted garments. By 1660 even the word 'hose' meant stockings.[19] A transformation in modes of dress had taken place, comparable with the one we have witnessed in the last four years as stockings for women are being replaced by tights. A new fashion had created a new industry.

Yet from the beginning this new industry was not one but several. As soon as it emerged into the light of better documented history in the 1570s its products were remarkably diverse, varying according to the types of yarn and the dyes used, and the districts in which the stockings were made. Moreover, strong influences were continuously exerted from abroad, for the industry had an international base from the outset, and new ideas and techniques flowed between all west European countries. The Italians were already knitting a finer wool fabric from worsted yarn when in 1564 a pair of stockings knitted from this yarn was spotted by a smart young apprentice in London. They belonged to an Italian merchant from Mantua, who lent them to the Englishman. He had them copied, and thus, we learn from Stow, 'were the first worsted stockings made in England'. 'Within a few years began the plenteous making both of jersey and woollen stockings, so in a short space they waxed common.'[20] They did indeed; but jersey stockings, which were still finer than ordinary worsted, were originally a speciality of the islands of Jersey and Guernsey. A document of 1596 tells us that the fine quality of jersey knitting was achieved by spinning the yarn on a special small Guernsey or Jersey wheel.[21] This was another secret, which passed from the Channel Islands to England, and was exploited most of all in Norfolk. By 1600 Thomas Wilson maintained that in Norwich £12,000 a year was earned by young child knitters of jersey.[22] In short, the industry was constantly benefiting and changing its products by

[19] Cunnington and Cunnington, *op. cit.*, pp. 114, 122.
[20] Stow, *op. cit.*, p. 869.
[21] *Caesarea, or, a Discourse of the Island of Jersey* . . . , ed. W. Nicolle, Société Jersiaise, x (1889), p. 5; T. F. Priaulx and R. de Sausmarez, 'The Guernsey stocking export trade in the seventeenth century', *Trans. Société Guernesiaise*, XVII (1962), *passim*; P.R.O., SP 15/33/71. I am grateful to Mr K. G. Ponting for showing me this document, originally found by Miss Mann.
[22] Thirsk and Cooper, *op. cit.*, p. 754. Yarmouth knitters seem also to have made jersey stockings. See below p. 250.

learning from others. But the search for an even finer knitted fabric did not squeeze out other branches of the industry. There were always people who wanted more durable, thicker stockings made from coarse, hairy wools.

At this point we are driven to make some conjectures about the diverse products of the stocking knitters, because we have no samples of local wares. But we can draw some reasoned inferences from contemporary descriptions, from known facts about the wools of different sheep breeds and farming regions, and from the geographical dispersal of the stocking knitting industry. By the beginning of the seventeenth century stockings were made in Wales, Cheshire, Gloucestershire, Cornwall, Devon, Nottinghamshire, Northamptonshire, Yorkshire, Northumberland, Cumberland, Westmorland and Durham. The local wools of these counties ranged from fine Cotswold to hairy, coarse Welsh and northern yarn. The texture of the stockings must have varied similarly.

Stockings made from the coarser, northern yarns were of the warm but tough hard-wearing kind, probably similar to those which are worn nowadays under wellington boots. In the early eighteenth century Defoe described the stockings made in Richmond as 'woollen or yarn stockings . . . very coarse and ordinary'. At the end of the eighteenth century (1792) Lord Torrington described a pair which he bought at Askrigg as 'coarse stockings for my wet expeditions'. They sold cheaply: a seventeenth century rhyme refers to 'stockings made of the northern hue which scarce cost 12*d*'.[23] Northern products suited the needs of soldiers, children, labourers and peasants who had to be out in all weathers. The same description probably holds good for Welsh stockings and may also hold true for those made in Cornwall.

Worsted stockings were finer, though the term 'worsted' evidently covered a wide range of qualities, some being finer than others. They were made from combed long wool of Midland long wool sheep, and the knitting yarn was of the same fineness as that used to produce smooth, worsted cloth.[24] Worsted stockings were worn by well-to-do merchants who took a pride in being well dressed, and by yet more

---

[23] Hartley and Ingilby, *op. cit.*, pp. 22, 34; C. W. and P. Cunnington, *Handbook of English Costume in the Seventeenth Century* (1955), p. 61.

[24] Despite Dr Bowden's statement that noils were used for knitted stockings, it does not seem to have been the usual practice, except to make a debased type of worsted stocking, which contemporaries regarded as a false and deceitful abuse. See Peter Bowden, *The Wool Trade in Tudor and Stuart England* (1971 edition), p. 42 n.; P.R.O., SP 12/231/11.

fastidious creators of fashion. On the scaffold Mary Queen of Scots wore a pair of blue worsted stockings, embroidered with silver silk.[25] Still finer stockings were known as jersey stockings. As we have seen, they were made from worsted wools, but were more delicate in texture, for the adjectives 'fine' and 'jersey' were almost inseparable in contemporary descriptions of them. On the scaffold Mary Queen of Scots wore a pair of fine white jersey stockings next to her skin, *underneath* the more decorative blue worsted stockings.[26]

A catalogue of grades of knitting yarns does not exhaust the variety of stockings that were on the market by 1600. Peasant craftsmen take a pride in producing work that is individual in its style and bears some token of its maker's special skill or idiosyncratic artistry. Stockings, like other peasant craft goods, were never standardised wares. As the industry became commercialised, and permanent trading links were forged between country knitters, sharp-minded city merchants and distant customers, we may fairly suspect that the variety of styles multiplied rather than diminished. The knitter had the incentive to produce a better and more attractive article, the merchant had to persuade his clients to go on buying, even when they had enough stockings in the closet to last them for several years. When the New Draperies won favour the same collective name continued to be used to embrace an ever-lengthening list of varieties of cloth.[27] New types were constantly being devised, all borrowing from each other ideas about spinning, yarn mixtures, weave, colour and methods of finishing. They became the subject of countless experiments and even guileful salesmanship, for when new ideas failed, their makers resorted to changing the names of the old cloths to make them sound like new.[28] In exactly the same way knitted stockings became as varied in design, colour and decoration, as well as in kind of yarn, as the New Draperies. They could be short or long, stretching to the knee or above it. They could be yellow, red, green, blue or violet, as well as white, black or grey. The welts could be plain or have innumerable different kinds of patterns knitted into them. The edges of the welts could be straight or scalloped. Alternatively, the stockings, after knitting, could be embroidered with gold and silver or decorated with clocks. One contemporary list names coarse

[25] H. K. Morse, 'Elizabethan pageantry', *Studio*, spring 1934, p. 16; Cunnington and Cunnington, *Handbook of English Costume in the Sixteenth Century*, p. 181.
[26] Cunnington and Cunnington, *loc. cit.*
[27] P.R.O., E 134, 44/45 Eliz., Mich. I.
[28] *Ibid.*

white woollen stockings, men's stockings with scalloped tops, men's stockings with large welts and of mingled colours, and children's coloured stockings.[29] Phil;ip Stubbs, describing fashionable stockings, named only the most luxurious and flamboyant styles, of jersey worsted, crewell and silk thread, and 'so curiously knit with open seam down the leg, with quirks and clocks about the ankles, and sometimes haply interlaced with gold or silver threads as is wonderful to behold'. Women's stockings were more daring in their colour: of 'wanton light colours, green, red, white, russet, tawny and else what not', 'cunningly knit and curiously indented in every point with quirks, clocks, open seam and everything else'. This did not, of course, run the full gamut. Stubbs merely described the most outrageous examples, the frippery that 'no sober chaste Christian can hardly, without suspicion of lightness, at any time wear'.[30] But we may judge subsequent trends from the array of worsted stocking types that were made to the order of one stocking dealer alone on the island of Guernsey in the 1670s. Thirty-three different code numbers were used to identify them, and although some of these may have differentiated sizes only, the correspondence of the stocking merchant (Matthew de Sausmarez at St Peter Port writing to his cousin, Michael, in Paris) gives a glimpse of some of the many designs and colours available. Some were *à l'écaille* (shell-patterned?), *mancheté*, marbled, fine marbled, very fine marbled, striped with a fiery red colour, plain white, white striped with blue, greyish white, greyish white striped, greyish brown, iron-grey, blue and white, and black.[31] Moreover, their prices establish that these stockings were offered principally to the well-to-do nobles and bourgeoisie of Paris.[32] Another type of stocking entirely was needed for the labouring classes.

Indignant commentators like Philip Stubbs maintained that labourers wore silk stockings. 'To such impudent insolency and shameful outrage it is now grown that everyone almost, though otherwise very poor, having scarce 40s of wages by the year, will not stick to have two or three pairs of these silk nether-stocks or else of the finest yarn that may be got, though the price of them be a royal or 20s or more, as commonly it is.'[33] Doubtless it was true that everyone

[29] Joan Thirsk (ed.), *The Agrarian History of England and Wales*, IV, *1500–1640* (1967), p. 46.

[30] Stubbs, *op. cit.*, pp. 31, 47.

[31] Priaulx and Sausmarez, *op. cit.*, pp. 213–4.

[32] See below, pp. 69 ff.

[33] Stubbs, *op. cit.*, p. 31.

enjoyed an occasional touch of luxury. But Stubbs's exaggerations obscure what for economic historians must be one of the most significant features of this flourishing industry, namely that many different kinds of stockings were made to suit all purses and purposes. Stubbs reckoned that the silk ones cost a royal or 20*s*. A contemporary, writing in 1590, complained of the high price of worsted stockings, at 8*s*–9*s* a pair. In 1582 the Book of Rates valued short (almost certainly woollen) hose at 8*d* (signifying a true value of perhaps 1*s* 4*d*) and long hose at 3*s* 4*d* (perhaps worth 6*s* 8*d*). A stocking dealer of Kirkby Lonsdale had a wide range of northern stockings in store at his death in 1578 that were valued per pair at 22*d*, 20*d*, 18*d*, 16*d*, 14*d*, 12*d* and 7*d*. A century later an Arkengarthdale hosier's stock (1680) valued boys' and children's woollen hose at 8*d* and 10*d* a pair; Leicester worsted stockings (1690) cost 1*s* 6*d*–2*s* 6*d* a pair; high quality worsted stockings made in Guernsey (1670s) were sold by wholesalers at prices between 2*s* 6*d* and 10*s* 10*d* a pair. Silk stockings worn at Charles II's court cost 10*s*–18*s* in the 1670s.[34] These are random price quotations, but they are sufficient to fix the two extremes of costly and cheap stockings made in England.

The growth of the stocking knitting industry created employment for a large and increasing number of knitters, most of whom were peasant farmers in pastoral areas, working on a part-time basis. Some of the principal knitting centres were the forests and the northern fells, but knitting was also found in other pastoral areas like the Ouse-Humber marshes near Doncaster, the Vale of Tewkesbury in Gloucestershire, and the dairying districts of Cheshire. It was also a by-employment in fishing centres, especially Yarmouth in Norfolk. In the course of the seventeenth century, however, as the industry expanded, it did not recruit new knitters only in the old centres. Other centres already existing in hitherto undiscovered places were sought out by merchants and drawn into their trade; and sometimes no doubt, knitting was deliberately introduced by enterprising traders and teachers into new areas.[35]

Hand knitting became a supplementary source of income that

[34] P.R.O., SP 12/231/11; Willan, *op. cit.*, p. 67; J. Raine, *Wills and Inventories of the Archdeaconry of Richmond*, Surtees Society, XXVI (1853), pp. 276–7; Hartley and Ingilby, *op. cit.*, pp. 23–4; S. D. Chapman. 'The genesis of the British hosiery industry, 1600–1750', *Textile History*, III (1972), p. 11 (I regret that I did not see Dr Chapman's article until a very late stage in the preparation of this paper); Priaulx and Sausmarez, *op. cit.*, p. 221.

[35] Chapter XIII above, p. 217 and *passim*. For knitting schools in Lincoln by 1591, in York by 1590, and in Leicester by 1591, see Hartley and Ingilby, *op. cit.*, pp. 7–8; M. and A. Grass, *Stockings for a Queen* (1967), p. 62.

meant a great deal to peasant labourers living near the margin of subsistence. But not only did it supply vital cash, it preserved for them some illusion of independence as well. Knitters could buy their own materials and sell their goods freely, and in this way felt themselves less exploited than those who were engaged to do outwork under contract to a factor who supplied all the necessary materials. The economic and social benefits of the stocking knitting industry are aptly summed up in the report of an anonymous writer in 1615, describing the old and new way of using the wool of north Buckinghamshire. Under the old way when the wool went to the making of Old Draperies the spinners and weavers worked for a clothier 'for small wages, so that they lived very poorly'. To work up three tods of wool into cloth fourteen people were employed, and their wages amounted to £1 13s 6d. Under the new way the wools were divided between the New Draperies and stockings, two-thirds of the wool being used for the first, one-third of the wool for the second. To work up the same three tods of wool, between forty and fifty people were needed, three times the number used on the Old Draperies, and their wages amounted to £7, four times as much. Better still, 'all sorts of these people are masters in their trade and work for themselves. They buy and sell their materials that they work upon so that by their merchandise and honest labour they live very well.'[36]

In the period between 1580 and 1630 the largest knitting centres can be identified through the aulnage records and the port books. The first sign that the aulnage collectors were taking an interest in the stocking industry was in 1580, when the farm of the aulnage in Norwich passed to the city council and its officials began to claim payments on knitted stockings. In the first quarter of that year, they collected dues on 732 pairs.[37] But the claim to aulnage was a novelty, and knitters did not willingly accede to it.[38] By the last quarter of the year they had been induced to pay on 2,640 pairs (perhaps the work of about 100 knitters).[39] In 1595 the farmers of the aulnage throughout England turned their attention to Yorkshire and carried out a survey of all drapery made in that county. The knitting centres were identified as Doncaster, where 120 knitters were at work, Richmond, with 1,000 knitters, and sixteen towns and villages within twenty miles of Richmond, including Askrigg and Middleham in Wensley-

[36] Thirsk and Cooper, *op. cit.*, p. 204.
[37] Norwich Record Office, aulnage accounts, 1580–1610, press D, case 17.
[38] P.R.O., E 134, 35 and 36 Car. II, Hil. 19.
[39] For output per knitter, see below, p. 248.

dale, and Barnard Castle in Teesdale, where another 1,000 knitters were at work.[40]

In 1605 a patent to collect the aulnage was granted to Ludovic, Duke of Lennox, and was renewed in 1619 for twenty-one years. Although searchers were appointed in other counties, including Middlesex and ⁻Hertfordshire, attention remained focused on Norfolk and Yorkshire. Lennox was plaintiff in a suit in 1606 against stocking dealers in Norwich who were evading payment. The Duke's representatives waylaid carts travelling to London and searched their hampers for goods that had not been sealed, some of which had been made in Yarmouth.[41] In 1626 the Duke's widow prosecuted the Yorkshire merchants: they were summoned from the north Yorkshire townships of Richmond, Barnard Castle and Askrigg, but allusion was also made at the hearing of the case to the stocking merchants of Doncaster and Rotherham. Another centre for aulnage payments existed by then in Northampton.[42]

Although by the 1620s the Lennox family was clearly prosecuting its searches further afield, it had not taken the full measure of the industry in the north and west of England, and it is only from chance references in scattered places that we can identify other centres. Cornwall and Devon were producers of stockings before the end of the sixteenth century: the London port book of 1598–99 shows them being despatched to Flushing, Amsterdam and Dieppe.[43] In the early years of the seventeenth century George Stratford, factor to a London salter, was earning his living buying Cheshire cheese and Cheshire stockings to sell in London.[44] In Westmorland, in Dentdale and Garsdale in 1634, the inhabitants were said to be heavily dependent on stocking knitting as a by-employment because their holdings of land were small and were continually subject to fragmentation through partible inheritance.[45] After the Restoration knitting was widespread in the Vale of Tewkesbury. Tewkesbury became the market whence stockings were sent down the Severn to Gloucester and thence to Bristol.[46]

[40] P.R.O., SP 12/252/2.

[41] P.R.O., Stac. 8, bdle. 90. No. 19.

[42] P.R.O., E 134, 2 Car. I, Mich. 38. An extract from this case is printed in Thirsk and Cooper, *op. cit.,* p. 342.

[43] I am indebted to Dr G. D. Ramsay for allowing me to use his transcript of this port book, P.R.O., E 190/10/11.

[44] P.R.O., Stac. 8, bdle. 266, No. 24.

[45] Chapter XIII above, p. 217.

[46] Chapter XII above, p. 204; Thirsk and Cooper, *op. cit.,* p. 296; D. Defoe, *A Tour through England and Wales* (Everyman edition), II, p. 42.

In the 1670s knitting had a foothold in Somerset, at Wells and Taunton, and at Tiverton in Devon; all three towns were supplied with wool by the blanket makers of Witney in Oxfordshire, who discarded the long fell wool which was unsuitable for blankets, and passed it on for the making of worsted stockings in the south-west.[47] Stockings were also knitted in Wales and were regularly offered for sale at Farnham in Surrey by the 1670s.[48] How the link was forged between these two widely separated groups of makers and buyers can only be guessed at, but Farnham was a major hop-growing centre at this time, and it is possible that Welshmen came to Farnham to help with the picking and brought their stockings with them. A principal characteristic of all pastoral economies throughout England was the combination of farming with industrial by-employments. Thus some of the seemingly unrelated commodities in which city merchants and factors specialised fit neatly into the jigsaw of a local peasant economy, where they were made by the same people. We have already noticed the London factor who bought Cheshire cheese and stockings: he was buying from dairymen who were also part-time knitters.[49] Large quantities of cheese and cloth appear together in the storehouses of early seventeenth century Kentish clothiers: the latter were evidently dealing with Wealden dairymen who were also part-time cloth weavers.[50] The pressing need for seasonal help with the harvesting of hops may well account for the presence of both Welshmen and their stockings at Farnham. Finally, in the last decades of the seventeenth century knitting appears to have spread to Essex, where 'wadmal' stockings—coarse textured articles, probably of small value—were made. They appear in small quantities in the port books of Colchester: 360 pairs went overseas in 1685, 840 pairs in 1700, and 120 pairs in 1715.[51]

By the end of the seventeenth century the hand knitting industry was geographically widely dispersed. It is not surprising to find it flourishing in many areas where a wool cloth industry already existed, for the two occupations were associated, and sometimes complementary, in their use of wool. But the two industries did not coexist everywhere, and the presence of local wool was not the

---

[47] Thirsk and Cooper, *op. cit.*, p. 296.
[48] *V.C.H. Surrey*, IV, p. 457.
[49] See above, p. 246.
[50] *The Agrarian History of England and Wales*, IV, p. 58.
[51] K. H. Burley, 'The economic development of Essex in the later seventeenth and early eighteenth centuries', University of London PhD thesis (1957), appendix 3, p. 409.

determining factor. The common denominator in nearly all rural stocking knitting communities was a large population of smallholders, pursuing a pastoral system of farming which gave them time to spare for a by-employment. With this they supplemented their income from their small farms.[52] The towns which were renowned stocking centres were the markets lying within or near these farming regions, where traders gathered and additional knitters were recruited.

The quantity of work which the stocking knitting industry afforded can be measured only in an impressionistic way. The population of the kingdom was between $4\frac{1}{2}$ and $5\frac{1}{2}$ million in the seventeenth century, and we can reasonably estimate that everyone wore out at the very least two pairs of stockings a year. Between 9 and 11 million pairs of stockings had to be produced somehow, and large numbers of people did not expect to make them for themselves. The aulnage collectors in 1595 reckoned that one knitter made two pairs of stockings per week.[53] On this basis the domestic market could have employed between 90,000 and 110,000 people working for fifty weeks a year. Reckoning one knitter per household, the whole of Gregory King's class of cottagers, day labourers, and paupers in 1695 could have been so employed.[54] This calculation is extremely rough and ready; the market was served not only by English knitters but by Welsh and Irish as well, and they are omitted from this reckoning. Cloth stockings continued to be worn as well as knitted stockings. But we started with a conservative estimate of the number of pairs of stockings required per person. Two pairs per year could quite reasonably be doubled,[55] thus doubling the demand to 18–22 million pairs a year, and providing work for 180,000–220,000 knitters. We could, if we wished, further refine our calculations, since knitting was described on at least one occasion as a seasonal occupation. Abraham Dent, hosier, facing competition from other kinds of employment during the summer in Kirkby Stephen, maintained in 1784 that knitting was done from September to February when there was no other work, and labour was consequently cheap.[56] There is no evidence that this was always so; the port books indicate otherwise,

[52] Chapter XIII above.
[53] P.R.O., SP 12/252/2.
[54] Thirsk and Cooper, *op. cit.*, p. 768.
[55] It was not unusual to wear more than one pair of stockings at once, in order to achieve warmth and elegance at the same time.
[56] T. S. Willan, *An Eighteenth-century Shopkeeper: Abraham Dent of Kirkby Stephen* (Manchester, 1970), p. 64.

since exports overseas continued all the year round, though they may have fluctuated in quantity. However, enough has been said to demonstrate that the knitting industry was a substantial employer of labour and a considerable branch of the clothing trades.

In addition to the domestic demand, knitters found a smaller sale among foreign buyers. Overseas trade built up steadily from a measurable beginning in the 1570s until by the end of the seventeenth century between 1 and $1\frac{3}{4}$ million pairs were being exported.[57] To establish the pattern of the trade overseas requires more detailed analysis than can be undertaken here. The following account is based on a small sample of the port books. The trade cannot be documented until the 1570s, for before then the customs officers at the ports did not record details of 'small goods'. Thus it *appears* (and appearances may be deceptive) that one of the earliest established trade routes for stockings ran between Chester and Ireland. Between Michaelmas 1576 and Michaelmas 1577 they were despatched in packs of two, three, four, fourteen and twenty dozen pairs. They included worsted stockings, kersey (i.e. woven) stockings of unspecified places of origin, and 'woollen stockings'. Since the latter often accompanied packs of Kendal cottons and northern kerseys, it is probable that these came from the Kendal neighbourhood, or, more exactly, from Dentdale. Their destination was Dublin.[58] A more spasmodic trade in stockings to Ireland proceeded from Bristol: in 1600–01 woollen, and less often kersey, stockings went to Cork, Waterford, Limerick and Kinsale, while occasionally worsted, and some cloth, stockings were loaded on vessels bound for London. But the Bristol trade was of small importance and probably reflected the relatively small attraction of knitted goods made in the west Midlands; in 1605, and in 1720 and 1775 (when stockings sometimes went to America), they were only an occasional item.[59]

Port books from the south-west have yielded no evidence that locally knitted stockings were sent from local ports overseas, though Irish stockings were sometimes imported and re-exported to France.[60] Instead, stockings made in Devon and Cornwall were sent overseas from London and Dover. At Dover the trade was

---

[57] Thirsk and Cooper, *op. cit.*, p. 587.

[58] P.R.O., E 190/1324/17.

[59] P.R.O., E 190/1132/11; W. E. Minchinton, *The Trade of Bristol in the Eighteenth Century*, Bristol Record Society, xx (1957), pp. 48, 76.

[60] The trade in Irish stockings is represented in the port book of Poole, Christmas 1631–Christmas 1632, P.R.O., E 190/875/2. I have also sampled the port books of Dartmouth and Exeter.

developing rapidly in the last decades of the sixteenth century. Between 1576 and 1577 vessels carrying cloth goods made in Devon and Yorkshire to Calais also carried some 'netherstocks'. By the late 1590s (Michaelmas, 1598–99) worsted, kersey and woollen stockings featured regularly on their way to Dieppe and Calais. A century later (Christmas 1697–Christmas 1698) the trade had swollen considerably. Children's and men's worsted stockings were the most regular exports, while some cotton stockings also made their appearance. They were all bound for Calais, or more rarely Ostend. In two months between 18 July and 18 September 1698 nearly 900 pairs were shipped to the Continent.[61]

From the port of London knitted stockings formed by 1600 a regular item in the cargoes assembled for despatch to France, Holland and Germany. In the record of exports between September 1598 and April 1599 stockings appeared every week, frequently three and four times a week, and sometimes in two or three different cargoes recorded at the customs house on the same day. They were packed in 'small trusses' of forty or sixty pairs, or in larger consignments, in barrels and chests, containing 320 pairs, 500, 600 and 750 pairs. Norwich worsted stockings were in the majority, and can often be recognised as such because they were stowed alongside Norwich cloths. They went to the French ports of Rochelle, Rouen and Bayonne, and to Holland and Germany via Amsterdam and Hamburg. Jersey stockings of uncertain provenance (probably from Norwich, too) were sent to Dieppe. Cornish knit stockings went to Flushing and La Rochelle. Knit stockings packed up with Devonshire dozens, and so perhaps coming from Devon too, were despatched to Dieppe and Amsterdam.[62]

Along the east coast Yarmouth was the main port of East Anglia for despatching white jersey stockings. In 1600 the standard type made in Yarmouth and Norwich and district went to Rouen, Rochelle, Flushing and even Civitavecchia, while a batch of coarse jersey stockings went to Rotterdam. The difference in quality between plain jersey and coarse jersey was evidently considerable: plain jersey stockings were valued in the customs house at 4s a pair, the coarse at 2s 8d.[63]

Farther north, Newcastle had become a stocking-exporting centre

[61] P.R.O., E 190/640/1; E 190/647/3; E 190/675/2.
[62] P.R.O., E 190/10/11.
[63] P.R.O., E 190/480/12. Mr. A. R. Michell of Hull University has a thesis on Yarmouth in preparation which will treat its stocking knitting industry in more detail.

by the 1630s, though none had appeared in cargoes registered in the early 1590s. Despatched at infrequent intervals, they nevertheless represented large consignments. During 1639 they were packed in units of 127 dozen, 130 dozen, 179, 196 and 222 dozen. Their place of manufacture is never stated, but they were almost certainly woollen stockings—men's and children's only—made in the northern counties.[64]

Thus the regional distribution of the stocking knitting industry was matched by a regional pattern in its overseas trade. Norfolk stockings were despatched from London and Yarmouth, northern stockings from Newcastle and Chester, Tewkesbury stockings from Bristol, those from the south-west from Dover and London. Which were their destinations? In the early years of the seventeenth century cheap English woollen stockings were bought by Spanish merchants, who exchanged them for tobacco in Trinidad and Orinoco. But a pamphleteer describing this trade in 1615 believed that the West Indian market was by then saturated, and the later port books do not give much sign of a continuing trade to Spain in these wares.[65] The main overseas markets for English stockings until the 1670s lay in Ireland, France and Flanders. This is the impression conveyed by the port books and confirmed by the casual comments of contemporaries. All three countries took an assortment of all types, though the English reputation in France and Holland rested on its worsted stockings. 'Our worsted stockings are in great request all Europe over, especially in France and Flanders', wrote Belasyse in 1657, in his enumeration of the most celebrated products of England's agriculture and industry.[66] Ireland did not interest itself in jersey stockings but bought the more durable woollen stockings of the north country as well as Cheshire stockings, which were probably of worsted. Its purchases were a much valued item in English trade, but they were largely lost when the Irish Cattle Act, passed by the English Parliament in 1663, deprived England of Irish store beasts and thereby deprived the Irish of the money to buy English stockings. English knitters in the north and west were the sufferers.[67] Henceforward the hand knitting industry looked mainly to France and Holland for its overseas sales, but Colbert's restrictive measures and

[64] P.R.O., E 190/185/6; E 190/192/4.
[65] C. T., *An Advice how to plant Tobacco in England with the Danger of the Spanish Tobacco* (1615), pages not numbered.
[66] H.M.C., *Var. Coll.*, II, p. 200.
[67] *The Grand Concern of England explained* . . . (1673), *Harleian Miscellany*, VIII (1746), p. 534.

increased tariffs between 1664 and 1671 curtailed English stocking imports into France, leaving the French trade to Holland. For a while between 1672 and 1678 the French war against the Dutch, by reducing France's domestic stocking production, improved the chances of English imports, but at the peace England again had to contend with an expanding French industry.[68] Despite these blows to trade, official English stocking exports amounted to $1\frac{3}{4}$ million pairs in 1697–98; and the French, at least, firmly believed that many more were illegally smuggled into their country.[69]

It remains to put William Lee, the inventor of the knitting frame, in his correct place within this diversified industry. In doing so we shall underline the strong contacts that were maintained throughout the sixteenth and seventeenth centuries between the makers of stockings in all west European countries. The industry had a strongly international character from the outset, and while it might appear that the English industry had developed a stable structure, with well defined regional sectors, by the 1630s, in fact the component parts of that industry were in a continuous state of change. Foreign influences, ever-changing fashions, and the invention of the knitting frame were responsible for the continually shifting relationships between the various sectors.

William Lee was born in Sherwood Forest at Calverton. After attending Cambridge University he returned to the forest to take up a curacy in his native parish. No evidence survives concerning a knitting industry in Sherwood, but there must have been knitters, else how would William Lee have been inspired to make a stocking frame? It was evidently a knitting centre which escaped the merchants' attention. Why? We can only speculate on the local wools, but the forest lies on Bunter sandstones, the soils are sandy and poor, and arable farming depended to a large extent on sheep for maintaining fertility. It is, therefore, a reasonable guess that the local sheep were of the small, heath breed, producing a short, fine wool, similar to that found on the sandy downlands of Herefordshire, in the Clun forest of Shropshire, and on the heaths of Staffordshire.[70] If so, then it follows

[68] C. W. Cole, *Colbert and a Century of French Mercantilism* (1939), I, p. 427; II, pp. 222, 207, 229, 566, 212, 230.

[69] Thirsk and Cooper, *op. cit.*, p. 587; Cole, *op. cit.*, II, pp. 561, 229.

[70] R. Trow-Smith, *A History of British Livestock Husbandry to 1700* (1957), p. 164. Henson commented on the fine staple of the wool of Sherwood Forest sheep, but his view that it had an unusually long filament is not confirmed by other writers (G. Henson, *History of the Framework Knitters* (1831), pp. 57–8). Cf. W. Youatt, *Sheep, their Breeds, Management and Diseases* (1837), pp. 303–4.

that when William Lee watched the womenfolk of his native village at their knitting, and conceived the design for a stocking frame, he saw them using a softer but thicker yarn than worsted.[71] This would explain why the merchants showed small interest in Sherwood's products; the latter would not have been sufficiently hard-wearing. But their softness may have been of some consequence in Lee's subsequent career, for when he sought royal support for his invention, he quickly won the patronage and support of nobility, like Lord Hunsdon, gentry and well-to-do merchants. This fact is more readily understood if we suppose that Lee was using the same wool and showing them samples of a soft knitted fabric having a texture that his influential patrons fancied and were prepared themselves to purchase.[72] Queen Elizabeth's reaction to Lee's request, denying him a patent for knitting wool stockings on a frame but urging him instead to perfect one that would knit silk stockings, may also be interpreted in this way. She too may have recognised in his frame-knitted stocking a soft fabric that was reminiscent of silk and so reacted to his proposal in pure self-interest: he should try what he could do with silk yarn on the frame. The stocking knitting trade was already highly differentiated in its products, and Elizabeth must have known this as well as any. It is much less likely that she knew the social basis of stocking knitting in Sherwood Forest. The story that she discouraged Lee from persisting with his frame because it would impoverish her poor subjects was a tradition among old stocking knitters whose memories went back to the early eighteenth century, and whom Gravener Henson heard and recorded in 1831.[73] It is not supported by any documentary evidence, and we are therefore justified in suspecting that it is a garbled version of the truth.

We can only tentatively suggest that Lee experimented with the knitting of a soft wool fabric, but it is certainly noteworthy how early he attracted the interest of well-to-do clients. Even if his attention was not turned in their direction from the outset, it certainly turned that way when he settled in London with his brother in 1589–90, immediately after he had completed the first prototype, Lord Hunsdon supported his claim to the Queen for a patent, and Lord Hunsdon's son became one of his apprentices. By 1599 he had perfected his knitting frame for making silk stockings, and henceforward was commonly described as a weaver of silk stockings; he

[71] I am grateful to Mr K. G. Ponting for technical advice on this subject.
[72] Grass, *op. cit.*, pp. 98–9, 108–9.
[73] Henson, *op. cit.*, pp. 39, 45.

appears as such in the Book of Admissions to the Freedom of the Weavers Company of London in 1608. He was then living at close quarters with the French silk weavers of Petty France and Spitalfields.[74]

The pioneers of the improved stocking knitting industry, as we have seen, had been French, Italians and Spaniards. Silk and worsted were the specialities in Italy, linen and worsted were knitted in France in the 1520s, though silk was being developed by 1560.[75] Knitters on the islands of Jersey and Guernsey also shared in the early rise of the industry, before England had much of a role to play in the production of fashion goods, probably because their merchants maintained close links with the towns of northern France, especially Paris and Rouen.[76] Foreign techniques spread rapidly in England after 1560. Some, as we have seen, were communicated in the ordinary course of trade; some were brought by persecuted Dutch and French refugees; some reached England via Guernsey and Jersey. Guernsey stockings were regularly imported into Southampton.[77] Jersey stockings, originally made on the island of Jersey, were being made in large quantity in Norwich by 1600.[78]

Yet the fact that English stockings were being exported to France, Holland and Flanders by 1600, when all these countries made their own, suggests that the English designs found favour, either because of their price or their design or both. Many of Norwich's stocking exports even went to Rouen, which was itself a major knitting centre.[79] What did the English article have which the French lacked? As far as worsted stockings are concerned, it appears to have been their fine texture. According to the *Declaration d'Exportations* of Rouen in 1603, the knitters of Rouen were then manufacturing hand knit stockings of *very fine worsted, façon d'Angleterre*.[80] Although Frenchmen had passed some of their technical secrets to England, yet even so the English knitters had something to teach them.

Meanwhile silk knitters from Rouen were settled in London, living as near neighbours of William Lee. Among them Lee met Salomon and Pierre de Caux, influential brothers in mercantile and governmental circles in France. The exchange of technical skill between

[74] Grass, *op. cit.*, pp. 93, 112, 125, 121.
[75] *Ibid.*, p. 54.
[76] Priaulx and Sausmarez, *op. cit.*, pp. 211, 213.
[77] P.R.O., E 190/824/2.
[78] See above p. 240.
[79] See above, p. 250.
[80] Grass, *op. cit.*, p. 129.

English and French resulted in some English silk knitters going to Rouen: in the early years of the seventeenth century three English apprentices were working for Gédéon Langlois. In 1608–09 Lee also decided that his prospects in France were better than in England. In 1611 he signed a contract with Pierre de Caux in Rouen to make stockings of silk and of worsted on his knitting frame.[81]

According to Thoroton, writing in 1677, Lee left one of his frames with an apprentice named Aston in Nottinghamshire before he crossed the Channel. This young man continued to exploit, and indeed added to, his master's invention. However, Lee's death in France *c.* 1611 caused seven out of the nine fellow knitters who had accompanied him to return home. They settled in London—not surprisingly, since it was still the principal centre in England for silk knitting, and was presumably also the city with the most buyers. But James Lee, William's brother, is said to have returned to Nottinghamshire and joined forces with Aston. This suggests that while they were in France James's speciality may have been worsted knitting, while William's was silk. James's prospects in England were thus more promising in the Midlands than in London. However that may be, the wider use of the knitting frame in Leicestershire and Nottinghamshire is clearly traceable in documents from the late 1630s onwards. There it was at first used for knitting *worsted* stockings. It spread rapidly in Nottinghamshire and in the western half of Leicestershire in the 1640s.[82] The coming of the frame to London and the east Midlands thenceforward developed another branch of the knitting industry on a mixed social basis. The knitters now lived increasingly in towns, and had less part-time interest in farming. Some could afford a frame and were their own masters, but those who could not, worked for other frame-owners, and never tasted the independence of the hand knitters. From the outset they were enslaved, like the spinners and weavers of cloth, working for a clothier 'for small wages, so that they live very poorly'. It is unlikely that William Lee envisaged this outcome when he invented his frame.

By 1655, when the London framework knitters sent a petition for incorporation to Cromwell, they were manifestly an articulate and relatively cohesive group, cherishing a strong tradition of Lee's pioneer efforts in England and France. But they were wholly concerned with the knitting of silk. They claimed, no doubt correctly,

---

[81] *Ibid.*, pp. 129, 134, 142–4, 169–71.
[82] *V.C.H. Notts.*, II, p. 353; *V.C.H. Leics.*, III, pp. 2–3; C. Holme, *A History of the Midland Counties* (1891), p. 22.

that their skill had greatly improved since his day, and that they had won such international repute that they sold more stockings abroad than at home. For the purposes of the petition they showed no interest in the activities of the Midland framework knitters, but were acutely anxious lest their secrets should be betrayed to foreign competitors. Intruders were growing in number, impostors were offering to teach knitting, and at any time a young man was liable to depart in dudgeon to a foreign country, taking his knowledge with him.[83]

By 1655, then, the knitting industry was regrouping itself into three sectors. Framework knitting in silk was entrenched in London, producing the highest quality goods of which English knitters were capable, in the most expensive yarn silk. Silk knitters claimed to be able to supply all domestic needs without the necessity of imports, but their sights were set on the foreign market, and they were content to leave the 'common tedious way' of knitting (their words) to common knitters, who supplied the home market 'in great part'.[84] A framework knitting industry, using worsted yarn, was slowly making headway in the Midlands, using the local long wool of Midland sheep. This was the wool that had furnished the main supplies of the Norfolk hand knitting industry. Stockings knitted on a frame doubtless competed on grounds of price with hand knitting, and also perhaps in uniformity of stitch. By the early eighteenth century, not surprisingly, observers were mourning the decline of hand knitting in Norwich.[85] The demand for woollen stockings of the northern variety continued at a high level, and they remained, as before, the cheapest. For rough working purposes they were superior to worsted. Later than anyone else the army came to terms with the fashion for knitted stockings, and during the eighteenth century was a large buyer from the northern knitters. Yet it bowed to the dictates of fashion in as much as it differentiated between the ranks of its soldiers, specifying different lengths and designs for sergeants' hose, guards' hose and those for the marching regiments.[86]

Other sectors of the industry regrouped themselves yet again during the eighteenth century. Nottinghamshire framework knitters, who had turned to silk in addition to worsted in the second half of the seventeenth century, turned increasingly to cotton lace in the later

[83] B.M., Thomason tract E 863 (4). Part of this petition is printed in Thirsk and Cooper, *op. cit.*, pp. 259–64.

[84] *Ibid.*, pp. 263–4.

[85] Hartley and Ingilby, *op. cit.*, p. 10.

[86] T. S. Willan, *An Eighteenth-Century Shopkeeper*, p. 66.

eighteenth. Derbyshire took up silk knitting in the early eighteenth century, and improved on the frame, while a cheaper silk stocking that was *woven*, and sold at half the price, began to compete with the knitted variety.[87] Another new partner also appeared on the scene: the Shetland hand knitting industry was 'discovered'. Its very fine wools and attractive new patterns caught the eye of the smart London and Oxford set.[88] The wheel of fashion continued to turn, assuring as it did so a fresh demand for knitted products, but also demanding a high price for its favours: it insisted on the frequent reconstitution of the industry. Thus although a trade in stockings was maintained, the geography and the social basis of the industry were permanently unstable. Both frame knitters and hand knitters were at the mercy of inventors or designers who copied their styles, cheapened their products and captured their markets. Their survival depended always on their ability to retaliate with a new design, or to tap a new market patronised by a different class of purchaser. The trade was continuous, but the livelihood of local communities of knitters was not continuously assured, unless they could constantly adapt and keep fickle fashion satisfied.[89]

[87] *V.C.H. Notts.*, II, pp. 355–6; *V.C.H. Derbys.*, II, p. 367; Thirsk and Cooper, *op. cit.*, p. 322.

[88] A. O'Dell, *The Historical Geography of the Shetland Islands* (1939), pp. 155 ff. Mr K. G. Ponting is preparing a fuller study of the Shetland knitting industry.

[89] I wish to thank the Pasold Research Fund for a grant to assist research for this essay.

XV

NEW CROPS AND THEIR DIFFUSION: TOBACCO-GROWING IN SEVENTEENTH-CENTURY ENGLAND

SUBSTANTIAL changes in the structure of agriculture and in the quantities of food produced have been brought about at different times in man's history by the introduction of new crops. Englishmen could cite as examples the introduction of clover and turnips; Irish, German and Polish historians the potato; French, Spanish and Italians maize. Sometimes the innovation is attributed to one man, as Sir Walter Raleigh is credited with the introduction of the potato in Ireland.[1] Sometimes it is attributed to its first publicist, as the introduction of clover as a field crop is attributed to Sir Richard Weston, or turnips to Lord Townshend. But while these attributions make colourful biographical history, they do not go to the heart of the matter. Explorers who bring back plants from their voyages, and the writers of persuasive books are only individuals singled out for obvious reasons from a large company of players. In reality the success of a new crop depends on its cultivators. It is they who experiment with it, measure its contribution to their food resources, decide if it will find a ready sale at the market, and judge how its cultivation can be fitted into their pattern of agricultural work. They are the supreme arbiters; it is they who determine whether the crop shall spread rapidly, slowly, or not at all.

But who are 'they', and what governs their decisions? 'They' are cultivators, but they are not always one homogeneous class. Their enthusiasm for an innovation must survive the test of the crop's economic attractiveness, *and* the demands it makes on their technical skills, their capital, and their labour resources. If enthusiasm does survive, it will vary in degree among different classes of farmers according to the social framework in which their lives are set. If the new crop takes hold among the peasantry, it may be counted a minor

---

[1] G. B. Masefield, 'Crops and livestock', in E. E. Rich and C. H. Wilson, eds, *The Cambridge Economic History of Europe*, iv (Cambridge University Press, 1967), pp. 277–8.

miracle, so notoriously slow are they in adopting novelties. In short, a successful new crop has a complex economic and social history involving several layers of explanation. The deeper layers are rarely explored for our sources of information are too meagre. We have to be content usually with a superficial account of its progress, studded with the names of one or two astute plant importers or eloquent writers. The phases of the story that involve the cultivators are shrouded in mystery.

Tobacco-growing in England, however, is a different case. It began to take hold early in the seventeenth century, and was almost immediately banned by the government. Yet the crop proved to be remarkably tenacious and popular, being taken up with alacrity by large numbers of peasant cultivators. In fifty years it spread into twenty-two counties in England and Wales, and to the islands of Jersey and Guernsey. Since the government had to fight a long-drawn-out battle, lasting over seventy years, before tobacco-growing was eradicated, its history is unusually well documented. An exceptional opportunity occurs of observing how a novel crop was first introduced, and, more remarkably, how it became firmly established among poor husbandmen, the group normally most reluctant to risk its fortunes on new-fangled ventures.

Ralph Lane, the first governor of Virginia, and Francis Drake are usually given credit for bringing tobacco to England in 1586. They introduced Sir Walter Raleigh to tobacco-smoking, and he became its first publicist. Seed was brought from America in the sixteenth century for the interest of English botanists, to be grown in their physic gardens and nurseries. But it does not necessarily follow that cultivation on a large scale began under their impetus. It is possible that field cultivation was encouraged by observations and experience of growing tobacco picked up by someone in another country in Europe. The plant (*nicotiana tabacum*) had been brought from Brazil to Portugal probably before 1530. In 1560 the French ambassador in Lisbon, Jean Nicot, was given some seeds by the distinguished Portuguese archivist and historiographer, Damião de Goes, and despatched them to France. It is thought that commercial tobacco cultivation did not start in France, despite Nicot's action, until 1626, seven years after it had begun in England.[2] If any country in Europe is to have credit for teaching English growers, it is more likely to have been Holland, where the crop was growing in 1610, and where by

[2] Sarah A. Dickson, 'Panacea or Precious Bane. Tobacco in Sixteenth Century Literature', *Bulletin of the New York Public Library*, vol. 57 (1953), 549–66.

1615 it was firmly established around Amersfoort, later to become a principal centre.[3]

Nevertheless, the influence of European experience on English tobacco-growers still remains in doubt, since the first book of instruction on the subject, *An Advice how to plant Tobacco in England... with the Danger of the Spanish Tobacco* by C.T., published in London in 1615, is clearly written by someone with an accurate knowledge of the methods used to grow and cure it in the West Indies.[4] In the next four years much experience was to be had from Virginia too. The Virginia plantation had been in existence since 1607, and tobacco was the staple crop from 1616 onwards.[5] By 1619 when the Tracy family of Toddington, Gloucestershire, was engaged in tobacco-growing around Winchcombe, one younger member, William Tracy of Hailes, near Winchcombe, was actively associated with the Virginia Company, recruiting men for the Virginia plantation. He sailed to Virginia in the first half of 1620 and was appointed a member of the Council of Estate there in June. His correspondence in 1620 included at least one letter from his 'cousin' Timothy Gates, parson of Winchcombe, whose wife allowed some of her land to be used to grow tobacco. He also wrote many letters to John Smyth of Nibley, who was ordering good tobacco seed from Virginia in 1619, and who sold English tobacco to Virginia in 1621.[6]

The impetus to grow tobacco commercially in England, therefore, could have come from one of a number of different sources or from the combined influence of several. By 1619 tobacco was finding its way into an increasing number of yards and gardens in Westminster and London, where the apothecaries were willing purchasers, and it was no longer certain that their purposes were only medicinal.[7] The first commercial grower of tobacco on a large scale had trading connections with Holland. But the strongest evidence is that which links Gloucestershire gentry with the Virginia Company. The full

[3] V. R. I. Croesen, 'Tabakscultuur in Nederland', *Agronomisch-Historisch Jaarboek* (1940), 3–4.

[4] The author also speaks of the results already achieved by growers in England and France, but since he names Gerarde's *Herbal* and the French writers, Olivier de Serres and Car. Stephanus (Charles Estienne), his remarks could have been derived from a reading of French and English herbals and horticultural textbooks.

[5] A. Rive, 'The consumption of tobacco since 1600', *Economic History* (1926–9), p. 59.

[6] S. M. Kingsbury, *Records of the Virginia Company* (1906), i, pp. 296, 303, 139, 141, 143, 379, 144; H. Willcox, *Gloucestershire: a study in local government* (Yale University Press, 1940), p. 159. For Timothy Gates, see p. 83.

[7] C. M. MacInnes, *The Early English Tobacco Trade* (Kegan, Paul, Trench, Trubner, 1926), p. 79.

significance of this association is elaborated below.

The first firm evidence of tobacco cultivation on a field scale in England dates from 1619, with some slight hints that a trial crop had been grown in the previous year.[8] The land used for tobacco lay in the neighbourhood of Winchcombe, Gloucestershire, and the promoters of the enterprise were two Londoners, John Stratford, salter, and his partner Henry Somerscales, gentleman, of Gray's Inn. The identity of these two gentlemen repays closer investigation.

When Henry Somerscales entered Gray's Inn in 1605 he was described as the son of Robert Somerscales, esquire, of Gains-borough, Lincolnshire.[9] In a subsequent lawsuit two London salters who sold English tobacco wholesale claimed their first acquaintance with Henry in 1618. This is a slender but corroborating clue that the tobacco venture with John Stratford was first planned in that year and not earlier.[10] Henry Somerscales had doubtless acquired his skill with tobacco through the similar interests of his brother. In May 1619 Robert Somerscales was seeking a patent 'about tobacco' from the Crown, much to the alarm of the Virginia Company. When the Company's officers investigated the scheme, they decided that it was 'very prejudicial' to them, and must be stopped. They seem to have succeeded, for, after a meeting was arranged in May 1619 with the Attorney General and Mr Somerscales, no more was heard of it. A year later, in May 1620, Robert Somerscales concocted another project which he put before the Virginia Company. It required a capital sum of £15,000 which was to be raised from among adventurers in the Virginia Company, and was concerned with 'the curing and ordering of tobacco'. Somerscales was introduced to the Company as 'a very fit man ... who is very skilful in curing that plant, whereby it may be made more profitable than it is'. The scheme was approved by the Company in June 1620, but it is not referred to again in the Company's records and Robert Somerscales thereafter disappears from sight.[11] Meanwhile his brother, Henry, was engaged in tobacco growing in Gloucestershire. From January until December 1619 it was a legal activity; thereafter it was banned.

[8] One witness, John Ligon, in a lawsuit discussed more fully below, made ambiguous reference to a crop before that of 1619 (Public Record Office [PRO] C2, Jas. I, S28/18).

[9] J. Foster, *Register of Admissions to Gray's Inn, 1521–1889* (1889), p. 110. Three branches of the Somerscales family, of gentle birth, lived in the Grimsby area of Lincolnshire (A. R. Maddison, *Lincolnshire Pedigrees*, 1902–6, iii, pp. 906–9).

[10] PRO Req. 2/308/44.

[11] Kingsbury, *op. cit.*, i, pp. 218, 219, 370, 364–5, 398, 403.

In 1625 Henry Somerscales petitioned the Privy Council from Coates in Nottinghamshire, a small hamlet a few miles from Gainsborough, claiming to be a poor man who had spent his whole estate in 'finding out and perfecting the mystery of planting and curing tobacco'. His 'impoverishment' was that of a gentleman rather than a labourer, however, for he admitted having just spent £30 travelling twice to London to reclaim confiscated tobacco. He had been hard hit by the government's ban on tobacco-growing, and he now sought a new but associated occupation. He wanted a warrant to seize all English and Spanish tobacco and suppress all tobacco plantations throughout England, his reward being half the tobacco so seized which he could then sell for the support of himself and his family.[12] Three months later, in September 1626, the Privy Council gave Henry Somerscales, 'gentleman of the county of Nottingham', the job he desired: he was ordered to search and seize all tobacco found growing in Buckinghamshire, Lincolnshire, Yorkshire, and elsewhere.[13] No more is heard of him after this and he may have died at Lincoln in 1634.[14]

Such meagre biographical information does nothing to explain how the Somerscales family learned the mystery of tobacco-growing. They could have talked to the gardeners of London, read C.T.'s book, lived in Virginia, the West Indies, or Holland, or even, perhaps, learned from Dutch settlers in England or from Dutch traders. They lived near Gainsborough, which was a modest but developing trading port on the Trent, which had regular contact via Hull with the Netherlands.[15] Speculation on this point is unprofitable, but some additional facts concerning Henry Somerscales's circumstances should be noted here, for though in the mid 1620s he stood at the centre of a fragile web of tobacco-growing connections in Lincolnshire, he had been more firmly established in this business in Gloucestershire in 1619, and some of the social and geographical features of his Gloucestershire partnership are repeated here.

Somerscales's home was in Coates, possibly Coates Hall, an address which seems to make modest claim to being a manor house.[16]

---

[12] PRO SP 16/2, no. 117.

[13] *Acts of the Privy Council, Colonial, vol. i, 1613–80*, p. 109.

[14] *Calendar of Administrations in the Consistory Court of Lincoln, 1540–1659*, Index Library (1921), p. 338.

[15] I. S. Beckwith, 'The river trade of Gainsborough, 1500–1850', *Lincolnshire History and Archaeology*, no. 2 (1967), 3–4.

[16] Information reaching the Privy Council in 1626 named Henry Somerscales of Goatshall as a persistent tobacco-grower (*Acts of the Privy Council, June–Dec. 1626*, p. 194).

But Coates was only a hamlet in Habblesthorpe parish, and even Habblesthorpe itself was not a fully fledged village, never having had a church though it once possessed a chapel. These two townships comprised a small parish of just over a thousand acres consisting of low-lying land along the banks of the river Trent. The manor of Habblesthorpe and Coates was already divided between two lords in the early fourteenth century, and subsequently the land became further subdivided.[17] In 1612 one landowner was Michael Bland, gentleman,[18] and it seems reasonable to suppose that there is a connection between him and the Michael Bland who was also sought out in August 1626 by an emissary of the Privy Council because he was suspected of growing tobacco at Utterby in the Lincolnshire marshland. Bland was not at home when his august visitor called, for he was being pursued by his creditors and dared not show his face in his own house. The royal messenger judged him 'very poor', and so fearful that he had to live away from home, leaving his wife and children alone at Utterby. His crop of tobacco, intended for medicinal purposes, occupied only a tenth of an acre.[19]

In tracing Henry Somerscales's associates, we have been led into a byway. But the fragments of his story seem to associate tobacco growing with parish gentry, even poor gentry, making their way not in the congenial environment of deferential village society, where the gentry were acknowledged leaders, but in a less propitious countryside, on the damp, ill-drained lands of river floodplains and in marshland, where they lived alongside tough peasant communities endeavouring to get a living from their pastures and meadows. Only the shadowy outline of the story emerges here, but it gains in clarity when set beside the story from Gloucestershire, where a few years earlier Somerscales had grown tobacco on a grander scale in partnership with John Stratford.

John Stratford was a member of the London Salters' Company. Several other members of his family were also making their way in the same company in the first two decades of the seventeenth century when, by all accounts, the company was at the height of its

---

[17] W. White, *History, Directory, and Gazetteer of Nottinghamshire*, (1844), under Habblesthorpe.

[18] Thoroton's *History of Nottinghamshire*, republished by John Thoresby, vol. iii (1796), p. 302. Richard Bland of Habblesthorpe was a Treasurer of the county in 1627, an office usually filled by gentlemen and esquires (H. Hampton Copnall, compiler, *Nottinghamshire County Records. Notes and Extracts from County Records of the Seventeenth Century* (1915), p. 13).

[19] PRO SP 16/34, no. 40.

prosperity.[20] John Stratford's business interests were multifarious: as an acquaintance put it later, when Stratford fell on evil days, he had 'too many trades and occupations'. In partnership with his brother Ralph and two others he was engaged in soap-boiling and soap-trading. At the same time he was buying land with borrowed money and paying out substantial sums each year in interest.[21] He also traded in broadcloth, which he sold to the Eastland merchants, taking in exchange wheat, rye, linen yarn, and rough flax. In his own account of his career, he described flax as the chief commodity of his trade, which he put out to be dressed by the poor in London and the country. The Netherlands merchants ruined his business when they started to bring in flax ready dressed, and so he turned to tobacco-growing.[22]

John Stratford was first and foremost a merchant of London, and in his partnership with Somerscales it was he who was responsible for the despatch of tobacco from Gloucestershire to London for subsequent resale. But John Stratford's native county was Gloucestershire, for he was a younger son of an old gentry family living at Farmcote, two miles east of Winchcombe. His forebears had been gentlemen in Leicestershire and Nottinghamshire, but he came of a prolific junior branch which had struck roots in Gloucestershire some two or three generations earlier.[23] His tobacco-growing enterprise, therefore, brought him to Winchcombe, in part, a least, because he could there enlist the cooperation of a great number of kindred and neighbours.

The division of function between Somerscales and Stratford as 'co-partners and parting fellows' was nowhere made explicit, but everything points to a working arrangement whereby Somerscales attended to the planting and curing while Stratford was the more experienced salesman. Partnerships to grow tobacco, however, did not depend on merchants alone, but involved others in a larger co-

[20] J. Steven Watson, *A History of the Salters Company* (Oxford University Press, 1963), p. 54.

[21] Req. 2, Bdle 308/45.

[22] PRO SP 14/180, no. 79.

[23] The Stratford family was so prolific that it is difficult to establish from the Stratford pedigree of 1623 which John Stratford was the salter of London. In lawsuits his brother Ralph is mentioned, also the fact that he married one of the daughters of Peter Robinson of London. The most likely candidate in the pedigree is John Stratford, the seventh son of John Stratford, but he is shown to have married Margaret, daughter of William (or Robert) Tracy, and his family tree omits two brothers of John, Giles and Ralph (H. Chitty and John Phillipot, *The Visitation of the County of Gloucester, 1623*, Harleian Soc. xxi (1885), 157). For additional information on John's family, see PRO Stac 8, Bdle 266, no. 24; Req. Bdle 308/45; C2 Jas. I, S3/11.

operative enterprise: the merchants owned little or none of the land which they selected for planting.

The crop was best grown on land that had lain under grass for many years, and since leases of old pasture and meadow contained clauses forbidding ploughing under penalties, landowners had to be consulted and their permission given to grow the crop. The cultivator of the land might be an employee of the merchant if the merchant chose to lease the land direct from the landlord, but just as often he was a tenant farmer who agreed to cultivate the land for tobacco on contract with the merchant. His role was a responsible one, for planting, transplanting, watering, weeding, and pruning were laborious tasks, and required care if the plants were to be nursed into full production. In the early autumn the leaves had to be picked individually as and when they ripened; the harvest could last a month or more from the beginning of September until early October. The cultivator, therefore, had to be in constant attendance and employ extra labour at busy times.

The curing of the tobacco was another skilled operation which the grower was not necessarily competent to undertake alone. The leaves were left to dry in the sun, and then heaped together until they began to ferment. They were then hung up to dry for three or four weeks, taken down and heaped again until fermentation started a second time, and then again spread out to dry. Curing occupied about six weeks altogether until the beginning or middle of November, when the crop was ready for despatch to the salesman in London. The merchant knew most about curing, and curing was critical in determining the final value of the crop. He kept a close eye on the last stages in the process to see that nothing went wrong; he or his representatives were at hand in the autumn, if not all through the summer as well. Tobacco cultivation in these pioneering days, therefore, usually (though not invariably) established a partnership between three groups of people, landlords, cultivators and merchants, and they shared the expenses and profits equally between them. Since Stratford and Somerscales were already partners with their own division of function, their contracts divided the profits equally between four persons.[24]

The merchant initiated the planting of tobacco by seeking out suitable land and negotiating with landlord and tenant. John Stratford's first contacts were made in February 1619 with

---

[24] This and the following paragraph are based on information in two lawsuits, PRO Req. 2, 308/44 and Req. 2, 399/68.

Gloucestershire gentry, whom he already knew and who knew each other. The plan to grow tobacco evidently caused something of a stir in the district: high rents were being offered for tobacco land, and the gentry kept each other up to date with the gossip about the new crop's lucrative possibilities. The gossip and the bargaining came to light in a lawsuit in 1621 when local people were called to give evidence at an enquiry at Winchcombe. Such a congerie of distinguished gentry assembled on one day in 1621 in Winchcombe that the rest of the townsfolk could well have mistaken the gathering for the opening of Quarter Sessions.

The dispute about tobacco contracts set John Stratford and Henry Somerscales at loggerheads with Thomas Lorenge, gentleman of Cleeve. Lorenge had an interest in eight acres of land in Bishops Cleeve which had been leased for tobacco. Two of these acres he occupied himself, six he let to John Lorenge, yeoman.[25] Both had been parties to the negotiations with Stratford and Somerscales,[26] and they produced many knowledgeable witnesses.

Evidence was given by Giles Broadway, esquire, of Postlip, owner of Bishop Cleeve manor[27] where several pieces of land had been taken for tobacco growing. His daughter was married to another younger John Stratford of the same family.[28] Broadway had made a tobacco-growing agreement with Stratford and Somerscales, and had also persuaded Alice, wife of the parson of Winchcombe, Timothy Gates, to do likewise. Bartholomew Smyth, gentleman of Tewkesbury, gave evidence because he had surveyed and measured land designated for tobacco. Christopher Merret, mercer and gentleman of Winchcombe and landowner at Cleeve, was called because he was well informed, through conversation with neighbours, on the tobacco contracts. He was, incidentally, the father of Christopher Merret, who later became a prominent member of the Royal Society and joined its Georgical Committee in 1662.[29] Henry Izod, gentleman of Toddington, Gloucestershire, gave evidence because he was present (whether as

---

[25] That John and Thomas Lorenge were kinsmen is made clear in John's will, though the exact relationship is not specified (Gloucester Public Library, Will dated 8 Dec., 1626).

[26] PRO Req. 2, 308/44.

[27] *Victoria County History, Gloucestershire* [*VCH Glos*], viii, (1968) 8.

[28] Probably grandson of John Stratford, who was the cousin of our John Stratford.

[29] The express purpose of this committee was to promote agricultural improvement, and spread a knowledge of new crops. Christopher Merret undertook to compile a list of plants grown in England, and this is doubtless the origin of his *Pinax Rerum Naturalium Britannicarum* (1666), a list of plants and animals found in Britain. Under tobacco he simply says 'cultivated in several places, especially in Winchcombe, Glos'.

witness, party or scrivener, is not made clear) when bonds were drawn up binding tobacco merchants, growers and landlords.[30] John Parsons of Overbury, Worcestershire,[31] was present to explain how he had contemplated letting some of his land for tobacco but had fallen out with John Stratford on the terms of the agreement, and had settled with someone else instead. Francis Thorne, gentleman of Sudeley in Winchcombe parish, disclosed that he was in partnership with others who had made offers to take up land for tobacco in competition with Stratford.[32] Other witnesses included yeomen growers of tobacco, and a husbandman and labourer who had helped with the planting and weeding.

Since tobacco-growing depended upon partnerships, much bargaining and bond-taking accompanied them. John Stratford, planning well ahead to ensure that he had enough land in successive years to grow a worthwhile crop, negotiated some leases for four years. He soon learned the error of pledging to pay such high rents into the uncertain future. His first crop in 1619 occupied one hundred acres altogether,[33] but in December 1619 the government banned tobacco-growing, and Stratford was saddled with obligations entered into by bond to pay for another three years rents which were only justified if the land bore this one uniquely profitable crop.

In a second lawsuit, in which John Stratford tried to wriggle out of another obligation to pay a high rent for four years, we see the other side of the coin, the calculated risks taken by landlords who allowed their land to be used for a novel crop. John Ligon, gentleman, was persuaded after much cajoling by Ralph Wood, his tenant, to permit ten acres of his land at Arle Court, Cheltenham, to be used for tobacco. The land was good pasture, situated near the farmhouse, and the owner hesitated before he allowed it to be ploughed up, since

[30] Christopher Merret's will shows that Henry Izod was his uncle (Gloucester Public Library, Will dated 31 Dec., 1624).

[31] This John Parsons is almost certainly the one whose family had been buying up land in Kemerton parish since the end of the sixteenth century, and became resident and influential landowners there until the present century (though the name was changed to Hopton). Kemerton was a tobacco-growing village, lying next door to Overbury, Worcs. In Overbury parish, Conderton was named as a tobacco-growing township in 1627 (*VCH Glos.*, viii, 212; *Acts of the Privy Council, Jan–August, 1627*, p. 409).

[32] This is one of two or three hints that other contractors besides Stratford were looking for tobacco land at the same time. On this, see note 46 below.

[33] PRO SP 16/57, no. 14. That John Stratford planted 100 acres is also implied in his statement of the costs he anticipated, when he planned his first year. He reckoned on a labour cost of £1400. Another £1800 for rent and land was itemised separately (PRO C2 Jas. I, S3/11).

little other grazing ground was available so near at hand. The ploughing involved the destruction of a good orchard and the felling of forty or fifty trees. But the high rent offered—£80 in place of the £13 per annum paid by the sitting tenant—swayed him. When Stratford had taken one crop of tobacco and could plant no more, he grew a crop of barley. After that the land was abandoned, and Ligon was left with a weed-ridden plot, tumbling down to grass, for which his tenant would now only offer half the previous rent of £13.[34]

Ligon's information on the comparative rents paid for 'deep, good' grassland and for tobacco—£13 compared with £80—sheds our first glimmer of light on the economics of the new crop. It was a subject on which witnesses were prepared to be expansive, and on which they offered remarkably consistent evidence. The contracts evidently did not all take the same form. Sometimes the merchant offered a larger rent and took all the responsibility for cultivation, planting, harvesting, and curing.[35] In at least one case the occupier of land appears to have cultivated the tobacco and then sold the growing crop to the merchant. But more often than not the merchant offered landlord and tenant a partnership before the ground was planted. On this footing the tenant took responsibility for cultivation, paid all labour costs as they occurred, and the partners settled up at the end, sharing expenses and profits equally.

Land chosen for tobacco was old pasture or meadow whose average value was reckoned at £2 an acre, though sometimes it fetched only 25–30s, and sometimes was worth as much as £4. Tobacco merchants, offering a partnership with landlords and growers, rented it for £5, £6 13s 4d and even £8 an acre. Such rents included payment for buildings too, for barns and storehouses nearby were essential for drying the tobacco leaves after picking.[36]

John Lorenge's two acres of land yielded 819 lb of tobacco or almost 410 lb an acre.[37] It was taken to London by carrier in February 1620 and received by Thomas Drinkwater, salter of Friday Street, on Stratford's behalf.[38] He valued it at 2s per pound or £81 18s altogether. Rent and the costs of cultivation had amounted to £29 leaving a clear profit of £52 18s. Since there had been four parties to

---

[34] PRO C2 Jas. I, S 28/18.

[35] *Ibid.*

[36] PRO Req. 2, 308/44; Req. 2, 399/68; C2, Jas. I, S28/18.

[37] The yield of an average crop of tobacco in Ireland in the early nineteenth century was 1200 lbs, three times the yield quoted here (BPP 1830 (565) x, 12).

[38] A Thomas Drinkwater was Master of the Salters Company in 1663 (Watson, *op. cit.*, p. 145).

this enterprise, John and Thomas Lorenge, and John Stratford and Henry Somerscales each received £13 4s 6d.

In this example, rent and cultivation per acre had cost £14 10s; the net profit amounted to £26 9s per acre. In another example, Edward Stratford, Somerscales's local representative, who supervised the cultivation and curing of 15–16 acres in a parish next to Cleeve,[39] claimed that rent and charges amounted to £16 an acre, while the crop sold for only £10 an acre. Thus a loss of £6 an acre had been incurred. In a third example, Somerscales wanted to dissolve a partnership at the eleventh hour and carry on on his own because a crop growing on eight acres of Sir John Tracy's land promised a bumper harvest. He offered Tracy £450 plus 50 lb of tobacco plus £25 as a gratuity to Sir John's daughter, Anne. If we value 50 lb of tobacco at 2s per lb, making £5 in all, Somerscales was offering £480 for eight acres or £60 an acre. Tracy had pledged himself to bear the costs of cultivation, which by the end of the harvest would have amounted (at an average of £15 an acre) to £120, of which he had expected to recoup half from Somerscales. On the most unfavourable reckoning, namely, that Tracy was now expected to bear the full cost of cultivation, harvesting and rent, he would have finished with a profit of £45 an acre. Somerscales still had to make his profit; and we may well ask on what basis he arrived at his offer. He could expect a crop of at least 410 lb per acre, or 3,280 lb altogether, for which, at 2s a lb, he would have received only £328, a good deal less than the price he had offered Sir John Tracy. However, there are many speculative calculations in this example. Tobacco valued at 2s a lb was a very moderate, even low, wholesale price; prices varied widely between good, medium, and poor quality. Another grower of tobacco, John Ligon, alleged that in the same year that Lorenge's crop was sold, some English tobacco was selling for 10s, 12s, 16s, and 18s per lb. Presumably these were retail prices. It is difficult to be exact about the price range since wholesale and retail prices cannot always be disentangled,[40] but there is such a large gap between a moderate wholesale price of 2s and a high retail price of 18s that the merchant grower evidently had the possibility of getting substantially more

[39] Edward Stratford, gentleman of Winchcombe, was almost certainly one of John Stratford's many kinsmen.

[40] For other evidence from 1621 of poor quality tobacco, worth 2s and 2s 6d per lb, and of good quality at 6s 8d, see PRO Req. 2, 397/122. Thorold Rogers gives some illustrations of widely varying prices for different qualities at later dates in the seventeenth century (*A History of Agriculture and Prices in England*, (7 vols, 1866–1902), vol v; *1583–1702*, (Oxford), pp. 467–8).

than 2s a lb for a good crop. This is doubtless why Somerscales tried
to buy Sir John Tracy's crop outright. He had only to sell it for 4s a lb
(£656 altogether) to be handsomely in pocket.

The possibility of high prices for good quality tobacco makes sense
of another contemporary statement by John Ligon that on his crop
of ten acres of tobacco at Arle Court, John Stratford made a profit
above all charges of servants, labour, and rent of £600–700. Ten acres
could have produced 4,100 lb of tobacco, which, at 2s a lb, would
have earned only £410. But at 4s it would have earned £820, thus
covering all charges and leaving, as Ligon claimed, just under £600
clear profit.[41] In short, a reasonable net profit on an acre of tobacco in
1619 was £26 9s, but on a very good crop it could easily be four times
as much, reaching nearly £100 an acre.

Tobacco-growing was thus a highly speculative venture which, at
its most successful, could bring in superlative profits, even by the
standards of London merchants. The hazards, of course, were many.
The English weather was unreliable—1619 was a good year, but the
years 1620–22 were wet and cold and wholly unkind to the ripening
crop.[42] Moreover, although the domestic demand for tobacco was
rising rapidly, supplies from Spanish America, the West Indies and
Virginia fluctuated sharply, and so affected unpredictably the price of
English tobacco. One of John Stratford's opponents in law claimed
that in 1620 an excessive supply caused prices to fall. But when the
Virginia Company secured the ban on the growing of English
tobacco, a shortage was anticipated, and instead of drawing in his
horns, John Stratford hastened to buy large stocks from all and
sundry, to bide his time until the price rose.[43]

In the event the hazards involved in tobacco-growing turned out to
be greater than any of the merchants and growers anticipated,
because of the inordinate influence exerted by the Virginia Company
on the government. In no other European country did merchants and
planters manage to secure a total prohibition on domestic cultivation
for the sake of the colonial trade, and it is not perhaps surprising that
English merchant-growers were caught unawares. But it is also clear
that tobacco-growing had developed within one or two years of the
first experiments all the attributes of a wild speculation, which was
of the merchants' own making. The trials were not cautiously entered
into; the merchants dreamed of making a quick fortune before too

[41] PRO C2, Jas. I, S3/11.
[42] PRO C2, Jas. I, S28/18.
[43] *Ibid.*

many others caught on to the same idea. They burst upon farmers and landlords in Gloucestershire with the same excitement with which they might have entered Ali Baba's cave, couching their proposals not in cautious terms, but offering high rents and the promise of high profits. They imported into the farming community a mentality and a commercial ethos which was the very air they breathed in London, but was surely alien to agricultural society. London merchants were not, of course, entirely guileless when they offered to share their profits equally with their neighbours in Gloucestershire—in fact, they were sharing the risks as well. They were also using their farming partners to supply liquid capital they did not wish to find for themselves. And they had ways of changing their contracts midstream when they saw in a growing crop the promise of a super-abundant harvest. But what the London merchants offered was profit far in excess of any that farmers normally received in agriculture, whether from dairying, cattle-raising, or corn-growing. The profit from a thirty-acre farm in the early seventeenth century has been estimated at £14 10s. The average annual earnings of a farm labourer was £9.[44] Compared with these sums, £26 9s clear profit from one acre of tobacco land was riches indeed.

For a short while the merchants held the whip hand while they alone knew the full mystery of cultivation, and they strove to keep it a mystery as long as possible. In the lease with Thomas Lorenge, Stratford and Somerscales insisted on a promise that he would not grow tobacco anywhere else within ten miles of Cleeve.[45] They had other yet more devious ways of guarding their secrets. When Somerscales decided to buy out Sir John Tracy's interest in eight acres of tobacco, it was, he later maintained, because he wished to take full charge of the drying process and prevent Sir John and his servants from learning anything about it. In renting Lorenge's land moreover, he believed that he and Stratford had forestalled two other gentlemen of Winchcombe parish who were trying to rent it because it adjoined another of their plantations, and their rivals wished to spy on them.[46]

[44] Peter Bowden in Joan Thirsk, ed., *Agrarian History of England and Wales, vol. iv., 1500–1640* (Cambridge University Press, 1967), pp. 653, 657.

[45] It may be that in imposing this condition Somerscales was anticipating that his brother would receive a patent of monopoly for growing tobacco. See above, p. 262.

[46] There are some slight references in PRO Req. 2, 308/44 to tobacco-growing ventures that did not involve Stratford. A Mr Harris had been in partnership with Francis Thorne of Sudeley 'in a former year', and they had made £70 an acre on tobacco. John Harvey had also been in partnership with Thorne at some stage. But Thorne was described as a servant of Giles Broadway who co-operated with Stratford

It is not essential to know whether the suspicions of Somerscales and Stratford were justified or baseless; the fact that they nursed them reveals the atmosphere in which London merchants pursued their schemes and enlisted others. They imported into the countryside of the West Midlands a commercial and speculative boldness, with which they infected gentlemen and other well-to-do farmers. But while the latter played their due part as compliant agents of London adventurers, they did not abandon their country caution. They insisted on bonds, four-year contracts, and the like before they agreed to surrender their land for tobacco, and these were upheld in the courts when tobacco growing was no longer permitted. Stratford had to fulfil his promises, even though it bankrupted him, while the local gentry emerged unscathed. When Stratford and his associates gave up tobacco and embarked on yet another scheme—flax-growing this time—they left in the hands of the local population a store of knowledge which did not go to waste.

At this point a closer look at the economy and structure of society in this part of Gloucestershire makes a necessary prelude to the later history of tobacco-growing there. Winchcombe lies in the Vale of Tewkesbury, a broad vale watered by the rivers Severn and Avon and numerous smaller streams. Tobacco-growing proved successful throughout this vale and the contiguous Vale of Evesham.

Most of the land consists of liassic clays that are heavy and difficult to work under the plough. Large areas consisted of ancient pastures and meadows, and those which lay along river banks that were liable to flooding were bound to remain so.[47] Whenever enclosure took place in the sixteenth and seventeenth centuries it usually resulted in the land being converted from arable to pasture.[48] At the same time a generally easy-going attitude towards small piecemeal enclosures prevailed in pastoral country like this, and people expected their neighbours to assent to small adjustments.[49] Thus the chief characteristic of the vale parishes was their extensive grasslands, which often included extensive commons, shared between townships.[50] These were the mainstay of their economy despite the

Continued

in growing tobacco, so that it is impossible to distinguish with any certainty an independent venture.

[47] *VCH Glos.*, contains numerous illustrations. See vi, 195; viii, 114.

[48] See, for example, *VCH Glos.*, vi, 189, (1965).

[49] PRO Req. 2, 308/44; C3, 227/58.

[50] *VCH, Glos. passim.* Deerhurst common, shared between Deerhurst and Leigh was four miles in length even in 1779 (*VCH Glos.*, viii, 42). Cleeve Hill, consisting of 1002a. of common land, was shared between four townships in the late nineteenth century. It was still common in 1964 (*VCH Glos.*, viii, 2).

presence of islands of sand and gravel on which the settlements and some of the arable lay, and despite the persistence of common fields, many of which were not enclosed until the eighteenth or nineteenth century.[51] The farming specialities of the region were dairying, cattle-raising, and -feeding, while those villages on the Cotswold slopes which had extensive sheep pastures kept many sheep. As in all pastoral regions other sidelines were welcome: the vale lands boasted fruit orchards, some hops, flax, and a linen industry, as well as other handicraft occupations like glove and clothmaking and stocking knitting.[52]

The agricultural conditions for tobacco were, therefore, entirely suitable. Contemporaries believed that it grew best on a moist loam, and that it needed animal dung in great quantity.[53] The Vale of Tewkesbury could provide both, though it was one of the (probably justified) complaints of those who opposed tobacco-growing that so much dung was put on the land that the corn fields suffered.[54] The necessary agricultural work also interlocked neatly with that of other arable crops. The seeds were sown in prepared seedbeds in February and were ready for planting out in the middle of April or even May, when other arable crops were safely in the ground and did not demand much attention, and before the hay harvest was ready. Picking began when the corn harvest was finished, in the second half of August, and continued until the end of September when drying began. This lasted until the beginning of November.[55] Tobacco could not have been a more convenient crop for employing casual labour without interfering with the cultivation of essential food crops.

The labour demands of tobacco-growing were readily met in a community having plenty of unused or underused casual labour. And while this was a common characteristic of pastoral communities generally, few possessed the almost unlimited supply of the Vale of Tewkesbury. The explanation for this situation lies in the past history of the Vale, which contains some unusual, perhaps even unique, features. A first look at the structure of its society shows none of the clear cut hierarchical features associated with the classic villages of Midland England. The pattern of settlement was that associated with scattered hamlets. Winchcombe parish accommodated eleven

[51] Doubtless because of the many freeholders.
[52] *VCH Glos., passim*; Thirsk, *Agrarian History*, pp. 67–8.
[53] A sandy loam is nowadays considered most suitable for tobacco.
[54] PRO SP 18/98, no. 16.
[55] BPP 1830 (565) x, 9, 113, 114, 136.

hamlets; Bishops Cleeve had seven; most other parishes had at least three. Nor did the villages invariably hold the commanding position one expects to find at a parish centre. Sometimes the villages themselves seem to have started as two hamlets that coalesced, rather than as a single community.[56] Such resident gentry as there were in the parish often lived in the hamlets and not in the village.[57] Some hamlets grew in size in the sixteenth and seventeenth centuries at a faster rate than their parent villages. Authority, such as it was, did not reside uncompromisingly and permanently in one place, but was liable to waver as people moved around from one township to another in the parish.

This impermanence of power reflected other impermanences in the structure of landed society in the region. Much land had belonged to the religious houses of Westminster Abbey, Deerhurst Priory, and Evesham Abbey until the Dissolution. These estates passed to new owners in the mid-sixteenth century. But so also did many manors belonging to the bishops of Worcester and Hereford, whose consolidated properties were compulsorily exchanged by Queen Elizabeth in 1560–61 for a collection of rents from impropriate rectories. A remarkable number of estates in this area thus came on to the market in the second half of the sixteenth century, and were sold by the Crown to absentee owners who forged no permanent attachment to their new acquisitions. In James's reign many of them changed hands yet again, sometimes twice over.[58] Some were dismembered in the process, and the freeholders became firmly entrenched as the ruling class in the community.[59]

The strength of the freeholders could, however, be traced back to a longer chain of causes. Their ranks had not been thinned in the fourteenth and fifteenth centuries by land consolidations that occurred elsewhere. Rather the reverse had happened: demesnes had been leased out, lands in villeinage enfranchised, and many holdings fragmented.[60] One ecclesiastical landlord, at least—Westminster

[56] See, for example, Alderton (*VCH Glos.*, vi, 189); Elmstone Hardwicke (*VCH Glos.*, viii, 50); Kemerton (*ibid.*, p. 209); Apperley (*ibid.*, p. 34).
[57] See, for example, *VCH Glos.*, vi, 190.
[58] As at Broadwell (*VCH Glos.*, vi, 52), and Bishops Cleeve, Southam, Stoke Orchard, Prestbury, Uckington, and Elmstone (*VCH Glos.*, viii, 8, 10, 72, 52, 53).
[59] As at Broadwell (*VCH Glos.*, vi, 52–3), Beckford, Ashton under Hill, and Woolstone (*VCH Glos.*, viii, 254, 246, 247, 107). Woolstone is my identification of the tobacco-growing township named 'Worston' in the Privy Council's list of 1627 (*Acts of the Privy Council, Jan.–Aug., 1627*, p. 409).
[60] See, for example, Bishops Cleeve, Southam, Stoke Orchard, Gotherington, Prestbury, and Woolstone (*VCH Glos.*, vii, 14, 47, 106).

Abbey—was remarkably lenient in its demands for rent and permissive in its attitude to the subdivision of land.[61] Thus the freeholders remained an influential and numerous group; customary tenants on some estates claimed unusual liberties; and no concerted effort by the gentry in the sixteenth century, thrusting or patiently striving, undermined this state of affairs.

Without the constraining influences of watchful and status-minded landlords, the peasantry sought their livelihood in pursuits which exploited their principal asset, their labour resources. Labour intensive crops (not only tobacco, but fruit and vegetables as well) enabled them to hold their own in the sixteenth and seventeenth centuries, and to survive into the nineteenth and twentieth—to the astonishment of modern observers, so accustomed to recording another turn of events.[62] As the writer of the Land Utilisation Survey of Worcestershire remarked of the adjoining Vale of Evesham:

> The development of the vigorous peasant communities of the (Avon) valley, though one of the most fascinating chapters in the rural history of the last hundred years has attracted little attention from the outside world, and detailed information on the course of events is meagre in the extreme. It is nevertheless an aspect of Worcestershire life that cannot be passed over.[63]

The towns of the region matched the rural areas: authority spoke in muted tones, as tradesmen with an independent turn of mind ran their own affairs. Tewkesbury became a self-governing community in 1610; the two large estates of Tewkesbury Abbey and the Honour of Gloucester were both divided and sold in the sixteenth century, and the latter handed over to Tewkesbury Corporation by the Crown in that year. Thereafter its inhabitants governed themselves and developed their economy in a way that suited poor rather than rich men. The river traffic on the Severn maintained a volatile population of bargemasters, trowmen, and fishermen. A cloth industry persisted, and although by the early eighteenth century it was said to be in decline, stocking knitting took up the slack when cloth manufacture

[61] Barbara Harvey, 'The leasing of the Abbot of Westminster's demesnes in the later middle ages', *Econ. Hist. Rev.*, xxii, pt 1 (1969), 22, 26.

[62] For the survival of market gardening, see *VCH Glos.*, viii, *passim*. The nineteenth-century gazetteers commonly describe property in these villages as 'much subdivided'. Enclosure and tithe awards give more precise information: for example, at Prestbury in 1732, 77 people received allotments of land, of whom 61 received less than 20 acres apiece (*VCH Glos.*, viii, 76); Elmstone Hardwicke in 1839 had 80 holdings of less than 50 acres out of a total of 93 (*VCH Glos.*, viii, 55).

[63] K. M. Buchanan, *The Land of Britain, Part 68, Worcestershire* (Geographical Publications, 1944), pp. 649–50.

lost impetus. Wild mustard seed was gathered in the surrounding countryside to make the famous mustard balls which attracted notice from every traveller. Further employment was found in market gardening—the excellence of Tewkesbury carrots was widely proclaimed—and the growing of other labour intensive crops, among which was tobacco. All these were activities which required small cash resources but many pairs of hands.[64]

Winchcombe was a smaller market town in the Vale that was losing its trade in the seventeenth century, probably in favour of Tewkesbury. Tobacco was introduced at a time when the manorial lord showed little interest in the place. Winchcombe Abbey had owned the manor till the Dissolution when it passed to the Crown. In 1610–11 James I sold it to Sir George Whitmore, a London merchant and later lord mayor, and his brother Thomas, absentee owners who did nothing to assert their authority. Courts were not regularly kept, and when tobacco-growing started, labourers flocked into the town without let or hindrance. When another Whitmore took over the estate and showed an unwonted interest in the rents in 1636, he found a few docile tenants who were prepared to pay more for their houses. But effective power over the tenantry lay with less accommodating tradesmen who could rally the townsfolk to put on a fine display of enraged resentment. It started with a chorus from the fiery tongues of scolds, raising their voices to 'God save the King and the laws, and they and their ancestors had lived there, and they would live there', and moved on to more spirited action with hot spits and scalding water. A court case in 1638 revealed that many single family houses had been turned into tenements in the previous twenty years to house two, three, and even four families. The lord's agents also accused the recalcitrant tenants of spoiling orchards, and converting orchards and gardens into arable land—a form of words that seems to contain a veiled reference to tobacco cultivation.[65]

Sir William Whitmore's idea of lordship did not coincide with that of Winchcombe's inhabitants. But it also seems to have been at odds with the accepted conventions of the local gentry, who were modest, unpretentious men, who felt strong bonds of sympathy and fellowship with their neighbours of all classes. William Higford, a gentleman of Alderton, another tobacco-growing parish, who before

[64] *VCH Glos.*, viii, 110 ff.
[65] PRO E 134, 14 Chas. I, Mich. 31. The date of this dispute is 1638, not 1662 as I wrongly stated in 'Seventeenth-century agriculture and social change', *Agricultural History Review* xviii (1970), Supplement, 165.

his death in 1657 wrote some advice for his grandson, seemed to speak for them all when he urged his heir 'to make yourself rather less than you are', to keep his first place in his affections for his friends, and then for his neighbours (by which he meant the gentry). But then he added:

> The next companions will be your tenants who are your neighbours . . . . they hold of you by fealty (that is fidelity) to be faithful unto you for the lands they hold. You must in relation (= return?) give them protection whereby they may follow their excessive labours. Your ancestors have been moderate in their fines, and I trust God will bless you the better for it. Let these men of bread enjoy and eat the bread, which they dearly labour for and earn.[66]

Society in the Vale of Tewkesbury was not a rigid hierarchy with clearly defined, even widening, gaps separating the classes. It had its share of gentry, but they were modest, parish gentry without class pride, or the desire or means for ostentation, and entirely without ambition 'to rule over their neighbours as vassals'.[67] They identified themselves with the interests of their neighbours and tenants, who were independent-minded peasants, smallholders and tradesmen of no more than middling wealth. And in this egalitarian society labourers moved around freely without interference, indeed with the connivance, of lords.

It is difficult to capture in words the spirit of a local community which mirrors the truth and is not an illusion of the biased beholder. But this account is similar to that of a contemporary, John Corbet, chaplain to the Gloucester garrison, who described the civil war struggles in Gloucestershire and portrayed the same people.

> There was no excessive number of powerful gentry. . . . But the inhabitants consisted chiefly of yeomen, farmers, petty freeholders, and such as use manufactures that enrich the country, and pass through the hands of a multitude; a generation of men truly laborious, jealous of their properties, whose principal aim is liberty and plenty; and whilst in an equal rank with their neighbours, they desire only not to be oppressed, and account themselves extremely bound to the world if they may keep their own. Such, therefore, continually thwart the intentions of tyranny. . . . The countryman had of his own, and did not live by the breath of his great landlord; neither were the poor and needy at the will of the gentry, but observed those men by whom those manufactures were maintained that kept them alive.[68]

[66] W. Higford, 'Institutions or advice to his grandson', *Harleian Misc.*, ix, (1810), 585, 588–90. William Higford was a signatory to a petition in 1626 on John Stratford's behalf, when Stratford sought protection from his creditors (PRO SP 16/57, no. 14, II).
[67] *A True and Impartial History of the Military Government of the City of Gloucester . . . , 1647, Somers Tracts*, v (1811), 303.
[68] *Ibid.*

Social egalitarianism in the Vale of Tewkesbury goes a long way to explain the unusual phenomenon which so hampered the Cromwellian Council of State, and later the Privy Council, in their fierce efforts at stamping out tobacco-growing between the 1650s and 1690. The gentry were in firm alliance with the peasantry, and none of them cared a fig for government orders. Rarely has a government acted so directly at variance with the opinion of *all* classes in the local community as in its determination to stamp out tobacco-growing.

Lawsuits show that gossip about tobacco and the economics of growing it circulated freely among neighbours in the Winchcombe area of Gloucestershire. To believe that the mystery of cultivating and curing it could long remain a secret was a vain hope. Since one acre of tobacco land properly planted requires 10,000 plants,[69] a veritable army of helping hands is needed in the planting season. Moreover, much of the work could be done by women and children, and who are more observant and adept at prying out and remembering the secrets of any skilled task than children? But the factors which ensured the survival of tobacco in the Vale of Tewkesbury when the government banned it and the capitalist entrepreneurs had departed, were economic and social: first, the continuing financial rewards—not any longer on a scale that was sufficiently enticing to fortune-hunting London merchants, perhaps, but still eminently satisfactory to West Midland family farmers; secondly, its use of the one factor of production which they had in abundance, hand labour; thirdly, the persistence of a ready market for English tobacco which survived alongside the demand for Virginian tobacco for another seventy years. Tastes were not yet highly developed for any one leaf, and since tobacco smoking had quickly become a habit among all classes, a wide range of prices was paid for it. Different markets were known to take different qualities: it was sold locally, and in London, exported to Ireland, and the Low Countries, or it was mixed with Virginian or Bermuda tobacco, and found its way into tobacconists' shops under the guise of pure West Indian or American tobacco.[70]

The Privy Council's ban on tobacco, first announced in December 1619, was only fitfully enforced for the next few years. In 1626–27 the Council became aware that the crop had spread from the Winchcombe area and was being grown in thirty-nine places in

---

[69] *BPP 1830 (565) x, 111–12.*
[70] PRO C2, Jas. I, S3/11; *CSPD 1631–3*, p. 224; *Harry Hangman's Honour. . .* , (1655), Thomason Tract, E 842 (13), p. 3.

Gloucestershire, seventeen in Worcestershire, and one in Wiltshire.[71]
In 1628 it was growing 'in very great quantity' in Jersey and
Guernsey.[72] From then until 1639 Gloucestershire along with
Worcestershire (that is, the Avon valley and Vale of Evesham) were
deemed the principal centres, but in the latter year it was newly
reported growing in Monmouthshire.[73] After 1640 official attention
was diverted to other matters, and the tobacco growers persisted with
their illegal tobacco cultivation.

In April 1652 the Council of State in the course of a new and
thoroughgoing survey of its commercial policy passed a fresh Act
forbidding tobacco-growing. When the growers raised an outcry, a
conciliatory Act in September 1653 allowed them to continue to grow
the crop on payment of excise. Such a compromise was not to the
taste of the Virginia merchants, who promptly intervened to procure
a fresh ordinance in April 1654 ordering the act to be fully enforced.[74]
A year later they seem to have feared some weakening of the
Council's resolve, and this time pressed their attack on to the enemy's
ground by describing the harmful effects of tobacco-growing on local
agriculture.[75] The Council of State, swayed by the trading arguments,
but more by its fiscal interest in the import duties on tobacco, decided
in March 1655 not to grant any further suspensions of its orders.[76]
Meanwhile tobacco-growing had spread still farther afield. In 1665 it
was reported in fourteen English and Welsh counties: Oxfordshire,
Sussex, Gloucestershire, Worcestershire, Herefordshire, Warwickshire, Wiltshire, Shropshire, Staffordshire, Somerset, Monmouthshire, Radnorshire, Montgomeryshire and Denbighshire.[77] All
official efforts to stamp it out met with tough local resistance,
especially in Gloucestershire. At the Restoration the Virginian
merchants again weighed in quickly with a fresh petition against
tobacco-growing.[78] Again they won the ear of the Privy Council, and
an Act prohibiting the crop was duly issued late in 1660.[79] Its
enforcement engaged the personal attention of the Privy Council for

[71] *Acts of the Privy Council, Jan.–Aug., 1627*, p. 409.
[72] *CSPD 1628–9*, p. 329.
[73] PRO PC 2/50, p. 564. Between 1636 and 1640 the Privy Council gave more attention to the licensing of tobacco retailers than to the iniquities of growers.
[74] PRO SP 18/72, no. 65; SP 25/75, p. 712; SP 25/76a, pp. 43–4.
[75] PRO SP 18/98, no. 16. It is suggested that Cromwell favoured a gentler policy towards the tobacco growers because Royalist agents were active in Gloucestershire and the neighbouring counties (MacInnes, *op. cit.*, p. 103).
[76] SP 25/76a, pp. 43–4.
[77] PRO SP 25/76a, pp. 44, 130; SP 25/76, pp. 123–4.
[78] PRO PC 2/55, pp. 140, 171.
[79] *Statutes of the Realm*, v, 297 (12 Car. II, c. 34).

the next twenty-eight years, as tobacco spread into still more counties: Brecknockshire was mentioned for the first time in 1666, Yorkshire and Essex in 1667, and Flintshire in 1668. 'A much greater quantity than in former years' was growing in 1666; 'many large plantations' were described in seven counties in 1667; ten counties received reminders of the law in 1668.[80] But it was always the customs officers at Bristol who were the recipients of more letters than anyone else, and the counties of Gloucestershire, Worcestershire, Herefordshire, Warwickshire and Monmouthshire, which were singled out for the most assiduous attention. The last order from the Privy Council against tobacco-growing was given in 1688–89. Gloucestershire was still ordering the crop's destruction in 1690.

Is it fanciful to think that, when William of Orange came to preside at the Council Table, it was he who brought the campaign quietly to an end? Throughout the 1660s and 1670s troops of horse had been used every summer against poor men and women who were scraping a livelihood from small plots.[81] William III came from a country where tobacco supported many small peasants, and where, far from being an illegal crop, it was the basis of a modest but flourishing industry. To an outsider, the draconian measures of the Privy Council must have seemed out of all proportion to the offence. At the same time, it must be admitted that by 1688 the ferocity with which the policy had been pursued throughout the 1660s to 1680s, had brought it close to success—it had already intimidated growers in areas where it was less firmly established than in Gloucestershire.[82] Furthermore, the price of Virginian tobacco was falling and the public taste for this, rather than any other, leaf was growing. When the government dropped its more ferocious expedients against tobacco growers, it was on the verge of victory after a prolonged and bitter war.

One final question remains to be answered. Who were the assiduous growers of tobacco in the years between 1620 and 1690, and how did the alliance of landlords and cultivators survive the withdrawal of the London merchant entrepreneurs? It is difficult to

[80] PRO PC 2/59, pp. 62, 507; PC 2/60, p. 36; PC 2/58, p. 396; SP 29/212, no. 108; PC 2/60, p. 36.

[81] PRO PC 2/57, pp. 57, 117; PC 2/58, p. 165; PC 2/59, p. 529; PC 2/69, pp. 32, 312. The last order about destroying tobacco from the Customs Commissioners is dated 27 June 1689—*Acts of the Privy Council, Colonial II, 1680–1720*, p. 135. For destruction of the Gloucestershire crop in 1690, see Glos. RO, QSO/2, Easter 1690.

[82] Those who defied the law were brought personally to the Privy Council Table (PRO PC 2/59, pp. 530, 539, 561, 562; PC 2/60, p. 58).

discover much about the growers in counties other than Gloucester-shire. The lists of their names which the Privy Council regularly demanded, and sometimes actually received, do not seem to have survived. But in the Vale of Tewkesbury, tobacco growers can some-times be identified personally. By 1634 tobacco was avowedly a poor man's crop: poor men claimed to be excused by their poverty from observing the prohibition on its cultivation.[83] The sympathy if not active participation of landlords, however, continued to be reflected in the reluctance of JPs to heed the Privy Council's orders. In 1634 and 1636, these orders were addressed to men such as Sir John Tracy, lord of Toddington, and Timothy Gates, parson of Winchcombe, both of whom had been involved with John Stratford in the tobacco-growing contracts of 1619.[84] They clearly had no heart for the task, and yearly reminders from the Privy Council did not change their attitude. 'All the justices do refuse to give warrant for the peace and is rather a hindrance than always helpful', wrote a melancholy soldier in 1658. He was saddled with the responsibility of destroying tobacco around Cheltenham, assisted by a cornet who would not act, and without a major to turn to for advice. His horsemen from the county had to be hand picked since so many were themselves 'dealers and planters'.[85] In the 1630s the appointed destroyers of tobacco had been labouring men from the neighbourhood, hired by the constables at a daily rate.[86] Doubtless, some of these also had had a hand in planting the very crops they were asked to destroy. No wonder that no one could be found to enforce the law with enthusiasm. As late as 1667 John Vaughan, high sheriff of the county of Herefordshire, was handed an order from the Privy Council, but 'seemed by his action to slight it and refused to receive it'.[87]

When the Council of State issued its ordinance against tobacco in April 1654, 110 Winchcombe tobacco growers signed a petition in protest. They were of all classes. One was John Harvey, reputed to have £60–80 per annum of free land, and a ringleader in the battle against higher rents demanded by the manorial lord in 1638.[88] He and nine other growers had contributed to the subsidy of 1641–42, which

[83] PRO PC 2/44, p. 109.

[84] PRO PC 2/44, p. 109; PC 2/46, p. 266.

[85] PRO SP 18/182, no. 50. For other examples, see HMC 12th Report, Appendix VII, 52; *Cal. Treas. Books, 1676–9*, v, pt 1, 330.

[86] PRO PC 2/45, pp. 27–8.

[87] PRO PC 2/59, p. 532.

[88] PRO SP 18/72, no. 65. A John Harvey was bailiff of Winchcombe in 1632 (Gloucester Record Office. Winchcombe Bailiffs' Accounts, P 368 M I 1/2).

did not fall on poor men.[89] In 1671 it is possible to identify among hearth tax payers twenty-five people of the same names as the petitioners of 1654: one had a four-hearth house, five had three hearths, eight had two hearths, three had one, and eight were too poor to pay.[90] The wills of other signatories to the 1654 petition similarly suggest that growers were a socially mixed group, some belonging to the middling ranks of the peasantry with sufficient cash to employ labour in busy seasons, while others were men who could plant only a rod or two of tobacco, and found the necessary labour within the family circle. Some were styled yeomen, some were craftsmen who thus had more than one source of income. No one openly referred in official documents to tobacco land, but bequests such as those made by Christopher Merret, mercer, of properties possessing 'courts, orchards, and gardens', and 'one barn adjoining the same orchards and gardens' seem to be euphemisms for tobacco plantations.[91]

No one in the later seventeenth century was so treacherous as to suggest that the Justices of the Peace were themselves growing tobacco, but it was certainly growing on their land. And the risks of the crop were still shared—indirectly by landlords, who collected high rents and faced the possibility of non-payment by unsuccessful growers, but directly now by tenants and poor labourer-planters, the latter taking the ground from tenants in return for half the crop. Thus cooperative agreements were still the order of the day, but they had spread down the social scale and involved an even poorer class of labourers working tiny plots. Such men did not hedge their risks with bonds and covenants, and so have left no records behind, but an informer in 1667 makes the position clear. He found tobacco growing

> upon the High Sheriff's land, the bishop's land, and scarce one of the justices but on their land tobacco is planted, possibly without their privity. The tenants set their ground to planters that are poor people who plant and give half the crop for the use of the ground. So, if destroyed, the planter loseth, the tenant loseth his half of the crop, and thereby is disabled to pay his rent.[92]

Directly or indirectly, all classes in the community, landlords, tenant farmers, and labourers had an interest in tobacco. It was still a crop that passed 'through the hands of a multitude'.

[89] PRO E 179/116/528.
[90] PRO E 179/247/14.
[91] Gloucester Public Library. Will dated 31 Dec. 1624.
[92] PRO SP 29/212, no. 108.

Three conclusions of wider significance emerge from this study of tobacco growing. While it seems an almost invariable rule that innovations in agriculture in the early modern period were first adopted by well-to-do gentry or merchant-entrepreneurs who could afford to take risks, the peasantry evidently were not slow to take them up when they suited their economic and social circumstances. This conclusion obliges us to look more carefully at innovations which did not spread quickly, for it is likely that the explanation for their poor success lay in the economic and social constraints of cultivation and marketing rather than in the ignorance and stubbornness of peasants.[93]

Secondly, well authenticated figures on the profits to be had from tobacco oblige us to pause before we reject what otherwise would seem to be extravagant claims by contemporary writers of the profits to be drawn from other special crops. Walter Blith, writing in 1653, gave examples which historians have tended to dismiss as wild exaggerations. Saffron, he said, might cost £4 an acre to cultivate, yield anything from 7 or 8 to 14 or 15 lb per acre, and bring in an average return of £36 an acre, or, for a very good crop, over £70. One acre of indifferent liquorice might sell for £50–£60, excellent liquorice for £80–100. At the best price of £14 per cwt one acre of hops could sell for £168 and yield a clear gain of £100. A gardener could make £100 an acre out of vegetable growing. In the light of the evidence on tobacco, these rates of profit are not incredible.[94]

Thirdly, the wide range of prices for different qualities of product is of vital importance for understanding the market in horticultural, industrial, and other special crops. Saffron sold at anything between 24s and £14. Tobacco prices varied just as widely according to the quality, and according to what Blith called 'the ebbings and flowings of the market'.[95] In short, anyone who strikes an average price for these crops is ironing out most of the evidence so carefully garnered for us by contemporaries to show why horticulture, market gardening, and other specialised crops secured such a following among the farming population of seventeenth-century England.

---

[93] A conclusion to which Professor Mendras was led in a recent investigation into the resistance of French peasants to hybrid maize (H. Mendras, *La Fin des Paysans*, Colin, 1970 edn., pp. 121 ff., esp. pp. 125–8).
[94] Walter Blith, *The English Improver Improved* (1653), pp. 249, 225, 247, 273.
[95] *Ibid.*, p. 225.

POSTSCRIPT

Since this essay was written, I have learnt much more about the
Stratford family tree from a descendant, Mr. G. H. Stratford, 109
Markfield Drive, Bramley, Yorkshire. His family records show that
John Stratford, the tobacco-grower, was the seventh son of John
Stratford and Margaret, daughter of William Tracy of Toddington
and Stanway. John and Margaret Stratford lived, not at Farmcote,
but at Paynes Place, a timbered house at Bushley, on the north-west
side of Tewkesbury. Their son John, the tobacco-grower, rented a
house on the site of Hailes abbey, and tobacco is said to have been
grown there. I am much indebted to Mr. Stratford for this
information.

XVI

PROJECTS FOR GENTLEMEN, JOBS FOR THE POOR: MUTUAL AID IN THE VALE OF TEWKESBURY, 1600–1630

A fierce political controversy raged in Parliament between 1586 and 1624 around the granting of monopoly privileges by the Crown. These privileges were accorded to individuals who promised to set up new industrial and agricultural enterprises or to engage in new branches of overseas trade. The abuse of these privileges by some holders aroused deep anger in the country at large, and gave rise to monopolies debates in the Commons which developed into trials of strength between Crown and Parliament. They raised serious constitutional issues, and it is in this light that historians have generally discussed them. But considered from the economic standpoint, the monopolies scandal was a small shadow lying across an impressively large and constructive effort to introduce new occupations to the English economic scene. New crops and new industries created employment for the labouring poor; when they succeeded and their full potential came to be more widely understood, enthusiasm developed for setting up similar enterprises in colonial territories, first of all in Ireland, and then in America. The economic consequences were far-reaching.

In this paper I propose to explore the impact of these agricultural and industrial innovations in one district of Gloucestershire, the eastern half of the Vale of Tewkesbury.[1] First, it will reveal the relative unimportance in the provinces of the monopolies scandal— monopolists were a bane in London and some provincial cities but they made only rare appearances in rural areas. Secondly, it will illustrate the pronounced and beneficial impact that new economic projects made in one country district far from London, where the

[1] The same theme in a national setting was explored in my Ford lectures, given at Oxford in Hilary term, 1975. These are now published, *Economic Policy and Projects*, Oxford, 1978. I wish to thank Mr. C. R. Elrington and the Rev. Canon J. E. Gethyn-Jones for their comments on this paper.

social circumstances were favourable. So many projectors thronged the streets of London and the corridors of power in royal palaces that the very term 'projector' became an insult carrying with it overtones of malpractice. But the ideas of projectors were nevertheless carried to country areas with remarkable speed, and in a purer air were translated into practical realities which had nothing but healthy economic consequences.

The eastern half of the Vale of Tewkesbury in the sixteenth century was a region peculiarly receptive to new economic ventures. It had been the centre of four religious houses—Tewkesbury Abbey, Winchcombe Abbey, Deerhurst Priory, and Hailes Abbey, all dissolved in 1539.[2] It is unfashionable to believe that abbeys and priories had given much charity to the poor. Nevertheless, they had employed labour and stimulated local trade, and their dissolution helps to explain the extreme poverty which characterised the population in this area in the later sixteenth century.

In the early seventeenth century, poverty in the eastern half of the vale was a byword. Thomas Dekker claimed that a beggars' fair was held at Deerhurst near Tewkesbury every year on the two Holy Rood Days, at which 'you shall see more rogues than ever were whipped at a cart's arse through London, and more beggars than ever came dropping out of Ireland'.[3] A satirical pamphlet, claiming to be the work of Harry the Hangman, and published in 1655, described how the author had been accustomed regularly to visit Deerhurst Fair, 'a place in Gloucestershire famous for three things, old clothes, lice, and shitten stiles'.[4] The old clothes were abundant at the fair because 'the comers thereunto wanted money to buy new', the lice were so 'goodly fat, and tall that a louse from that fair . . . hath carried as much tallow as an ox that comes within Smithfield bars'. The shitten stiles were 'done out of state policy to preserve the place from any infection or contagion that might be left there by means of clothes coming from diseased parts and places'. Harry the Hangman used to look forward to attending Deerhurst fair because he collected so many customers there. 'Then 'twas a merry world with me', he sighed nostalgically, referring to former days when there was no work to employ idle hands in the Vale. 'Before tobacco was planted, there being no kind of

    [2] See the *Map of Monastic Britain, South Sheet*, Ordnance Survey (1950).
    [3] A. L. Beier, 'Vagrants and the Social Order in Elizabethan England', *Past and Present*, vol. 64, p. 24, quoting *Thomas Dekker*, ed. E. D. Pendry (1967), p. 287.
    [4] *Harry Hangman's Honour: or Gloucestershire Hangman's Request to the Smokers or Tobacconists in London*, British Library, E 842 (13).

trade to employ men and very small tillage, necessity compelled poor
men to stand my friends by stealing of sheep and other cattle,
breaking of hedges, robbing of orchards, and what not; insomuch
that the place became famous for rogues, as 'twas taken up in a
proverb by many that stood on the top of Breedon Hill viewing the
country would say, 'Yonder is rich Worcester, brave Gloucester,
proud Tewkesbury, beggarly Evesham, drunken Pershore and
roguish Winchcombe. And Bridewell was erected there to be a terror
to idle persons.'

The Vale of Tewkesbury's economic difficulties stemmed, as Harry
the Hangman explained, from its small tillage and absence of
industry. It was a pastoral region with an excess of unused or underused labour. Its towns suffered the same poverty as the countryside
around. Winchcombe was a very poor town in Elizabeth's reign,
when the grant of a fair and market recited that the borough was
'fallen into so great ruin and decay that its inhabitants were not able
to support and repair it for the great poverty that reigned amongst
them'.[5] When a list of Gloucestershire's male inhabitants was drawn
up in 1608, it was plain that Winchcombe had not yet discovered a
new economic role. Some were glovers and clothmakers but no other
occupations seemed to command the labours of many.[6]

The geographical handicaps which left the Vale of Tewkesbury in
this forlorn state were not irreparable. It is true that many rivers and
streams that wend their way through the Vale make its lower-lying
land wet and unsuitable for crop cultivation. Its abundant pasture
was frequently of poor quality and its spacious commons were not
attractive to fine gentlemen, though they were ideal for supporting a
poor population. But a new attitude to poor pastoral country began
to take hold in the early seventeenth century as campaigns to improve
fens, forests and chases got under way and improvers began to look
upon run-down pastoral areas with fresh eyes. Elizabeth encouraged
a start on the fens and James's ministers began to improve the forests.
This concern for their royal estates reflected a general interest in the
possibilities of improving pastoral country. Whether this was a
consideration influencing Londoners to take an interest in land in the
Tewkesbury Vale at this time is not definitely established. But it is
noticeable that when dissolved monastic estates came onto the
market in James's reign, together with other Crown lands earlier

[5] S. Rudder, *A New History of Gloucestershire* (1779), p. 825.
[6] John Smith, *Men and Armour for Gloucestershire in 1608* (1902), pp. 77–8.

acquired by Elizabeth from the Bishop of Worcester (in exchange for the rents of impropriated rectories), some notably vigorous and able London merchants appeared as purchasers. Baptist Hicks, London mercer and moneylender, bought the site of Tewkesbury Abbey, and although this property was settled on his daughter, and he went to live in Chipping Campden (whence he took his later title of Viscount Campden), he retained a strong interest in Tewkesbury's affairs. He was M.P. for Tewkesbury in 1624, 1626 and 1628 and, at his death, left money for Tewkesbury's poor as well as funds for the support of a preaching ministry.[7] Two of the estates of Deerhurst Priory, namely Uckington and Staverton manors, along with other properties in Bishops Cleeve parish, passed *c.* 1608 to Paul Bayning, later Viscount Bayning, a London merchant trading to the Levant, who was worth £20,000 in goods at his death.[8] Finally, Winchcombe manor was bought by the two brothers, Sir George and Thomas Whitmore, sons of William Whitmore who had been a London haberdasher, Merchant Adventurer, and charter member of the Spanish and Portuguese Company. Sir George Whitmore was master of the Haberdashers' Company, a member of the Virginia Company, and later Lord Mayor of London. His eldest brother, William, who later took over sole possession of the manor from George and Thomas, was also a freeman of the Haberdashers' Company, lent money to the Crown and bought its land, but did not become deeply involved in City affairs.[9]

There is no evidence to show that these London merchants set about improving their estates in the conventional manner of new brooms sweeping dusty corners clean. At Winchcombe, indeed, the reverse occurred: until the mid-1630s the new landlord let sleeping dogs lie. Nevertheless, industrial and agricultural schemes, which were being hotly canvassed in London and which employed the poor, were imported into the Tewkesbury Vale at the same time that the Londoners became landowners there. It is unlikely that this was simply a coincidence.

The merchants-turned-landowners did not achieve this result single-handed, however. Many of the indigenous gentry at this time were far from munificently endowed, and they consorted readily with

---

[7] *DNB, sub nomine; VCH. Glos.*, viii, 136, 153, 155, 168, 239.

[8] *VCH, Glos.*, viii, 52, 91; R. G. Lang, 'Social Origins and Social Aspirations of Jacobean London Merchants', *Economic History Review*, xxvii, 46; *Cal. S.P.D., 1591–4*, p, 400.

[9] *DNB, sub nomine*; Lang, *op. cit., p. 32.*

the new arrivals in their midst. Moreover, being markedly modest parish gentry, they were disinclined to develop a self-conscious pride that separated them from the lower orders. For one thing, they lacked the means to set themselves apart; for another, the geography of settlement was a discouragement. In parishes like Winchcombe and Cleeve, numerous hamlets dispersed the gentry in many different centres; their neighbours were few but for that very reason, they met at close quarters. At Farmcote, George Stratford, esquire, lived with 10 servants and only 2 husbandmen. At Postlip, Giles Broadway was lord, employing 11 servants but having no other neighbours.[10] In such an environment, a gentleman had no opportunity to cut a fine figure and overawe those around him. On the contrary, he might well develop a strong paternal concern for servants and the one or two tenant farmers who depended on him and on whom he in turn depended.[11]

Many complex factors explain the varied relationships between the social classes in different regions of England, and in this paper no general discussion is appropriate. But facts drawn from some parishes in the eastern half of the Vale of Tewkesbury suggest that a single stereotyped image of the gentry irons out interesting and important differences. It is an image drawn from examples in southern and eastern England where the village was the principal, and sometimes the only, centre of population, and where the manor house and parish church stood as twin symbols of authority in the community. In the west and north of England, people distributed themselves in a different geographical pattern, and while authority and deference were elements in the relationship of gentlemen with their humbler neighbours, they obtruded less sharply, since men held permanently in mind another fact of life, that in small communities survival depends on mutual aid. Mutual aid, indeed, was the most conspicuous common factor underlying all the employment schemes introduced into the Vale of Tewkesbury in the early seventeenth century. The new occupations gave work to the poor *and* yielded an income to their gentlemen-undertakers. The partnership benefited both sides, and both parties acknowledged their mutual advantage.

Some clues to the economic standing of the gentry who engaged in new projects explain their interest in the partnership. They were often the younger brethren of gentle families, who could only maintain their father's rank in society by their own efforts. This is revealed in

[10] John Smith, *op. cit*, p. 88.
[11] This argument is developed at greater length in Chapter XIV above, pp. 273-9.

an analysis of the six families who were involved in the project of tobacco-growing, when it was first introduced into the Vale in 1619. They were parish gentry with little land outside their home parish, claiming gentility, but lacking the generous means to support it. One was Giles Broadway, esquire, of Postlip, who was among the first to lease his land for tobacco-growing. At the Heralds' Visitation in 1623 he traced his pedigree no further back than his grandfather and claimed no grand connections. He had bought the manor of Bishops Cleeve in 1606 from Peter Vanlore, and with this land (newly on the market at the beginning of the seventeenth century after centuries in the dead hand of the church) Giles Broadway was raising the status of his family.[12]

The second owner of land for tobacco-growing was the wife of Timothy Gates, the parson. She owned land in Bishops Cleeve. Timothy's forebears were established gentry in East Anglia, of whom one son in an earlier generation had married Francis Walsingham's sister. The main branch of the family remained in the eastern counties, but Timothy's father was a younger son who moved off into the Midlands, and there Timothy too remained, marrying a Herefordshire woman and becoming the parson of Cleeve.[13]

A third local landowner who allowed some of his land to be sown with tobacco was Thomas Lorenge, gentleman, of Haymes in Bishops Cleeve parish. He was the owner of a modest estate and the heir of a family that had lived in the same place since before 1500.[14] He had a firm attachment to the local community but kept out of the limelight.

The fourth family was that of John Ligon, esquire, who leased twelve acres of his land at Arle Court, Cheltenham for tobacco. He was the younger son of Sir William Ligon, head of a Worcestershire gentry family, living at Beauchamp Court, Madresfield. The Worcestershire property had been inherited by the family as a result of a marriage alliance in the early sixteenth century between Richard Ligon and the second daughter of Lord Beauchamp of Powick. The main estate, in due course, passed to the elder son of Sir William, who also inherited the precious heirlooms of the family, its armour, weapons, books, and manuscripts. John Ligon, however, the younger son, was given a start in life by receiving from his father

[12] H. Chitty and John Phillipot, *The Visitation of the County of Gloucester, 1623*, Harleian Soc., xxi (1885), *sub* Bradway; subsequently referred to as *1623 Visitation*; *VCH, Glos.*, viii, 8.

[13] *1623 Visitation*, *sub* Gates.

[14] *VCH, Glos.*, viii, 13; Gloucestershire Record Office: D 127/46/48–54.

before his death a detached piece of family property in Cheltenham. It was from this land that he selected twelve acres to let to the tobacco-growers.[15]

The fifth and most illustrious family was the Tracys. The main branch lived at Toddington, the parish next to Winchcombe, and in the sixteenth century counted four generations living in the same place.[16] They were successful at rearing many sons, and more than one of these established himself on his own estate in a neighbouring parish, for they were a closely-knit family. The eldest son, Sir John Tracy, became the tobacco-grower, and his higher status in local society may explain the more advantageous terms he was given when the lease of his land for tobacco was negotiated. But his willingness to enter upon the project may in part be explained by the friendship subsisting between the Tracys and the Stratfords who pioneered the crop. Paul Tracy (later Sir Paul) of Stanway was executor of the will of George Stratford, the senior representative of the Stratford family, and Tracys and Stratfords more than once sold land to one another.[17]

This catalogue of tobacco growers ends with John Stratford, the principal undertaker. The Stratford family as a whole claimed a long ancestry in the Midland counties. The family pedigree in the seventeenth century was traced back to John Stratford, member of Edward II's Parliament in 1319–20, at which time the family's marriage alliances were being forged with Nottinghamshire and Staffordshire families. The association with Gloucestershire seems to have started later with a John Stratford who described himself as a gentleman of Farmcote, in Winchcombe parish, and whose children thereafter married into Gloucestershire families. Like the Tracys, they were a healthy stock and produced many sons. Thus John Stratford, who married Mary Throckmorton, had five sons. Of these George, the eldest, inherited his father's seat at Farmcote along with the title of gentleman. Robert, the second son, went on an expedition with Sir Francis Drake, during which he died. Anthony went to live in Ireland and married there. (Was he perhaps the Lieutenant Anthony Stratford who was deputy governor of Duncannon fort in Ireland in 1614?[18]) Finally, there was John, the tobacco-grower, the son who is described in the pedigree as of Prestbury. He was apprenticed in

[15] *VCH, Glos.*, viii, 91; *VCH, Worcs.*, iv, 187, 120; Worcestershire Record Office: Will of Sir William Ligon of Madresfield, 6 November 1618. I wish to thank Mr. Peter Large for this reference.
[16] *1623 Visitation, sub nomine.*
[17] *1623 Visitation, sub* Tracy; *PRO*: Prob. 11/148, will of Sir Paul Tracy of Stanway.
[18] *1623 Visitation, sub* Stratford; *Cal.S.P. Ireland,* 1611–14, p. 434. Anthony

London to a salter and duly became a member of the London Salters' Company. No further details concerning the careers of John's brothers are vouchsafed to us. But even on this meagre evidence, it is not altogether surprising to find this family in the forefront of the tobacco-growing enterprise in Winchcombe and the neighbourhood. Its sons were all of an adventurous spirit, not one of them being inclined to live at home 'like a mome' knowing 'the sound of no other bell but his own'.[19]

The three Stratford brothers who chose such different walks of life in which to make their careers reached their late teens in the 1580s or 1590s. In London this was the age of daring projects, which inspired many young men with hopes of easy fortune. Their impact may be gauged from the career of John Stratford whose life story is comparatively well documented. John arrived in London in the 1580s when a war with Spain was brewing, and the preliminary skirmishes were already interfering with the supply of some essential imports from Spain such as oil, wine, woad and soap. The flow of other goods that came from France, including woad and salt, was also being disrupted by that country's internal struggle against the Huguenots. For these reasons projects were being energetically set on foot to produce these essential commodities in England. Oil, wine, woad, salt, and soap provide, as it were, the orchestral accompaniment to the projects which emerge as dominant themes in the Vale of Tewkesbury in the next forty or fifty years.[20]

Salt was one project high on the projectors' list and was, we must suppose, a prime concern of the salters, in whose company John Stratford found himself on his arrival in London. Already in 1549 the author of the *Discourse of the Commonweal* had expressed apprehension at the insufficiency of salt produced at home, and had deplored England's dependence on overseas supplies. Threatened shortages were accompanied by threats of steeply rising prices because the French kings were also increasing the salt tax. The search for ways of evaporating sea salt had therefore started in England and in Scotland in the 1550s and 1560s, and though energy flagged when French supplies resumed at the peacemaking, anxiety revived again c. 1575. French saltpans were then in decay as a result of the civil war in

Stratford started life as a salter in London. See *PRO*: Stac 8, Bdle 266, no. 24. For further references to John Stratford's career, see also Chapter XIV above, pp. 264 *et seq.*
[19] Joan Thirsk and J. P. Cooper, *Seventeenth-Century Economic Documents* (1972), p. 756.
[20] See Thirsk, *Economic Policy and Projects* (Oxford, 1978), *passim.*

France, troubles in the Netherlands had destroyed Dutch saltpans, salt arrived in England in uncertain quantity, and was high in price. The government was forced to the conclusion that foreign supplies could no longer be relied upon to furnish English needs.[21]

The parish of Winchcombe is traversed by a salters' route and has a Salters Hill. Indeed, saltways criss-cross the area, and it is tempting to think that they had some bearing on the Stratford family's close association with the Salters' Company.[22] However, John Stratford does not, himself, appear to have taken an active interest in the salt trade, though he undertook business in other related commodities. His first experience of independent trade, on completing his apprenticeship, was gained from dealings in Cheshire cheese and woollen stockings, which chapmen collected in the provinces and brought for him to sell in London. At first sight this statement, coming from Stratford himself, suggests that he bought his stockings in Cheshire along with the cheese, but since confirmatory evidence of a stocking industry in that county is lacking, we may speculate whether, even in his early days in business, Stratford turned to his native parish for some of the wares he sold in London. Stocking knitting was certainly carried on in Winchcombe after the Restoration.[23] Was it introduced fifty years earlier?

Stratford next turned his hand to the Eastland trade to the Baltic. *Circa* 1601 he began to sell English broadcloth in northern Europe and to import undressed flax. This enterprise was markedly successful, and, having started with a capital of £200, he built up a fortune of £1,200 in two years. He then agreed to hand over the broadcloth trade to his partners and concentrate on flax, which he put out to be spun in and around London. But the flax trade did not last. The Netherlanders were even more adept than the English at developing labour-intensive occupations to employ their poor, and they began to send to England flax that was ready dressed, rather than the undressed, raw flax. They outpriced the English flax dressers and Stratford's business fell away.[24]

[21] *A Discourse of the Commonweal of this Realm of England*, ed. E. Lamond, pp. 42, 44, 61; E. Hughes, 'The English Monopoly of Salt in the Years, 1563–71', *English Historical Review*, xl, *passim*, but esp. pp. 334–5, 348–9; British Library: Lansdowne MSS. 21/23; 86/72; 52/53.
[22] A. H. Smith, *The Place-names of Gloucestershire*, i, 19–20, English Place-Name Society, xxxviii.
[23] For John and George Stratford's dealings in stockings and cheese, see *PRO*: Stac 8, Bdle 266, no. 24.
[24] *PRO*: C2, Jas. I, S3/11.

At the same time, however, John Stratford had other irons in the fire. He conducted a trade in miscellaneous goods that were traditionally salters' business—tallow, potash, soap ashes, and oil.[25] By 1616 he was in partnership with his half-brother Ralph who was also a salter[26] and they set up a soap boiling house. New ways of making soap greatly interested projectors when the high cost of imported oil began to make soap expensive. A search for substitutes in the 1570s had already produced an answer in 'specle soap', made of tallow instead of oil. This proved to be sufficiently cheap to win favour among the 'common people'.[27] By 1616, however, yet another solution was in sight as Benedict Webb's experiments with growing rape and pressing the seeds for oil began to show promising results both in the making of soap and the fulling of cloth. At a later date, *c.* 1624, Stratford compiled a document showing his familiarity with Webb's work[28] (it was, after all, being conducted in Gloucestershire) but whether Stratford was himself experimenting with the use of rape oil in 1616 is not clear. He certainly used both tallow and oil in his business, but did not explain the source of either.[29] Nor did he explain the source of his soap ashes: were they imported from Danzig or were they soap ashes produced experimentally at home? Suffice it to say that he had a soap boiling business in London at a time when soap manufacture was passing through a highly experimental phase.[30]

Soap boiling, however, was not sufficiently remunerative to compensate Stratford for the shrinking flax trade from the Baltic. The latter struck a heavy blow at his livelihood and his fertile brain turned to other schemes. He was buying land avidly in the Winchcombe area, and his partners in business watched his extended financial dealings with some misgivings. 'He charged himself with too many trades and occupations' said one of them later.[31] They urged him to reduce the number of his enterprises by handing over the flax trade to them. No doubt the reasons that persuaded John Stratford to

---

[25] *PRO*: Req. 2, Bdle 308, no. 45.
[26] *PRO*: Stac 8, Bdle 266, no. 24.
[27] British Library: Lansdowne MS. 18, no. 63. Dated (in pencil) 1574.
[28] *PRO*: SP 14/180/79.
[29] *PRO*: Req. 2, Bdle 308, no. 45.
[30] The description of three kinds of soap made in England in 1574 specified Danzig soap ashes as one ingredient in every case— British Library: Lansdowne MS. 18, no. 63. By 1624 'new soap' and 'soap with home materials' and 'work with home ashes' were being discussed, suggesting that the ashes were being produced at home (from bracken and weeds perhaps, as they were in the eighteenth century?), in addition to the oil. See, for example, *Cal. S.P.D., 1623–25*, pp. 127, 272, 330.
[31] *PRO:* Req. 2, Bdle, no. 45.

accept their advice were more complex than he described, but the upshot was that Stratford decided to try his hand at tobacco-growing.[32] Where else more suitable as the scene for his experiments than his native heath, the Vale of Tewkesbury, which offered the right sort of land (old pasture long unploughed) *and* plentiful labour?

Tobacco-growing, then, appears as the first firm project offering new employment in the Vale of Tewkesbury. But was it really the first? A possible forerunner of tobacco-growing as an employer of labour was woad-growing.

Woad-growing was a project that spread rapidly in southern England in the early 1580s when woad supplies from the Azores were interrupted. It was quickly taken up in many southern counties, including neighbouring Oxfordshire and Wiltshire. Unfortunately, the careful census taken of this crop in 1586 does not enumerate the acreage so employed in Gloucestershire.[33] But at Painswick, in the more specialised clothmaking area around Stroud, tithes were being paid on woad in 1615; at Over Guiting, close to Winchcombe, a woad mill was at work in 1634; and later still in 1656 a woad mill was working in Slaughter Hundred.[34] The Vale of Tewkesbury had plenty of suitable land for woad, and woad-growing was highly commended as a means of employing many poor. Against this background, one small piece of evidence—that land let out by Thomas Lorenge for tobacco-growing in 1619 in Cleeve had been used to grow woad shortly before—takes on a larger significance.[35] This clue, set in the wider context, gives some ground for suspecting that an experiment with woad had already been undertaken, before the growing of tobacco was introduced. We can only speculate on its scale, however, and must regard tobacco-growing as the first fully identified project in the Vale of Tewkesbury.

The first season of tobacco-growing in 1619 in Winchcombe, Cleeve and Cheltenham, started with a crop of 100 acres. John Stratford leased fragmented pieces of land from different owners to make up this acreage and paid out £1,400 in labour costs in the first year. At 8d. a day this represented the labour of 42,000 man days, and if we roughly estimate daily toil on the crop for 7 months from 1 May to 30 November (214 days) it must be reckoned that about 196 men were at work in the tobacco fields each day, or, at the rate of 6s. a day,

[32] *PRO*: C2 Jas. I, S3/11.
[33] Thirsk, *op. cit.*, contains fuller details on woad-growing. See pp. 28–30.
[34] *VCH, Glos.*, ii, 159; *PRO*: E 134, 10 Car. I, Mich. 9; *VCH, Glos.*, vi, 75.
[35] *PRO*: Req. 2, 308/44.

262 women. These figures give a rough indication of the work afforded by the tobacco-growing enterprise in its first year. As John Stratford later described his venture, he took himself to Gloucestershire 'where poor people do much abound' and thereby relieved them.[36] Winchcombe's total population was 340 families in 1650, and that of Cleeve at the same date 200. If we estimate that one third of the population was in need of such employment, then work in the summer for 200 labourers could have engaged a member of every single poor family in Winchcombe and Cleeve, thus making a substantial contribution to their relief.[37]

Tobacco-growing undertaken by merchants and gentry, however, was a short-lived affair. At the end of 1619 the government banned tobacco-growing in England in order to improve the chances of the growers in Virginia. John Stratford promptly ceased his operations. But his year's work had been enough to teach many poor men in the Vale of Tewkesbury how to cultivate tobacco and it continued as a poor man's crop in the region for another 70 years as well as spreading to twenty-two other counties. A seemingly brief experiment had created a new kind of work for the poor that was to last for many decades.[38]

Meanwhile, however, John Stratford had to find himself another occupation. The government's ban on tobacco had left him in deep financial trouble since he had pledged himself to pay high rents for four years ahead for tobacco. It was known as a profitable but exhausting crop, and landlords expected to be compensated. Though tobacco could no longer be grown, the courts of law insisted that he continue to pay the same high rents. He had to find another project and turned to flax-growing. His earlier business ventures had given him experience of the trade in flax from the Baltic and of flax dressing around London. He became convinced that England could produce a better quality flax than that imported; again he could count on a good supply of labour and suitable land in the Vale of Tewkesbury.[39]

Thus began John Stratford's next venture, growing flax on 40 acres

[36] *PRO*: C2 Jas. I, S3/11; SP 14/108/79.

[37] C. R. Elrington, 'The Survey of Church Livings in Gloucestershire, 1650', *TBGAS*, lxxxiii, 89, 90. In 1609 Winchcombe manor was said to have 80–100 tenements, but two and three families occupied one tenement in the later 1630s. In 1650 it was said to have 340 families. In the 1620s even a population of 340 families may be on the low side: Winchcombe was much damaged in the Civil War. David Royce, *Landboc sive Registrum Monasterii . . . de Winchcumba* (1892), pp. lxii, lxvii.

[38] Chapter XV above.

[39] *PRO*: SP 14/180/79; SP 16/57/28.

of land in Winchcombe and Cockbury. For growing and dressing the flax, he employed a labour force of 200 people. Needless to say, he made himself unpopular with his former partners in London who were still counting on imported flax to give them their living.[40] However, he held to his conviction that it was desirable to employ Englishmen 'for their better relief and the good of this commonwealth, seeing an inconceivable distress and misery increasing amongst the multitude of poor people that live in cities and towns where no clothing or help of other work is'. With the same flax, he also tried making a small quantity of linen cloth, though 'only for trial'.[41]

Stratford was not unique at this time in arguing the case for labour-intensive crops and providing careful estimates, based on personal experience, of the numbers employed. Forty acres of flax, grown and made into linen cloth, employed 800 people in one year, he maintained.[42] It was his belief that oil from flax seed was capable of being used to make sweet soap, just as Benedict Webb had used rape oil. Had he, one wonders, attempted to crush the flax seed which he stored in his barns for this purpose.[43] Or did he, perhaps, send it on to Benedict Webb? The tangled connections between projectors engaged in various enterprises makes it a tempting guess that Benedict Webb and John Stratford had more than a passing acquaintance with each other.

Benedict Webb was a contemporary of Stratford and a man of the same stamp, energetic and enterprising. Webb had high hopes for the future use of rape oil both for soap and in the cloth industry, and had been conducting experiments with an oil mill at Kingswood since 1605. He even grew his own crop of rape on land in the Forest of Dean, leased to him by Sir William Throckmorton, and by 1618 he had successfully persuaded clothiers to use rape oil in cloth manufacture. He had other high achievements to his credit. He had perfected the manufacture of a multi-coloured cloth, known as medley or Webb's cloth. All this had followed from his early training with a linen draper in London, followed by travels in France. From these beginnings he had built up a trade with France, principally in cloth but also in salt.[44] Stratford, for his part, could claim to have

[40] *PRO*: C2 Jas. I, S3/11.
[41] *PRO*: SP 14/180/79.
[42] *Ibid.*
[43] *PRO*: C2 Jas. I, S3/11.
[44] Esther Moir, 'Benedict Webb, clothier', *Economic History Review*, x, 256–64.

started tobacco-growing in Gloucestershire, now flourishing as an illicit crop, and was looking ahead to a great future for the linen industry. 'The more flax we sow, the greater quantity of tillage it will beget, as the sowing of woad does prepare the land better for corn afterwards', he wrote. In other words, flax, like woad-growing, paved the way in some places for a more general improvement of agriculture on poor pasture. They offered the chance to put to better use 'mean land such as the uplands of remote forests, chases, and other commons which doth now increase and nourish idle people and is the breed [breeding ground?] of weak and unserviceable horse and the bane of sheep'.[45] Surely, as Stratford wrote, he was thinking especially of the Vale of Tewkesbury, which had so much common and waste and offered such scope to improvers? Surely he was thinking of Winchcombe's poor when he wrote of the work afforded by such crops. 'If our idle poor had flax raised here, as they might have, and [were] compelled to work, if they will not willingly otherwise, whereas now they are an intolerable burden to the abler sort by begging and stealing, they would contrariwise become profitable to the commonwealth, paying for food and clothing and live according to God's ordinance by the sweat of their face in a more religious order.'[46] Stratford's aspirations were not distant dreams, but drew their strength from his own experience.

The flax-growing enterprise in Winchcombe which started in 1623 was still under way in 1627 when Stratford claimed that it had enabled him to pay off £8,000 of the debts he had incurred in tobacco-growing. A lawsuit in 1634 adds supporting evidence for this claim, by revealing that Giles Broadway, who had leased his land for tobacco in 1619, had received 300 sheep (worth £10 a score) in 1622–3 in payment of the rent that Stratford owed him; while on another occasion in 1623–4, he had taken payment in 20 cwts. of flax. Broadway had thereupon engaged flax-dressers in Winchcombe. At one time he had three dressers, dressing 33 lbs. apiece each week for three weeks; in the following 9–10 weeks, he had seven dressers.[47]

Giles Broadway, it will be recalled, lived at Postlip and owned Cleeve manor. He had a local surname, but no grand pedigree. He had once spent three months in France, and although we are not told what business took him there, it may be significant that the informa-

[45] *PRO*: SP 14/ 180/79.
[46] *Ibid.* See also similar words in another of John Stratford's appeals for the growing of hemp and flax. *PRO*: SP 16/57/28.
[47] *PRO*: SP 16/57/14; E 134, 10 Car. I, Mich. 9.

tion was given to the court of Exchequer by Humphrey Kirkham, a labourer, from the woad mill at Over Guiting, who had been his servant in France.[48] Was Broadway perhaps in France to learn skills that might serve to improve the Englishman's dyeing of flax? It may seem overspeculative to put such questions, but the proven interconnections of projects and projectors show that these were possibilities.

In this case we cannot proceed beyond guesswork. But a chain of friendship and mutual support linked projectors who had various different schemes afoot, to grow new crops, start new industries, improve old skills, and, above all else, provide more work for the poor. The circle of Winchcombe tobacco- and flax-growers has introduced us to one such group of projectors and friends. The activities of that same group invite us to look still further afield to colonising schemes overseas. Members of the same families were interested in the settlement of Virginia, and depended on Winchcombe and its neighbourhood to produce colonists to assist that venture. In short, they were involved in yet another scheme offering work and a new future for the local population.

The Virginia plantation first aroused the enthusiasm of Gloucestershire gentry from another part of the county before those in the Winchcombe district took any serious interest. Richard Berkeley of Stoke Gifford, John Smyth of North Nibley, Sir William Throckmorton of Clearwell,[49] and George Thorpe of Wanswell Court in Berkeley had been responsible for sending a ship *The Margaret* with 36 men to Virginia in September 1619.[50] The vessel sailed in the autumn of the year in which the first tobacco crop was being harvested at Winchcombe. The intention was to build in Virginia a new town, to be called Berkeley, its name indicating clearly that the gentry from the Vale of Berkeley were the principal promoters. However, it is doubtful if all the four original partners ever intended to go personally to Virginia. In March 1620 one of them, George Thorpe of Wanswell, had certainly set sail to direct affairs on the

---

[48] *PRO*: E 134, 10 Car. I, Mich. 9.

[49] Sir William Throckmorton had leased some land in the forest of Dean for growing rape to Benedict Webb (see p. 299). The Throckmortons held one manor in Deerhurst, formerly belonging to Deerhurst Priory, until 1604, and another in Apperley hamlet, belonging to Westminster Abbey, until 1613. *VCH, Glos.*, viii, 34ff. Sir John Tracy of Toddington was married to Anne, daughter of Thomas Throckmorton of Coscourt. *1623 Visitation, sub* Tracy.

[50] *Records of the Virginia Company of London, iii, 1607–22.* ed. Susan Kingsbury, p. 379. This venture was the subject of the Rev. Canon J. E. Gethyn-Jones's presidential address to the Bristol and Gloucestershire Archaeological Society in 1975.

spot, but in May Sir William Throckmorton withdrew from the partnership, and William Tracy, esquire, was brought in.[51] The Tracys and the Throckmortons were related by marriage, but in addition to this, William Tracy's brother, Sir Thomas Tracy, was a member ot the Virginia Company, and in May 1620 attended a Quarter Court of the Company.[52] The gentry of the Winchcombe area were now firmly involved in the scheme for colonisation.

We have already met the Tracys as a large and ramified family in the Vale of Tewkesbury. Sir John Tracy of Toddington leased some of his land for tobacco-growing. Other members lived in close proximity, at Stanway, and at Hailes. William Tracy was living at Hailes when he entered upon his agreement to take his wife and two children to Virginia, and his letters to John Smyth make clear his eagerness to start a new life overseas. With his own household of 16–30 people, he planned to take others, making a party of about 65 settlers, of which he would be governor and captain.[53]

A circle of influential friends in London and in Gloucestershire rallied to Tracy's aid. Sir Edwin Sandys, Treasurer and Governor of the Virginia Company, promised to lend cows when the party arrived overseas, and Lady Delaware, whose land lay next to the proposed plantation, promised goats and silkworms.[54] The colonists were recruited in Gloucestershire. A gardener, a glover, and a husbandman came from Wotton-under Edge,[55] much nearer Berkeley than Winchcombe. But the passage of another 20 men and women was paid 'from the parts of Hailes to Bristol', from which we may perhaps reasonably infer that they were recruited locally. Certainly Giles and Alexander Broadway came from the same neighbourhood (the Broadways lived at Postlip). The surnames of others who arrived safely in Virginia include familiar Winchcombe families like the Halls and the Pages.[56]

Organising the supplies for the voyage caused Tracy endless

[51] Kingsbury, *op. cit.* 271–4, 379–81.

[52] See above, n. 50; Conway Robinson and R. A. Brock, *Abstract of the Proceedings of the Virginia Company of London, 1619–24*, Virginia Historical Society (1888), i, 60.

[53] Kingsbury, *op. cit.* 368–70.

[54] Kingsbury, *op. cit.* 293, 290, 291. In December 1621, the Deputy Governor of the Virginia Company ordered a translation of a treatise on silkworms and silkmaking, written by a Frenchman who was master of James I's silkworms at Oatlands. The book was to be sent to Virginia by the next ship. This is another example of a project being simultaneously pursued in England and America. See E. D. Neill, *History of the Virginia Company of London* (New York, 1869), 250, 258.

[55] Kingsbury, *op. cit.* 393–4.

[56] *Ibid.*, 392, 426.

trouble and anxiety, but his problems shed more light on his circle of
Gloucestershire friends. Thirteen broadcloths were delivered to him
at Bristol by Benedict Webb.[57] When money to pay the bills was hard
to find, Tracy gave up all hope of help from 'his cousin', Richard
Berkeley of Stoke Gifford, and sent urgent letters to John Smyth at
North Nibley.[58] But on the eve of Tracy's departure, when he was
thrown into gaol for debt, one of his most effective helpers was
Timothy Gates, the parson of Cleeve, whose wife had leased her land
to John Stratford for tobacco-growing. Timothy Gates addressed
William Tracy as his good cousin and referred similarly to his 'cousin
Bridges'.[59] Cousin Bridges was John Brydges, a member of the family
of Grey Brydges, fifth lord Chandos of Sudeley Castle. Grey Brydges
was renowned for his hospitality ('twice a week his house was open to
his neighbours') and for his generosity to the poor.[60] When Tracy was
released from gaol and the good news was passed on by John
Brydges, he likewise referred to Tracy as his 'cousin'.[61]

The many threads that linked these adventurers and projectors
linked their numerous projects. Tracy's contract with the gardener
from Wotton under Edge promised him houses and land in Virginia
for orchards, gardens, grain and grass, and also for vineyards,
tobacco-growing, woad, silk, flax, and hemp-growing.[62] In short, the
new crops that were the subject of experiments at home were also to
be grown in Virginia. Meanwhile in London, the governing court of
the Virginia Company entertained grander and more official schemes
to promote the same crops and industries that were occupying the
energies of the Gloucestershire projectors. John Stratford's partner
in tobacco-growing at Winchcombe had been Henry Somerscales; his
brother, Robert Somerscales, engaged the Court in discussions about
a plan for 'the curing and ordering of tobacco'—evidently in Virginia,
since the plan was approved in July 1620, after tobacco-growing in
England had been banned. Other projectors urged upon the
Company plans for making in Virginia soap ashes, and potash, and
for establishing improved methods of sowing and managing flax and
hemp.[63]

[57] *Ibid.*, 390, 391.
[58] *Ibid.*, 373–4, 266.
[59] *Ibid.*, 409.
[60] *DNB: sub* Grey Brydges, fifth Lord Chandos.
[61] Kingsbury, *op. cit.* 410.
[62] *Ibid.*, 393–4.
[63] *Records of the Virginia Company of London, i. 1619–24*, ed. S. Kingsbury, 364–5,
403. Another contract was made with Thomas Prirse, who professed skill with hops
and woad, but travelled on a different ship. Kingsbury, iii, 197.

William Tracy's party for Virginia patiently endured their trials and tribulations before they could leave England. Their ship lay becalmed for several days at Bristol, and as Tracy surveyed the cargo being stowed on board and the passengers installing themselves, he wrote, on 24 September 1620, a melancholy description of the prospect before them. The middle and upper decks were so overcrowded that no one could lie down comfortably. 'The best is purgatory that we shall live in till landing and long after.' More people had offered themselves for the voyage than Tracy could accommodate, and at least ten had been turned off the ship and had to stay for the next boat. As the ship waited for a favourable wind, Tracy's money worries loomed again. His party could not live on air, and ''tis not a little fifty persons at least will spend,' he observed wistfully.[64] When the ship did sail, it sprang a leak in the Irish Channel and had to put into Kingfall [Kinsale?] in Ireland for repairs. The party finally arrived safely in Virginia in January 1621, and in July 1621 the master of the vessel was back in England with a cargo of tobacco from Virginia, some sassafras, some 'pieces of walnut tree' (perhaps cuttings?), and members of the crew claiming the remainder of their wages for transporting Tracy and his company to their journey's end.[65]

Meanwhile in Gloucestershire, John Smyth and Richard Berkeley settled up the account and kept in close touch with the new planters in Virginia. Smith ordered tobacco seed from Virginia, and in October 1621 sold his crop, presumably grown from the same seed, to John Stratford. Stratford, being now prevented by statute from growing tobacco, continued in England to trade in the commodity.[66]

What was the net result of all this economic effort in the Vale of Tewkesbury? William Tracy's party of colonists settled in Virginia. William Tracy himself died there in April 1621; his daughter lived there long enough to marry, but died in the massacre of March 1622. However, William Tracy had taken his wife Mary and his son Thomas, and the Tracys who appear in Virginian land grants in the 1650s and 1660s may well be descended from Thomas. Mary Tracy, who appears in 1654, may even have been the widow of William.[67]

---

[64] Kingsbury, iii, 410–12.
[65] *Ibid.*, 403–5, 426–7.
[66] *Ibid.*, 402–4, 195, 509–10; i, 150.
[67] *Ibid.*, i, 520, 535; E. D. Neill, *op. cit.*, 189; Kingsbury, *op. cit.*, iii, 405; N. M. Nugent, *Cavaliers and Pioneers. Abstracts of Virginia Land Patents and Grants, 1623–66* (Baltimore, 1969), i, pp. 227, 250, 279, 293, 300, 307, 512.

Giles Broadway, who travelled with the same party to Virginia (his family came from Postlip), was reported slain soon after his arrival, but other members of the family must have followed him thither, for a number of Broadways were involved in land grants in the 1640s, 1650s and 1660s.[68] Two members of the Stratford family participated in land grants in 1657; and a Robert Lorenge (the Lorenges lived at Haymes in Cleeve parish and had leased some of their land for tobacco in 1619) was in Virginia in 1664.[69]

The dispersal of the Ligon family overseas carries us into yet another area of colonial enterprise. John Ligon of Arle Court, Cheltenham, had leased some of his land for tobacco to John Stratford in 1619. He was alleged to have promised Stratford that, if tobacco-growing was prohibited, he would engage his influential friends to procure an exemption for Stratford from such tiresome legislation.[70] He proved not to be as influential as he thought. But the Ligons, like the Stratfords, were vigorous adventurers. At least one member of the Ligon family, Thomas, was buying land in Virginia in the 1660s.[71] Yet another representative of the family, Richard Ligon, having lost his property in what he termed 'a barbarous riot' in England in 1647, set sail from England, he cared not whither, in a vessel that was bound for the Caribbean. He stayed in Barbados from 1647–50, and on his return wrote his remarkable history of the Island of Barbados, published in 1657, to inform and persuade other Englishmen to settle there.[72]

In these fragmented scraps of information, we see the offspring of the Gloucestershire gentry dispersing themselves overseas and encouraging others to make a new life there. Other members of the same group of gentry families created more work at home. We have traced the beginnings of a successful new occupation—tobacco-growing—that became so firmly entrenched that it could not be rooted out—illegal though it was—until 1690. We have found evidence of at least ten years of flax-growing, and have suggested reasons for adding the occupation of woad-growing. None of this enterprise completely solved the problem of poverty. The structure of these communities militated against such a possibility. Winchcombe, Cleeve, and Deerhurst were open villages; Tewkesbury was an open

[68] Kingsbury, *op. cit.*, iii, 397; Nugent, *op. cit.*, 146, 296, 356, 458, 450.
[69] Nugent, *op. cit.*, pp. 357, 452.
[70] *PRO*: Req. 2, Bdle 399, no. 68.
[71] Nugent, *op. cit.*, pp. 440, 516.
[72] Richard Ligon, *A True and Exact History of the Island of Barbados* (1657), Dedication, 1–2.

town. As soon as a project was successfully launched and labour was recruited to it, it attracted a throng of poor people from elsewhere. The large number of subdivided tenements in Winchcombe in 1638, housing two and three families in place of the single families for which they were built, bore witness not only to the success of projects in creating work, but to the fresh problems created by the influx of more people.[73] A visitor to Winchcombe from Oxford in 1641 dubbed it 'a poor beggarly town'.[74] But Harry Hangman's testimony in 1655 was not altogether frivolous when he claimed that tobacco-growing had put him out of business. This and other labour-intensive occupations had brought work into an area where there had been almost none in 1600.

Similar successes in providing work for the poor, not only in Gloucestershire but elsewhere, taught the political economists new lessons about the value of occupations requiring small capital resources but many willing hands. After the Restoration they wrote in new and more appreciative terms about the role of labour in an expanding economy. Carew Reynel in 1674 even urged a relaxation of the government's prohibition on the growing of tobacco because of its beneficial effect in employing the poor.[75] The consequences of projects thus went far beyond the expectations of their founders.

The most impressive efforts in starting new agricultural and industrial occupations were made by a generation of men at work in the period 1580–1630. In the Vale of Tewkesbury they worked to most effect in the period 1610–20, though the consequences of their labours were felt throughout the seventeenth century. In how many other poor towns and villages in England did the same generation of men try to work the same miracles? Benedict Webb's labours in Kingswood and in the Forest of Dean have impinged upon this story at several points. Dr. Paul Slack has recently described the efforts of the town officials of Salisbury, who, in the 1620s, embarked on ambitious schemes for providing work and food for the poor— organising jobs in lacemaking, pinmaking, stocking knitting, cloth weaving, hemp and flax spinning, and also establishing a brewhouse and storehouse of cheap food.[76] It is unlikely that these are the only

---

[73] *PRO*: E 134, 14 Chas. I, Mich. 31.

[74] John Allibond of Magdalen College to Dr. Peter Heylyn, cited in Eleanor Adlard, *Winchcombe Cavalcade* (1939), p. 28.

[75] Carew Reynel, *The True English Interest* (1674), p. 19.

[76] Paul Slack, 'Poverty and Politics in Salisbury, 1597–1666', *Crisis and Order in English Towns, 1500–1700: essays in urban history*, ed. P. A. Clark and P. A. Slack (1972), p. 181ff.

examples of business enterprises mixed with philanthropy, of projects devised by gentlemen that created jobs for the poor. Parliamentary history in the years 1600–30 sheds a harsh light on many speculations that went awry and created scandals. In the provinces, however, some men experienced the more constructive consequences of these projects. How many more are waiting to be uncovered?

XVII

STAMFORD IN THE SIXTEENTH AND SEVENTEENTH CENTURIES

THE history of Stamford in the sixteenth and seventeenth centuries is something of an anti-climax after the drama and the splendour of the Middle Ages. Stamford had risen to a place of international repute as a cloth manufacturing centre and wool market in the thirteenth century. It had been the resort of many Spanish and Italian merchants, who frequented its fairs to purchase supplies of Stamford's splendid scarlet cloth for sale in the Mediterranean. Moreover, the local wool used for this cloth was held in such high esteem that buyers came regularly from Flanders to the wool market at Stamford to secure it for their own native cloth manufacture. Lest there be any doubt about Stamford's prosperity in its hey-day, we have only to name its many religious foundations, its priories, nunneries, hospitals, and colleges which bore eloquent testimony to its wealth and importance. Stamford had the accoutrement of a fine city, in which wealth flowed freely. But its economy was insecure, for it leaned heavily on an industry that was undergoing revolutionary change. And the change which brought new life to some lesser cloth centres and many villages dealt Stamford a bitter blow. By 1500, its trade and industry had declined, and the town was left with the architecture and institutions of its illustrious past, while its population was on the verge of destitution. As if to pile blow upon blow, the town was burned in 1461 by the Lancastrian army as it passed through on its way south to St Albans. Among other things, most of its medieval records were destroyed.[1]

It is necessary, then, to show how the economy of Stamford gradually recovered, and how its people eventually found employment and contentment. But the process was slow and painful, and not particularly well documented, and the more deliberate attempts by its citizens to bring new industry to the town did not all bear fruit. The final revival of Stamford, which was postponed until the second half

[1] R. Butcher, *Survey and Antiquity of the Town of Stamford*, 1646, reprinted 1717, p. 44.

of the seventeenth century, resulted from developments which the town could hardly have foreseen.

In some ways, the long-drawn-out process of recovery in the sixteenth and early seventeenth centuries presents a challenge to the historian, for it runs counter to the experience of most towns. Generally speaking, the Tudor period, at least, was a prosperous age for town dwellers. Farming was exceptionally profitable, and this led to a great increase in the sale of agricultural produce, which, by governmental regulation, was compelled to be carried on in recognized markets, mostly in the towns. Hence, they benefited from expanding enterprise in the countryside, and their markets attracted more and more business. In some cities, too, this century saw a great expansion of industry. But even without this, the development of marketing alone might have set Stamford on its feet once more, had the town created for itself a niche in the marketing organization of the region. But it did not. And if we are to explain why, we must look briefly at the countryside around Stamford.

Before Stamford occupies all our attention, however, it is worth noting that it was not the only city in this part of the Midlands to face serious economic difficulties at this time. Its neighbour, Lincoln, was another great medieval city which had thriven on the international reputation of its cloth, but found itself at the beginning of the sixteenth century full of empty, falling houses and disused churches. Some interesting parallels can be found in the fortunes of these two nearby towns.[2]

To substantiate the statement that Stamford was a depressed town in the sixteenth century, some facts are necessary. The first and most conspicuous sign of its poverty was the decision to amalgamate some of its parishes. So little money was available for the support of its many churches, that in 1548 a drastic reorganization was carried out, and the parishes were reduced from eleven to six. In 1574, nearly thirty years later, the town council was so disturbed by unemployment and poverty in the town that it issued an ordinance that no one should give work to any stranger so long as there were native citizens without jobs. In particular, they desired that no one should employ a stranger in threshing corn, but should give the work to town labourers only—a reminder that towns at that time still had many of the attributes of the country village. A decade later, in 1548, when the town council had to raise money to pay the fifteenth—a tax on the movable property of all the queen's subjects—it decided, since 'the

[2] J. W. F. Hill, *Medieval Lincoln*, 1948, pp. 286–8.

poverty of this town is great,' that the only way the money could be raised was by leasing the common tenter meadows, where tenter bars were set up for drying the cloth after it had passed through all the processes of weaving and fulling, and using the money paid by the lessee of the meadows towards the payment of the tax. In 1624, forty years later, the town still invited pity; it was described by Lord Keeper Lincoln as 'a poor decayed town.'[3]

Some information about the population of Stamford in these two centuries supports this evidence, and also carries us a little further by indicating the period at which recovery began. In 1524, when a new subsidy assessment was made, involving all but the very poorest, 199 taxpayers were listed for Stamford, and 43 for St Martin's. This makes a total of 242 households. Stamford was evidently not a large town: Spalding boasted eight more households at the same date, and some of the fenland villages of Lincolnshire had populations that fell not far short—Pinchbeck, for example, with 226 families. Nearly forty years later, in 1563, Stamford's population showed little change. By that time, the town, not counting St Martin's, accommodated 213 families. If we allow for another 50 families in St Martin's, we have 263 families altogether. It was thus a little more than half the size of Boston with 471 families, and about the same size as Grantham with 252 families. By the end of the century, when a census of communicants was taken (1603), the population, again excluding St Martin's, had risen slightly by some 33 families from 213 to 246—this at a time when in other townships of the Midlands the increase of population was sometimes of the order of 40 or 50 per cent. By 1665 another increase brought the total to about 282 families, but still progress was slow. Grantham's population had risen by 38 per cent in a century. Spalding had more than doubled its population. Many villages in Lincolnshire and Leicestershire had experienced the same dramatic rise in numbers. The large village of Wigston Magna in Leicestershire, for example, doubled its population from 80 to 161 families between 1563 and 1670. Stamford, on the other hand, had increased its numbers by rather less than a third.[4]

[3] Butcher, p. 10; John Drakard, *History of Stamford*, 1882, pp. 215–16; Stamford Corporation Archives, Hall Books (= HB), i. fols. 206, 225; *Calendar State Papers Domestic*, 1623–5, p. 317.

[4] P.R.O., E 179/136/330 and 315. The population figures for St Martin's are not available, since, unlike the rest of Stamford, it lay in the diocese of Peterborough. For the 1563 census, see B.M., Harleian MS.618; for the 1603 census, see C. W. Foster, ed., *The State of the Church*, L.R.S., 23, p. 325; for the Hearth Tax return of 1665, see P.R.O., E179/140/754; W. G. Hoskins, 'The Population of an English Village, 1086–1801,' *Trans. Leics. Archaeolog. and Hist. Soc.*, XXXIII, 1957, pp. 19, 25.

The mid-seventeenth century, however, was the turning point. Between 1665 and 1705 the population rose from 282 families to 470 and by 1788 to 856 families. These figures are only a rough-and-ready guide, and they all exclude the population of St Martin's, but it is clear that the period in which we must look for Stamford's great revival was the second half of the seventeenth century, and that this growth continued at a steady rate throughout the eighteenth century until, at the end, the total population was three times as great as it had been four generations before.[5]

If we are to find a satisfactory explanation for the long spell of economic depression in the town's history, and then to account for its eventual recovery, we must look closely at its industries and trade. A town can justify its existence and support its citizens, only if it serves one or more of four functions. It may be an administrative centre of government; it may have an industry or industries, and if these serve a national market as well as local needs, then so much the better for the prosperity of the town; thirdly, it may flourish by virtue of its markets, dealing in commodities made in the town, or brought in from the neighbourhood; fourthly, if it happens to be conveniently situated on the main road, it may serve as a halting place for travellers, and so develop an inn-keeping business.

At this period, Stamford was not an administrative centre—it did not have to accommodate officials and their volumes of records of local government—but it performed all the three other functions of a town. In other words, it played the same role in the economic life of the neighbourhood as many another modest market town. But having had a more celebrated past, it was discontented with its present lot. None of its activities was on a sufficiently large scale to compensate for the loss of its medieval cloth trade.

As an important halting place on the Great North Road, Stamford has always catered for travellers. Everyone passing from north to south had the choice of this road as one of the main thoroughfares, and if Stamford's position brought disaster in 1461 when the Lancastrian soldiery passed through and left it burning in their wake, it also, and more often, brought business. Leland and Camden, two travelling journalists of the sixteenth century, anxious to describe the face of the countryside in their own day, passed through it in turn and admired its antiquity. In Elizabeth's reign, the town was a post station—the eighth stage on the postal service journey from London

⁵ *Speculum Diocesos Lincolniensis*, ed. R. E. G. Cole, L.R.S., 4, 1913, pp. 114–16; L.A.O., Speculum, 1788–92.

to Berwick—and so bedded and boarded all the mail riders passing this way. It was frequently visited by kings, whose coming compelled the council to issue hasty orders for all dirt and rubbish in the streets to be swept away to allow His or Her Majesty a 'more easy and convenient passage.' Henry VIII passed through in 1528, 1532, and 1539, Queen Elizabeth dined at the Whitefriars in 1566, James I passed through on his way from Scotland in 1602, and Charles I visited it in 1633 and 1634. Thus the needs of travellers both eminent and humble brought business to the inns, to the food shops, and to those who groomed and shod the horses. But the number of travellers on the road until the mid-seventeenth century was still relatively small, for nearly all travellers came on foot or on horseback. Only kings and rich nobles had private coaches. Hence, people did not travel for pleasure as we do today, and the government officials, merchants, chapmen, and drovers were not the sort of clientèle that could rescue a town from poverty. It needed rich patrons and the fashionable set, who were attracted to the spa at Tunbridge Wells, for example, in the second half of the seventeenth century, to set a town firmly on the map. Stamford, unfortunately, had no health-giving waters of which to boast.[6]

As for the industries of the town, it is clear that no single craft leapt into prominence to supplant the staple industry—cloth—which had served the town so well in the past. On the other hand, the trades were varied enough. When business began to improve towards the end of this period, fifty-four different occupations were represented in the list of craftsmen who were made free of the town after 1663.[7]

Is it possible to gauge the importance of the different crafts? The best piece of evidence is the list of freemen of the town, mentioned above. It gives the occupations of all who were made free after 1663 up to about 1721—the final date is a matter of conjecture. One thousand and seventy-nine people are listed, of whom 35 were gentry, and 407 (38 per cent) had no occupation given. This leaves 637 people. Among these there were 80 (12½ per cent) leather-workers of all kinds, 75 (12 per cent) weavers of wool, hemp, and hair, 69 (11 per cent) craftsmen in stone and wood, and 45 (7 per cent) metal workers of many kinds (blacksmiths, farriers, pewterers, goldsmiths and silversmiths, cutlers, and gunsmiths). The remainder represented

---

[6] Geoffrey Grigson, 'Stamford, 1461–1961,' *Geographical Magazine*, XXXIV, May 1961, pp. 45–6; W. G. Stitt Dibden & L. Tebbutt, *Stamford Postal History*; B.M., Add. MS. 29727, p. 27; HB., II, fol. 179.

[7] HB., II, fol. 1 *et seq.*

miscellaneous and less common skills, such as tobacco pipe-making, trunk-making, and parchment-making. Caution is necessary in drawing conclusions, but this list, together with probate inventories showing the property of fifty citizens of Stamford between 1560 and 1640, provides some information about the two principal occupations. One definite conclusion, therefore, seems permissible, namely that, while no craft dominated the rest, the two which engaged most workers were the leather and fibre industries. The term fibre industries is used here in order to include the weavers of hemp, hair, and ribbon, as well as wool, and the total includes ropers and tailors who made up the finished articles from these fibres. The third group of industries of almost equal importance with the first two comprised the wood and stone-working crafts.[8]

The fact that leatherworkers were numerous reflects the importance of cattle and sheep-fattening in the countryside around Stamford. Did not Justice Shallow in *Henry IV* enquire of 'a good yoke of bullocks at Stamford Fair'? In fact, the whole of the east Midlands was the home of the grazier and sheepmaster at this period. Northamptonshire, Lincolnshire, and Leicestershire all were specializing increasingly in cattle and sheep-farming. Hence, the towns in these three counties could rely on a ready supply of skins and hides. It was for this reason that the leather industry established itself firmly in this region, and in some towns permanently. Apart from Stamford, Leicester and Northampton both had thriving leather industries, and the last two have prospered to this day.[9]

The other industry of prime importance was the fibre industry. This is not as surprising as at first it seems, for although the broad-cloth manufacture had declined and left no hope of recovery in the sixteenth century, the town continued to pin its faith on a revival of the weaving industry, but on a new basis. The efforts of the town council to relieve the problems of unemployment were all directed to this end. Two such attempts were made in the 1560s. The first scheme, supported by Lord Cecil, was for the setting up of a canvas-weaving industry. It prompted a private proposal for the erection of a hemp-beating mill which would beat enough hemp to employ three hundred to four hundred people. This was too grandiose a scheme; the town did not have this number of workers available (the whole population of Stamford did not approach three hundred households) and the

---

[8] *Ibid.*; L.A.O., Probate Inventories, *passim*.
[9] W. Shakespeare, *Henry IV, Part 2*, Act III, scene 2; V.C.H., *Leicestershire*, IV, pp. 83–5.

authorities turned it down. Instead they proposed to make a more modest start by buying twenty to forty stones of hemp and setting the poor to work. It is almost certain that hemp suggested itself as a suitable raw material because Stamford lay on the doorstep of two considerable hemp-growing regions, the Fens around the Wash and Rockingham Forest in Northamptonshire. Whether the plan succeeded does not appear, but at the end of the seventeenth century Stamford's freemen included only nine hempdressers and one roper.[10]

The second project of the 1560s, and one which did bear fruit, was for settling Dutch immigrants in Stamford. A number of towns in eastern and southern England at this time were inviting refugees, persecuted for their religion, to come from France and Flanders and settle in their midst. Usually the towns issuing such invitations had fallen on hard times and were anxious to attract artisans who would bring new skills and hence new wealth to the city. The craftsmen who were invited to Stamford in 1567 were the weavers of bays, says, stammets, fustians, carpets, fringes, linsey wolseys, tapestry, silks, velvets and linen; hatters; makers of rope, coffers, knives and locks; and workers in steel and copper. Sir William Cecil gave a house for the Dutch to dwell in and invited ten households to live there. The Dutch received the invitation gratefully and asked for permission to bring twenty households, since a smaller number would not have been able to support a preacher, and to have two hundred to three hundred acres of ground to rent for the growing of hops and other crops. The scheme made headway and in 1572 correspondence was in progress between Lord Burghley and Caspar Vosbergh concerning the endowment of a German church in the town.[11]

The full consequences of the Dutch immigration are a subject which deserves more research than I have been able to give it. Did these people settle permanently and prosper? Did their families quickly become integrated with the native population and cease to be regarded as foreigners within a generation or two? Has any evidence survived in local surnames of this immigration, and what lasting influence did the Dutch have upon the trades of the town? We know that they did not succeed in re-establishing a wool cloth industry. Early evidence of this is given in the council minutes of 1584, which tell us that Richard Shute was then engaged in *setting up* 'the

---

[10] P.R.O., SP 12/18/22; SP 12/43/11; *Cal. S.P. Dom.*, 1547–80, pp. 293, 380; HB., II, fols. 1 *et seq.*, 227.
[11] B.M., Add. MS. 29727, p. 18.

profitable science and occupation of clothing' and that Lord Burghley had given two hundred marks towards the expenses together with certain trees for the making of looms and beams. The aliens in Stamford clearly had not had much success with their New Draperies; they had better fortune in this respect in Colchester and Norwich. Nevertheless, in the later list of freemen there is a remarkable number of metal-workers, and since the Dutch had been invited to bring such craftsmen, their ancestry may be linked with the arrival of the Dutch.[12]

As for Stamford's third function as a market for local farm produce, few places at first sight seem as well situated as Stamford for a market, since it lay at the junction of three different farming regions. And since each region was becoming more highly specialized in this period, and each brought different commodities to the market, Stamford had the opportunity to become a central exchange for local farm produce. Moreover, it had good facilities: a corn market in front of Browne's Hospital, a hay market alongside, a white meat market in Red Lion Square, a sheep market at the end of Castle Street, and a beast market next to the corn market.[13] But it never secured any outstanding reputation for its traffic in food, and it never specialized sufficiently in any one commodity to draw merchants from far afield to its markets. Some of the reasons for this failure emerge from a closer examination of the position of the town in relation to the farming regions around it and the markets in the neighbourhood.

To the north-east, east, and south-east lay the flat countryside of the fens. It was the home of a large population of graziers who made use of the lush meadows and summer pastures to fatten cattle, feed dairy cows, breed horses, keep geese, and on the saltmarshes of the Wash to fatten sheep. Some of the fens lay under water in winter, and this was doubtless true of fens like Deeping Fen nearest to Stamford, but on the drier parts in mild winters cattle were kept outdoors the whole year round. The winter-flooding was not a curse, but a blessing, for it enriched the grass with a deposit of silt. The amount of arable land was small in relation to the acreage of fen pasture although it was larger in the fen villages of Kesteven than in those of Holland. In both divisions barley occupied more than half the arable land. Hemp was grown in crofts behind the house and gave employment to many poor people, not only in the curing of hemp, but in the

---

[12] HB., I, fol. 227.
[13] Speed's map of Stamford in 1600.

weaving of canvas as well. Thus Stamford received from the fens the products of a pastoral region: butter and cheese, beef and mutton, horses, and geese, as well as wildfowl, osiers, reeds, and sedge for thatch.[14]

To the south of Stamford lay the forest region of east Northamptonshire. Rockingham Forest once came right up to the very edge of Stamford, and included the village of Wothorpe, but the trees had been felled, and the clearings turned into grassland. This too was a pastoral region yielding good grazing for cattle and sheep, and pannage in the woods for pigs. Horse-breeding was also carried on, and Fotheringhay and Rothwell, near Kettering, were noted horse fairs.[15]

On the limestone heath to the north, north-west, west, and southwest of Stamford, the farming was based on corn and sheep, and much of the ploughland still lay in common fields. Sheep grazed on the hill pastures, and were folded on the arable. In this way, fertility was maintained, and the heathlands were able to produce large crops of barley. The sheep flock had once yielded wool for Stamford's medieval cloth industry, and if the town had less need of this now, its butchers still needed mutton.[16]

The notable contrast between the farming of the fens and forest on the one hand and the heathlands on the other was matched by equally striking differences in the social structure of their villages. The fens and forests were extremely populous, for they had abundant commons, which yielded valuable natural resources for the support of the landless poor. In the forests people could gather sticks for fuel and browse for winter feed, as well as pasture their beasts. In the fens they had unlimited grazing, could catch fish and wildfowl, and gather peat. The Elizabethan surveyor of the forest village of Apethorpe thought this generous provision for the poor was the cause of all the poverty and idleness in the neighbourhood. In fact, of course, it was the shortage of land in other districts in the east Midlands which attracted the landless to the fens and forests. He wrote indignantly:

In these fields tenants and cottagers have common of pasture for their horses, oxen, kine, and other great beasts without any rate amongst themselves cessed or appointed, which is a great hindrance to the husbands, and a maintaining of the idlers and beggary of the cottagers, for the liberty of the common of pasture and the gentleness that is showed in the forests to

[14] Joan Thirsk, *English Peasant Farming*, 1957, pp. 6–48.
[15] *Ibid.*, p. 176.
[16] Chapter IX above.

the bribers and stealers of woods and hedge breakers without punishment
is the only occasion of the resort of so many naughty and idle persons into
that town and others adjoining.

The fens and forests, then, possessed large villages, populated by
many small peasants and no very rich gentry. There were no sharp
class divisions, but rather a multitude of different grades of wealth
between the larger yeoman and the landless commoner.[17]

On the heath, the villages wore a different aspect. They were small
—in Beltisloe wapentake, at the southern end of Kesteven, for
example, they accommodated on average only twenty-six families
apiece in the mid-sixteenth century, whereas in the fens of Holland,
half the villages had more than seventy families. Class divisions in the
heath villages, moreover, were prominent. A resident squire, who was
notably richer than anyone else, headed the list of villagers. Below
him came a group of yeomen and husbandmen—independent
farmers of varying degrees of wealth—and below them again a group
of wage labourers, comprising about a third of the village population. In such a society, the resident gentry were the acknowledged
leaders, in contrast with the situation in the fens where men
complained of 'the want of gentlemen here to inhabit.'[18]

These differences in the social structure of the regions around
Stamford had a bearing upon its situation as a market. It might have
served as a meeting-place for these three different communities, but
in fact the town derived little advantage from the proximity of the fen
and forest. Their inhabitants were not such as to produce a great
many clients making frequent journeys to the larger town markets.
Few of the peasantry were rich, and some were so poor that they
rarely disposed of ready cash. Moreover, the communities of fen and
forest were large, and they made their own markets within their
regions. Their populations were numerous enough to make this
possible; indeed, it was essential, since the ordinary peasant could not
afford the luxury of leisure or shopping in the town.

The only region which had many gentry and rich yeomen with
enough cash to wander far afield to markets was the heathland.
Thomas and John Hatcher, gentleman farmers of Careby, near
Castle Bytham, for example, frequently made their way to Stamford
in the early seventeenth century to buy and sell wether sheep, to buy
heifers for meat for the family, and to sell oxen, to buy hemp (the

[17] Thirsk, *English Peasant Farming*, p. 10; Northants. R.O., Westmorland,
Apethorpe Coll., 4, XVI, 5.

[18] Thirsk, *op. cit.*, p. 47; Chapter IX above, pp. 142, 147.

produce of the fens and forests), and to lay in a store of domestic provisions such as pickling, cheese, raisins, nutmegs, cinnamon, rice, sugar, prunes, currants, fustian, canvas, buttons, and a child's saddle. It is fair to assume that their neighbours and friends in the same class made similar journeys. But such well-to-do farmers were specialists in the marketing of surplus produce. They chose their markets carefully, and were prepared to travel far afield if they thought advantage could be gained thereby. For the Hatchers, Stamford was only one among many markets. They went to Newark, Grantham and Nottingham for oxen, bullocks, and bulls. They went to Stow Green, Spilsby and Waltham, all in Lincolnshire, for steers. They bought cows at Corby in Northamptonshire and at Market Harborough, horses at Rothwell, Melton Mowbray and Fotheringhay, fruit trees at Apethorpe, and even went into Derbyshire in 1629 to buy a young bull. Like all wealthy farmers they were prepared to travel. And in this part of the east Midlands, there was a host of markets to choose from. The Hatcher's diary lists sixteen places apart from Stamford where they bought farm and household produce.[19] And all but one of these lay within twenty miles of Stamford. Is it then surprising that Stamford, while serving as a fair country market town, did not leap ahead of its fellows and surpass them by its reputation for one or other farm commodity? It had too many competitors. Moreover, its attention had long been riveted on the cloth industry. Indeed, to some extent, as we have seen, its hopes for the future lingered there throughout the sixteenth century.

A further drawback which the inhabitants considered to be of vital importance in hindering their commercial activity was the fact that the River Welland was no longer navigable as far as Stamford. In a petition to Queen Elizabeth in 1570, its alderman and burgesses alleged that the former wealth of its merchants (so evident, they emphasized yet again, in the ruins of their ancient buildings and parish churches) had depended on the river and the outlet it gave them to the sea. The cause of the silting was not explained, but it was no doubt due to the diminution of traffic on the river, following upon the decline of the wool and cloth trade, aggravated by neglect. It was evidently the result of long, slow deterioration, for the same petition tells us that by that time six or seven watermills had been erected between Stamford and Deeping and all had divided the river into streams in order to drive their wheels. Clearly, it was a long time since

---

[19] L.A.O., Holywell, 97, 22, 1.

the Welland had been navigable.[20]

The loss of this waterway seemed to contemporaries to put considerable obstacles in the way of the revival of Stamford's trade. It is noteworthy that Lincoln which suffered similar economic decline at this period thought itself hampered in exactly the same way by the silting up of the Fossdyke. Lincoln's dyke had connected the city with the Trent at Torksey, and so given it water communication with the Midlands and Yorkshire. Although an attempt was made to reopen the Fossdyke in 1518, success was not achieved until some time in the course of the next century, the exact date being unknown. Vague information also prevents any firm date being given to the opening up of the River Welland. An Act of 1570 gave Stamford authority to make the river navigable in its old course or to make a new cut, but the plan was not immediately fulfilled. Some progress was made, however, for in 1620 a new grant mentioning the difficulties that had prevented the execution of the previous plan, and giving permission for a new cut to be made, decreed that it should run along the north side of the Welland starting between the east end of the town and Hudd's Mill 'where a cut is already made.' Thence it was to proceed across Newstead river through Uffington, Tallington, West Deeping, and Market Deeping, and so back to the river again. The existence of a cut already on the east of Stamford suggests that something had been done in Elizabeth's reign.[21]

Work on the river was actively in hand between 1620 and 1623, for the minute books of the town council tell a woeful tale of the financial difficulties into which it plunged the town. In 1625 promises were made that the work would be completed by 1627, but they were not fulfilled. In 1633 the town council agreed to sue out another commission for making the river navigable. David Cecil offered to undertake the task in 1636, but could not agree with the town council on terms. Two other offers in 1637 and 1638 raised hopes and then dashed them again. The matter was taken up again in 1651–2, and still nothing was settled. Finally, in 1664 Daniel Wigmore, gent., bravely undertook the venture and received a lease of the tolls on the river for eighty years. His efforts seem to have met with success for Richard Blome, in a description of England in 1673, remarked upon the traffic passing up and down the river 'now made navigable, which affordeth

[20] *The Antiquities of Stamford and St Martin's from the Annals of the Rev. Francis Peck*, ed. W. Harrod, 1785, p. 535 ff.
[21] Hill, *Medieval Lincoln*, p. 313; Hill, *Tudor and Stuart Lincoln*, 1956, pp. 24, 129–34, 206–9; Harrod, *op. cit.*, p. 535 ff.

no small advantage to the town and adjacent places.' By that time too, he said, the inhabitants were driving a considerable trade in malt, 'which is here made in great plenty.' Moreover, they had markets well supplied with corn, as well as cattle and other provisions.[22]

It is almost certain that the development of the malting trade was a direct result of the resumption of traffic on the Welland. Most of the corn of the kingdom was carried by water at this period (while stock travelled by road) and no malting town was without its river communications. The towns of north Hertfordshire, for example, specialized in malting and used the River Lea to transport it to London. Leicestershire farmers, on the other hand, resigned themselves to the lack of river transport for corn, and concentrated on growing fodder crops, and feeding cattle, sheep and pigs for the market. While Stamford was without river communication, therefore, it too was barred from participation in the corn trade. But when once the Welland was made navigable once more, it was able to malt and transport the barley crop of the countryside around. As we have seen already, barley was the main arable crop on the heathlands and in the fens, and a subsidiary one elsewhere.[23]

By the second half of the seventeenth century, malting and the malt trade were two of Stamford's more thriving activities. Another development which brought good business to the town was the improvement in modes of travel after the Restoration. Public coaches were put on the streets of London in Charles I's reign, and in 1636 there were said to be six thousand in use there. By 1658 long-distance coach services were available, carrying passengers from London to the north of England. And whereas the old public coaches had been able to travel only ten to fifteen miles a day, because they were drawn by one team of between six and eight horses, by the end of the century the system of changing horses on the journey enabled passengers to travel fifty miles in a day's travel of twelve to thirteen hours. This placed Stamford within two days' journey of London, and resulted in a notable increase of travellers on the road.[24]

Although it is difficult to pass final judgement on the reasons for

[22] HB., I, fols. 329v, 330, 331v, 332v, 335v, 342–3, 373, 384, 388v, 391v, 437, 438v, 439; II, fols. 22v, 69v; R. Blome, *Britannia*, 1673, p. 144. I wish to thank Mr Alan Rogers for kindly allowing me to use his notes on the Welland navigation. The new cut is still visible on the ground. Its present condition is described in J. M. Palmer, 'The Stamford Canal: a Seventeenth Century Navigation,' unpublished paper presented to the Conference of the C.B.A. on Industrial Archaeology, December 1959.

[23] *Cal. S.P. Dom.*, 1619–23, p. 124.

[24] Joan Parkes, *Travel in England in the Seventeenth Century*, 1925, pp. 66–84.

the town's improved condition by 1700, it is fairly certain that great benefits accrued from the growth of coaching activity. The number of innkeepers who were made freemen of the town after 1663 was fifteen, while another hundred people, including butchers, bakers, fishmongers, victuallers, grocers, maltsters and vintners, were engaged in supplying food. Moreover, the town began to take an interest in the improvement of its water supply, and in 1694 Daniel Dennill of Gloucester was commissioned to carry water by engines and other instruments from the river to the market cross, to erect cisterns there, and convey the water thence by pipe through the streets to the various houses whose owners were prepared to pay the charge. No time limit was specified for this work, but Dennill evidently did not fulfil his contract for a fresh agreement was made in 1697 with William Yarnold of St Albans to do the same thing, and, provided that he finished before the end of September 1698, he was promised a lease for nine hundred years. The provision of water laid on to the houses undoubtedly improved the comfort of travellers at the inns, and suggests that the town was now recovering its prosperity.[25]

Writers on Stamford at this time also began to indulge in more cheerful descriptions of its appearance. Whereas Richard Butcher, town clerk of Stamford, had harped on the glories of its past when writing its history in 1646—'this town hath in it eleven indifferent fair streets, well replenished with houses, but in former times (as appears by the ruins of many ancient buildings) it was much more populous than now it is'—Defoe in 1724 called it 'a very fair, well-built, considerable and wealthy town,' while Francis Howgrave, writing in 1726, could see both its illustrious past and its flourishing present. 'In former times,' he observed, 'as appears by the ruins of many ancient buildings, it was much more populous, though it is now very fully inhabited.'[26]

By the early eighteenth century, then, Stamford had pulled through its troubles, and its roads and river had once again put it on the map of the kingdom's more thriving towns. Even when its fortunes were at their lowest ebb, however, it was never without wealthy citizens to bestow generous gifts upon it. Indeed, in some ways, it is difficult to reconcile the wealth of these individuals with the penury of the town as a whole. William Ratcliffe, alderman of the town on four different

[25] HB., II, fols. 1 *et seq.*, 173, 180.
[26] Butcher, p. 11; Daniel Defoe, *A Tour through England and Wales*, Everyman edn, II, p. 105; Francis Howgrave, *An Essay on the Ancient and Present State of Stamford* (1726), p. 11.

occasions between 1495 and 1522, gave all his houses and lands in Stamford to maintain a free grammar school, which was thus founded, or refounded, in 1532. William Browne, merchant of the Staple and alderman of Stamford, founded Browne's Hospital and gave lands in Swayfield and elsewhere to maintain it. John Haughton, alderman in 1558, built the new Town Hall athwart the bridge, demolished in 1776; and in 1597 Lord Burghley founded a hospital in Stamford Baron. A number of benefactions provided money, interest free, to tradesmen and artificers.[27]

The beneficent citizen, whose family established the most enduring connection with Stamford, however, was David Cecil, alderman in 1504, 1515, and 1526. No account of Stamford would be complete without some reference to this family. Just as Lincoln owed much to the patronage of Cardinal Wolsey when it fell on evil days in the early sixteenth century, so Stamford's fortunes were closely linked with those of the Cecil family. David Cecil, the first of the family to settle in Stamford, was the younger son of a Herefordshire family, and like all younger sons of his class had to make his own way in the world. Another younger son, Thomas Wilson, described in coarse but forceful terms the plight of these unlucky members of a family—'the elder son takes all, leaving to the younger that which the cat left on the malt heap . . . But,' he added philosophically, 'this I must confess doth us good someways for it makes us industrious to apply ourselves to letters or to arms, whereby many times we become my master elder brother's masters, or at least their betters in honour and reputation, while he lives at home like a mome, and knows the sound of no other bell but his own.'[28]

David Cecil ran true to type and did not stay at home. By his own efforts he paved a smooth way for his distinguished grandson. What brought him to Stamford we do not know, but he married Alice, daughter of John Dicons, a well-to-do Stamford merchant, who was alderman of the town in 1493. In 1506 he acquired an estate in the county, and in the next ten years was favoured with a number of crown offices, including that of sergeant-at-arms in 1513, and escheator of Lincolnshire in 1516. And in 1531 he became sheriff of Northamptonshire. His career was notably different from that of

---

[27] Butcher, pp. 61, 62, 45, 63; Harrod, *op. cit.*, pp. 154, 265; W. Marrat, *History and Antiquities of Stamford*, 1814, p. 257; B.M., Add. MS. 29727, p. 42; Thos. Blore, *Account of the Public Schools, Hospitals, and other Charitable Foundations in the Borough of Stamford*, 1813, pp. 225–7.

[28] Butcher, pp. 82–3; Thomas Wilson, 'The State of England, 1600,' ed. F. J. Fisher, Camden Soc., *Miscellany XVI*, 3rd Series, LII, 1936, p. 24.

other distinguished Stamford citizens, for his success rested upon crown offices. David's elder son, Richard, had the conventional career of a modest country gentleman. He became sheriff of Rutland two years before his father died, and consolidated the family's Stamford possessions by buying the manor of Little Burghley in 1527 and dissolved monastic land, consisting of the site of St Michael's priory and two hundred and ninety-nine acres in St Martin's parish, in about 1539. In 1543 he became steward of the king's manors of Nassington, Yarwell and Upton in Northamptonshire, and in 1545 he bought the manor of Essendine.[29]

Richard's wife was Jane Heckington of Bourne, and it was at Bourne that she gave birth to her son and heir, William Cecil, in 1520. He was educated at local schools, like many gentlemen's sons at this time, first at the grammar school in Grantham and later at Stamford. From there he went to St John's College, Cambridge, and thence to Gray's Inn, London, where he had the good fortune to win the favour and patronage of the duke of Somerset. Through Somerset's good offices, he made his way to court, and must have shown unusual ability for at the age of twenty-eight years he became Somerset's personal secretary. At the fall of Somerset, he suffered temporary disgrace, but found favour with the duke of Northumberland, Somerset's successor, and was released from prison. At Elizabeth's accession, he was appointed Principal Secretary of State. In his long service to the Queen, he showed himself possessed of all the qualities of an admirable secretary—a tactful but firm way of handling his mistress, a capacity for hard work, and care for meticulous detail. Some of the most informative documents of government in this reign are William Cecil's careful notes upon a problem of State, beginning with a statement of the situation, and continuing in the form of a debate on the *pros* and *cons* of a certain course of action. They hold a mirror to the mind of this outstanding statesman.[30]

Despite his heavy duties at Westminster, William Cecil never lost touch with Stamford. His home was there, and it is clear from the correspondence that passed between the alderman and town council and himself that he kept as sure a grasp upon the town's affairs as upon business in London. And in about 1575 he took upon himself the enormous task of building the new palace at Burghley, which William III, visiting it in 1696, was to call 'too great for a subject.'[31]

---

[29] W. H. Charlton, *Burghley*, 1873, pp. 2–4, 160–1; Northants. R.O., List of Exeter MSS., 47, 9.

[30] Charlton, *op. cit.*, pp. 5–14.

[31] B.M., Add. MS. 29727, pp. 18, 32.

This survey of Stamford's history in the sixteenth and seventeenth centuries has carried us through an uneasy period when the town was slowly adjusting itself from being a centre of international trade to the life of a local market town on one of the main roads of the kingdom. It was a painful transformation, for contemporaries had nothing but contempt for local market towns. 'Touching the present estate of Lincoln,' wrote William Lambarde in 1584, 'I think it pitiful . . . the condition thereof is little better than of a common market town.'[32] Is it any wonder that Stamford could not submit to this ignominious fate without doleful complaint? Memories of the past lingered long because there were sermons in the stones of its old decaying buildings. The townspeople still clung to the idea that the town would once again build its fortunes upon the weaving of cloth, if not the old scarlet cloth, then the New Draperies or even hard-wearing canvas. These dreams died hard. As it turned out, Stamford found its salvation in other activities, in the processing of commodities produced in the countryside around, in the curing and working of hides and skins from the backs of Midland cattle and sheep, and later on in the malting of locally grown barley. And as more and more Englishmen took to travelling in the second half of the seventeenth century, Stamford enjoyed greater benefits than ever before from its position on the Great North Road, and made its innkeepers happy. When Stamford's career as a great industrial centre was cut short in the Middle Ages, a grievous blow was struck at the economy of the town. But at this distance of time, we can see compensations. Something of Stamford's medieval splendour was preserved and has not since been destroyed by industrial development.

---

[32] Cited in Hill, *Medieval Lincoln*, p. 288.

XVIII
THE FAMILY

Iт is perhaps no great exaggeration to say that 'the whole of our history and of our civilization depends on the family'.[1] And yet the historian, fixing his attention upon the more obviously influential institutions of society, has so far ignored its humble history. This attitude of indifference was once common among French scholars, but it has now given way to enthusiastic interest. In 1954 the historians held a conference on the history of the family; in 1955 the sociologists followed with a conference on the comparative sociology of the modern family.[2] And now we have two books dealing in whole or in part with the same subject: *L'Enfant et la Vie Familiale sous l'ancien Régime* by Philippe Ariès, now translated into English under the title *Centuries of Childhood*; and *Introduction à la France Moderne. Essai de Psychologie Historique, 1500–1640* by Robert Mandrou—a study of the physical environment and mental attitudes of men in the sixteenth and first half of the seventeenth centuries, dealing in turn with each of the four communities that commanded their loyalties: the family, the parish, their professional, religious, and similar associations, and the nation. No one can read these absorbing studies without deploring the absence of any comparable work, or even slight signs of concern for the subject in England.[3]

French interest in the family was first stimulated by the work of demographers. Their investigations disposed of the idea that the family was an immobile institution in society. On the contrary, as many other scholars with different approaches have since confirmed,

---

[1] Régine Pernoud in R. Prigent, ed., *Renouveau des Idées sur la Famille, Institut National d'Études Demographiques*, Cahier 18, (Paris, 1954), p. 21.
[2] R. Prigent, *op. cit.; Sociologie Comparée de la Famille Contemporaine*, Colloques Internationaux du Centre National de la Recherche Scientifique, (Paris, 1955).
[3] Philippe Ariès, *L'Enfant et la Vie Familiale sous L'ancien Régime*, (Paris, 1960); *Centuries of Childhood*, (Cape, London 1962); Robert Mandrou, *Introduction à la France Moderne*, (Editions Albin Michel, Paris, 1961). This article, it should be said, does not do justice to Mandrou's book which is wider in scope, and full of provocative ideas concerning the unspoken assumptions of men in the sixteenth and early seventeenth centuries.

the family throughout history has been undergoing continuous change. Are these changes to be described in terms of the gradual destruction of a once solid institution, torn apart since the eighteenth century by individualism, the growth of industry, urbanization, and the emancipation of women? This was the melancholy suggestion of one speaker at the conference in 1954.[4] Ariès—the one writer to pass judgment at the conclusion of his investigation—takes the opposite point of view. The family in industrialized societies, he argues, occupies a more influential place than ever before. It has never 'exercised so much influence on the human condition'. And certainly, when we contemplate the advisory services and multitudes of books on child psychology and family life, when we consider the strength of the modern notion that the family is essential to the child, it is clear that the idea of the family has never been more assiduously fostered and carefully analysed than now.[5]

The silence of the family in history will always frustrate the historian. But French scholars have shown how much can be inferred from meagre evidence: in frescoes and portraits; in title deeds of property, which by the number of their signatories distinguish between family-owned and individually-owned property; in literature, whether that of the medieval epic, which glorified the lineage, or of the early nineteenth-century novel, which romanticized childhood; and, finally, in the law, which at the Revolution secularized marriage, permitted divorce, and thereafter laid down a strict legal framework for family life. To these sources we might add others—family papers, family correspondence, and wills, faithful mirrors in England, at least, of the quality of family life.

Although most French writers are concerned with the small conjugal family, the decay of the patriarchal family, whose traditions persisted long in some parts of France, makes first call upon their attention. Georges Duby has rescued it from the shadows in a most skilful reconstruction of society in the Mâcon region in the eleventh and twelfth centuries. His story does not support the idea of a progressive diminution in the size of the family from large clan to conjugal family, but of a series of contractions and expansions in family size and solidarity as the security offered by the state waxed and waned. The tenth-century family was a small unit, which allowed its members the utmost liberty. Husbands and wives each owned and

---

[4] Prigent, *op. cit.*, pp. 9–11.
[5] Ariès, *op. cit.*, p. 10.

disposed of their property as they pleased. The Frankish state guaranteed enough protection to the individual at this time to enable him to slacken the reins of kinship. With the dissolution of the state after 1000, however, family links were tightened. 'The family', writes Duby, 'is the first refuge of the individual when the state fails him'. Property became the joint concern of all members of the family, and at first was not physically divided among heirs until the second or third generation. Grants of land required the consent of all, and wives surrendered control over their property to their husbands.[6]

This situation was gradually transformed again between the mid-twelfth and mid-thirteenth centuries. The expansion of the economy and the increasing efficiency of the state once more encouraged the conjugal family to assert its independence. But the complete individualism of the tenth-century family did not reassert itself. The disadvantages of partible inheritance were manifest. In its place, the custom of primogeniture began to find favour. By this means, the integrity of the family estate was preserved, and, incidentally, the father's authority maintained and increased. The modern family began to take shape.[7]

Duby's analysis of changes in family structure in the eleventh and twelfth centuries relates, of course, to the nobility and bourgeoisie. The peasant family, he argues, pursued a different course. When the state failed to guarantee him security, the peasant sought protection from his lord, and found satisfaction for his social needs in the solidarity of the village rather than the family. This argument deserves further investigation since it suggests that the village did not develop its corporate sense, and may not have begun to engage in cooperative activities until this period. If this were so, we should have to revise our notions about the origins of common field farming. Certainly, the emphasis placed on the role of the lord in indirectly promoting village solidarity seems to be justified by English experience, for a clear distinction can be observed between the weakly-manorialized districts of England and Wales, where family cohesion was aided by the practice of partible inheritance, which involved much cooperation within the family in the working of jointly-owned land, and the highly manorialized areas, where the family observed primogeniture and farming cooperation was not a

[6] Georges Duby, *La Société aux XIe et XIIe Siècles dans la Région Mâconnaise*, (Paris, 1953), pp. 136–7, 263–4, 270–71, 278. Cf. also David Herlihy, 'Land, Family and Women in Continental Europe, 701–1200', *Traditio*, xviii (1962).
[7] Duby, *op. cit.*, pp. 279, 481–500.

family, but a village concern.[8]

Philippe Ariès and others take up the later history of the conjugal family in France. The growing authority of the father over his family led in the fourteenth century to a marked deterioration in the status of women. Whereas they had earlier had the right to administer their husbands' affairs in their absence, now they had to have their acts authorized by a judge. By the sixteenth century they could do nothing without the sanction of their husbands. The father thus came to be master in his house at a time when the phase of childhood was being prolonged. In the medieval family, boys reached their majority at fourteen years and girls at twelve. At this early age they were given their freedom and encouraged to seek adventure—how else, writes Régine Pernoud, could one understand the Crusades? But by the sixteenth century maturity was not reached until twenty-five years, so that for a longer period of life than ever before, the child had to submit to the increasingly severe discipline of the father. It was for this reason that daughters frequently chose to go into a convent rather than resign themselves to an arranged marriage.[9]

At the same time, however, the child began to benefit from a more sympathetic understanding of his nature. Using the evidence of frescoes, paintings, contemporary treatises and encyclopaedias, Ariès demonstrates how parents slowly learnt to treat children as children. In the early Middle Ages they had been dressed as adults and depicted in paintings as such. In medieval epics they were expected to show the bravery of the mature warrior. Beginning in the thirteenth century, another image of childhood gradually took shape. In Italian paintings of the virgin and child, children were painted as children and not as little men. Instead of being sent at the age of seven or eight years to serve an apprenticeship or work in the house of a noble, where they were encircled by adults, children began after the fifteenth century to be educated at school with others of their own age, and to live for many more years under their parents' roof. By the seventeenth century, the family portrait began to be planned around the children, and they were even deemed worthy of portraits to themselves. The child ceased to be dressed like a grown-up, childish speech was thought deserving of comment and record, and adults who had previously allowed children to see all and hear all, began to pay heed to their innocence and to exercise restraint in their presence. Pedagogues made much of the respect that ought to be paid to

---

[8] Duby, *op. cit.*, pp. 281–2.
[9] *Sociologie Comparée, op. cit.*, p. 13; Prigent, *op. cit.*, pp. 30–31.

children, and by the eighteenth century their ideas had become commonplace.[10]

As children came into their own, primogeniture fell out of favour, its legitimacy disputed by moralists and educationists who argued that all children should be treated equally. Subsequent attempts in the early nineteenth century to restore primogeniture were strenuously resisted. Thus the old idea of the family as a house of kindred, possessing a surname that must be preserved at the cost of the individual's personal interests, disappeared. The family was henceforth held together by the simple bond of affection between parents and children.[11]

Attitudes to illegitimacy are summarily discussed by the French but have not yet been fully investigated. Differences of class as well as of time already suggest themselves. In the Carolingian age, bastards among the nobility were never banished from the family circle, but this practice was at variance with canonical law which recognized only legitimate children, though the illegitimate could be legitimized by the subsequent marriage of the parents. In the sixteenth century moral disapproval was still not conspicuous among the nobility, but we know nothing of the attitude of ordinary folk. At a later period one aspect of changing moral attitudes is revealed in the fact that it was an honour to serve as a royal mistress in the seventeenth century, but a dishonour in the eighteenth. But perhaps royal mistresses were different. If so, at what period did all classes come to share the church's attitude of moral disapproval of bastardy?[12]

This discussion of French writing on the family prompts comparison with the history of the English family. We can see at once that in many respects ours has run a different course. If the family, in which two and three generations lived together under one roof, ever existed in England, we seem to have an intermediate type of household before the emergence of the conjugal family in those rural establishments, well attested in the sixteenth and seventeenth centuries, in which the old people shared the farmhouse with their married heir, but occupied a room or two at the end of the building and had access to other parts of the house—to the well or the kitchen—when necessary. Such an arrangement implies that the ageing parents had given up active control over the farm but took a share perhaps in the income from it. But the precise nature of the agreement between the old and young is a matter of guesswork. Our

[10] Ariès, *op. cit.*, p. 33–5, 36–9, 40–43, 47, 50, 109–10.
[11] Ariès, *op. cit.*, pp. 371–3.
[12] *Sociologie Comparée*, *op. cit.*, pp. 10, 15.

knowledge of the architectural layout of the farmhouse is clearer than our notions about the division of labour and authority.

Another striking contrast with French development concerns the position of women. Their status in England certainly did not deteriorate in the sixteenth or early seventeenth centuries. Indeed, in some ways it temporarily improved. Although in theory wives were expected to show complete obedience to their husbands, in practice they were far from being dutiful, dependent slaves. Their freedom to go where they pleased, and accept invitations without their husbands was a source of surprise to foreigners. 'The females have great liberty and are almost like masters', wrote Jakob Rathgeb after a visit to England in 1592. No wonder it was said that the country was a purgatory for servants, a hell for horses, but a paradise for women. During the Interregnum some of the Separatist sects gave new responsibilities to women by proclaiming their spiritual equality with men and allowing them to debate, vote, and preach at religious assemblies, but the influence of these sects did not survive the Restoration. Clarendon thought that the Interregnum had disrupted the family, that it was no longer held together by the obedience of its members. But if so this relaxation of paternal discipline did not lead on to the emancipation of women. Among the working classes women may have maintained their economic independence through toiling alongside their husbands, but middle-class women by the late eighteenth century were swooning, docile, dependent creatures.[13]

But in saying this, we return again to the question of class differences. It is almost certainly true that the history of the rich family was not also that of the poor. Differences in the size of the household, differences in the form of education available to the children, differences in the amount of leisure of the parents were all class distinctions. And there were regional contrasts too. French scholars distinguish between the parts of France dominated by customary and by Roman law, the latter preserving longest the patriarchal Roman tradition of the family. Other local differences have been observed by historians of English society such as Professor G. C. Homans and Dr. Titow. Professor Homans has drawn attention to the contrast between the dispersed communities of Kent and E. Anglia with their joint families practising partible inheritance, and the small family practising primogeniture in nucleated villages in

---

[13] W. B. Rye, *England as seen by Foreigners*, (London, 1865), p. 14; E. Gurney Salter, *Tudor England through Venetian Eyes* (London, 1930), p. 121; Keith Thomas, 'Women and the Civil War Sects', *Past and Present*, No. 13 (April, 1958), pp. 44, 46–7, 57.

central England. Dr. Titow's description of land shortage on the Somerset manor of Taunton in the thirteenth century shows an unusual age relationship among members of families living on this estate which cannot but have influenced the status of each. For widows with land were at a premium among landless young men. This must surely have affected the status of women in the neighbourhood, irrespective of what was happening in other parts of Somerset outside this fertile vale. In our knowledge of local societies, it seems we may be better equipped than the French to spot local refinements in the quality of peasant family life.[14]

In explaining the general circumstances which shaped the modern family, however, we are not likely to dissent from the argument of French scholars. So long as the social life of the village community flourished, it swamped and stifled the life of the family and inhibited the growth of family solidarity. Mandrou argued, indeed, that sociability was forced upon the individual: his house was so cold that he had to move about and visit his neighbours to keep warm. The idea of the modern family and family privacy therefore first evolved in the houses of the rich and spread downwards. To this analysis the best contribution we can make is the notion that the peasant's receptiveness varied in different agrarian situations. Many pasture farmers had lived in relative social isolation for centuries, perhaps had already developed another concept of the family of which we as yet know nothing. It was in the countryside of villages that upper-class influence was strongest, but even there the notion of family privacy could not take complete hold until the economic basis of village unity was destroyed, until the fields were enclosed and cooperative farming—the forceful fosterparent of village solidarity—came to an end.[15]

[14] *Sociologie Comparée, op. cit.*, pp. 15, 14; G. C. Homans, 'The Rural Sociology of Medieval England', *Past and Present*, No. 4 (Nov. 1953), pp. 32–43; J. Z. Titow, 'Some Differences between Manors and the Effects on the Condition of the Peasant in the Thirteenth Century', *Agric. Hist. Rev.*, x (1962), pp. 1–13.

[15] Ariès, *op. cit.*, pp. 398–400, 406–7; Mandrou, *op. cit.*, p. 42.

POSTSCRIPT

Interest in family history has increased remarkably since the above essay was published in 1964; a full bibliography would be voluminous. Mention may be made of the following, which contain references to many more recent publications.

Michael Anderson, *Approaches to the History of the Western Family, 1500–1914*, Studies in Economic and Social History, London, 1980.

Vivian C. Fox and Martin H. Quitt, *Loving, Parenting, and Dying: The Family Cycle in England and America, Past and Present*, New York, 1980.

L. Stone, 'The Rise of the Nuclear Family in early modern England. The Patriarchal Stage', in Charles Rosenberg, ed., *The Family in History*, Pennsylvania, 1975, pp. 13–57.

L. Stone, *The Family, Sex, and Marriage in England, 1500–1800*, London, 1977.

For a comparable French study, see

J.-L. Flandrin, *Families in Former Times. Kinship, Household and Sexuality*, Cambridge, 1979.

XIX

YOUNGER SONS IN THE SEVENTEENTH CENTURY

THE changing fortunes of the gentry have been the subject of several recent historical studies. Their rising influence as a class is not seriously in dispute. The question at issue is how the more successful individuals among them gained in fortune and distinction. Was it by the ownership and efficient management of land, by trade, or by crown offices? And at the expense of whom—of their less enterprising peers, of the nobility, of the yeomanry, or the church.[1]

On the face of it, this discussion among present-day historians was not one which provoked vociferous debate among contemporaries. It is true that the crown in the sixteenth century deplored 'the confusion of degrees' and took steps to arrest social mobility, but its policy cannot be said to have echoed strong popular complaint. And it was as ineffectual as that of Canute trying to stem a rising tide. Some generalized observations offered by James Harrington, Henry Neville, Edmund Ludlow, and others in the later 1650s on the increasing landed wealth of the gentry suggested that the gains of this class were made at the expense of the nobility, but they have been discounted by Professor Trevor Roper as the slogans of active Republican politicians rather than statements of fact. Nevertheless, their conclusions have found support in Professor Stone's study of the peerage, and this, no doubt, is part of the explanation of the rise of the gentry.[2] But is it the whole answer? If we do not finally conclude that the gentry achieved economic and political success *wholly* at the expense of the nobility, where do we look for other supplementary

---

[1] I wish to express particular thanks to Mr. Christopher Hill for his interest in this article and the many references he gave me on the subject. I also have to thank Mr. Richard Grassby and Mr. Keith Thomas for their helpful criticisms and guidance on a number of points though none are responsible for my conclusions.

[2] C. B. Macpherson, *The Political Theory of Possessive Individualism* (Oxford, 1962), pp. 164–5; Lawrence Stone, *The Crisis of the Aristocracy, 1558–1641* (Oxford, 1965), pp. 152–7; H. R. Trevor Roper, *The Gentry, 1540–1640*, Econ. Hist. Rev. Supplement, no. 1, pp. 45–7.

explanations? There is one which rests entirely upon contemporary discussion, but which has hitherto been strangely ignored. This is because our questions have been clumsily formulated. The gentry in our debates are the elder sons of gentle families who inherited their fathers' estates in accordance with the rule of primogeniture. As we know, some enlarged them, some dissipated them. The absence of many strong expressions of opinion by contemporaries on the fortunes of this class suggests, perhaps, that their economic gains and losses were thought to cancel each other out. But what of the other children of such families, what of the younger sons? They were also gentry born and bred, but in manhood they had to fend for themselves, and they did not necessarily die as gentlemen. Primogeniture sacrificed them for the sake of their elder brothers. On this aspect of the fortunes of the gentry contemporaries had many observations to offer and held very strong views. Indeed, when one puts to them the question how and at whose expense the gentry rose in the sixteenth and seventeenth centuries, their answer is unambiguous. They rose at the expense of their younger brothers.[3]

It is not the purpose of this article to suggest that this is the full explanation, but rather one of several elements in the situation; the contemporary literature of protest by and for younger sons is so plentiful, its language so vehement, and its authors so unanimous, that it clearly deserves closer scrutiny.

Throughout the sixteenth and seventeenth centuries younger sons were singled out for special comment and commiseration. Shakespeare, himself an elder brother, but with the will and sympathy to see things from the younger brother's point of view, launched Orlando on his adventures in *As You Like It* with a powerful protest against the iniquity of primogeniture. Orlando was the younger son of Sir Rowland de Boys, and was wholly dependent for his living on the charity of his elder brother, Oliver. 'He keeps me rustically at home, or, to speak more properly, stays me here at home unkept: for call you that keeping for a gentleman of my birth that differs not from the stalling of an ox?' In a quarrel that ended in a scuffle between the two brothers, Orlando voiced the familiar complaint of many of his kind. 'My father charg'd you in his will to give me a good education: you have train'd me like a peasant obscuring and hiding from me all gentlemanlike qualities: the spirit of

---

[3] If we follow the calculations of E. Chamberlayne, there were in England in 1669 8100 baronets, knights, and gentlemen, and 16,000 younger brothers. *Angliae Notitia* (London, 1669), pp. 486–7.

my father grows strong in me, and I will no longer endure it: therefore allow me such exercises as may become a gentleman, or give me the poor allottery my father left me by testament, with that I will go buy my fortunes.'[4]

On another occasion, Shakespeare made a more disparaging reference to younger sons which expressed the contempt in which they were commonly held. Falstaff, reviewing a bedraggled company of soldiers in *Henry IV, Part I*, hurled at them the most abusive epithets he could summon: 'slaves as ragged as Lazarus in the painted cloth, where the glutton's dogs licked his sores; and such as indeed were never soldiers, but discarded unjust serving-men, younger sons to younger brothers, revolted tapsters and ostlers trade-fallen'. Younger sons were pitiable enough, but younger sons of younger brothers were plainly the very lowest of the low.[5]

Thomas Wilson's description of *The State of England, 1600* gives a more subjective but not less pungent account of the same problem, written from hard personal experience, since he was another younger son of a gentleman. 'Such a fever hectic hath custom brought in and inured amongst fathers and such fond desire they have to leave a great shew of the stock of their house, though the branches be withered, that they will not do it, but my elder brother forsooth must be my master. He must have all.' The younger brethren were left with 'that which the cat left on the malt heap, perhaps some small annuity during his life, or what please our elder brother's worship to bestow upon us if we please him and my mistress his wife'. There was only one consolation: 'This I must confess doth us good someways, for it makes us industrious to apply ourselves to letters or to arms whereby many times we become my master elder brother's masters, or at least their betters in honour and reputation, while he lives at home like a mome and knows the sound of no other bell but his own.'[6]

The most succinct and yet gracious literary portrait, however, is that written by John Earle in his *Microcosmography* (1633). A younger son, he maintained, was born a gentleman, expected to play the role of a gentleman, but lacked the wherewithal. If his annuity was sufficient, he went to the university, and then with great heart-burning into the ministry—a profession he was condemned to for lack of any other. His last refuge was the Low Countries where he

[4] *As You Like It*, Act I, Scene 1.
[5] *Henry IV, Part I*, Act IV, Scene 2.
[6] F. J. Fisher (ed.), *The State of England Anno Dom. 1600 by Thomas Wilson*, Camden Miscellany, XVI, Camden Soc., Third Series, LII (1936), p. 24.

lived a poor gentleman of a company and died without a shirt. He was commonly discontented, and desperate, and the exclamation most frequently on his lips was 'that churl my brother'. His only hope of bettering his fortune was to marry a widow. 'He loves not his country for this unnatural custom', Earle concluded, 'and would have long since revolted to the Spaniard but for Kent only which he holds in admiration.'[7]

During the sixteenth century to describe anyone as '*a younger son*' was a short-hand way of summing up a host of grievances. Just as the mention of a *stepmother* to children brought up on a diet of traditional fairy tales conjures up a picture of a harsh, spidery woman without love for her step-children, and the term *mother-in-law* on the music-hall stage conjures up the image of another nagging creature without any agreeable qualities, so *younger son* meant an angry young man, bearing more than his share of injustice and resentment, deprived of means by his father and elder brother, often hanging around his elder brother's house as a servant, completely dependent on his grace and favour.

Until the 1620s the tone of all literary lamentations on the plight of younger sons was mostly light-hearted and always resigned. They bewailed the tyranny and injustice of primogeniture, but they did not envisage or discuss the possibility of putting the injustice right. The temper of the literature changed noticeably in the middle of James I's reign, and subsequently developed into a more serious debate on the disadvantages of primogeniture for society as a whole and on the practical measures that might remedy the situation. Two questions call for answer. How did things work out in practice for younger sons; was life really as cruel as the pamphleteers complained? And how and why did the literature of the subject grow in size and urgency in the course of the seventeenth century?

The first question opens up a problem which is too large to be answered in this article. The careers of younger sons and the fortunes of their families call for closer examination at all class levels. The impression derived from a superficial survey of wills suggests that primogeniture did not exercise a tyranny over classes below that of the gentry. It was not, of course, unknown for yeomen, husbandmen, and labourers—in rural areas at least—to advance their eldest sons at the expense of the rest, and certainly this was the law for socage land in cases of intestacy, unless it was held by gavelkind tenure. But as a

---

[7] John Earle, *Microcosmography*, ed. A. S. West (Cambridge, 1951), pp. 69–70.

general rule people of lower rank divided their property, though not necessarily equally, between their sons and sometimes between their daughters as well. One method was to leave the freehold land to one son, the copyhold to another, and the leasehold to another. Another method, where the land was small in area, was to leave it all to one or two sons, while stipulating that they should pay certain sums of money, or give certain crops and animals, to their brothers and sisters. Primogeniture, as John Earle and many others agreed, was an 'unnatural custom', and people without social pretensions saw little merit in it.

It was otherwise with the gentry. Contemporary writers seemed to think that primogeniture had not always held such undisputed sway as now. Thomas Wilson vaguely implied this when he spoke of 'such a fever hectic' that custom 'hath brought in'. It was also implied in the words of another early seventeenth-century writer: 'I must confess that the custom of leaving the child estate to the eldest son hath of latter times been much imbraced by our gentry for the preservation of their families for which it was invented.'[8] This is not convincing proof that primogeniture in the sixteenth century noticeably displaced a more common practice of partitioning land in the fifteenth century and earlier. But it is a sign that the subject requires further investigation. Clearly something had changed or there would have been no reason for this literature of protest. Either the custom of inheritance had altered or the economic circumstances of younger sons had deteriorated for other reasons, making them more conscious of the injustices they suffered through primogeniture. Contemporaries conducted their discussion on the assumption that both factors played a part, without assigning more blame to one cause than the other.

Pamphleteers were concerned with the sons of gentry rather than of the nobility, but the ideals and prejudices of the latter were not without influence on the gentry, and it is therefore worth summarizing Professor Stone's conclusions on their practices when bequeathing land. He does not commit himself to any view about their habits in the fifteenth century, but is clear that in the sixteenth and seventeenth centuries the eldest son took the lion's share of the estate, while the younger sons were provided either with a small property in land, which reverted to the elder brother at death, or an annuity which also terminated at death. A career in trade or the

[8] J. A(p. Robert)., *An Apology for a Younger Brother* . . . (Oxford, 1641), p. 29.

professions was open to all with inclination and energy to pursue it, but no one took it for granted that he had to earn his living in this way. Yet paternal benevolence was frequently not sufficient to assure a comfortable living to younger sons who chose to support a wife and children. In consequence, they tended to marry late and have fewer children, or they remained bachelors.[9]

The testamentary habits of the gentry deserve similarly careful study before generalizations can be attempted. There may well have been significant local variations. For example, the Kentish gentry still held much land by gavelkind tenure, and many continued to uphold the spirit and the letter of this custom, resisting any attempt at change. A bill to abolish gavelkind in Kent in 1597 was refused the Queen's assent, though it had passed the Commons without much debate; and when revived again in 1601 was firmly rejected by the Commons by 138 votes to 67.[10] Some Kentish gentlemen, it is true, had already succumbed to the arguments in favour of primogeniture, and it became increasingly common in the sixteenth century for Kentish gentlemen to apply to Parliament for an act to disgavel their lands.[11] Despite these examples, however, the old customs died hard.

Recent studies of the gentry in other counties imply that primogeniture held sway over the majority; and yet there are also contrary examples from counties more remote from London which reveal the strenuous efforts of some heads of families to provide a sufficiency for all sons.[12] Would a larger sample of these families, particularly from the north and west country, where there was less purpose in ostentatious spending, show a stronger preference for partible inheritance than is presently allowed for? It is impossible as yet to say. As the evidence stands at the moment, we can only repeat the impressions and prejudices of the *literati* and politicians of the age. They believed that younger sons of gentlemen were ill provided for, that they had a hard fight to make good, and many did not succeed. Two illustrations bear this out. Sergeant Yelverton, elected

[9] Lawrence Stone, *The Crisis of the Aristocracy, 1558–1641* (Oxford, 1964), pp. 599–600.

[10] *House of Lords MSS., XI, N.S., Addenda, 1514–1714* (1962), pp. 32–3; Sir Simonds D'Ewes, *Journal of all the Parliaments during the Reign of Queen Elizabeth* (London, 1682), pp. 272, 533, 676. I wish to thank Mr. Keith Thomas for these references.

[11] A. M. Everitt, *The Community of Kent and the Great Rebellion, 1640–60* (Leicester, 1966), pp. 46–7; Idem, 'Social Mobility in early Modern England', *Past and Present*, no. 33 (1966), pp. 60–1, 66–8.

[12] J. P. Ferris, 'The Gentry of Dorset on the Eve of the Civil War', *Genealogist's Mag.*, XV, no. 3 (1965), p. 107.

Speaker of the House of Commons in 1597, was a relatively successful younger son, but looked pessimistically to the future. He described his life's struggle thus: 'My estate is nothing correspondent for the maintenance of this dignity, for my father dying left me a younger brother and nothing unto me but my bare annuity, then growing to man's estate and some practise of the law, I took a wife by whom I have had many children, the keeping of us all being a great impoverishing of my estate and the daily living of us all nothing but my daily industry.'[13]

An account of the fortunes of the younger brothers of one Northamptonshire gentry family, although fragmented in the pages of several antiquarian histories and genealogies, has been conveniently brought together in Mary Finch's study of the family. Euseby Isham was the representative of a minor Northamptonshire gentry family. The eldest son inherited the estate, sat in Parliament, and became steward to the Earl of Bedford. There were four younger brothers, of whom one went into the church, and three were apprenticed to London mercers, Gregory and John becoming Merchant Adventurers. Gregory died young, but John made a success of his business in London and later in life set up as a landed gentleman in his native county, employing his priestly brother as rent collector. John passed on his wealth to his eldest son Thomas, and did his duty by his other sons: Henry was apprenticed to a mercer, and Richard was educated at Cambridge and the Middle Temple. But already the younger sons were slipping down the social ladder. Henry had six sons and three daughters, but only one son married, choosing a wife of yeoman stock. Richard had three sons and four daughters, but he could only find a marriage portion for one daughter, and three went without. Only one of the sons married and, having received a university education, became a parson in Suffolk. The parson's son became a Suffolk grocer. In short, the eldest branch of this landed family maintained its standing in Northamptonshire society throughout this period. The younger branches clung to the tradition of giving their sons a good education or at least an apprenticeship in trade, but failed to maintain it beyond the second generation. Their heirs settled into the middle class of rural yeomen and shopkeepers, and many did not marry.[14]

---

[13] A. F. Pollard and Marjorie Blatcher, 'Hayward Townshend's Journals', *B.I.H.R.*, XII (1934–5), p. 7.

[14] Mary Finch, *The Wealth of Five Northamptonshire Families, 1540–1640* (Northants. Rec. Soc., XIX, 1956), pp. 5–6, 23–30. For a similar verdict on the younger sons of Dorset gentlemen, see J. P. Ferris, *op. cit.*, p. 107.

These are random illustrations only, but they suggest that the prospects and problems of younger sons of gentlemen were hardly different from those of the nobility while differing sharply from the experience of all classes beneath them. How were they mirrored in contemporary literature? Much writing in the sixteenth century observed the melancholy facts but did no more than rail, often light-heartedly, at the law. But in the second half of James I's reign the subject ceased to be merely a laughing matter for dramatists and essayists. A more serious tone was struck by the publication of John ap Robert's *An Apology for a Younger Brother*, the first known edition of which was published at St. Omer in 1618. It was reprinted at Oxford—the meeting place of many younger sons in their most impressionable years—in 1624 and 1634, in 1641 and again in 1671. It was evidently popular.

By this time a substantial body of literature had accumulated on the Continent, notably in France, Spain, and Germany, on the merits and drawbacks of different inheritance customs.[15] The writer of the *Apology* began his argument in the manner generally favoured by Continental writers of enumerating the many Biblical examples of partible inheritance. Jacob and Esau; Noah dividing his property between his three sons; David giving his kingdom to Solomon, his youngest son—all were paraded before the reader. It is tempting to infer from this that he was familiar with some of the pamphlets from abroad. However, he disclaimed any knowledge of the existing literature—'Let not any expect many quotations of authors; for I never read any of this subject'—and we must take him at his word. He was prompted to write his discourse after joining in a discussion with friends over dinner concerning the temperament and character of elder and younger brothers. It seemed to the assembled company that their characters were often moulded by their position in the family and their expectation, or otherwise, of inheriting their father's fortunes. Elder brothers were inclined to be selfish, younger brothers selfless. The debate was stimulating and without further ado our author was prompted to embark on his essay.[16]

Much of the central part of the discourse was taken up with the question of the legal rights of owners of land to devise it as they pleased. As a general rule, he alleged, they observed primogeniture, not appreciating their full rights in the matter. Most landowners

[15] For the bibliography of this literature, see J. S. Pütter, *Litteratur des Teutschen Staatsrechts* (Göttingen, 1783), III, pp. 754 ff. See also Chapter XX.
[16] John Ap Robert, *op. cit.*, pp. 1–5.

understood and used their right to bequeathe freely land which they had acquired by purchase. But people felt conscientious objections about devising freely land acquired as patrimony, and the gravest doubts of all surrounded their moral right to cut off an entail. But in fact, John ap Robert assured his readers, a father had in all cases power to dispose of his property freely 'to a good end and upon a just cause'. If he wished to divide land among all his sons, the law permitted him to do so.[17]

Throughout the pamphlet ran the underlying conviction that younger brothers deserved and urgently needed maintenance in the form of land from their fathers, and that they had not always faced the hardships of which they now complained. The practical reasons why primogeniture had gained such a strong hold were twofold. It preserved the family name; and it conferred on one person the means for supporting brothers, sisters, and other members of the family. On both counts, ap Robert argued, these advantages were illusory. Far from preserving the family name, primogeniture often quickly extinguished it: if the family of the privileged elder child produced no male heirs, the family's name and prestige were abruptly destroyed. The results, he claimed, were obvious in county society: for every one family in a county with a history going back three hundred years, there were many others 'scarce of five descents in a blood'. Secondly, the tradition of elder brothers supporting their younger brothers in comfort was now more honoured in the breach than in the observance. Eldest sons accepted their rights with alacrity but ignored their obligations. They were ready to spend more in a year idly than would maintain a whole family nobly.[18]

Although ap Robert gave pride of place in his narrative to the failure of fathers to endow their younger sons with land, he did not consider that this fully explained their plight. The roads leading to alternative careers were not as attractive, or as smooth to the tread as once they had been. For one thing, the church as a career was 'not so grateful to our English gentlemen's natures as anciently it hath been'.

---

[17] In fact, the Statute of Wills (1540) allowed tenants in fee simple to dispose by will of 2/3 of land held by military tenure and the whole of land held in socage. Frederick Pollock, *The Land Laws* (2nd ed. London, 1887), p. 100. But Thomas Wilson also believed in the existence of legal obstacles. He claimed that fathers could not give a foot of land to their younger children in inheritance 'unless it be by lease for 21 years or for three lives (or unless his land be socage tenure whereof there is little, or gavelkind such as is only in one province, in Kent) or else be purchased by himself and not descended'. Thomas Wilson, *op. cit.*, p. 24.

[18] John Ap Robert, *op. cit.*, pp. 18 ff.

For another, 'the trade of merchant, soldier, and courtier advanced many more than now they do'.

Recent work by historians of the sixteenth and seventeenth centuries sheds some light on the issues raised here, and at many points lends substance to the author's main arguments. There seems no doubt that primogeniture was moulding county society into a certain familiar pattern, which became more readily recognizable in the later seventeenth centuty when still stricter legal measures were devised for keeping family estates intact. The landed class came to be composed of a few single branches of ancient gentry families who had the luck to survive, supplemented by others who had moved in from outside through their success in other walks of life. Intermarriage forged ties between them, but they were a small select company. This contrasted with what might be called the Kentish pattern of landed society, shaped by gavelkind, where the gentry were numerous but possessed only modest estates. Each family was represented by many branches; hence the saying that 'all Kentish men are cousins'.

The charge against elder brothers of stinted and even grudging hospitality to their relations rings true. Inflation had straitened their resources and raised the cost of keeping relatives. They faced many temptations to vie with their fellows in conspicuous consumption. The measures taken by the nobility to meet competing claims on their income, as Professor Stone has demonstrated, included a reduction in the size of their retinues. Households employing between 100 and 400 servants in the sixteenth century made do with between 30 and 50 by the mid-seventeenth century.[19] By the same token it is reasonable to guess that the gentleman's household was also curtailed; certainly, the complaints of contemporary pamphleteers about declining hospitality seem to be directed at them as much as at any other class. If, then, there was truth in the charge that younger brothers were being elbowed out of place in their elder brothers' houses, they suffered a double hardship, since it was at this time that their chances of picking up a job as a servant in a noble house were also disappearing. Their two prospects of enjoying a life of comfort and leisure without hard work were destroyed at one blow.

What of the professional occupations available to them? The church, ap Robert tells us, was now less attractive than before. There were no longer any monasteries, and the church was no longer attracting many recruits from the gentry. Christopher Hill's work on

---

[19] L. Stone, *op. cit.*, pp. 212–13.

The Economic Problems of the Church offers two explanations for this development: the gentry were losing interest in this career because the financial rewards in the lower ranks of the profession, at least, were not keeping pace with the rise in the cost of living; and, since the intellectual demands made upon the parson were steadily rising, the gentry's sons were suffering from the competition of educated men of lowlier birth.[20]

This competition between the gentry and middle classes touches upon the larger crisis in the universities, which has already been discussed by Professor Mark Curtis in his study of alienated intellectuals in early Stuart England. The vigour and effectiveness of the universities at this time created new problems for the men they educated. More and more were being trained for offices in church and state without any corresponding increase in the number of jobs.[21] Not all the disappointed young men who failed to find a satisfying career for the exercise of their talents were younger sons of gentlemen. But since the conventions of family life among the gentry class did not threaten the eldest sons with unemployment—they were fully occupied in managing and enjoying their estates—it was the younger sons who were the only competitors from this class in the labour market. As the pamphleteers explained with monotonous regularity, fathers felt that they had discharged their obligations if they gave their younger sons a good education. It was they who constituted a high proportion, perhaps even a majority, of the alienated intellectuals of seventeenth-century England.[22]

The last three occupations for gentlemen, mentioned by ap Robert, which had formerly 'advanced many more than now they do' were those of merchant, soldier, and courtier. Many younger sons continued to be apprenticed to merchants, and there is nothing to suggest that trade was acquiring a social stigma which deterred recruits. But it is probably true that merchants in international trade, at least, found it more of an uphill task in the seventeenth than in the early and mid-sixteenth century. Political and economic trends made business more hazardous, and the youthful apprentice, who

[20] Christopher Hill, *The Economic Problems of the Church* (Oxford, 1956), pp. 108 ff., 206 ff.

[21] Mark Curtis, 'The Alienated Intellectuals of early Stuart England', *Past and Present*, no. 23 (1962), pp. 25–41.

[22] The proportion of younger to elder sons of the gentry at the university is discussed, but not settled, in Joan Simon, 'The Social Origins of Cambridge Students, 1603–40', *Past and Present*, no. 26 (Nov., 1963), p. 62; L. Stone, 'The Educational Revolution in England, 1540–1640', *Past and Present*, no. 28 (July, 1964), p. 63.

embarked on this career, could not feel such whole-hearted hopes as the aspirant of an earlier generation. For the soldier expectations of rapid advancement in England were small, and so those who persisted in this career went to the Low Countries as mercenaries. Whether the pickings at Court were less plentiful in the later years of James I's reign is not certain. James I's finances were precarious, and opportunities for honour and profit were not expanding. Of a positive reduction in court offices, there is no evidence. But for other reasons the serious-minded politician may well have found the life at James's court less satisfying than under Elizabeth.[23]

The significant omissions from ap Robert's list of careers for younger sons were medicine and law. Medicine was only just beginning to attract the sons of gentry. Its status in the hierarchy of the professions was still ambiguous, mainly because it drew recruits from two layers of society—from among the humble apothecaries, without formal education, but with a good working knowledge of the uses of herbs and of the latest imported drugs, and from among graduates educated either at English universities or abroad.[24] Law, on the other hand, was among the most popular careers for gentlemen's sons and offered a comfortable niche to increasing numbers. Contemporary jibes at this 'Egyptian plague of caterpillars' are too well known to require repetition. It is sufficient to say that with every passing decade their enemies grew more eloquent in denouncing them.[25]

It cannot be said that occupations were lacking in the early seventeenth century for younger sons with the will to work, and it would be idle to pretend that anyone was forced to be unemployed. Sir George Sondes unwittingly enumerated most of the openings available to them (though he omitted the church) when he described in 1655 what he had done in his early life to launch his brother and step-brothers on their careers. One brother received an annuity of £100 and studied law. The eldest step-brother received an annuity of £100 and chose to travel. Another, who was 'something of a scholar', went to Leyden to study medicine; another went as a soldier to the

[23] Professor Aylmer's study of office-holders lends support to the pamphleteer's argument for Charles I's reign when some economical reforms were attempted but not for James I's reign. G. Aylmer, 'Office Holdings as a Factor in English History, 1625–42', *History*, 44 (1959), p. 233.

[24] R. S. Roberts, 'The Personnel and Practice of Medicine in Tudor and Stuart England, Part 1, The Provinces', *Medical History VI*, i (1962), pp. 363, 369, 375.

[25] See, for example, *A Modest Plea for an Equal Commonwealth against Monarchy*, 1659, B. M. Thomason Tracts, E999 (11), pp. 71–2.

Low Countries and received money to buy his promotion; another was apprenticed to a merchant; another to a merchant of the Russia Company; yet another to a woollen draper in the City of London.[26]

The law, the army, medicine, the church, and trade could all find a place for younger sons of gentlemen in the early seventeenth century, if they were willing to work. Other more novel propositions were also canvassed. The planting of settlements in northern Ireland had been commended in Elizabeth's reign as a means of occupying younger brothers who were no longer able to enter the monasteries. Colonization schemes for the New World were advocated in 1623 as a means of finding 'worthy employment for many younger brothers and brave gentlemen now ruined for want thereof'.[27] But the habit of working for a living was not ingrained in younger sons of this class, and no amount of argument could convince them of the justice of treating them so differently from their elder brothers. The contrast was too sharp between the life of an elder son, whose fortune was made for him by his father, and who had nothing to do but maintain, and perhaps augment it, and that of the younger sons who faced a life of hard and continuous effort, starting almost from nothing. Many persistently refused to accept their lot, and hung around at home, idle, bored, and increasingly resentful.

Although John ap Robert's essay proved popular with the reading public, it did not offer any very constructive remedies for the plight of younger sons. In its first pages the author had suggested that the law should be amended. But as his argument proceeded he came to the conclusion that fathers had all the remedies they needed within their grasp. They merely had to be persuaded to exercise powers they already possessed of devising land as they pleased. This argument may, indeed, have persuaded some individuals to alter the provision of their wills, but its general effect was not noticeable.

The situation deteriorated visibly during the Civil War and Interregnum. Parliamentarians and Royalists all suffered financial hardships, which were liable to fall unequally on their children. A steady stream of petitions, directly or indirectly reflecting on penniless younger sons, flowed into Westminster. Fathers had

---

[26] 'Sir George Sondes, his Plaine Narrative to the World . . . . 1655', Harleian Miscellany (London, 1813), X, p. 54.

[27] *A Letter sent by I. B. Gentleman unto his very frende, Mayster R. C. Esq. wherein is conteined a large Discourse of the peopling and inhabiting the Cuntrie called the Ardes, and other adjacent in the North of Ireland* . . . (London, 1572), (no page numbers); Exeter City MSS. Ref. in H.M.C. vol. 73, City of Exeter MSS, p. 167. I am indebted to Mr. J. P. Cooper for this reference.

sacrificed their fortunes in the Parliamentary cause by making loans
or taking up posts for which Parliament failed to pay the salaries; or
they were taxed, sequestrated, and decimated for their Royalist or
recusant sympathies.[28] Clearly, the gentry were still wedded to the
idea of advancing their eldest sons at the expense of the rest, and as
their resources were now much reduced, younger sons were worse off
than ever before. At this point the Levellers took up the cudgels on
their behalf.

It is at first sight surprising to find the Levellers so exercised by a
matter which was entirely the concern of the gentry and noble
classes.[29] But William Walwyn and John Lilburne were both younger
sons of modest gentry families, and the Leveller movement was
heterogeneous in composition, drawing support from this class as
well as from the urban tradesmen and independent peasantry. Their
proposals for modifying the rule of primogeniture figured in a
broader programme for the reform of the law, which the Levellers
considered a matter of the greatest urgency. An ambitious prospectus
drawn up in 1649, proposed among other things that the rule of
primogeniture be modified so that elder sons should have two-thirds
of their father's inheritance, and the rest be equally divided between
the rest of the children.[30] It was a modest proposal in the right
direction.

The tide of Leveller hopes surged swiftly forward between 1647 and
1649, but it quickly ebbed away. This issue, however, did not pass
into oblivion in the fifties. Indeed, the year 1655 saw the outline of a
gentlemanly pressure group casting its shadow across the pages of the
ephemeral pamphlet literature. A younger brother, calling himself
Champianus Northtonus, wrote a tract entitled *The Younger
Brother's Advocate, or a Line or two for Younger Brothers with their
Petition to Parliament.* The last words of the title suggest that a
petition to Parliament was actively under consideration in 1654 or
1655, but I have failed to find any other evidence for it at this date.[31]

[28] See, for example, *CSPD*, 1656–7, p. 277; *CSPD*, 1655, pp. 63, 311.
[29] The Diggers turned the terms 'elder brother' and 'younger brother' into
synonyms for the propertied, and unpropertied classes. Covetous landlords and lords
of manors generally were referred to as elder brothers and the poor commoners,
cheated of their commons, as younger brothers. B. M. Thomason Tracts E557 (9);
E669, f. 15 (23).
[30] B. M. Thomason Tracts E541 (16): *The Representative of Divers Well-Affected
Persons in and about the City of London*, 1649, p. 15.
[31] B. M. Thomason Tracts E234 (5). It does not seem to be connected with the
petition to Parliament in June 1652 'signed by many thousands and setting forth the
miseries of the war endured by them', although this does complain of 'unjust descents

The author, disappointed in his hopes of reform of the law through Parliament, had decided to argue the case in print. A series of statements followed which made more explicit than ever before the miserable plight of younger brothers. The very name, he averred, was a word of such contempt that younger sons often wished they had been born sons of yeomen. (We may surely infer from this that the problem was in truth peculiar to the gentry and wealthier classes.) If a kindly father granted his younger sons a small competence, it was commonly insufficient or they could not use it to best advantage. They had been deprived by their ancestors of the monastery as a possible retreat. The idea of living in the household of an elder brother in subservience to him had become wholly distasteful and in practice unworkable; the younger was at the mercy of the elder brother's humours and upon the slightest pretext found himself 'cashiered and left to the four winds'. Younger brothers had no prospects; they must remain bachelors, or if they married, keep their children in poverty.[32] The author's final rallying call to younger sons was a plan for action if their appeal to Parliament failed. They should seek a plantation abroad where they could frame a policy and a government 'according to our own mode and establish decrees and constitutions of our own'.[33]

The idea of a more egalitarian commonwealth on the Leveller model lurks in the background of this pamphlet, but its arguments bear stronger marks of having been written by a younger son of the gentry class with a personal axe to grind. Indeed, we may wonder whether Champianus Northtonus is not perhaps a pseudonym for the younger son of a Northamptonshire gentleman, for Northamptonshire was one of the best examples of a county where primogenitire stabilized and preserved a small group of rich county families while steadily squeezing out the lesser ones.

Leveller opinions continued to find expression, and in 1659 another pamphlet kept the debate alive within the wider context in which the Levellers chose to place it. A discussion on forms of government, written by William Sprigge, another younger son, and entitled *A Modest Plea for an Equal Commonwealth against Monarchy* contained an appendix with a title which makes plain the general drift of the argument: *An Apology for Younger Brothers, the Restitution of*

to the eldest son only'. Bulstrode Whitelock's *Memorials of the English Affairs* . . . (Oxford, 1853), III, p. 434. I owe this reference to Mr. Keith Thomas.
[32] Thomason E234 (5), *op. cit.*, ff. 2, 4–5, 15.
[33] *Ibid.*, f. 16.

Gavelkind, and Relief of the Poor. It treated the plight of younger sons as an illustration of the evils of allowing land to be engrossed in the hands of a few. Had anything been gained, its author asked bitterly, by throwing down bishops when all their lands were accumulating in the hands of elder brothers? The distribution of wealth was as unequal as ever. The hereditary nobility were as privileged as ever, and would continue to maintain their position as long as the rule of primogeniture was preserved.[34] In consequence, younger sons swelled the numbers of claimants for poor relief. The monasteries had long since ceased to entomb 'those of a less mercurial genius', and now the bishops and the court had gone as well, leaving nothing to take their place. The professions were overstocked: the lawyers were far too numerous and were driven to make their living by multiplying suits. Final blow of all, trade was dead and gave no encouragement to hopeful merchants' apprentices. Education, it concluded, had become a curse instead of a blessing. Two constructive suggestions to relieve the poverty of this section of the community were to set up Protestant monasteries to encourage chastity and the single life among the poorer sort; and to institute gavelkind throughout the kingdom. Gavelkind, the author boldly asserted, was the ancient custom of the island before it was subjugated to the Norman yoke, but it had survived only in Kent. It might be thought necessary to give eldest sons a double portion or some other advantage, but gavelkind was clearly the answer.[35]

In the varied arguments of these pamphlets published between 1618 and 1660 we have a discussion covering most aspects of the problem of younger sons. Legally, there was nothing to prevent the bulk of land being divided among all children. But a convention had grown up among the gentry class, which had gradually hardened into a kind of law, favouring primogeniture and preventing the wider practice of partible inheritance. Even the lawyers most strongly in favour of primogeniture could not base it clearly and firmly in the law. John Page, a one-time Master of Chancery and doctor of civil law who wrote an angry reply to John ap Robert's work, tried hard in legal verbiage to impress but could not persuade. Indeed, the weakness of his argument was a strong defence of his opponent's

---

[34] Thomason Tracts E999 (11), Epistle to the Reader, and p. 59. These remarks echo the view put forward in Harrington's *Oceana* that it is only when land is partitioned that 'a nobility cannot grow'. *James Harrington's Oceana*, ed. S. B. Liljegren (Lund, 1924), p. 90.

[35] Thomason Tracts E999 (11), ff. 59, 64, 69–70.

case. He admitted the existence of the problem of younger sons: parents left too small annuities to them, and, since they were not trained to labour, they were driven into dishonest courses in consequence. 'I heartily wish it were otherwise and that parents would be better advised,' he observed lamely. Page did not accept ap Robert's interpretation of the law: he held that the Bible, canon, and civil law all supported the doctrine of primogeniture; but the law was not dogmatic or extreme—it did not absolve fathers of the duty of providing something for all their children. In fact, our Master of Chancery's conclusions were nothing but a gentle assertion of tendencies in the law that were in no way emphatic or positive.[36]

In practice, if not in theory, then, the law was depriving younger sons of any inheritance save perhaps an annuity which terminated on their death and did not benefit their descendants. The extent of public sympathy for younger sons was made abundantly clear in 1655 when rumours and flysheets 'raised a dust in Maidstone and the adjacent parts' following the murder of George Sondes, elder son of Sir George Sondes of Lees Court, near Faversham, Kent, by his younger brother Freeman. The public leapt to the conclusion that Freeman was a deprived younger son, ill-treated by his father, despised and rejected by his elder brother. The rumours were so wild that Sir George Sondes, the unhappy father, was stung into writing a circumstantial account of the upbringing of his two sons in which he described their contrasted temperaments, and their petty quarrels. It is one of the most moving testaments of a tender, not to say indulgent, seventeenth-century parent, who fervently upheld the spirit of gavelkind in its ancient stronghold. Both boys had been equally cherished, more especially since their mother had borne and lost many children, but the elder was of a gentle, amiable disposition, the younger was envious and quarrelsome. And it was true that in a moment of anger their father had reminded the younger boy that if he died, he would be beholden to his elder brother.[37]

This tragic story contained a clear lesson for society. It brought home the social waste and the social danger of rearing and educating younger sons without assuring them an acceptable place in society as adults. A number of careers were open to them, but if they showed no spontaneous interest in them, there were no strong conventions compelling them to take up work. Freeman Sondes had received a

[36] Thomason Tracts E1669 (3), p. 34 *et passim*.
[37] Harleian Miscellany, X, pp. 40, 52–3, 59–61.

good education at school and university. When the plans for his brother's Tour of Europe were made he did not want to travel, and so it was arranged that he should enter the Inns of Court. But when political unrest in France caused his elder brother to abandon his plans, Freeman declined to go to London, deciding 'to keep with his brother'. His father pressed him to study law, to become a merchant, or take up some employment. He rejected every suggestion. On the eve of his execution, Freeman recognized the root cause of his tragedy. His message to the world contained two injunctions: that all gentlemen should read the Bible frequently and pray daily; and that parents should 'not suffer their sons to live in idleness (which exposes a man to temptation) but to employ them in some honest public calling'.[38]

The tragedy of Freeman Sondes brought to the centre of the stage one younger son more desperate and wretched than the rest. But in the fifties thoughtful people reflecting on the causes of the Civil War and the uneasy peace nursed a suspicion that this political unrest was much aggravated by the resentment of the gentry's younger sons. William Sprigge, the author of *The Modest Plea for an Equal Commonwealth* (1659), attributed the 'murmurings of the common-wealth' to their discontent, which was made more dangerous by their education in arming them with formidable weapons for revenge. The English system of inheritance, he hinted darkly, was the cause of many shakings and convulsions of these later ages. Who could blame younger sons, if, in their valiant efforts to build up their own fortunes, they purchased the ruin of the commonwealth's peace and govern-ment?[39]

There was doubtless some truth in all this. Younger sons were brought up as members of a class which expected to supply the majority of political leaders, and influential administrators in local government. They received an education which qualified them to follow the example of their fathers in this respect. But the doors which seemed to be thrown wide in their youth, were shut upon them when they reached their majority. Did these experiences drive them into extreme positions in the Civil War? There are hints in the history of the Kentish gentry during the Interregnum that this was so—that younger sons tended to take up extreme partisan positions, either in the Cavalier or the Parliamentary party, and to eschew the

---

[38] *Ibid.*, pp. 53–4, 64, 39.
[39] Thomason Tracts E999 (11), *op. cit.*, pp. 61, 63.

moderation of those who were financially comfortable and secure.[40] But this question can only be broached here; it would probably be more profitably explored in counties where primogeniture exerted a stronger influence.

By the late 1650s the subject of younger sons bade fair to become a controversial political issue worthy of discussion in Parliament. Francis Osborne in an ambiguous passage in his *Advice to a Son, The Second Part* (1658) seemed to view the prospect of a solution pessimistically so long as elder brothers formed the majority in all Parliaments.[41] But public opinion was nevertheless being guided towards the notion of serious debate. William Somner, a Kentish scholar, published in 1660 his *Treatise of Gavelkind, both Name and Thing*—an attempt inspired by antiquarian interest to trace the historical development of the custom in Kent. Although without ostensible propaganda purpose, it nevertheless bore upon the possibility of changing the law.[42] A second treatise on gavelkind with more direct allusions to the social consequences of primogeniture and gavelkind was being written at the same time by Silas Taylor. Taylor was a former Captain in the Parliamentary army, and a sequestrator in Herefordshire. At the Restoration he was saved from ruin by the intervention of Royalist friends whom he had obliged during the Interregnum, and as a commissary for ammunition accompanied Sir Edward Harley, father of Robert Harley, to Dunkirk in 1660. His book on gavelkind was dedicated to Sir Edward, 'his much honoured patron'. Already under way when Somner's treatise appeared, Taylor's study was almost certainly prompted, in part, at least, by his observations of the custom of gavelkind in operation in the Irchenfield district of Herefordshire. Other examples he drew from a much wider area of England than Somner and from Europe too, and

[40] This subject is lightly touched on in A. M. Everitt, *The Community of Kent and the Great Rebellion, 1640–60* (Leicester, 1966), p. 101. Thomas Fuller also emphasized the single-mindedness of younger brothers in their pursuit of a fortune, though in more peaceful times, in *The Holy State* (Cambridge, 1642), p. 49. 'They make the court their calling and study the mystery thereof, whilst elder brothers, divided betwixt the court and the country, can have their endeavours deep in neither, which run in a double channel.'

[41] Or did his words mean that younger sons were in the majority in the House of Commons and that hope of reform was imminent? His style of writing was tortuous, and it is impossible to be sure. B. M. Thomason Tracts E1887 (2). In the Long Parliament and the Rump, roughly a quarter of members were younger sons. D. Brunton and D. H. Pennington, *Members of the Long Parliament* (London, 1954), p. 45.

[42] William Somner, *A Treatise of Gavelkind, both Name and Thing* (London, 1660), pp. 91, 98–9, 77, 81. The treatise was written in 1647.

interspersed were comments which underlined the contrasting consequences of different inheritance customs for the structure of society. He even pointed a moral for the benefit of the English colonists in America, particularly in Virginia, for he aligned himself with those who believed that gavelkind was a proper custom for planting and settling an uninhabited country, but held that in well-populated kingdoms it caused the destruction of lands and lineage. On several grounds this work has greater interest for the historian than Somner's. Although it was not finally published until 1663, it clearly embodies arguments arising from the debates of the late fifties.[43]

The subject of inheritance customs, then, was under active discussion and investigation when Cromwell's death thrust it into the background. The Restoration of Charles II brightened the horizon for younger sons, for overnight the hopes of buying or begging preferment at court were revived, bishops were reinstated, and advancement in the church once more became a practical possibility. In the later seventeenth and early eighteenth centuries some professions were upgraded and some new ones came into existence, thus affording further relief to younger sons. The practitioners of medicine and surgery won a higher status for themselves. So did the solicitors, differentiating themselves from the lawyers, and asserting their claims to be equally useful and respectable members of society. The navy became a profession; the land stewards turned themselves into a profession which was amongst the most highly paid of any in the eighteenth century. Meanwhile, merchandise continued as before to accommodate a substantial number of younger sons; indeed, it was alleged by one pamphleteer that the Turkey trade was 'managed by the younger sons of our gentry'.[44]

[43] Silas Taylor, *The History of Gavelkind with the Etymology thereof* (London, 1663), *passim*, but especially the Preface and pp. 151, 27, 81. Some of Taylor's judgements—for example, 'I believe there is scarce a county in England but hath this tenure (i.e. gavelkind) more or less' (p. 151) rings true in the light of modern research. On customs of inheritance in the American colonies, see G. L. Haskins, 'The Beginnings of Partible Inheritance in America', *Yale Law Jnl*, LI (1941-2), pp. 1280 ff.

[44] Sir George Clark, *A History of The Royal College of Physicians*, vol. II (Oxford, 1966), pp. 435-7. For examples of bishops and doctors among the Dorset gentry, see J. P. Ferris, 'The Gentry of Dorset on the Eve of the Civil War', *Genealogist's Mag.*, XV, no. 3 (1965), p. 106; G. E. Mingay, 'The Eighteenth-Century Land Steward', *Land, Labour, and Population in the Industrial Revolution*, ed. E. L. Jones and G. E. Mingay (London, 1967), pp. 8-9; *The Interest of England considered in an Essay upon Wool, on Woollen Manufactures, and the Improvement of Trade* (1694), p. 28. The occupations of younger sons in Kent and Northamptonshire are compared in A. M. Everitt, 'Social Mobility', *Past and Present*, no. 33 (1966), pp. 60, 67-8.

Meanwhile the citadel of primogeniture, far from falling to the attack of younger sons, was strengthened into a seemingly impregnable fortress, thanks to the increase of entails and the legal devices used to safeguard them. Professor Habakkuk's analysis of the landed families of Bedfordshire and Northamptonshire is the classic illustration of how the wealthiest nobility and gentry closed their ranks with the aid of the strict settlement. Nevertheless this legal device, widely used after 1660, conferred certain benefits on younger sons by ensuring that some financial provision was made for them even before they were born, and in such a way that elder sons were unable to frustrate it. Since elder sons could not sell or give away land, the portion given to younger sons was usually a cash sum. It killed vain hopes, since the sum was sealed and settled at the marriage of the parents, but at least it guaranteed to younger sons a sum of money with which they could make a start in business or a profession.[45] As the tide flowed ever more strongly in favour of the preservation of undivided estates, younger sons turned their attention more and more to exploiting the rise of the professions.

Faint echoes of the livelier debates of the 1650s returned fitfully. Although some writers continued to point to the professions and trade as sufficient to meet the needs of younger sons, these did not satisfy everyone. Carew Reynel, for example, proposing ways of stimulating the economy in the 1670s still deplored the lack of employment for young gentlemen, and urged some novel system of financial relief for them. Josiah Child, a wealthy and highly experienced merchant in the East India trade, held up for admiration the custom of gavelkind in Holland, arguing that primogeniture and poor commercial opportunities in England still obliged many young men to remain bachelors.[46] The debate did not again move into the political arena at Westminster until the mid-nineteenth century.[47]

[45] H. J. Habakkuk, 'Marriage Settlements in the Eighteenth Century', *Trans. R.H.S.*, Fourth Ser., XXXII (1950), pp. 15 ff.; 'English Landownership, 1680–1740', *Econ. Hist. Rev.*, first ser., X (1939–40), pp. 6–7 *et passim*.

[46] Carew Reynel, *The True English Interest* (London, 1674), p. 72; E. Chamberlayne, *Angliae Notitia* (London, 1669), pp. 487, 512; Josiah Child, *A New Discourse on Trade* (London, 1693), pp. 2, 29. Bachelorhood may have been more common among Catholics than Protestants, since professional openings for Catholics were fewer. See Rosamond Meredith, 'A Derbyshire Family in the Seventeenth Century: the Eyres of Hassop and their Forfeited Estates', *Recusant History*, VIII, no. 1 (1965), pp. 56–7.

[47] Thomas Robinson published a handbook on gavelkind in Kent and Borough English in 1741. It began as a guide for his own use in legal practice, but it contained some personal judgements on the, to him undesirable, social effects of gavelkind in bringing people 'to a low kind of country living', and encouraging them to neglect the 'greater advantages of enriching themselves and the kingdom', *The Common Law of Kent* (London, 1741), pp. 23–4.

The history of the younger sons of the gentry touches tangentially on so many aspects of economic and social life, religion and law that it is surprising that historians have not yet confronted it directly. This article has concentrated on one chapter in that history—the political debate in the first half of the seventeenth century. It has used recent work on the professions to illuminate, and in general to support, the polemical arguments of the pamphleteers. But many of their allegations cannot yet be substantiated for lack of sufficient knowledge of the testamentary conventions of the gentry, not only in the sixteenth and seventeenth centuries, but, more important perhaps, in the fifteenth. More family histories that take all children, and not merely the eldest, into their purview are sorely needed. Without them we shall never be able to measure fully the actual problems of younger sons against the polemical literature.

Finally, to give the seventeenth-century debate a longer perspective, it may be helpful to offer a brief reminder of the later phase of the debate on younger sons. A fresh campaign was waged in the House of Commons against the tyranny of primogeniture by Mr. Locke King between 1850 and 1869. He did not win sufficient support to secure a change in the law, but a debate continued spasmodically in print and in Parliament into the late seventies.[48] As in the seventeenth century, it was accompanied by renewed discussion on the dearth of careers open to younger sons of the gentry and middle-classes, now passing in increasing numbers through the public schools, but emerging still unfitted for a working life, though well equipped to play cricket and write classical verse. Some now blamed the content of their education, others, including Thomas Hughes, who had done so much to spread the fame of the public schools in *Tom Brown's Schooldays*, blamed society. In 1879 Hughes collected a capital sum of £150,000 and launched a colony to provide a home and a living for younger sons in a deserted spot in Tennessee, to be known as Rugby. The tennis and drama clubs flourished exceedingly, and the fishing was excellent, but no one wanted to work. The vine-growing, poultry-farming, and horse-breeding, the brick and tile works, and the canning factory all failed. The local paper described the set-up in biting, satirical terms: 'They are Englishmen of culture and refinement, and at one period their supply of Worcester sauce became

---

[48] An instructive debate in print includes the following: G. C. Brodrick, 'The Law and Custom of Primogeniture', *Cobden Club Essays*, 2nd Ser. (London, 1872); C. S. Kenny, *The History of the Law of Primogeniture in England* (Cambridge, 1878); Eyre Lloyd, *The Succession Laws of Christian Countries* (London, 1877).

exhausted and their agonies were terrible to witness. But even this disaster was followed by a greater. This was the failure of London Punch to arrive on time . . . Then again the country was not favourable for the playing of lawn tennis. This, of course, had a most depressing effect on the pioneers in culture, high art, and mutton chop whiskers.' The scheme fell in ruins in 1881.[49] Would Champianus Northtonus, who had had a similar idea in 1655, have been any more successful? The solution to the dilemma of younger sons plainly did not lie here. It came instead several generations later, with the change in the law of property in 1925, the emergence of our managerial society, and the further proliferation of the professions.

POSTSCRIPT

For other, more recent discussions of this theme, see D. R. Hainsworth, 'Manor House to Counting House: the Gentry Younger Son in Trade in the Seventeenth Century', in F. McGregor and N. Wright, eds., *European History and its Historians*, Adelaide, 1977.

L. A. Montrose, ' "The Place of a Brother" in *As You Like It:* Social Process and Comic Form', *Shakespeare Quarterly*, 32, 1981.

---

[49] M. B. Hamer, 'Thomas Hughes and his "American Rugby",' *North Carolina Hist. Rev.*, V (1928), pp. 391–413; Edward C. Mack and W. H. G. Armytage, *Thomas Hughes. The Life of the Author of Tom Brown's Schooldays* (London, 1952), pp. 227–41.

XX

THE EUROPEAN DEBATE ON CUSTOMS OF INHERITANCE, 1500–1700

ANY discussion of the inheritance practices of the upper classes in the sixteenth and seventeenth centuries calls for a preliminary survey of the considerably body of European literature on primogeniture produced at the same time. Most of it takes the form of legal treatises, and is part of a genre of legal dissertations that attempt to sum up present law and custom. But it may be possible to learn more from them than this. They are a quite new literary form in the sixteenth century, and they contain more than factual statements on the law of primogeniture; they include arguments for and against primogeniture, and some brief observations on its consequences. Do they shed any light on assumptions, expectations, or changing practices?

This brief essay does not dig very far below the surface. Many of the treatises are not available in English libraries. One needs to have deeper knowledge than the present writer concerning the testamentary preferences of the upper classes, especially in Spain, France, and Germany, before the treatises were written, in order to judge actual practices against the lawyers' statements on practice; specialists in the study of the European nobility and gentry are needed to illuminate these aspects of the question. But it may broaden our perspective if the debate is summarized, and some suggestions are offered concerning its significance.

The treatises are lawyers' statements about inheritance practices, but the writers were not simply lawyers. Some were administrators in government, and hence were intelligent observers and thinkers on the practical consequences of current practice. They necessarily had opinions, and the writing of such essays could not be divorced from practical considerations.

However, it is necessary to be cautious when interpreting these treatises. Mary Dewar has some sobering remarks on what should, and should not, be read into Sir Thomas Smith's description of the workings of the English Commonwealth (*De Republica Anglorum*,

1565),[1] and the same cautionary words could be uttered with regard to the many treatises *De Iure Primogenito*. Stimulated by his personal observations of French governmental institutions (he was in France on government business in 1551, 1562–6, 1567, and 1572), Sir Thomas Smith planned to describe the government of England in order to make clear 'the principal points wherein it doth differ from the policy or government at this time used in France, Italy, Spain, Germany, and all other countries which do follow the civil law of the Romans'. He wished to illustrate those 'points wherein the one [country] differeth from the other, to see who hath taken the righter, truer and more commodious way to govern the people as well in war as in peace'. In Smith's work, says Miss Dewar, 'we are listening to a learned civilian expounding the formal structure of English society, not the experienced Secretary analysing the realities of power'. Smith was, of course, an experienced Secretary of State, perfectly capable of analysing the realities of power, yet that experience was firmly kept out of his text. Later historians have claimed for Smith a special place in the development of the concept of the sovereignty of Parliament, reading into his words meanings which were not there. We may be tempted to read more into the writings on primogeniture than is really there.

Nevertheless, primogeniture was practised in many different European countries, and it prompted comparisons. Like the constitution, it demanded to be judged by its long-term practical consequences. The writers of treatises strove, like Sir Thomas Smith, to separate theory from practice. They described the rule of primogeniture formally, but did not describe reality in detail. How much, then, do contemporaries betray in their writings of their concern for inheritance customs?

The first noticeable fact is that civilians in the sixteenth and seventeenth centuries wanted to write on primogeniture when no one pontificated on it in the fifteenth century. This is surely significant. Moreover, by the very fact that they were writing down something on the law, they were pressing for its acceptance and promoting conformity. They admitted that primogeniture was not observed by everyone; it therefore had to be justified. No matter how hard kings and princes were trying to commit their descendants and their subjects to primogeniture, moral pressures were being ignored. English writers explained how primogeniture was evaded in England.

[1] Mary Dewar, *Sir Thomas Smith. A Tudor Intellectual in Office* (London, 1964), pp. 111–13.

Nevertheless, they wrote in the conviction that primogeniture was the right and proper practice for great families. Every treatise went out of its way to justify it. No writer hammered his argument home, but by gentler methods of debate, usually by question and answer, each spoke with authority, and helped to harden attitudes in its favour.

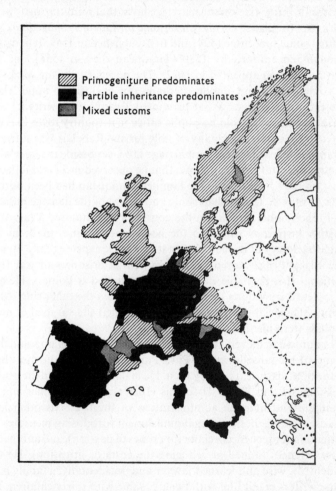

Figure 1. Inheritance customs in Western Europe (after Wilhelm Abel, *Agrarpolitik,* by permission of Vandenhoeck & Ruprecht)

Note: This is the only attempt of its kind to map inheritance customs and the results are of course extremely generalised. Every country could show refined regional distinctions.

Among the first authorities on primogeniture, quoted by all subsequent writers, was André Tiraqueau, of whose early life little is known except that he was born at Fontenay-le-Comte, capital of Lower Poitou, and spent most of his life there as *juge-châtelain* and then as *lieutenant*. He first attracted attention with an essay written at the age of thirty-five on the marriage laws, that went through twelve editions. His treatise *On the Nobility and the Law of Primogeniture* was written some time after 1524, and first published in 1549. It had gone through ten editions by 1580 (Tiraqueau died in 1558), and the fifteenth edition appeared in 1622.[2] The popularity of the work tells us something about public, perhaps not exclusively upper class, interest in the subject. What prompted Tiraqueau to write it?

He was a lawyer holding public office in a country town that was noted for its select company of able jurists. Rabelais was a friend. Tiraqueau's first treatise on marriage laws, set beside the later work on primogeniture, clearly shows that he observed most and reflected most on the fortunes of noble families. Tiraqueau had been born in 1488; it may be that he had some knowledge of the damage inflicted on French noble families in the course of the Hundred Years War. English historians dwell on the handsome fortunes made by the English gentry out of the war, but it was at the expense of the French. The Black Prince raised £20,000 by selling prisoners of war from Poitiers.[3] It is probable that Tiraqueau studied at Poitiers. He may have heard something of this experience from the other side. At all events, the social institutions that determined the survival of noble families were his main preoccupation.

Tiraqueau achieved such a reputation that he was appointed by Francis I a counsellor in the Paris Parlement in 1531; he must have been about sixty years old by then. He is said to have won the respect of Francis I and Henry II for his efficiency as a reformer and his equitable and humane administration of the law. His other legal treatises included one on legal punishment (proposing measures for mitigating sentences especially for crimes of passion), and another on petty offences (aimed at reducing the costs of litigation). He was evidently a wise and learned lawyer and, incidentally, a family man; some writers credit him with twenty. some with thirty children. But all in all this biographical information is insufficient to explain Tiraqueau's interest in the law of primogeniture.

[2] For these and the following remarks on Tiraqueau's life, see Jacques Brejon, *André Tiraqueau* (Paris, 1937), *passim; Biographic Universelle*, under Tiraqueau.
[3] G. A. Holmes, *The Later Middle Ages, 1272–1485* (Edinburgh, 1962), p. 162.

In any case, Tiraqueau is not the first writer on the subject. Cooper identified a fifteenth-century Italian jurist, Martini Garrati da Lodi, and all sixteenth-century writers knew of Jean le Cirier, who wrote *Tractatus Singularis de Iure Primogeniturae vel Maioricatus* in 1521. He too was a counsellor in the Paris Parlement, though little seems to be known of his history.[4] The form of the essays by both Le Cirier and Tiraqueau was the same, and it set the pattern for all that followed. They first recited all the Biblical instances of inheritance practices, and decided that the Hebrews partitioned their estates, but that convenience led the Jews in the end to prefer the eldest son. Then followed a series of questions relating to primogeniture in practice: who is the eldest son?—who is the eldest of twins?—should the eldest succeed to the whole patrimony?—what is the correct way to treat adopted sons, bastard sons, etc.? Le Cirier's work passed through a number of editions, of which the British Library has those of 1521, 1549, and 1584. When Tiraqueau's treatise followed, it was much more popular, and more frequently cited.

Two Frenchmen, therefore, stimulate, if they do not start, the literature, but after that it was taken up enthusiastically by the Spaniards. A treatise on primogeniture in Spain was published in 1571 by Christian de Paz de Tenuta, another in 1575 by Melchior Palez a Meris, and another by Didacus de Simancas also in 1575. More Spanish essays followed in 1611 and 1612. German writers began to take an interest in the early seventeenth century: the first was Johannes Mehlbaum's *De Iure Primogeniturae* in 1611, followed by two more in 1614 and 1615. Fifteen treatises by German authors are bound together in one volume in the Bodleian Library.[5] Starting with Mehlbaum, they run on to the last publication in 1740.

The German essays clearly describe a changing situation, which is not made explicit in the French literature. They report on the spread of primogeniture among the German principalities. It was ordained among Electoral families by the Golden Bull of Charles IV in 1356. Other princes gradually adopted it, or strove, not always successfully,

---

[4] J. P. Cooper did not, in the end, mention Garrati de Lodi in his essay, 'Patterns of Inheritance and Settlement by Great Landowners from the Fifteenth to the Eighteenth Centuries', in *Family and Inheritance. Rural Society in Western Europe, 1200–1800*, ed. J. Goody, J. Thirsk, and E. P. Thompson, 1976, pp. 192–327. Mehlbaum described Le Cirier as a counsellor in the Paris Parlement. He does not appear in biographical dictionaries.

[5] The Bodleian Library reference to this volume is Diss. H. 129. The European literature as a whole is listed in J. S. Pütter, *Litteratur des Teutschen Staatsrechts* (Göttingen, 1783), iii, pp. 754ff.

to tie down their successors to adopt it. By natural law, said Mehlbaum, all free men should succeed equally; the children are all the offspring of the same parents. But the division of a kingdom is the worst misfortune that can befall it, and so, amongst the ruling class, it has become the custom to favour the first-born. It is difficult to say what is just and what is unjust in any absolute sense, says Mehlbaum; it depends on the circumstances. Primogeniture has become a strong custom because it has fewest drawbacks. Yet as he admitted, usage differed everywhere. His manner was to coax gently. His discussion was calm and temperate, without passion.

Tiraqueau had taken the same line: the customs of Poitou were one thing, other customs differed. But primogeniture was essential for the preservation of families. Despite certain injustices, it was necessary to tolerate primogeniture because of the common benefit that resulted from it. It prevented the morcellation of property. At the same time French and German writers all stressed in primogeniture the father's duty to provide for his younger sons. Their food should be provided and sometimes a small estate. Elder brothers were far from being the absolute heirs. They held a privileged place in the family, but they had serious obligations towards their younger brothers.

The writers of all these treatises sounded complacent about the growing strength of primogeniture. Clearly they approved of the trend, and by their writing they forwarded it. The stability of the state depended on the existence of well-rooted, well-endowed families commanding authority. The lawyers looked with satisfaction and pleasure on the rock-like solidity of great estates and great noble houses. Superficially all these essays by citizens of different countries in Europe seem to constitute a unified whole, speaking with the same voice, in the same style, and with the same aims. Yet in practice the workings of primogeniture cannot have been the same in all Continental countries. The French were among the first writers on the subject to be widely read; were they defending primogeniture because of some mild questioning of its wisdom? There is nothing polemical in these treatises. But, as Jack Goody points out in his paper, in every society, there is always tension between the equality pushing up from below and the inequality thrusting down from above. The tensions will be weak or strong at different times, and the literature will flourish or wither accordingly. In view of Professor Le Roy Ladurie's description of the growing strength of egalitarian sentiment in France among classes below the nobility, should we interpret the literature on inheritance as a response to mild upper-class apprehension—to put it no stronger—concerning the expediency of primogeniture?

In Germany, on the other hand, the argument in favour of primogeniture plainly had a purpose to bring all principalities into line, establish primogeniture as a rule of inheritance, and so enable princely power to be consolidated along with the stability of the state. The German treatises had an aggressive propagandist purpose, whereas the French may have been written in a more defensive mood. Such an interpretation of the literature, however, must be tentative.

In England, it seems fair to say that primogeniture was noticeably gaining ground among the gentry in the early sixteenth century. The preservation of estates in noble families had been made more effective since the early fourteenth century by means of joint feoffments and family trusts. Within this more secure legal framework, elder sons were advanced, but younger sons were also provided for.[6] These tendencies favouring the eldest son had been somewhat weakened in the later fifteenth century by the use of recoveries to bar entails, but the use made of this device did not challenge the growing primacy of primogeniture. The supporting literature written by jurists in France and Germany, however, did not yet exist in England. What was heard in England at a notably early date in the sixteenth century were rumblings of a controversy against its harsh consequences. It was plainly presented in Thomas Starkey's *Dialogue between Cardinal Pole and Thomas Lupset*, written about 1532–4. Starkey, it should be emphasized, wrote part of it in Italy when he visited Padua in 1533–4.[7] Its argument on customs of inheritance strongly suggests that his travels and discussions in Europe had revealed differences between the workings of primogeniture in England and other countries.

Starkey criticized primogeniture for the injustice of disinheriting younger sons.[8] He was saying this at a time when European writers were underlining the fact that younger sons were *not* disinherited thereby. Was English and Continental practice moving in different directions? Cardinal Pole in the *Dialogue* expressed vehement disapproval: 'utterly to exclude them (i.e. younger sons) from all as

---

[6] G. A. Holmes, *The Estates of the Higher Nobility in Fourteenth-Century England* (Cambridge, 1957), pp. 40–1, 53–4, 57.

[7] G. R. Elton, 'Reform by Statute: Thomas Starkey's Dialogue and Thomas Cromwell's Policy', *British Academy Proc.*, liv (1968), p. 169.

[8] T. Starkey, *Starkey's Life and Letters*, ed. Sidney J. Herrtage (*Early English Text Soc.*, No. 12, 32, 1878), pp. 108–13.

though they had commit some great offence and crime against their parents is plain against reason and seemeth to [di]minish the natural love betwixt them which nature hath so bounden together'. Primogeniture, he concluded was a 'misorder in our politic rule and governance'. The defence of primogeniture fell to Lupset, who claimed that good order and peaceful rule in the realm were promoted by it. People needed heads and governors to temper their unruliness. 'If the lands in every great family were distributed equally betwixt the brethren, in a small process of years the head families would decay and by little and little vanish away. And so the people should be without rulers and heads . . . [whereby] . . . you shall take away the foundation and ground of all our civility. Besides that you shall in process of years confound the nobles and the commons together after such manner that there shall be no difference betwixt the one and the other.' Thus primogeniture preserved a class of people with authority. Pole conceded Lupset's point that the nation needed governors and heads, but he wanted some compulsory legal provision for younger children. This was taken for granted in France, Flanders, and Italy, Lupset pointed out, and hence you never saw younger brothers begging as you did in England. Evidently in England things were working out differently from the theory as accepted on the Continent. Moreover, in England primogeniture had penetrated more deeply into the ranks of society below the nobility. Pole accepted the expediency of this custom of inheritance for princes, dukes, earls, and barons, but he did not think it tolerable among 'all gentlemen of the mean sort. For this bringeth in among the multitude overgreat inequality which is the occasion of dissension and debate'.

In short, Starkey's *Dialogue* seems to bring out two different stages in the development of primogeniture: having taken firm hold in England, it was failing to preserve a just balance between the claims of elder and younger sons; also, it was tending to spread down the social scale to 'gentlemen of the meaner sort'. The two developments were doubtless linked with one another. As lesser gentlemen espoused the idea of primogeniture for the sake of building up their family's status, so some had to neglect the younger children for lack of means to provide handsomely for all. In other European countries where primogeniture was just as strong, for example, among the nobility of France, this extreme development had not occurred.

The difference in the rigour with which primogeniture was adopted in England and other Continental countries seems also to be brought out in the comments of travellers from abroad. They overstated the facts of the English case, but in so doing, they tell us something more of their own prejudices. Lupold von Wedel, travelling in England in 1584 and 1585, said that the eldest sons of the nobility inherited all, while the younger took up some office or pursued highway robbery.[9] An anonymous Italian author in Mary's reign described primogeniture as the preferment of the eldest son leaving the other sons 'with no help from the eldest brother whatsoever'. Though land bought in the father's lifetime was sometimes conferred on younger children, this happened very rarely.[10] Continentals thought the practice in England very harsh compared with what they knew at home.

The literature on primogeniture in England after Starkey was slow to accumulate. People were not galvanized into action until they experienced the practical problems of younger sons of gentlemen almost begging in the streets. Then for several decades they offered solutions that had nothing to do with changing the laws and customs of inheritance, but were much more practical and down-to-earth: they suggested new careers. The settlement of Ireland was recommended in 1566 by Sir Humphrey Gilbert as a means of providing for younger sons.[11] Their misfortunes were referred to by Sir Edwin Sandys in a Parliamentary speech in 1604, and his concern in the matter must surely be linked with his active promotion of the Virginia Company and encouragement of younger sons in that enterprise.[12] On the other hand, it must be remembered that some experiences were pulling men towards another point of view: the Island of Jersey petitioned the Crown in 1617 for liberty to entail estates, 'the island being much weakened by partitions of lands'.[13]

[9] Gottfried von Bülow (trans.), 'Journey through England and Scotland made by Lupold von Wedel in the years 1584 and 1585', *Trans. Roy. Hist. Soc.*, NS. ix (1895), p. 268.

[10] See C. A. Sneyd (ed.), *A Relation... of the Island of England*, Camden Soc., vol. 37 (1847), p. 27, for the evil effects of primogeniture in England; also C. V. Malfatti, *Two Italian Accounts of Tudor England* (Barcelona, 1953), p. 64, though this text seems to be derived from Thomas Wilson's account of primogeniture. See also *Cal. S.P. Venetian*, iv. p. 345 (1551); vi, p. 1670 (1557). These pitying comments on the plight of younger brothers depict a deteriorating situation as the century wears on. Finally in *Cal. S.P. Venetian, 1632–6*, p. 370: 'Equally cruel, not to say unjust, is the law that only one among brothers shall inherit the paternal property.'

[11] D. B. Quinn, *The Elizabethans and the Irish*, Folger Shakespeare Library, Folger Monographs on Tudor and Stuart Civilization (Washington, D.C., 1966), p. 107.

[12] J. R. Scott, *Joint-Stock Companies* (New York, 1951), pp. 123–4.

[13] *Cal. S.P. Domestic, Addenda, 1580–1625*, p. 582.

When the debate took on a much more angry tone in the 1630s, it reverted to a discussion of law and custom and focussed clearly on the gentry class. The inheritance customs of classes below the gentry did not give rise to controversy: practices were as varied as the circumstances of families. Primogeniture in the original sense of advancing the eldest son, but nevertheless providing for the others, was common, perhaps the commonest custom among yeomen and below, but it did not exercise a tyranny. Among the nobility primogeniture was most common, and it seems to have been deemed by common consent the most acceptable practice for family and for state reasons. It reduced strife among brothers when the eldest automatically took the leading position: it maintained the status of the family; and it preserved a class of rulers in society. In general it did not cause excessive hardship to younger sons because the nobility had the means to provide adequately for all. The hardships were felt most keenly among the gentry because their means were not sufficient to provide decently for younger sons. Standards of living had risen sharply among the gentry in the course of the sixteenth century and elder brothers had greater expectations, and could not spare so much for their younger brothers. Younger brothers in their turn required more if they were to maintain social equality, or something approaching it, alongside their elder brothers.[14]

The debate that resumed in the 1630s now produced academic studies similar in form to the Continental treatises. John Selden interested himself in the origins of laws of succession, and wrote *De Successionibus* in 1631, using the Bible to establish the inheritance practices of the Hebrews. His earlier work, *English Janus* (1610), had tried to identify the earliest inheritance practices in Britain. He had decided that partition among sons was usual at the beginning of settlement, and that it remained the custom of the Saxons. It was allowed to continue in Kent after the Conquest, by permission of the Norman kings, and it continued in Wales. Nowhere in all this, however, did Selden make any allusion to the practical issues raised by contemporary customs in England or Europe.[15]

The polemical treatise that was widely read and acclaimed was John ap Robert's *Apology for a Younger Brother*, published in 1634.[16] The author was overwhelmed with indignation at the injustice dealt

[14] For a general discussion of this period, see Chapter XIX above, pp. 335ff.

[15] John Selden, *Opera Omnia*, ed. D. Wilkins, ii, part 1 (London, 1725); *Tracts written by John Selden* (London, 1683).

[16] See Chapter XIX above, pp. 342ff.

out to younger sons of gentlemen. Like the academic writers, he drew on Biblical examples to show that equal shares had been the more favoured usage in the early history of man. He did not make comparison with Continental conventions: indeed, he disclaimed all knowledge of other writings on the subject. But he made it clear that the practice of primogeniture was now thoroughly debased among the English gentry. It gave the bulk of the property to the eldest, and an education or an apprenticeship did not save the younger children from sometimes open poverty. Not surprisingly, this polemical literature increased in quantity during the Interregnum when preferment at court and in the church became impossible and trade was depressed.

The sympathy of many members of Parliament for younger sons raised the hopes of a change in the law of primogeniture in the 1650s, but hopes were disappointed. In one sober and judicious appraisal of the problem by John Page, one-time Master of Chancery and doctor of civil law, replying to the angry polemics of John ap Robert, we see it again presented as something arising out of the debasement of the original concept of primogeniture.[17] It was never envisaged that primogeniture would leave younger sons with a mere pittance. But this was the way things had worked out.

Another dimension had been introduced into the English debate in the second half of the sixteenth century by the experience of colonization first in Ireland and then in America. The plan for New England in 1623 had been commended because it would find 'worthy employment for many younger brothers'.[18] Those younger brothers had now established themselves as landowners in a new country, and so the question arose: how was land to be transmitted after the first grants? An influential book in shaping opinion was H. Lloyd's *History of Cambria*, first published in Welsh in the thirteenth century, and now translated into English and added to by David Powell in 1584 (reprinted in 1602 and 1697). Powell argued that partible inheritance destroyed the Welsh nobility by causing the partition of estates and exacerbating strife between brothers. It was wholly appropriate in places where population was small and land plentiful. 'Partition is very good to plant and settle any nation in a large country not inhabited; but in a populous country already furnished with inhabitants it is the very decay of great families, and (as I said before) the cause of strife and debate.' When Silas Taylor, a one-time captain

[17] John Page, *Ius Fratrum, the Law of Brethren* (London, 1657), *passim*.
[18] *Hist. MSS Commission*, lxxiii, City of Exeter MSS, p. 167.

in the Parliamentary army, published in 1663 *The History of Gavelkind with the Etymology thereof* he quoted these words, and added in the margin, 'I could wish that those renowned English plantations in America would examine of what avail this in probability and policy may be to them and in particular the most famous plantation of Virginia.'[19] His advice came too late, however. By this time Virginia had formally adopted primogeniture.[20] In New England, on the other hand, Powell's point of view on the virtues of partible inheritance when settling a large, new country carried more weight. John Winthrop who had served as an attorney in the Court of Wards for $2\frac{1}{2}$ years before going to New England, disliked primogeniture, and had been responsible for a petition to Parliament in 1624 which enumerated primogeniture among a number of 'common grievances'. He believed it to be 'against all equity'. The Massachusetts legislature subsequently adopted partible inheritance, though it did give the elder son a double share.[21]

The idea of giving the elder son a double portion came from Biblical sources, and leads to a third theme in the debate on inheritance, namely, the positions taken by Catholics and Protestants on the issue. All writers had turned first to the Old Testament for wisdom and guidance, but in fact the Biblical instances were numerous and varied, and did not all point in one direction. In the end, Protestants took up different positions. The attitude of an English Puritan is expressed very firmly in William Gouge's work *Of Domesticall Duties*.[22] A father should love his children equally, but nevertheless give his first-born a greater patrimony than the others. Joseph, the first-born 'of the true wife' had a double portion. There is an excellency in the first-born, as Jacob declared in his words to his eldest son: 'thou art my first born, my might, and the beginning of my strength'. 'Houses and families by this means', Gouge continued, 'are upheld and continued from age to age'. The stability of the Commonwealth consisted in preserving such houses and families. Nevertheless, younger children should be trained for a calling or given land other than the main inheritance. Provision of this sort was essential, and training in a calling was perhaps preferred, since it benefited the

[19] Silas Taylor, *The History of Gavelkind* . . . (London, 1663), p. 27.

[20] C. Ray Keim, 'Primogeniture and Entail in Colonial Virginia', *William and Mary Quarterly*, 3rd ser., 25 (1968), pp. 545ff.

[21] *Winthrop Papers, I, 1498–1628* (Massachusetts Hist. Soc., 1929), p. 306; G. L. Haskins, *Law and Authority in early Massachusetts* (New York, 1960), p. 170.

[22] W. Gouge, *Of Domesticall Duties, Eight Treatises* (London, 1622), pp. 575–9. I wish to thank Dr Roger Richardson for this reference.

state to have trained people who expected to work for their living rather than encouraging young men to live easily on a piece of inherited land.

In Germany Protestant princes read their Bibles carefully and came to a different conclusion. The tradition in favour of partitioning estates among princely families had been strong in the Middle Ages, and although primogeniture gained ground in the sixteenth and early seventeenth centuries, there was much resistance to it. The testament of Duke Johann Wilhelm of Sachsen-Weimar in 1573 weighed up the *pros* and *cons* of primogeniture and partition and decided that partition was God's will, the exact portions of each brother being settled by lot. Philip von Hessen declared in his will that it fell heavily on his conscience to prefer the first-born to the other sons. Some Protestant rulers feared that by espousing primogeniture they would drive their disinherited children into the arms of the Catholic church, for it alone offered the refuge of a monastic life.[23] Religion was so closely bound up with politics that it is perhaps not surprising that Protestants came to such different conclusions.

The literature summarized in this essay reveals contrasting viewpoints on different customs of inheritance, and a pressing concern for their political and social consequences. It is a mirror of the political and social anxieties of the seventeenth century. At the same time, it underlines the fact that primogeniture was not one rule of inheritance, but two. In England it was so strictly operated that younger sons were often left with a pittance or nothing. On the Continent it was not understood as a rule for endowing the eldest son with the whole family estate; rather when lawyers defended it in noble families and urged it upon landowners, they had in mind a system that preferred eldest sons and yet dealt justly with younger sons. Thus interpreted, it seemed to be wholly advantageous to families and to the state. English landowners, especially the gentry, however, had too readily pushed it to extremes, and so were the first to experience the disadvantages of their excessive zeal. The English debate by the middle of the seventeenth century was charged with passion against primogeniture, whereas it was a calmer issue in other European countries.

This seems to be the message of the literature. But it should be

---

[23] Joseph Engelfried, *Der Deutsche Fürstenstand des XVI and XVII Jahrhunderts im Spiegel seiner Testamente, Inaugural-Dissertation . . . der Eberhard-Karls-Universität zu Tübingen*, 1961, pp. 118–26. I wish to thank Dr Henry Cohn for drawing my attention to this thesis.

stressed that the view of it given here is partial. It has concentrated on the academic debate on the Continent, while considering the polemical debate in England. Was there a polemical, popular literature attacking primogeniture in Europe? Did primogeniture in practice in France, Germany, Spain and elsewhere diverge from the seemingly moderate definition officially expounded? These questions have not been explored, though the second of these is illuminated by Mr Cooper's essay. A preliminary survey of the literature does no more than fill in a background, and by giving a glimpse of contemporary opinion, draw attention to controversial features within it.

As far as England is concerned, an explanation is required for the evident abuse of primogeniture in the sixteenth and seventeenth centuries. It may well have been caused by the greater fluidity of English society at this time, compared with the Continent. This dispersed aspirations and *mores* of the nobility too rapidly through the next lower rank of society, fostering pride in family and habits of conspicuous expenditure that could not yet be borne by all gentry on the average gentleman's income.

The English debate about primogeniture, of course, was far from being at an end. In the eighteenth century the aspirations of the gentry filtered down to the next class below, and produced yeomen who followed the rule of primogeniture and, in order to make assurance doubly sure, settled their estates.[24] Primogeniture gained ground among the middle classes and provoked another controversy, centring upon that class, in the nineteenth century. More treatises were written, and fresh comparisons were sought in European experience.[25] Yet another illuminating body of literature was assembled of great value for the study of inheritance practices in Europe in the nineteenth century.

---

[24] John V. Beckett, 'Landownership in Cumbria, c. 1680–1750' (University of Lancaster, Ph.D. Thesis, 1975), pp. 149–50. I wish to thank Dr Beckett for allowing me to quote from his unpublished thesis.

[25] See, *inter alia*, G. C. Brodrick, 'The Law and Custom of Primogeniture', *Cobden Club Essays*, 2nd ser. (London, 1872); C. S. Kenny, *The History of the Law of Primogeniture in England* (Cambridge, 1878); Eyre Lloyd, *The Succession Laws of Christian Countries* (London, 1877).

POSTSCRIPT

References in this essay to other authors' writings on inheritance, notably those by Mr. John Cooper, Professor Jack Goody, and Professor Le Roy Ladurie relate to their papers in *Family and Inheritance. Rural Society in Western Europe, 1200–1800*, ed. Jack Goody, Joan Thirsk, and E. P. Thompson, Cambridge, 1976.

XXI

HORSES IN EARLY MODERN ENGLAND: FOR SERVICE, FOR PLEASURE, FOR POWER

IN an early and rather rambling essay on *War Horses*, first published in 1580, Montaigne interpolated a revealing autobiographical sentence. 'I am loath to dismount when I am in the saddle for it is the place where I am most at home whether I am well or ill'.[1] This admission might equally well have been made by an English gentleman, merchant, tradesman, chapman or farmer.[2] Horses were as indispensable to men as is the car, the lorry, and tractor today, and their companionship in toil, travel and recreation brought much comfort to both: Lady Sarah Lennox was not the only wife who knew that while her husband loved her, he loved his horses more.[3] As for less wealthy men, it is not difficult to understand why they often found it more enjoyable to sit on a padded saddle out in the fresh air, in the silent company of a horse, rather than sitting on a hard bench in a dim room amid the noise of much company.

When we consider the age-long dependence of man on the horse, coupled with the dramatic expansion of economic activity in the early modern period, it is remarkable how little interest historians have shown in the way that horses were made available to meet more insistent and fastidious demands. The two centuries between 1500 and 1700 witnessed a steady rise in the volume of internal trade on roads and rivers, which multiplied the need for horses on both routes. Pack horses and horse-drawn carts had thronged the roads for a long time, but from Elizabeth's reign onwards, they had to make room for long wagons which carried a heavier burden of goods, but also required more horses to draw them.[4] At the same time the expanding

[1] E. J. Trechmann (transl.), *The Essays of Montaigne*, i (1935), p. 282.
[2] A similar sentiment was expressed by Henry Peacham in *The Worth of a Peny; or a Caution to keep Money* (1647), p. 30: 'Of recreations, some are more expensive than others . . . but the truth is, the most pleasant of all is riding with a good horse and a good companion . . . into the country'.
[3] L. Stone, *The Family, Sex, and Marriage in England, 1500–1800* (1977), p. 371.
[4] J. Crofts, *Packhorse, Waggon and Post* (1967), p. 7.

traffic on rivers, for river improvements were substantial in the seventeenth century, required more horse transport than before to get goods to the point of embarkation. On the farm, horses in some regions were displacing oxen for pulling the plough and for general draught purposes. Moreover, as the rising standard of living benefited the lower classes of society in the second half of the seventeenth century, even peasants began to ride horses instead of trudging for miles on foot. One of the Venetian ambassadors remarked with some surprise and disapproval as early as 1558 that English peasants (by which we should understand yeomen) usually rode on horseback: 'miserable must that man be who follows his cart on foot. Thus the rustic on horseback drives the oxen or horses of his team, and hence comes it that England is also called the land of comforts'.[5] After 1660 the same description would accurately have been applied to much poorer men. A carefully substantiated illustration is given in a recent survey of the property of peasants living in Yetminster, Dorset, in the seventeenth century. This was a dairying parish, populated for the most part by smallholders of modest, though plainly rising fortunes. In the 1590s only a fifth of its householders had horses, but by the 1660s, three-fifths owned them. Yet they did not plough a large acreage, and we are driven to conclude that some of the peasants' additional wealth was being spent on horses to enable them to ride instead of walk to market.[6]

The rising demand for horses for power went hand in hand with a new interest among the nobility and gentry in keeping horses for pleasure. They had long been used for hunting and hawking, but now they were needed for three further purposes, for training in dressage, in emulation of the great riding schools in Italy, Spain, Austria, and France; for horse racing, the new recreation of the upper classes, first popularised by nobility like the Earl of Pembroke, and made eminently fashionable when James I showed such a passion for it;[7] and for pulling coaches where the needs of pleasure and power were combined. The first coach in London was introduced by Queen Elizabeth's Dutch coachman in 1564.[8] Great ladies, and then great

---

[5] *Cal. SP Ven., VI, iii, 1557–8*, p. 1672.

[6] *Probate Inventories and Manorial Excepts of Chetnole, Leigh and Yetminster*, ed. R. Machin (Bristol, 1976), p. 16.

[7] Professor J. H. Plumb remarked in his Stenton Lecture in 1972 on the surprising fact that 'there is no work by a professional historian on horse-racing, or indeed on horses, vitally important as they are to the economic and social life of the time'. *The Commercialisation of Leisure in Eighteenth-century England* (Reading, 1973), p. 16, note 58.

[8] Crofts, *op. cit.*, pp. 111–17; John Stow, *The Annales . . . of England* (1615), p. 867.

lords, hastened to buy coaches, and quickly lost the habit of walking on foot in town streets, at least in southern England. By 1636 in London and the suburbs, coaches blocked the streets, in Harry Peacham's graphic words, 'like mutton pies in a cook's oven; hardly you can thrust a pole between'.[9] Since both coaches and horses were made the means of ostentatious display, an expensively decorated coach had to be set off by a handsomely matched pair of horses. For all these pleasurable purposes, nobility and gentry were prepared to scour Europe and beyond for horses, and to pay high prices for them. They also had to build large stables, and employ skilled grooms, keepers, and riders for whom they devised a rich vocabulary to differentiate their functions.[10] To satisfy their many different needs, monarchs like Henry VIII and Elizabeth I accommodated between 100 and 300 trained horses at any one time, not counting their breeding studs.[11] Nobles had 80 to 100 horses apiece; rich gentry, like Sir Henry Sidney of Penshurst, Kent, had 50 to 100, while parish gentry were content with 10 to 20.[12]

Everything in a gentleman's stable proclaimed the affluence of the master. Heavy expenditure was involved in keeping a veritable army of servants, ranked and clothed in uniform like a troop of soldiers.[13] Henry VIII needed 98 servants to look after 119 horses; Queen Elizabeth employed 83 servants to look after 98 horses.[14] But the wages of a man often cost less than the fodder for one horse. In 1562 the expense of feeding one horse for a week was reckoned at 5s., compared with 3s. 4d. paid to the average agricultural labourer, or 2s. 4d. to a horse boy, and 4s. 8d. to a groom in a well-to-do household

[9] Henry Peacham, *Coach and Sedan, pleasantly disputing for place and precedence, the brewer's cart being moderator* (1636), f. 1v.

[10] In the royal household, separate duties were performed by avenors, surveyors, purveyors, garnitors, saddlers, grooms, ferriers, esquires, and riders, while the gentry distinguished between saddlers, grooms, ferriers, yeomen, and riders. See *A Collection of Ordinances and Regulations for the Government of the Royal Household* (1790), pp. 206, 257 *et passim*. This was a world apart from that of working men, for whom a horse courser was anything and everything; he was a jobbing dealer in horses, he hired them, broke them, and he may even have raced them. See O.E.D. under *corser*, the 14th- and 15th-century term, and *horse corser*, which became current in 1550–80.

[11] *A Collection of Ordinances, op. cit.*, p. 200; PRO SP 12/240/79; SP 12/233/69.

[12] For the stables of Sir Henry Sidney, see Kent Archives Office, A54(i) and U 1475/015/12; for Sir Francis Walsingham's stable, see PRO SP 12/224/80. For parish gentry, see probate inventories, *passim*.

[13] Sir Henry Sidney's grooms in the 1570's, for example, wore black jerkins, with blue buttons, and yellow stockings. Kent Archives Office, U 1475/A56(3).

[14] *A Collection of Ordinances, op. cit.*, pp. 200–05; PRO SP 12/240/80.

like Sir Henry Sidney's.[15]

Five shillings for fodder per horse per week represented fairly generous feeding rates calculated for military horses under war conditions (fourteen pounds of hay a day, seven pounds of straw, one peck of oats, ahd half a peck of peas)[16], but gentlemen's standards of horse-keeping seem to have been just as high. Moreover, five shillings a week was cheap in comparison with the cost of foddering and stabling a horse while travelling on a journey. For just one night's stabling for one horse at Reading, in July 1574, Sir Henry Sidney of Penshurst paid 1s. 5d. (just over 7s. a week), and for one day and one night at Warwick, 2s. 7d. (or just over 18s. a week).[17]

Expenditure of this order in foddering horses has to be borne in mind when considering their third function—for service in war. The sharp rise in the demand for horses for war in the early sixteenth century represented a heavy outlay of money, totally upset the equilibrium of demand and supply which further raised their cost, and concentrated the minds of Henry VIII's statesmen on devising a firm policy of promoting horse breeding to ensure adequate supplies for the future. Henry VIII's reign has been called the *Age of Plunder*[18], and his extravagant folly in wasting England's and, indeed, Europe's stock of horses, offers one justification for that damning description. In April 1512 Henry made his first serious venture into the field of battle overseas, declaring war on France and intending, in league with Spain, to attack Aquitaine.[19] In the same year, his officials were scouring the countryside of southern and eastern England, buying up horses for cart and carriage to transport victuals to the troops. In every village in every county, royal buyers summoned sellers, and bought two here, four there. Usually one man could produce only one horse to their satisfaction, but sometimes two were chosen, and very rarely four or even six met the standard.[20] An average parish could find somewhere between five and ten horses, which meant that in a single year the horse population of a county could be drastically reduced by one royal shopping expedition. In 1513 Oxfordshire

---

[15] PRO SP 12/26/29; J. Thirsk, *Economic Policy and Projects* (Oxford, 1978), p. 3; Kent Archives Office, U 1500/A11/4; U 1475/A55.

[16] I wish to thank Miss Daphne Goodall who helped me to judge this ration. The hay ration she deemed average, the ration of oats and peas above average, and straw a bonus.

[17] Kent Archives Office, U 1475/A55.

[18] By W. G. Hoskins in the title of his book, *The Age of Plunder. The England of Henry VIII, 1500–1547* (1976).

[19] J. J. Scarisbrick, *Henry VIII* (1968), pp. 28–9.

[20] PRO E 101/107/27.

furnished 312 horses and Berkshire 246.[21] In that year 2,566 horses were procured from counties lying mostly between Lincolnshire and Kent, including Essex, Buckinghamshire, and Hertfordshire. On a buying tour in 1527 558 were bought in Oxfordshire and Berkshire.[22] When it is realised that these were fully grown horses of four years old and upwards, it is clear that such purchases could not continue indefinitely. Twenty-seven years after Henry began his first military campaign, alarms began to sound concerning the shortage of horses for war service, and with good reason. Yet an even more arrogant dissipation of resources was to follow in the 1540s, when the King was ageing, all his marriages were failing, and he was becoming a more reckless autocrat. The military campaigns in Scotland and France in the 1540s surpassed all others in their wild destruction of horses and men. Lightning raids on lowland Scottish townships in spring 1544, for example, involved 4,000 horsemen in burning Haddington and nearby places and 3,000 in burning Hawick and adjacent villages.[23] When an attack on Edinburgh was planned, five northern counties were ordered to supply 2,500 horsemen.[24] Every punitive raid destroyed, injured, or, at the very least, tired hundreds of horses, putting them out of action for weeks, if not for ever. To burn Jedworth, it required 500 horses (supplied from the bishopric of Durham), of which so many were injured that men and horses were obliged to rest for a month to six weeks thereafter.[25]

Yet the campaign against Scotland was nothing to that being planned at the same time against France. They were intended to run consecutively, but the plans went awry and they were in fact waged concurrently. Four hundred horsemen had to be summoned from the Scottish border to go to France,[26] and England was again scoured for horses. The musters of 1539 had earlier yielded a very thorough census of horses for service in every county, in every parish, and in every gentleman's stable. The exercise was repeated in 1544.[27] In addition, Henry took it for granted that horses from the territories of his ally, the Emperor, would be ready to assist him.[28] The Emperor's

---

[21] PRO E 101/107/17.

[22] *L. & P. Hen. VIII*, IV, ii, pp. 1668–9.

[23] *L. & P. Hen. VIII*, XIX, i, no. 223.

[24] *L. & P. Hen. VIII*, XIX, i, no. 140. In another letter on Henry's plans for this expedition 4,000 horsemen were said to be required. *Ibid.*, no. 223.

[25] *L. & P. Hen. VIII*, XIX, i, nos. 601, 684.

[26] *L. & P. Hen. VIII*, XIX, i, pp. 123, 217.

[27] *L. & P. Hen. VIII*, XIV, i, 652; XIX, i, no. 273 sqq.

[28] *L. & P. Hen. VIII*, XIX, i, no. 314 (p. 203).

Regent in the Netherlands, the Queen of Hungary, was peremptorily asked in 1544 for 4,100 draught horses, to be sent to Calais within six days. When she wrote a haughty reply,[29] Henry placed a private order for 400 to 500 mercenary horsemen to be found in Zealand, and when they did not turn up on time he placed the same order with another supplier.[30] When the Zealanders nevertheless arrived late, and found they were not wanted, they started to make trouble in Liège and Utrecht demanding their pay.[31]

The procuring of horses in the Low Countries was as complex a business as in England, yet Henry was wholly without understanding. He coldly told his Dutch allies that one wagon with its horses from every parish in Flanders, Brabant, Hainault, and Artois, would more than furnish his needs, and the Emperor could procure his requirements from Germany. The Regent of the Netherlands explained some of the practical problems: the Emperor was encamped in the Luxemburg area to which the French had access through Lorraine; they had already drawn away many horses from that area for their own use. The local people, having the Rhine for transporting their goods, did not keep an excessive number of wagon horses, and in any case it was not the custom in the Netherlands to commandeer horses; they had to be obtained by consent. Henry's demands made it appear that things were managed very differently in England.[32] Even Henry's first request to the Netherlands for 4,100 horses did not satisfy all his needs; another 7,200 draught and wagon horses were ordered to be at Calais one month later.[33] The Queen Regent had calculated that the Netherlands could supply no more than 10,000 horses to the Emperor and Henry combined, if husbandry and trade at home were to continue as normal. In fact, she supplied to Henry alone 9,660 draught horses. Piteous complaints reached her from her subjects who expressed a readiness to pay any tax in cash rather than lose more horses.[34]

[29] *L. & P. Hen. VIII*, XIX, 1, nos. 647, 877 (p. 546).

[30] *L. & P. Hen. VIII*, XIX, i, no. 866. The agent, engaged to supply the Zealand mercenaries, was Thomas Lightmaker, or Luchtemaker, a merchant at the Steelyard in London, who 'since bankruptcy' was said to have 'meddled in war'. The second order was placed with the Count of Buren. In the end both sets of mercenaries were used. *Ibid.*, nos. 583, 587, 622.

[31] *L. & P. Hen. VIII*, XIX, i, nos. 767, 832 (pp. 520–1), 834, 866.

[32] *L. & P. Hen. VIII*, XIX, i, p. 203. In the event the Emperor got his cart-horses from around Spier (Speyer). *L. & P. Hen. VIII*, XIX, i, no. 461.

[33] *L. & P. Hen. VIII*, XIX, i, p. 519.

[34] *L. & P. Hen. VIII*, XIX, i, nos. 877 (pp. 545–6), 832 (p. 521). Some of these draught horses came from beyond the Meuse and Namur. *Ibid.*

The contribution of the Low Countries to the war against France still left the English with heavy responsibilities. They had to find 5,226 horsemen for an army of 40,000 in all. Victualling called for another 10,500 horses to pull 1,500 wagons. A precise calculation of the cost had suggested that it was much cheaper to use English horses and wagons than to hire them in the Low Countries. But the expected economy disappeared in practice, for seven English horses were reckoned necessary to pull one wagon. The English subsequently discovered that the Dutch managed with four horses; and in the field, the English horses proved so weak that it often took fourteen or fifteen to draw one wagon.[35]

The English learned many hard but salutary lessons from this campaign about the poor quality of their horses for service, the losses that could be suffered, and the constraints imposed, by insufficient grass in a bad summer and, harshest lesson of all, that horses for service were not in inexhaustible supply either in England, France, or the Netherlands. One supplier of mercenary horsemen in the Netherlands alone had lost 700 horses in four months in 1544.[36] When Henry sent a fresh request to the Netherlands for draught horses in 1545 and 1546, therefore, he was coldly rebuffed, told that there were none to be had around Antwerp, and he must make the much longer journey to Oldenburg Fair, where he might buy them in the ordinary way of trade.[37] In 1546 Henry seems to have had recourse to Italian suppliers,[38] but rising costs created new problems.

At home the situation was equally bleak. In 1512 and 1513 Henry's officials had sought, and found, their horses for war service south of the Trent. But in 1539 a thoroughgoing enquiry for the musters showed that southern England could offer many foot soldiers, but now had practically no serviceable horses. A serviceable horse was, of course, a precise term, meaning a war horse of a certain size, *and,* it was hoped, of a certain stamina. Townships around Hastings in Sussex, for example, could furnish 1104 men on foot but only 27 horsemen (2.4%). Several districts in Wiltshire could find no more

[35] *L. & P. Hen. VIII*, XIX, i, nos. 271-6, and especially pp. 148, 146, 545, 465. The Venetians attributed the weakness of English horses to their being fed only on grass. *Cal. SP Ven.*, VI, ii, p. 1048.

[36] *L. & P. Hen. VIII*, XIX, ii, no. 259.

[37] *L. & P. Hen. VIII*, XX, i, no. 70; XXI, i, no. 340.

[38] *L. & P. Hen. VIII*, XXI, i, no. 643. This is a guess, based on the fact that two Italians, Nic. Cresia and Ant. Stranio, were paid for draught horses delivered at Boulogne. But it is possible that they were horse traders roaming all over Europe for their purchases.

than 3 to 6 horsemen for every 100 footmen.[39] England north of the Trent still had serviceable horses in some quantity, but they were not abundant in the Midlands, only in the north: in the Pennine districts of Derbyshire, for example, where small fell ponies were doubtless more useful than great horses, serviceable horsemen numbered only one third of the footmen.[40] Only in Yorkshire and beyond, on the North Yorkshire moors in Cleveland and Danby Forest, around Richmond and Sedbergh, and under the Hambledon Hills, were horsemen found that were almost equal in number to the foot soldiers.[41] It was, therefore, the horses from northern England which bore the brunt of warfare in Scotland and France in the 1540s with damaging consequences. By the end of the Scottish campaign of 1544, all the good campaign and cart horses in Northumberland and in the garrisons had been lost, and in Spring 1545 the north could find so few fit carriage and cart horses to draw guns and munitions that fresh supplies were called for from the south.[42] But the south was corn-growing country: it was not the place where horses could be bred cheaply in quantity, and all its fully-grown horses were needed for farmwork for most of the year. This was the urgent situation, out of which a constructive policy emerged in the 1530s and 1540s for increasing the number and improving the quality of English horses.

During earlier war campaigns, Henry had regularly looked abroad for great horses to stiffen the English force. In 1519, Gregory de Casalis of Bologna had been used as a messenger to visit the princes of Ferrara and Naples to buy war horses.[43] He had brought back eighteen horses from Naples, though evidently not from the Duke's stud, for even at this early date the breed of Naples and of Italy was thought to be degenerating, and good specimens were not easy to find.[44] At the same time Henry showed a delight in receiving fine riding horses as gifts, by exchange, or purchase. On his marriage to Katherine of Aragon in 1509, he had asked his father-in-law, Ferdinand of Aragon, for a Spanish jennet, a Neapolitan, and a Sicilian horse to be sent by the first messenger.[45] A steady flow of gifts and horses arrived for Henry from other kings and notabilities, some of whom even sent their grooms to teach Henry's stable-hands how to

[39] *L. & P. Hen. VIII*, XIV, i, pp. 264–319 *passim*.
[40] *Ibid.*
[41] *Ibid.*
[42] *L. & P. Hen. VIII*, XX, i, nos. 295, 339, 395.
[43] *L. & P. Hen. VIII*, III, i, pp. 63, 204.
[44] *Ibid.*, p. 63.
[45] *L. & P. Hen. VIII*, I, no. 127.

manage them.[46] Purchases for breeding purposes supplemented these gifts. One of Henry's household, Sir Griffith Donne, arrived back in England in 1517 with mares that he had been commissioned to buy in Naples and Turkey.[47] A purchase of 200 Flanders mares for Henry's private use in 1544 led to delicate negotiations with the Queen Regent for permission to export them. They too were almost certainly intended for Henry's breeding studs, since Flemish horses had shown themselves to be so much stronger than the English in the French campaigns.[48]

Royal interest in horsebreeding and the improvement of English breeds became public policy in the 1530s. First of all the export of horses was prohibited in 1531, because of their general scarcity and high price; then in 1532 the sale of horses to Scotland was banned likewise.[49] In 1535–6 and in 1541–2 the nobility and other large landowners were exhorted to arrest 'the great decay of the generation and breeding of good and swift and strong horses, which heretofore have been bred in this realm' by keeping mares and stallions in their parks, and ensuring that they were of a certain size. In all except the four northern counties, mares had to be at least thirteen hands high and stallions fourteen hands.[50] Another measure (1540) governed the size of horses kept in forests, chases, on moors, marshes, heaths, commons, and waste grounds where the mating of horses could not be controlled. No horses were to be allowed to graze in these places unless they were at least fifteen hands high, and in northern counties fourteen hands high. Smaller horses had to be killed or removed to enclosed grounds, though, as an afterthought, the legislators allowed them to graze common pastures where they were not in contact with mares and fillies. The avowed object was to breed 'good and strong horses' that would help the defence of the country—in other words, horses for war.[51]

Legislation was accompanied by a strong propaganda campaign among nobility and gentry, especially those employed in the royal household or involved in central and local government, to impress their responsibilities on them. In 1541–2 nobility, gentry, and churchmen, in descending order of rank and wealth, were ordered to keep so many saddle horses of a certain age and size. Dukes and

[46] *L. & P. Hen. VIII*, III, no. 181.
[47] *L. & P. Hen. VIII*, II, no. 3906 (p. 1218).
[48] *L. & P. Hen. VIII*, XIX, i, nos. 831, 832.
[49] *Statutes of the Realm*, II, 22 Hen. VIII, c. 7; 23 Hen. VIII, c. 16.
[50] *Statutes of the Realm*, II, 27 Hen. VIII, c. 6; 33 Hen. VIII, c. 5.
[51] *Statutes of the Realm*, II, 32 Hen. VIII, c. 13.

archbishops had to keep seven entire trotting horses for the saddle of three years of age and fourteen hands high while, at the bottom of the scale, gentry with an income of between 500 marks and £100 had to keep one horse.[52] Government officials conscientiously spread the government's message far and wide, and tried to execute the Crown's purposes in their native counties. Every measure that went into the making of this policy bears the imprint of Thomas Cromwell's methods. New regulations were drawn up for the King's own studs, laying down a chain of command and detailed procedures for their management.[53] Welsh horses seem to have been procured to infuse new blood into Henry's studs, judging by a cryptic Privy Council decision, taken in October 1540, to obtain a breed of horses and mares from Rice ap Morrice, almost certainly a servant of the Council of Wales.[54] His duty was evidently to enlist the cooperation of all Welsh owners of horse studs, and his success is indicated in a letter of November 1541, from the Privy Council to the Lord President of the Welsh Council and other Welsh gentlemen, thanking them for the mares given by them to the King.[55] In the reverse direction, John Uvedale, secretary to the Council of the North, wrote from York in April 1540, thanking Thomas Cromwell for the bay stallion he had sent him, thus fulfilling a promise earlier given in London. 'Would God that every county in the realm had but one such a fair stalland for the increase of the breed of horses which is sore decayed in these parts', he wrote, 'and all for want of good stallands.' He intended to run thirteen mares with the stallion that summer, and looked forward to the day, three or four years hence, when he would be able to present Cromwell with 'some colt of his own getting'.[56]

Many other gentlemen cooperated in smaller ways. Sir Edward Willoughby gave up his park at Henley for the King's stud in 1540.[57] In 1545, Sir Nicholas Strelley, a Warwickshire gentleman, took into his park for 4d. per week apiece thirty mares of the royal stud from Warwick Castle, perhaps because the royal park was short of grazing

[52] *Statutes of the Realm*, II, 33 Hen. VIII, c. 5. See also PRO SP 12/27/43.

[53] PRO SP 1/113, ff. 148–51.

[54] *L. & P. Hen. VIII*, XVI, no. 172. The letter was addressed to the Council of Wales. Wales was thought by one Venetian ambassador to be the best supplier of mettlesome, courageous horses, and of heavy horses for men-at-arms. *Cal. SP Ven.*, VI, ii, p. 1048.

[55] *L. & P. Hen. VIII*, XVI, no. 1355. Rice ap Morrice's interest in horses is indicated by the fact that he rode to war in France in 1544 with other men at arms in the retinue of the Master of the Horse. *L. & P. Hen. VIII*, XIX, no. 275 (p. 163).

[56] PRO SP 1/159, ff. 84–5; *L. & P. Hen. VIII*, XV, no. 648.

[57] *L. & P. Hen. VIII*, XV, no. 410.

at the time.[58] The full number of the King's own stud parks does not emerge clearly from the documents. But they impressed Marillac, the French Ambassador in England, who reported to his master, Francis I, in 1542 that Henry had two stables of 100 horses which he himself had seen, and that Henry could draw 150 animals yearly from his studs towards Wales and in Nottinghamshire.[59] In 1526 Henry VIII had 32 parks, but only in some of these did he have breeding studs.[60] However, the situation was liable to change rapidly: two new ones had been set up in 1519 in Upton, Worcestershire, and Budbrooke, Warwickshire,[61] and the number of parks at the Crown's disposal was greatly increased in 1536 and 1539 by the dissolution of the monasteries. As soon as monastic lands came into the King's hands, the royal surveyor cast a sharp eye over estates with parks suitable for more studs. Sir Arthur Darcy suggested Jervaulx Abbey as a good site, for there were horses that were the tried breeds of the north. Wigmore Abbey land in Herefordshire was inspected but deemed unsuitable because it did 'not stand in the most wholesome air', and horses would not eat the hay.[62] But parks which the Crown did not retain in its own hands might pass to Gentlemen Pensioners who were then expected to use them for their private studs.[63]

Gentlemen Pensioners came to play a key role as intermediaries between the King and the gentry at large. The King set the first example in keeping breeding studs; but Gentlemen Pensioners, members of the royal household, numbering fifty in all, whose duties at court were particularly concerned with the provision of horses on ceremonial and military occasions, were expected to follow the royal lead and keep fine breeding studs also. It is this responsibility which explains some of the leases of ex-monastic and other forfeited lands, especially of parks, to Gentlemen Pensioners. They were not random and capricious grants to court favouries, as at first sight appears, but purposeful measures to improve the number and quality of English horses for service. To contemporaries, indeed, they probably seemed deliberately designed to maintain the tradition that had hitherto been upheld by the monasteries of keeping the best horses. According to the Venetian ambassador, viewing the situation in 1557, English horse studs had been 'handsomer and better' before the monasteries

---

[58] *L. & P. Hen. VIII*, XX, i, no. 560.
[59] *L. & P. Hen. VIII*, XVII, no. 178.
[60] *A Collection of Ordinances, op. cit.*, pp. 263–6.
[61] *L. & P. Hen. VIII*, III, no. 581.
[62] *L. & P. Hen. VIII*, XII, ii, no. 59; XIV, ii, nos. 384, 375.
[63] See also below, p. 387.

were dissolved, because abbots and bishops had carefully attended to these matters.[64] The duty passed to men like Sir Francis Knollys, Gentlemen Pensioner, who received a grant of Caversham Manor— former monastic land—which included a park. Ralph Fane, another Gentlemen Pensioner, received a Crown grant in 1541 of lands, including parkland, formerly belonging to St John's of Jerusalem in the Tonbridge–Hadlow area, and was also appointed chamberlain of Postern and Cage Parks in Tonbridge in 1542, and chief governor of the herbage of the parks—this land having been surrendered to the Crown by the attainder of Edward, Duke of Buckingham.[65] This helps to explain how this young man from a far from wealthy gentle family could supply the unusually large number of thirty horsemen for the French campaign in 1543.[66]

The government's measures were impressively thorough in the planning, and although their implementation was far less efficient, the consequences were nevertheless far-reaching. Plainly not all the gentlemen of England were inspired with enthusiasm for improving England's stock of good horses. But in every county there were some, and they made their influence felt in the countryside around them. The Weald of Kent, for example, had twenty-two parks, and although it was not especially accessible to court influence, and not particularly congenial country for gentlemen to inhabit, yet in one small area it had three families promoting the government's policy with dedicated energy—the Fanes at Hadlow, the Astleys at Maidstone, and the Sidney family at Penshurst.

The grievous waste of English stocks of horses in the 1540s could not quickly be made good. For the rest of the century the government kept Henrician policy alive and in force by prohibiting the export of horses, initiating enquiries at the ports into illegal exports, and regularly reminding the nobility and gentry of their duty to the Commonwealth to breed good horses and maintain their numbers.[67] The continuation of Henry's wars in France and Scotland into Edward VI's reign made it necessary to compile a great new muster book in 1547, in which gentlemen were again rated to furnish a

[64]   *Cal. SP Ven.*, VI, iii, p. 1672. On the establishment of the Gentlemen Pensioners in 1509, modelled on the French *Pensionnaires*, see H. Brackenbury, *The History of His Majesty's Bodyguard*, 1905.
[65]   *L. & P. Hen. VIII*, XVII, nos. 47, g 71 (23) (p. 30); XVI, p. 729.
[66]   *L. & P. Hen. VIII*, XVIII, i, no. 832.
[67]   R. Furley, *A History of the Weald of Kent* (Ashford, 1874). II, ii, p. 743: *Statutes of the Realm*, II, 1 Edw. VI, c. 5; *CSPD 1547–80*, pp. 5, 137; PRO SP 12/136/38; SP 12/146/50.

certain number of horses each, based upon a new assessment of their income that did not rely on the old valuations of 1524.[68] In 1565 the Henrician statutes were called to notice once again, and Elizabeth announced her intention of taking a muster of horses for service every six months in future 'until the realm be replenished with horses'.[69] Thereafter, muster returns were compiled at frequent (though not six-monthly) intervals, especially in the 1570s and 1580s. In 1580 when rumours of war with Spain made horses a matter of urgent concern, the Queen set up a high-powered Special Commission for the Increase and Breed of Horses, to see the statutes properly executed, and particularly to ensure that each gentleman kept horses for service in accordance with his true ability.[70] This was no idle threat. The policy was put into execution in a chain of orders that involved sub-commissioners in rating men correctly, and assigning a day when they personally viewed all the stallions and mares in every county.[71] At the same time, the legislation about keeping so many mares and stallions in parks was also enforced.[72] The gentry clearly took the matter to heart: from Cheshire, for example, came a helpful letter pointing out the decline in the number of parks (many of which had originally been designed for deer, but were now disparked and turned into cattle pastures), and suggesting that the obligation to keep brood mares should be laid on *all* gentry irrespective of whether they had parks.[73] Regulations were also drawn up to ensure that on all common pastures a sufficient stallion was kept to produce progeny of a certain size.[74]

When gentlemen thus became continuously involved in the plan to promote the breeding of horses for service, they passed a more critical eye over their own horses. They were painfully abashed when their horses were turned down by the muster masters as being below standard.[75] A strong spirit of emulation is reflected, moreover, in the

[68]   PRO SP 15/1/64.
[69]   P. L. Hughes and J. F. Larkin, *Tudor Royal Proclamations*, II (New Haven and London, 1969), nos. 494 (p. 194), 534; *CSPD 1547–80*, p. 254.
[70]   PRO SP 12/137/17; SP 12/143/26. The full title of the Commission was 'For the increase and breed of horses and for the keeping of horses and geldings for service'. *CSPD 1547–80*, p. 685. Lords Lincoln, Warwick, Leicester, Sussex, Bedford, Huntingdon, and Hunsdon, Sir Christopher Hatton, and Sir Henry Sidney were members.
[71]   PRO SP 12/136/4.
[72]   PRO SP 12/136/42.
[73]   They suggested that all those who already had to furnish horses for demi-lances or light horsemen should also keep broodmares. PRO SP 12/143/1. Many returns from other counties are contained in PRO SP 12/140–144.
[74]   PRO SP 12/143, 23.
[75]   *CSPD 1601–3*, p. 121.

gifts of horses that passed between them. It was customary to give every horse in the stable a name that recorded its donor. Thus Sir Francis Walsingham's horses in 1589 included, among a hundred others, Grey Bingham, given him by Sir Richard Bingham, Bay Sidney, given by one of the Sidney family, and Pied Markham, given by Mr Robert Markham, the Nottinghamshire gentleman whose son, Gervase Markham, became the famous writer of books on horsemanship and husbandry.[76]

Of course, not all the 102 horses in the stables of Sir Francis Walsingham, or of other gentry, were capable of service in war. The gentry had diverse interests in horses, but for whatever purposes they kept them, high standards were sought after. This was evident when a long period of domestic peace in the 1550s, 1560s and 1570s allowed gentlemen to indulge in horsekeeping for recreation. Younger sons went off to Europe to learn something of the cult of horsemanship that was now so popular there, especially in Italy and France. Others did not go so far but learned at second hand in England from Italian grooms and riders, originally engaged by Henry VIII to serve in the royal stables. In 1526 Alexander de Bologna and Jacques de Granado were officers in the royal stable and were still on the payroll in 1544; in 1545 Mathew de Mantua was a studman in the royal stables.[77] Foremost among their pupils and associates, therefore, were the Gentlemen Pensioners, and this explains why the Gentlemen Pensioners produced from among their circle three out of the four authors of early works in English on horses and their high-school

---

[76] PRO SP 12/224/80. Robert Markham was a close friend of Walsingham. See F. N. L. Poynter, *A Bibliography of Gervase Markham, 1568?-1637*, Oxford Bibliographical Society, NS XI, 1962, pp. 6–8, 85. Other branches of the Markham family also prided themselves on their stables. Blundeville (see below, pp. 390–91) mentions another horse called Markham, owned at one stage by Master Thomas Markham of Ollerton and later by Lord Robert Dudley, Earl of Leicester. He originally came from the stud of Master Munday of Markeaton, near Derby, and was broken by John Astley's man, Abraham. This is an instructive example of the care taken to record the history of individual horses, a prelude to the keeping of pedigrees. T. Blundeville, *The Four Chiefest Offices belonging to Horsemanship* . . . (1609 edn.), p. 12.

[77] *A Collection of Ordinances, op. cit.*, p. 202; *L. & P. Hen. VIII*, XIX, p. 160; XVII, no. 220, item 39; XX, ii, p. 515. According to William Cavendish, Duke of Newcastle, writing in 1667, two of Federico Grisone's pupils were brought to England by Henry VIII. These may have been they. William Cavendish, *A New Method and Extraordinary Invention to dress Horses* (1667), p. 2. For Grisone, see further below, p. 391.

Others who employed Italian riders in their stables later in the sixteenth century were Sir Philip Sidney (who brought over two Italians, Signor Romano to teach his nephew, Lord Herbert, afterwards Earl of Pembroke, and Signor Prospero), the Earl of Leicester (employing Claudio Corte), and Lord Walden (who engaged Mr Hannibal from Naples). William Cavendish, *op. cit.*, pp. 2 and 4.

training, namely, Nicholas Arnold, Thomas Blundeville, John Astley, and Gervase Markham. The biographies of these four admirably illustrate the role of the gentry in focussing attention on the improvement of breeds and of horsemanship at court and in the country.

First was Nicholas Arnold of Highnam, Gloucestershire, a Gentleman Pensioner in Henry VIII's reign, who imported horses from Flanders in 1546, travelled in Italy in Edward VI's reign, and thereafter kept in his own stables a fine stud of Neapolitan horses for war service. William Harrison, in his description of English horses in Elizabeth's reign, singled him out for special praise: 'Sir Nicholas Arnold of late hath bred the best horses in England and written of the manner of their production', he wrote.[78] Unfortunately, the manuscript does not appear to have survived but some of his wisdom is almost certainly incorporated in the books of the next generation of Gentlemen Pensioners.

When the gentry turned to the enjoyment of horsemanship in the peaceful years between 1550 and 1580 books began to exert a stronger influence. The first printed work on horsemanship had been Spanish, published in 1495; the second, third and fourth were Italian, published in 1499, 1517, and 1518. Thereafter, Spaniards, French, and Germans joined enthusiastically in cultivating the arts of horsemanship, and books on the subject appeared thick and fast in the 1550's and 1560's.[79] The training of horses for recreation was at the expense of their role in war, but this was not all loss. The new principles taught a professional attitude to horsetraining, making clear to what heights of perfection horses could be schooled in obedience to their riders. They emphasised the wisdom and utility of training a horse by gentle persuasion, by sensitive use of the hand, rather than by cruel and harsh bullying and beating. And, in parenthesis, it is worth noting that the new doctrine was laid down at least half a century or more before the same principles were applied to the training of children. The first work read by English parents, advocating more gentle ways of educating their offspring, was Florio's translation of Montaigne's *Essays* in 1603; and the first *English* work to uphold this principle was published in 1656.[80] The

[78] V. C. H. *Glos.*, X, p. 18; DNB *sub nomine*; T. Blundeville, *op. cit.*, p. 7v; William Harrison, *Elizabethan England* (Scott Library edn.), p. 154.
[79] See the bibliography of F. H. Huth, *Works on Horses and Equitation. A Bibliographical Record of Hippology* (1887).
[80] L. Stone, *The Family, Sex, and Marriage, 1500–1800* (1977), pp. 435, 731, note 74.

first book on training horses in this way was published about 1560.

Thomas Blundeville gives us a lively picture of the average horse with his sloppy rider attending the musters: 'some sit on their horses like windshaken reeds, handling their hands and legs like weavors'. The horse 'spurred forward, went backwards; directed to turn on the right hand, he turned on the left'. Horses for service as well as those for pleasure could not but benefit from the new rules of horse training.[81]

If a stark economic explanation is required to account for the new doctrine, it lies in the fact that horses were becoming ever more expensive, and could no longer be taken for granted like rain from heaven. By rough handling many expensive animals were being ruined, maimed, and killed. But if economic interest played some part in the new fashion, it was much less prominent in discussion than the pride and satisfaction to be had from training a horse well. It was the joy of achievement, and the pleasure of riding a superbly trained animal, that fired gentlemen with enthusiasm, and became sufficient justification for their labour. Surely, wrote the translator of an Italian work by Claudio Corte on *The Art of Riding*, in 1584, surely, it was permissible for great persons to train horses for pleasure, 'to delight the lookers on, and make proof of the rider's excellency, as also thereby to show the capacity of the beast'.[82]

The first *published* book on horsemanship appeared in England *circa* 1560 and was concerned with horses for war service. Written by Thomas Blundeville, a Norfolk gentleman, who had spent his youth at court, it was part-translation, part-adaptation of Federico Grisone's Italian work on *The Art of Riding*. Alexander de Bologna, who had worked in Henry VIII's stables from at least 1526 until his death, had taught Grisone's rules, and Blundeville was their

---

[81] T. Blundeville, *The Art of Riding*, n.d., but *circa* 1560, Preface. John Astley wrote most eloquently on training horses to be responsive to the hand. 'This manner of riding is not usual, neither easy to be followed', he explained. People had lost the art for which Xenophon was renowned and had to learn all over again. Having become 'butchers rather than riders', they found that they had to use ever harsher methods of horse training, and their horses had become dull and unresponsive. Perfect horsemanship was achieved when rider and horse rode as of 'one body, of one mind, and of one will'. This teaching is commonplace today, but was fresh and exciting in the sixteenth century. J. Astley, *The Art of Riding* (1584), pp. 5, 8, 18, 56.

[82] Claudio Corte, *The Art of Riding* (1584), n.p.; see also H. Mackwilliam's Second Dedication in the same work. The Duke of Newcastle expressed the same sentiments in 1667. 'What can be more comely or pleasing than to see . . . so excellent a creature with so much spirit and strength to be so obedient to his rider'. W. Cavendish, *A New Method, op. cit.*, p. 13.

enthusiastic advocate. However, he found Grisone 'a far better doer than writer' and incorporated many changes in the text. Dealing with the riding and breaking of great horses, the book owed its appearance, in part, as the author explained, to the encouragement of William Cecil, Elizabeth's first minister, who read it in draft.[83] Blundeville next published a larger work, *The Fower Chiefest Offices Belongyng to Horsemanshippe* in 1565, in which he included new sections on breeding, dieting, and the treatment of diseases in horses. This time, he took nothing from Grisone but gathered his material from a variety of other authors (including perhaps Nicholas Arnold?), supplementing it with his own knowledge gained abroad, but adapting it (as he emphasised) to English conditions. The book passed through four more editions in 1570, 1580, 1597 and 1609.[84] Here was a practical, down-to-earth text, setting out the requirements of a good park for a breeding stud, the amount of ground needed, and the amenities such as water, buildings, and stocks of fodder. The novelty of some of the new precepts on breeding and breaking was emphasised, as against the old fashioned methods followed at the royal stud at Tutbury. At Tutbury they broke horses using force; Blundeville recommended persuasion. A mare at Tutbury that would not allow the horse to leap her was tied to a post, whereas Blundeville could achieve the same end by patient wooing of the mare. The young colts at Tutbury ran wild, and when ready to be broken were difficult to catch and halter; many were maimed in consequence. Blundeville preferred to handle them more when they were young.[85] Other differences of opinion concerned the design of the stables, types of floor, and the height of feeding racks. The moderns were arguing fine points with their out-dated elders, but the liveliness of the debate revealed the seriousness of their search for perfection in horsemanship.

[83] T. Blundeville, *The Art of Riding, op. cit.*; Arthur Campling, 'Thomas Blundeville of Newton Flotman, co. Norfolk (1522–1606)', *Norfolk Archaeology*, xxi (1920–22), 340–41, 343. I assume that Blundeville's reference to Old Alexander, Master of the Royal Stables, relates to Alexander de Bologna who served Henry VIII for many years, and perhaps continued under Elizabeth. His statement about Alexander's debt to Grisone does not make it absolutely clear whether Alexander simply read Grisone or worked under him.

[84] Campling, *op. cit.*, p. 343; Blundeville, *The Four Chiefest Offices* ... (1608 edn.), A3. Foreign travel was extremely valuable to English horsemen for other reasons: competent linguists were needed to deal with mercenaries in wartime. Thus Gentlemen Pensioners, put in charge of mercenaries, were chosen for their linguistic skills: Richard Knyvett commanded Italian mercenaries because he spoke Italian; likewise William Fulwood, who spoke Italian and Spanish. *L. & P. Hen. VIII*, XX, i, no. 872.

[85] Blundeville, *op. cit.*, pp. 14, 20.

Twenty years later, in 1584, Blundeville's friend and early companion at court, John Astley, another fervent admirer of Grisone and old Alexander de Bologna, wrote *The Art of Riding*. His father, Thomas Astley, had served as a Gentleman Pensioner in Henry VIII's reign and John became Master of the Jewel House. The book was prepared in collaboration with other Gentlemen Pensioners, and mingled their joint personal experience with the rules of the Italian riding schools.[86] In the same year, a translation was published of the Italian work of Claudio Corte on *The Art of Riding*, completed at the instigation of Henry Mackwilliam, another Gentleman Pensioner, and reflecting the influence of Corte's one-year sojourn in England in 1565 at the invitation of Lord Robert Dudley, Earl of Leicester, Master of the Royal Horse.[87]

Finally Gervase Markham produced the most popular book of all. One of his forebears, Henry Markham, had been a Gentleman Pensioner in Henry VIII's reign.[88] His father was Robert Markham, a country gentleman of Cotham in Nottinghamshire, and a close friend of Sir Francis Walsingham, who had presented Gervase's father with an expensive Arabian horse as a gift. Gervase as a young man was given the task of training it, having probably served some time in the Earl of Rutland's household at Belvoir Castle where he got his early training in horse keeping and horse sports. Gervase then had a course of instruction at Master Thomas Story's riding school at Greenwich where he too was taught by celebrated Italian riders. Markham wrote several books on horses, all of which embody much practical experience. None of his manuals, except perhaps those on the treatment of horse ailments, would lead any modern horse breeder, who wanted wise and good basic guidance, astray, and it is not surprising that his books turn up in so many gentlemen's libraries in the seventeenth century.[89]

Since much recent research on agrarian development from the later sixteenth century onwards underlines the cardinal importance of books in influencing the gentry and directing their actions, these works on horse breeding and training deserve careful study.[90] Not all books, of course, influenced all men; and some gentry managed to

---

[86] John Astley, *The Art of Riding* (1584); DNB *sub nomine*.

[87] Claudio Corte, *The Art of Riding* (1584); F. N. L. Poynter, *Bibliography of Gervase Markham, op. cit.*, p. 83.

[88] *L. & P. Hen. VIII*, XV, p. 5.

[89] F. N. L. Poynter, *Bibliography of Gervase Markham, op. cit., passim*.

[90] This is substantiated in *The Agrarian History of England and Wales, V, 1640–1750*, ed. Joan Thirsk (1984).

live without them altogether. But correspondence from the early seventeenth century onwards reveals many who pored over books, assimilated ideas eagerly, and corresponded about them. Useful page references were noted and sometimes whole passages copied into diaries and notebooks. The copies of books that survive in our libraries show passages underlined, and agreement or disagreement signified in marginal comments: one reader of *The Compleat Horseman and Expert Ferrier* (1639) by Thomas de Gray, esquire, so strongly disapproved of its advice that he crossed out 'esquire', and deleted the prefix 'ex' in the book's title to make it read *The Compleat Horseman and Pert Ferrier*. 'Oh the cretin', he wrote in the margin.[91] The printed word, and the ideas so publicized, were treated with more serious consideration than we can fully understand, who are overwhelmed with too many books and too many ideas.[92]

By 1600 the literature on horsemanship and the government's regular enquiries into horses for service were raising standards of horse training and, as contemporaries believed, increasing the number and size of serviceable horses. It is worth emphasising that nobility and gentry shouldered virtually all the responsibility for this. The Privy Council's letters and the practical arrangements for calling the musters assumed that only in desperate circumstances would freeholders or tenants be called on to bear the cost of providing horses for service.[93]

But the gentry's obligations frequently meant that they had to buy or hire horses to fulfil their duties towards the Crown. They did not succeed in breeding all horses for service in their own parks and stables. The demand for good horses thus gradually worked its way through to yeomen and husbandmen, enlivened the horse markets

---

[91] Thomas de Grey, *The Compleat Horseman and Expert Ferrier* (1684 edn., Bodleian Library copy (Vet A 3e 1069)).

[92] For an example of bookish guidance on horses, seriously treated, see *CSPD 1628–9*, p. 8. *The Council at War* in 1628 ordered that horses be trained for war by being made accustomed to the sound of guns and the sight and feeling of armour, in accordance with the recommendations of Monsieur de la Brove. On Solomon de la Brove's book on horsemanship, *Le Cavalarice françois* (1593), see William Cavendish, *A New Method, op. cit.*, p. 3.

[93] See, for example, *CSPD Addenda, 1580–1625*, p. 126; *CSPD Addenda, 1547–65*, p. 463. This is implied also in the order of 1544 (at the time of the French campaign) that horses were to be provided 'without disfurniture of necessary tillage and husbandry of any man'. *L. & P. Hen. VIII*, XIX, i, p. 147.

and fairs, and gradually encouraged them to specialise.[94] What influence, we may wonder, did the horse musters, held at Ripon, for example, exert on local horse traders and breeders when all the gentlemen of North Yorkshire were summoned there and had to produce large numbers of stallions or strong geldings to defend the realm against the northern rebels in 1569?[95] What was the effect on local horse owners in the fenland of Lincolnshire when the Privy Council's order arrived in 1560, requiring them to produce thirty cart-horses for the royal use? Thomas Ogle promptly had the best horses and geldings in East Holland brought before him, selected fourteen at Spalding, and another sixteen at Boston, and paid prices that varied between £2 and £3 6s. 8d. for each.[96] Nor were horses for war service the only ones being sought by gentlemen buyers. The high school training of horses in the *manège*, in vogue in the years of peace between 1550 and 1580, gave way to another fashion for horse-racing in which the nobility and gentry began to show marked interest from 1580 onwards.[97] It was already plainly a sporting fashion in 1585, when a horse-race at Salisbury was attended by the Earls of Cumberland, Warwick, Pembroke, and Essex, along with many gentlemen, and prizes of a golden bell and a golden snaffle were awarded.[98] James I is traditionally given most credit for establishing this fashion; he certainly gave it high status, and he established the race course at Newmarket.[99] But thereafter horse-racing developed its own momentum, and, in the later seventeenth century, it no longer

[94] For the notable development of the horse markets and fairs in the seventeenth century, see A. Everitt, in *The Agrarian History of England and Wales, IV, 1500–1640*, ed. Joan Thirsk (Cambridge, 1967), pp. 492, 495–6, 590; J. A. Chartres, *Internal Trade in England, 1500–1700* (1977), pp. 24–5; and especially Peter Edwards, 'The Horse Trade of the Midlands in the Seventeenth Century', *Agric. Hist. Rev.*, 27, 1979, pp. 90–100. A useful contemporary guide to the specialities of different fairs is given in William Cavendish, *A New Method, op. cit.*, pp. 69–61.

[95] *CSPD 1566–79, Addenda*, p. 170.

[96] PRO SP 12/11/26.

[97] Thomas de Grey, *The Compleat Horseman and Expert Ferrier* (1639) refers to 'the neglect of the horse of manège' in his dedication to James, Marquess of Hamilton, Master of the Horse.

[98] Racing at Salisbury is first recorded in 1585 and at Winchester in 1591 and 1605 when the Marquis of Winchester and the Earl of Southampton were evidently the main sponsors. *VCH Wilts.*, IV, p. 379; A. B. Rosen, *Economic and Social Aspects of the History of Winchester, 1520–1670* (Oxford D.Phil., 1975), pp. 231–2. But a horse race is recorded much earlier at York between William Mallory and Oswald Wolsthrope, in 1530 (*VCH Yorks., City of York*, p. 159); earlier still in 1527 between Lord Abergavenny and Mr Karey (Carew?) (*L. & P. Hen. VIII*, II, p. 1668); and at Chester in 1512 (James Rice, *History of the British Turf* (1879), ii, p. 75.

[99] There is a reference to the Scottish King (James VI, later James I of England) going to a horse race near the Scottish border in June 1599 (*CSPD 1598–1601*, p. 225)

required the presence of the king to be successful.[100] The country gentry and nobility organised their own meetings, and since they gave amusement to other classes of the population, they received support from town authorities, who in turn benefited by all the trade which such occasions promoted. Already in 1619 Salisbury Corporation had taken charge of a fund 'for the encouragement of the races'.[101]

This was not all; the nobility and gentry needed coach-horses to draw their splendid coaches. They had to be of the right conformation and size, and generally comely and suitable for their purpose. A specialised market for coach-horses developed, for the gentry were prepared to pay high prices, as the pride of display drove them on. Great esteem came to the man who owned good horses, and even more when he was known to be the breeder thereof. Fine horses always attracted great attention on the road, as admiring pedestrians stopped in their tracks and gazed upon them until they disappeared from sight.[102]

The gentlemen buyers at horse fairs required high quality horses that set a standard at the upper end of the market. At the same time, a much larger group of men wanted horses for the pack-saddle, to pull carts and wagons on the roads and on the farms, to serve as mill-horses, to pull loads from quarries and mines to river-ports, and to pull the plough, as well as padnags for everyday riding.[103] A population rising in number from $2\frac{1}{4}$ million in 1500 to $5\frac{1}{2}$ million in 1700 needed horses in much greater numbers for highly differentiated purposes. Moreover, by the later seventeenth century industry was far more widely dispersed over the whole countryside, in villages and hamlets, and less concentrated in towns than it had been in 1500. Thus while pedlars multiplied on the roads, so did hawkers and chapmen with packhorses.[104]

---

but the first reference I have found so far to racehorses kept by James I in England dates from 1617 (*CSPD 1611–18*, p. 493). For the history of the Newmarket racecourse, see *VCH Cambs.*, V, p. 279.

[100] See, for example, *The Diary of Thomas Isham of Lamport, 1658–81*, ed. Sir Gyles Isham (Farnborough, 1971), *passim* but especially pp. 30, 155. See also Nottingham Univ. Lib., Newcastle of Clumber MSS., Ne E8 1662.

[101] *VCH Wilts.*, IV, p. 379.

[102] Thomas de Grey, *The Compleat Horseman, op. cit.*, Epistle to the Reader.

[103] For the use of mill horses to drain mines, see Peter Edwards, *art. op. cit.* The padnags of Cornwall were specially protected from the effects of the legislation about keeping only horses of over fourteen hands in forests, heaths, and chases by a clause in 21 Jas I, c. 28. (1623–4). *Statutes of the Realm*, IV, ii, p. 1240.

[104] For the importance, and the rising number, of pedlars, see J. Thirsk and J. P. Cooper, *Seventeenth-Century Economic Documents* (Oxford, 1972), pp. 392–4, 417–9,

The horse-breeding areas were the pastures and woodlands,[105] and these were tending to shrink in size as the improvement of fens, forests, and chases for agricultural purposes went on apace throughout the seventeenth century. It made serious inroads into horse-breeding country, especially in the Midlands. On the Scottish border some alarm had been expressed as early as Elizabeth's reign at the reduced number of horses bred there when the Crown's policy took effect of establishing new farmsteads and cultivating more land under the plough.[106] In consequence, the pockets of moorland and fenland that remained became more conspicuously specialised horse-breeding areas than before,[107] and show up very clearly in probate inventories of the seventeenth century. To supplement numbers further, horse traders turned increasingly to Wales and Ireland, valuing especially the Merlins of Monmouthshire as pack animals and the hobbies from Ireland as comfortable riding horses.[108]

Thus, while the areas of country which retained their grasslands became more narrowly delimited, they attained for that reason greater renown. Parts of northern England won a singular reputation for their fine horses, in particular, the Vale of York between Malton and Ripon.[109] Ripon's reputation went back to the early sixteenth century, at least, but it may have been enhanced by the fact that the musters were regularly held there subsequently.[110] At all events, the Ripon colt was an English horse with a fine reputation in 1610, which

Continued

420–21. Dr Margaret Spufford is at present analysing a late seventeenth-century list of licences to pedlars and hawkers, showing the number on foot, and the numbers with horses.

[105] J. Worledge, *Systema Agriculturae* (1675), p. 160.

[106] Thomas de Grey, *The Compleat Horseman* (1639), Epistle Dedicatory; *CSPD Addenda, 1547–65*, pp. 416, 465; *Addenda, 1566–79*, p. 348; *1580–1625*, p. 123.

[107] For example, the Somerset moors which specialized in breeding colts that were then sold to the horse trainers of the north, and ended up as cart and coach horses in London. Peter Edwards, *art. cit.* The Wealdmoors in Shropshire broke, rather than bred, horses. *Ibid.* The fens around the Wash bred cart, wagon, and plough horses, and it was not unusual to find fen farmers in the 1680's owning over forty horses. Stephen Porter 'An Agricultural Geography of Huntingdonshire, 1610–1749', (Cambridge M.Litt., 1973), p. 76. Forest and fell ponies were chosen as pack-horses and pit ponies.

[108] On the merlins, see Peter Edwards, *art. op. cit.*

[109] Nicholas Morgan in *The Perfection of Horse-Manship* . . . (1609), pp. 19–20, thought that the horses of northern England stood in higher popular estimation than any others, though he did not himself share this view. For Malton and Ripon fairs, see William Cavendish, *A New Method, op. cit.*, pp. 58–60.

[110] Anthony Fitzherbert in his *Boke of Husbondrye*, n.d., (Bodleian Library, Douce XX 3(2), f. 44v) recalled the day (before 1523) when he went to Ripon to buy a colt. For Ripon musters, see *CSPD Addenda, 1566–79*, p. 170.

placed it alongside the Spanish Jennet and the Irish hobby.[111] Ripon stirrups were of a distinctive shape in the seventeenth century, specially made in Staffordshire.[112] The Earl of Cardigan's servants in the late 1720s went to Ripon to buy hunters and race-horses.[113] A high-class clientèle is implied by all this evidence, which explains why the northern grooms and breeders found it economically worthwhile to develop their horse-keeping, grooming, and training to such a fine art. They 'take such indefatigable pains with them', wrote Defoe in the early eighteenth century, 'that they bring them out like pictures of horses, not a hair amiss in them; they lie constantly in the stables with them, and feed them by weight and measure; keep them so clean and so fine, I mean in their bodies, as well as their outsides, that, in short, nothing can be more nice'. When they were sold, their pedigrees were paraded as though they were Arabians, and some sold for 150 guineas each.[114] These words echo the description given in the middle sixteenth century of the way the Spaniards kept their horses. The English had learnt a great many lessons since then.[115]

All accounts of the horse trade of the later seventeenth century describe a highly differentiated demand for highly differentiated animals at a wide range of prices. The ordinary run of prices for colts in the mid-seventeenth century was £1 to £1 10s., and in the second half of the century £2 10s. to £3. Yet two fine colts in 1679 were bought for £12 2s. and £13 5s. at the Midland fairs of Ashby and Hinckley. Mares generally cost somewhere between £1 and £2 10s. apiece in the first half of the seventeenth century, yet a gentleman student at Cambridge spent £9 on a brown mare for breeding in 1647 and £24 on a mare in 1648. By 1700 £8 was normally a fairly high figure to pay for a mare, yet two coach mares belonging to Sir William Haslewood of Maidwell, Northamptonshire, were valued in 1681 at £15 each, and a coach mare in 1701 fetched £19. Cart-horses in Northamptonshire and Leicestershire could be bought for £6 to £7 in the period 1680–1700, yet one special cart-horse was sold at Smithfield in 1689 for £17 10s. At much the same period, in 1681, a race-horse of Sir William Haslewood, called *Silversides*, was valued at £60. Finally, William Cavendish, Duke of Newcastle, knew of prize horses in the 1660s that had sold at Malton and Penkridge fairs for

---

[111] W. Folkingham, *Feudigraphia* (1610), p. 8.
[112] Robert Plot, cited in Thirsk and Cooper, op. cit., p. 313.
[113] Northants. RO, Brudenell Papers, Fiii, 183.
[114] D. Defoe, *A Tour through England and Wales* (Everyman edn.), II, pp. 78–9.
[115] W. Cavendish, *A New Method, op. cit.*, pp. 82–3, 33.

£100, £150, and £200.[116]

These wide discrepancies in horse prices are thoroughly familiar to us nowadays, and we could cite much more spectacular examples, but the significant contrast is not between the seventeenth- and the twentieth-century horse breeding business, but between the seventeenth century and *earlier* periods. Increasing differentiation encouraged expansion of the business through all ranks of society, for rich and poor alike were potential purchasers of horses now that there were so many prices and qualities to choose from, rather in the same way that the market for cars is nowadays highly differentiated. Taking the second-hand market along with the new car market, there is a car within the purse of everyone; you can pay £20 or you can pay £10,000.

Differentiation, as well as the increasing total demand for horses, made an impact on horse breeders down to the very lowest levels of society. Horses of all qualities, and for all purposes, would sell somewhere, but now and then poor men struck lucky and produced a shapely horse that sold exceptionally well; such horses could make a precious source of extra income for a husbandman. A writer in the late eighteenth century, describing the life of smallholders in the New Forest, put the point graphically: small New Forest ponies were fashionable, driven in a light carriage, and so 'it is a little fortune to a poor cottager if he happens to possess three or four colts that are tolerably handsome and match well'.[117]

Discerning buyers with long purses were not confined to Englishmen, moreover. The demand for English horses abroad had been insistent since the beginning of the sixteenth century. Foreign noblemen and statesmen had regularly sent buyers to England who took home ten, twenty, thirty horses at a time. The free export of horses was prohibited, but they could always procure licences, and English (or Irish) hobbies—easy riding horses with an ambling gait— were their favourite, for they were the most comfortable on short journeys.[118]

---

[116] Average prices are derived from a miscellany of probate inventories. Individual prices are taken from the following sources: Bucks. RO, Uthwatt MSS, D/U/4/7; S. Porter, 'An Agricultural Geography of Huntingdonshire', *op. cit.*, pp. 70–71; *The Flemings in Oxford, I, 1650–80*, ed. J. R. Magrath, Oxford Hist. Soc., XLIV, 1904, pp. 383, 391; Northants. RO, Finch Hatton MSS. FH1140; Leicester RO, Finch MSS. DG 7/1/19a; Leicester Museum Archives, 2 D31/187; William Cavendish, *A New Method, op. cit.*, p. 58.

[117] William Gilpin, *Remarks on Forest Scenery* (1791), p. 251.

[118] See, for example, *L. & P. Hen. VIII*, I, no. 941; XV, no. 705; *Cal. SP Milan, 1385–1618*, pp. 101, 147, 149–50; Fynes Morison, *Shakespeare's Europe*, ed. Charles Hughes (New York, 1967), p. 479.

How the different breeds of English horses were modified by energetic and enthusiastic crossbreeding with Neapolitans, Spanish Jennets, Friesland mares, Hungarian, Arabian, and Barbary horses in the sixteenth century is difficult for a historian without personal experience of horse breeding to assess. William Harrison, writing between 1577 and 1587, believed that breeders lost their way after the first experiments in Henry VIII's reign, and having 'for a time had very good success with them', finished up with a 'mixed brood of bastard races, whereby his [Henry VIII's] good purpose came to little effect'.[119] The same degeneration was attributed by more than one writer to the breed of Neapolitan horses. But perhaps this judgement was premature and unduly pessimistic. By the early seventeenth century it was recognised that for war horses Neapolitan, Sardinian, German or French blood was needed, crossed with English; to secure swiftness and endurance in war service, Arabian, Barbary, Spanish, or Greek blood was needed; for travel and war service, Hungarian, Sweathland (Swiss), Polish, or Irish horses had to be crossed with English mares; for draught, burden, and war service Flemish crosses were best.[120] By the middle seventeenth century, Englishmen seemed much more content with the size of English horses, fewer foreign animals were brought into England for breeding purposes, and the experts seemed to think that they now had a satisfactory stock that could be perfected by inbreeding. The judgement should not be attributed to ignorant self-satisfaction or empty national pride. It was made among others by William Cavendish, Duke of Newcastle, who spent many years in exile during the Civil War and Interregnum in daily contact with the most discriminating horse-fanciers of all Europe. His conclusion was that English horses were now the best all-purpose horses, having been 'bred out of the horses of all nations'.[121]

The stream of foreign buyers, coming to England from the mid-

---

[119] William Harrison, *Elizabethan England* (Scott Library edn., n.d.), p. 154. Nicholas Morgan in *The Perfection of Horse-Manship* (1609), pages unnumbered, also wrote of the difficulties how 'to keep and maintain your races in greatest perfection nearest their original and primary creation'. For Hungarian horses, see the imports of four by the Earl of Sussex, Elizabeth's representative in Vienna in 1567, and nine by John Dee in 1589. Dee made several trips to Hungary. *Agrártörteneti Szemle*, XIV, nos. 3–4, 1972, p. 355.
[120] This was Gervase Markham's brief summary of advice, inserted into his 1631 edition of Barnaby Googe's translation of Conrad Heresbach's *The Whole Art of Husbandry* (1631), p. 213.
[121] William Cavendish, *A New Method, op. cit.*, Letter to the Readers, and pp. 58–9.

seventeenth century onwards, seemed to share this opinion. English horses stood so high in their estimation that no legislation restricting export could withstand the determination of the foreigners to have them. They were shipped in large numbers from Rye, from Dover, and from Sandwich. At one enquiry, an informant testified to the export from Sandwich of 456 horses between 1631 and 1632, of which 378 departed without official record.[122] In the 1650s when exports were only allowed by special licence, a continuous stream of requests was considered by the Council of State to export 20, 30, 40, 100 horses on behalf of eminent men, such as the public minister of Sweden, the Vice-Chancellor of Poland, the Archduke of Austria, the Prince of Condé, the Chief President of the *Parlement* of Paris, the King of Portugal, and so on.[123] Men who were refused licences bribed the Customs officials. It seemed impossible to prevent private shippers of horses from getting their way in smuggling horses from Brighton to Dieppe. They were so determined that they moved around in armed companies, and abused and killed any who detected them smuggling their animals from Shoreham Cliff.[124]

Finally, common sense prevailed. The Commonwealth and Protectorate government was anxious to promote business at home and trade overseas. Horses were plainly much in demand abroad; it was only sensible to encourage the trade. Recognizing that 'if restraints were taken away and customs made easy, it would advance trade and manufacture', horses were allowed from 1 January 1657 onwards to be exported freely—at specified custom rates.[125] They were not a commodity with which the port of London concerned itself, and consequently they have not received any recognition from historians. But Sandwich offers a good example of the scale of the trade: in any one year over 500 might be exported.[126] Contemporary economic theorists, if not twentieth-century historians, recognised the opportunities and achievements clearly. 'Of all things this nation is capable to raise' [for foreign trade], wrote Samuel Fortrey in 1673, 'there is not anything of so great profit as the exportation of horses, which of all commodities is of least charge to be raised at home and of greatest value abroad'.[127]

---

[122] PRO E 134, 8 Chas. I, Mich. 20.

[123] See, for example, *CSPD 1652-3*, pp. 178, 267, 242, 477; *1653-4*, pp. 427, 430, 434, 435, 442, 446.

[124] *CSPD 1656-7*, pp. 112-13.

[125] *CSPD 1656-7*, p. 174.

[126] PRO E 190/675/2.

[127] S. Fortrey, *England's Interest and Improvement*, first published 1663, reprinted from 1673 edn. in J. R. McCulloch, *Early English Tracts on Commerce* (Cambridge, 1952), p. 237.

Thus the trade in horses at home and overseas flourished at the exalted levels required to meet the standards of gentlemen. But it had a firm, broad foundation for the simple reason that men of all classes had taken to riding. The discerning buyer, therefore, had a very wide range of choice. Before 1500 the horse rider on the road had been a singular individual: he was likely to be a gentleman of quality, an official in the service of the Crown, or at the very lowest perhaps a messenger on urgent business for His Majesty, or a gentleman's serving man. By the end of the seventeenth century the upper classes were still riding horses for sport, but for ordinary travel on the roads they were more likely to use coaches, and so keep their clothes clean. The middle classes rode in stage coaches, and riding on horseback on the roads on everyday business became increasingly the common man's way of getting about. Being now within the reach of everyman, riding on horseback was no longer the privilege and hallmark of the rich. Guy Miège, the Frenchman, summed it up succinctly in 1699: 'I may say the English nation is the best provided of any for land travel as to horses and coaches . . . Travelling on horseback is so common a thing in England that the meanest sort of people use it as well as the rest'.[128]

The horse-keeping business, in short, had become everyman's business. In the process of breeding them for service, for pleasure, and for power, men made them accessible to all classes, gave them a larger place in trade at home and overseas, created a highly differentiated pattern of demand and supply (in which quality mattered as well as quantity), and created work that distributed profits from the horse trade among large numbers of working people. It forms an instructive parallel with the car industry in the later twentieth century.

POSTSCRIPT

One of the themes of the Eighth International Economic History Congress at Budapest in August 1982 was 'Horses in pre-industrial and industrialized Economies'. The papers which were contributed to this lively discussion were published in 1983, edited by F. M. L. Thompson: *Horses in European Economic History: a Preliminary Canter*, British Agricultural History Society.

---

[128] Thirsk and Cooper, *op. cit.*, p. 428.

INDEX

DATE DUE